Exploring Gender Diversity
in the Ancient World

Intersectionality in Classical Antiquity

Series Editors: Mark Masterson, Victoria University of Wellington, Fiona McHardy, University of Roehampton and Nancy Sorkin Rabinowitz, Hamilton College

This series focuses on the intersection of gender and sexuality in the Greco-Roman world, with a range of other factors including race, ethnicity, class, ability, masculinity, femininity, transgender and post-colonial gender studies. The books in the series will be theoretically informed and will sit at the forefront of the study of a variety of outsiders – those marginalised in relation to the 'classical ideal' – and how they were differently constructed in the ancient world. The series is also interested in the ways in which work in the field of classical reception contributes to that study.

Editorial Advisory Board

Patty Baker, Alastair Blanshard, Susan Deacy, Jacqueline Fabre-Serris, Cristiana Franco, Genevieve Liveley, Mark Masterson, Amy Richlin, Carisa R. Showden

Books available in the series
Exploring Gender Diversity in the Ancient World, edited by Allison Surtees and Jennifer Dyer

Forthcoming books in the series
Women in the Law Courts of Classical Athens, Konstantinos Kapparis
Marginalised Populations in the Ancient Greek World: The Bioarchaeology of the Other, Carrie L. Sulosky Weaver

Visit the series web page at: edinburghuniversitypress.com/series-intersectionality-in-classical-antiquity

Exploring Gender Diversity in the Ancient World

Edited by Allison Surtees and Jennifer Dyer

EDINBURGH
University Press

Edinburgh University Press is one of the leading university presses in the UK. We publish academic books and journals in our selected subject areas across the humanities and social sciences, combining cutting-edge scholarship with high editorial and production values to produce academic works of lasting importance. For more information visit our website: edinburghuniversitypress.com

Edinburgh University Press Ltd
The Tun – Holyrood Road,
12(2f) Jackson's Entry,
Edinburgh EH8 8PJ

First published in hardback by Edinburgh University Press 2020

Typeset in 11/13 Adobe Garamond by
IDSUK (DataConnection) Ltd

A CIP record for this book is available from the British Library

ISBN 978 1 4744 4704 1 (hardback)
ISBN 978 1 4744 4705 8 (paperback)
ISBN 978 1 4744 4706 5 (webready PDF)
ISBN 978 1 4744 4707 2 (epub)

Contents

Acknowledgements

We have a number of people to thank, people without whose help, support or guidance this volume would never have come together.

First, we are grateful to the Women's Network of the Classical Association of Canada, the former for choosing the panel theme of 'Gender B(l)ending in Ancient Greek and Roman Culture and Society' and the latter for including it in the annual association conference held in Toronto, 2015.

We are indebted to the labour and time offered by our external reviewers. Because the essays included in this volume cover new interdisciplinary terrain in bringing together classical studies of literature, art and culture with queer, trans and feminist theories of identity and embodiment, and because they cover a broad array of topics, figures and histories from the ancient world, we required many especially insightful external reviewers for the essays, and we are most grateful to all of them: Sarah Blake, Sandra Boehringer, Marica Cassis, Fanny Dolansky, John Gilbert, Allison Glazebrook, Judith Hallett, Adam Kemezis, Rebecca Futo Kennedy, Sarah Levin-Richardson, Nikoletta Manioti, Hanna Sigmund Nielson, Mark Nugent, Katharine von Stackelberg, Caroline Vout and Connor Whately. Not surprisingly, with such an array of topics and temporalities from our authors, we are also most grateful to our Greek and Latin editors, Kathy Simonsen (Greek) and (again) Sarah Blake (Latin). We really could not have done this without your knowledge, support, advice and patience.

Of course, we thank our authors for being a true joy to work with; putting this collection together was a genuinely positive experience largely because our authors were such excellent colleagues.

We thank our editors at Edinburgh University Press, Fiona McHardy, Nancy Rabinowitz and Mark Masterson. Your support, advice and encouragement was truly appreciated.

We thank Joan Butler, who generously shared with us her knowledge and skill with editing and formatting this project into a book.

And finally, as one editor to another, I thank Allison for asking me to join her in developing this panel concept into a book. Not only did this answer to a real need I've found in queer and trans history studies, but it allowed me to learn and develop some profoundly interesting conceptual, historical and academic connections amongst disciplines and motifs. Moreover, we have a lot of fun working together, and that means a lot in this business!

Notes on Contributors

Evelyn Adkins is assistant professor in the department of classics at Case Western Reserve University. She specialises in the study of Imperial Latin literature and the ancient Greek and Roman novel, with particular interests in Apuleius' *Metamorphoses* or *The Golden Ass*, discourse analysis, gender and sexuality, and Roman social and cultural history.

Dalida Agri is a lecturer in classics at the University of Birmingham and has published on gender, emotions and intertextuality. She is currently completing a monograph on the textual representations of emotions in Flavian Epic within the framework of Stoic thought and their impact on depictions of gender, power and agency.

Rowan Emily Ash is pursuing a doctorate in classical philology at the University of Western Ontario. While she maintains broad interests in both Latin and Greek literatures and their receptions, her current primary focus is her dissertation project, a commentary on the so-called 'Paris Handbook' (PGM IV) among the late antique Greek magical papyri.

Linnea Åshede earned her doctorate at the University of Gothenburg. In 2016, her dissertation was awarded the Per Nyström prize for outstanding historical scholarship by the Royal Society of Arts and Sciences in Gothenburg. She subsequently underwent a scholarly identity crisis, which resulted in her changing professional track. She is currently part of the editorial staff of the digital database project *Swedish Women Online 2.0* (www.skbl.se). Dr Åshede is a self-professed feminist, theoretical geek and librarian-in-training, usually found wherever there are books.

Rebecca Begum-Lees completed her PhD in classics at the University of Cambridge in 2018. Before that she completed a master's in classics at the University of Durham and a bachelor's in classics at the University of Oxford. Her PhD thesis explored the relationship between grammatical gender, biological sex and social gender in Ovid's *Metamorphoses*. Rebecca now works in Diversity and Inclusion for the House of Commons in the UK Parliament.

Mary Deminion is a PhD candidate in the Department of Classical Studies at the University of Western Ontario. Her research interests include ancient Greek and Roman law and Roman political history. She is currently completing her dissertation on gender in Justinian's Digest of Roman Law.

Lisa A. Hughes is associate professor of classics and religion at the University of Calgary. Her research focuses on visual representations of non-elites in the late Republic and early Empire. Her latest SSHRC IG funded research project examines the role of small-scale theatrical performances in the gardens of ancient Roman residential contexts. The goal is to demonstrate how performances in garden settings complete with mythic sculpture, wall paintings, mosaics and architectural features can break down perceived social barriers between audience and performers alike.

Peter Kelly is a visiting research associate in the classics department at the University of Oregon, and is teaching in the Honors College at Oregon State University. He completed his PhD in classics at the National University of Ireland, Galway. His research explores parallelisms between cosmic and textual structures in Greek philosophy and Augustan poetry. He is currently finalising a monograph titled *The Cosmic Text: from Ovid to Plato*, and has published a number of articles on related topics.

Denise Eileen McCoskey is a professor of classics and affiliate of Black World Studies at Miami University (Ohio). She is the author of *Race: Antiquity & Its Legacy* and co-author, with Zara Torlone, of *Latin Love Poetry*. McCoskey is currently serving as editor of a forthcoming volume on the cultural history of race in antiquity, and is also at work on a project examining the role of eugenics in early twentieth-century American classical scholarship.

Kimberly Passaro is a PhD student in classics at the University of Cincinnati. Her research focuses on women, gender and sexuality, late antique literature and early Christianity.

Walter Duvall Penrose, Jr is associate professor of history at San Diego State University. He is the author of *Postcolonial Amazons: Female Masculinity and*

Courage in Ancient Greek and Sanskrit Literature (Oxford University Press 2016). Walter has also published essays and journal articles on Hellenistic queens, the Tomb of the Diver Paintings, pedagogy in the classics classroom, conceptions of disability in ancient Greece and the reception of Sappho, as well as homoeroticism and gender diversity in South Asian history.

Jussi Rantala (PhD) is a researcher at the University of Tampere. His publications include *The Ludi Saeculares of Septimius Severus: The Ideologies of a New Roman Empire* (Routledge 2017) and the edited volume *Gender, Memory, and Identity in the Roman World* (Amsterdam 2019).

Kelly E. Shannon-Henderson is assistant professor of classics in the Department of Modern Languages and Classics at the University of Alabama. She holds a bachelor's degree in classics from the University of Virginia, and a DPhil in Greek and Latin languages and literature from the University of Oxford. She is the author of *Religion and Memory in Tacitus'* Annals (Oxford University Press), a forthcoming commentary on Phlegon of Tralles' *On Marvels* (Brill) and various articles on aspects of Greek and Roman historiography and paradoxography.

Brian P. Sowers is assistant professor of classics at Brooklyn College of the City University of New York. His research focuses on early Christianity, late antique literature and gender and reception studies. He has published on late Latin reading communities and early Christian female martyrs, saints and poets, including Perpetua, Felicitas, Thecla, Justina, Aelia Eudocia, Ausonius and Proba. His current monograph project (forthcoming, Center for Hellenic Studies) examines the poetry of Aelia Eudocia, one of antiquity's best surviving female authors.

Tyson Sukava is assistant professor of classics at the University of Delaware. His research interests revolve around Greek and Roman science and medicine. He is currently concentrating on the transmission of ideas within and between various groups in antiquity.

Anna Uhlig is associate professor of classics at the University of California, Davis, where she is also a member of the Graduate Group in Performance Studies. She is author of *Theatrical Reenactment in Pindar and Aeschylus* (Cambridge 2019) and co-editor (with Richard Hunter) of *Imagining Reperformance in Ancient Culture: Studies in the Traditions of Drama and Lyric* (Cambridge 2017).

For all our gender-diverse colleagues.
AS

For Fenna and Adrian, my favourite explorers.
JD

Introduction: Queering Classics

Allison Surtees and Jennifer Dyer

BRINGING TOGETHER GENDER ANALYSIS AND CLASSICS

This volume was inspired by the recognition of two different yet connected needs that we found through our work in classics and in gender studies. In 2015, the Women's Network (WN) of the Classical Association of Canada (CAC) sponsored two panels at the CAC annual meeting, hosted by the University of Toronto. The topic, chosen by the WN membership, was 'Gender B(l) ending in Greek and Roman Culture and Society' and the panels consisted of seven papers – including both Agri's and Begum-Lees' contributions in this volume. The interest in and attendance at these panels indicated a need for analyses of the ancient world that do not assume a cisnormative, masculinist and largely heterosexual lens in order to better understand the various social and political roles occupied by people who did not seem to identify as cisgender men. From gender studies, we were driven by the need for a clear history of gender diversity that reveals both the existence and successes of gender-diverse and transgender people long before our current era's emerging recognition. The authors of the essays in this volume develop these concerns in their explorations of gender diversity, sexual diversity and the politics of the power of representation in the ancient world.

The discipline of classics has a long scholarly tradition which, for the bulk of its history, has been a history of men. With the exception of a few early works on women in the ancient world, women were treated largely as footnotes or extensions of the men to whom they were attached, if they were mentioned at all. The rise of the second-wave feminist movement of the 1960s and 1970s – a movement focused on labour rights, family structure, sexuality and identity politics – had a broad and significant impact on academic work. Not only did scholars increasingly focus on studying women's history, women and culture, and the socio-politics of sex and sexuality, but the discipline of women's studies was developed as a sustained critical response to this new focus and became increasingly integral to understanding any aspect of academic enquiry.

One effect of the integration of gender analysis in scholarly enquiries has been the recognition of the hyperbolic distinction between male and female gender roles found in the ancient world; another is the new appreciation of the considerable use of these roles in establishing and maintaining political identification and power hierarchies. Increasingly, particularly in the area of feminist gender archaeology, there is the recognition not just of gender roles but of the active construction of these roles. The more we recognise the social construction of gender or at least the biosocial interaction of biological sexes and social environments, the more visible are those who challenged specific gender roles and who challenged the oppositional gender binary itself.

The present work seeks to understand gender beyond the context of sex and sexuality as a focus of study in its own right, where gender is the range of identifications people have with femininity or masculinity as personal characteristics, comportments, sets of values or social roles. This volume explores these challenges to normative gender and gender role histories through critical analyses of texts and material culture. These essays work to (1) open a new understanding of the impact of under-recognised gender roles and gender diversity on ancient social and cultural history and (2) show how this may affect our understanding of gender in contemporary thought and society. More importantly, however, in exploring these challenges through specific analyses, this volume goes further to challenge the very heteronormative and cisgendered readings of the ancient world. These essays contest (mis)understandings of the past that present power, lived time, desire and social order in terms of some abstract and ahistorical norm that maintains a strictly naturalised, hierarchical binary division of genders, a norm that tends to see instances of diversity as outliers to an assumed norm. That is, these studies reveal that there is not only a clear diversity of sexualities in the ancient world, but a diversity of gender roles, of gendered bodies and of sexed bodies that have been overlooked or marginalised due not always to masculinist, cisgender and heteronormative lenses of the past, but often to those lenses the present brings to the past. The essays in this volume show that classical Greek and Roman history is the history of all genders, not just those of the cisheteronormative gender binary that dominates today, a history that includes identities that are gender-fluid or gender blending (varyingly feminine and masculine), non-binary (neither masculine nor feminine), intersex (born with sex characteristics that do not correspond with norms assigned to male or female) and transgender (identifying with a gender that does not correspond to the sex assigned at birth) (Halberstam 1998; Butler 1990). In this way, we bring together classics with feminist, queer and trans studies to reveal unexamined aspects of the past, and to use that past to open new ways of considering gender diversity in the present.

We put these theories in conversation with feminist, queer and trans theories because they afford classics the capacity to do a different sort of gender work. Specifically, queer theory, such as that put forward by Halberstam, Butler or Dinshaw, is speculative in nature because it does not set out a series of methods, categories or concepts that determine its objects. Quite the contrary, queer theory argues for the constructed, culturally situated and changeable nature of things which are considered sexual behaviours, the concepts linking those behaviours to certain identities, and the normative categories that are generated when those concepts stick. In this sense, queer theory argues against universalising, normative and therefore biological models of sexual identity or of gender. Any theory which prioritises, for instance, a two-gender model of society based on two biological sexes ignores the complexity of sexuality and sexual identity that involves far more than chromosomal variation, and it ignores the existence of societies with historically more than two genders and the recognition of a multitude of sexual identities. These differences must be construed as anomalies to a norm, or outliers, in order for the norm to function as such. Amongst other things, queer theory questions the construction of norms on these terms. In this respect, queer theory puts an emphasis on abductive reasoning: reasoning that moves from (an often surprising) observation to a theory that explains it (Huffman 2013). In an abductive argument, the argument is not a deduction, since it does not claim that its conclusion must be true if its premises are true (Bradley 2009). It is not inductive, since the statement referred to in the conclusion is not tested by sampling. Whereas induction tells us that a statement, true in some cases, is likely to be true in unobserved cases, abduction allows us to conclude to the likelihood of something unlike anything that is observed (Peirce 1992). It is inference to the best possible explanation. The procedure is fallibilist: repeated application of abductive inference may lead to continued revision of our hypothesis in the light of new observations, as has always been the case with explanatorist theories of actualisation (Bradley 2009). And the hypothesis is not just tested against experience. Experience is tested against the hypothesis, which has the status of a critical principle: do the putative observations, or our descriptions of the observed, display the characters posited by the hypothesis? Ostensive demonstration cuts both ways. Or, more precisely, it moves in a virtuous circle. In the context of this book, queer theory employs abductive reasoning to open the often surprising observations about the past that don't fit into the schemes by which we usually observe it. This then allows us to reconsider the intersections of gender identity, expression and roles with sex, sexuality and identity, and how those categories figure in what we (think we) know about the past but also how we know it. The essays in this volume hold focus to issues specifically of gender and sex in the ancient world in an intersectional way, such that no category is taken to be homogeneous or essentialising, and no description asks identities, bodies or roles to subordinate one aspect of themselves in favour of another. Each essay treats gender, sex and to some degree sexualities as complex coalitions of differences – from other people, from oneself over time, from social roles, from historical perspectives – that enact particular relations to power. Our aim is to unpack some of those relations and explore the ways they interact in order to come to those aforesaid surprising observations about the past.

REVIEW OF THE LITERATURE

In classics scholarship, a tradition of scholars turning their attention to women, sexuality and their respective roles in ancient society largely began with Sarah Pomeroy's 1975 book, *Goddesses, Whores, Wives, and Slaves.* This book represented a watershed moment for the study of women in antiquity. What followed were several works aimed at centralising women in ancient studies and placing the study of ancient women firmly in the classroom. Helene Foley (1981), Eva Cantarella (1987), Elaine Fantham et al. (1995) and Sue Blundell (1995) are key early exempla of this trend, followed more recently by Laura K. McClure (2002), Fiona McHardy and Eireann Marshall (2004), Janet Tulloch (2016), and Stephanie Lynn Budin and Jean MacIntosh Turfa (2016). Sourcebooks exclusively focused on women further facilitated both research and classroom study by making these sources accessible and contextualised (for example, Lefkowitz and Fant 1982; MacLachlan 2012, 2013). As women in antiquity became an accepted area of research, studies became more focused, speaking to women's role in specific aspects of the ancient world; such as, women as authors (Snyder 1989; DuBois 1995; Plant 2004; Greene 2005), women and theatre (Rabinowitz 1993; Stehle 1997; Foley 2001; McClure 2009), women in literature (Keith 2000; James 2003; Gilhuly 2008), women in myth and religion (Lyons 1997; Kraemer 2004; Connelly 2007), women in law and politics (Loraux 1981; Gardner 1986; Just 1989; Sealy 1990; Bauman 1992), women in marriage and family life (Patterson 1986, 1998; Treggiari 1991; Dixon 1992). This interest extended into material culture, as demonstrated by two roughly concurrent museum exhibitions; the Walters Art Museum presented *Pandora: Women in Classical Greece* (Reeder 1995), and the Yale University Art Gallery organised *I, Claudia: Women in Ancient Rome* (Kleiner and Matheson 1996).

This new interest in women in antiquity coincided with the new focus on studies of ancient sex and sexuality, beginning with Kenneth Dover's 1978 study, *Greek Homosexuality.* This book was followed by a spate of new works on ancient homosexuality or the male sexual experience. David Halperin's influential *One Hundred Years of Homosexuality and Other Essays on Greek Love* (1990b) was followed up with his 2002 work, *How to do the History of Homosexuality.* Other key works include Cantarella (1992), Craig Williams (1999, 2nd edition published 2010), Thomas Hubbard (2003) and James Davidson (2007). While much work focused on the male sexual experience, a number of works focused on sex, sexuality and desire more broadly (Winkler 1990a; Richlin 1992b; Davidson 1997; Skinner 2005; Ormand 2009). Increasingly evidence from material culture played a role in these works, resulting in a range of studies on sexual imagery (Jones 1982; Kampen 1996b; Clarke 1998, 2003). Of particular note are a series of edited collections which, taken together, offer a vast range of topics and evidentiary sources on sex and sexuality; *Before Sexuality: The Construction of Erotic Experience in the Ancient Greek World* (Halperin et al. 1990), *Roman Sexualities* (Hallett and Skinner 1997), *A Companion to Greek and Roman Sexualities* (Hubbard 2014), *Ancient Sex: New Essays* (Blondell and Ormand 2015), and *Sex in Antiquity: Exploring Gender and Sexuality in the Ancient World* (Masterson et al. 2015).

While much work still focuses on the male sexual experience, important works aimed to draw out and understand the female sexual experience among women (Rabinowitz and Auanger 2002; Boehringer 2007a), in sex work (McClure 2003; Faraone and McClure 2006; Glazebrook and Henry 2011; Glazebrook 2015), and as violence (Richlin 1983; Keuls 1985; Pierce and Deacy 1997). Moreover, the increasing use of broader and more complex theoretical frameworks has pushed the boundaries of the gender binary to explore the wider issues of women, sex and gender in more dynamic ways. *Feminist Theory and the Classics* (Rabinowitz and Richlin 1993) brought together essays that moved beyond the inclusion of and focus on women in scholarship to question traditional readings of women and gender through a theoretical lens. More recently, Lin Foxhall's 2013 work, *Studying Gender in Classical Antiquity*, applies a theoretical framework of gender to examine how gender itself shapes experience and interacts at the intersection of other socio-political characteristics (wealth, status, age). Brooke Holmes (2012), Jennifer Ingleheart (2015) and Dorota Dutsch and Ann Suter (2015) each examine underexplored links between ancient and modern notions of gender and sexuality.

As with the application of feminist theory, gender theory engages with the interconnections of gender and power in antiquity, broadening the scholarly scope of studies addressing women and sexuality in antiquity. The ties between gender, sex and sexuality have been a topic of inquiry for some time, from John J. Winkler's 1990a *The Constraints of Desire: The Anthropology of Sex and Gender in Ancient Greece*, to the recent volumes by Ruby Blondell and Kirk Ormand (2015), and Mark Masterson, Nancy Sorkin Rabinowitz and James Robson (2015). In these and other works, gender is understood as dynamic and without singular expression. Luc Brisson's *Sexual Ambivalence: Androgyny and Hermaphroditism in Graeco-Roman Antiquity* (2002) examines the fluidity of gender, while other scholars seek either to deconstruct gender representations or to engage with asexual bodies and identifications, as Penelope Allison does in 'Characterizing Roman Artifacts to Investigate Gendered Practices in Context without Sexed Bodies' (2015). In contrast, classical archaeologists are increasingly studying gender construction, working through the framework of gender archaeology (Gilchrist 1999, Sørensen 2000, Nelson 2007). Tied to the notion of gender construction are a series of edited collections focused specifically on the body. Two edited volumes by Maria Wyke, *Parchments of Gender: Deciphering the Bodies of Antiquity* (1998a) and *Gender and the Body in the Ancient Mediterranean* (1998b) focus on the body and gender construction through an interdisciplinary lens. Other collections aim to explore varied aspects, presentations and functions of bodies through liminality and embodiment theory, and while the volumes as a whole do not focus specifically on gender, they include individual essays that do (for example, Petersen, Lateiner and Lee in Fögen and Lee 2009; King, Shapiro and Bremmer in Boschung et al. 2015). Still other works challenge gender expectations through the exploration of transgender, masculinity, female masculinity and gender ambiguity (Gleason 1995; Foxhall and Salmon 1998a, 1998b; Valentine 2007; Penrose 2016; Campanile et al. 2017; Olson 2017). This review of sources is not exhaustive, but aims to highlight the general trends and some of the major works in classics of the last several decades that explore gender.

Concomitant with the development of feminist practices in classical interpretation, feminist, queer and trans theory have developed their own fields of study in the last two decades. Not only have these disciplines elaborated their own histories, literatures, methodologies, conferences, journals and monographs, but they have opened other disciplines to new forms of analysis and of self-critique. Thinkers such as Carolyn Dinshaw in medieval studies, Gayle Salamon in phenomenology/new materialisms, Susan Stryker in history, Jose Esteban Munoz in cultural studies and J. Halberstam in English literature, to name only a very few, have radically altered not only the methods of enquiry, the historical categories and the theories of representation in their own disciplines by bringing feminist, queer and trans theories into conversation with them; they have opened contiguous and overlapping disciplines as well. These theories take up concepts and methodologies introduced by thinkers such as Judith Butler, Eve Kosofsky Sedgwick, Michel Foucault, J. Halberstam, Elizabeth Grosz, Karen Barad and Sarah Ahmed. In this way, the means by which we consider the past in classics – from notions of time to cultural forms to ideas about authorship – change as well. They take up more social constructionist, new materialist or culturally critical arguments about categories such as male and female or cultural and natural, to show how these forms of representation are neither universal nor naturally occurring (see Sukava, Uhlig and Åshede in this volume).

In particular, the essays in this volume take up ways by which traditional binary notions of gender and of sexuality were challenged, subverted or 'bent' in the ancient world, ways that could only become recognisable when researchers took up these new methodologies in classical art history, literary analysis, archaeology and history. Following Betsy Lucal's (1999) descriptions, gender bending can be understood to be an everyday performance of self by which we code ourselves in culturally significant gender cues, traditionally as either man or woman. We cannot choose to refuse participation in gender, which means that even if one doesn't present oneself (consciously or unconsciously) as gendered, our society will nevertheless 'gender' a person by trying to read gendered cues anyway. This gendering that codifies one's actions, comportment, clothing and behaviours tends to be normatively folded into biological sex, such that one's maleness and femaleness is determined by biological sex, and maleness and femaleness appears inseparable from masculinity and femininity. To further solidify this apparent double-helix of binary sex and gender, they are treated as natural and irreducible. Now, we have known for some time that sex and gender are non-identical; otherwise, there would be little distinction amongst 'men' and amongst 'women'. But there are certainly varieties of masculinity and femininity, and varieties of what we call maleness and femaleness (Ainsworth 2015), and these are also historical and geopolitically variant. What seemed hypermasculine in the fifth century BC would almost certainly not seem so today. Furthermore, we know that the very binary categories of 'gender' support cisheteronormative and patriarchal social forms, for it is masculinity and the male that demand the least gendered coding work (Lucal 1999; Lorber 1996; Devor 1989) and that gain the most (sometimes invisible) social privilege and power (see Agri, Ash and Rantala in this volume). Bending the gender roles and blending gender norms are ways by which traditional forms of social power can be challenged and changed.

REFLECTIONS OF AND CHALLENGES TO GENDER EXPECTATIONS IN THE OLYMPIC PANTHEON

The essays that follow in this book explore non-normative enactments of gender bending and blending beyond the binary norms in ancient Greece and Rome. For this reason, it is crucial to lay out what those norms have been taken to be, based on both literary and material studies of the ancient worlds. They tend to begin with the Greek Olympian gods (a few recent introductory texts to Greek and Roman mythology include Buxton 2004; Harris and Platzner 2016; Morford, Lenardon and Sham 2018; on the portrayal of myth in art, see Carpenter 1991; Gantz 1993; Shapiro 1994; *Lexicon Iconographicum Mythologiae Classicae* (*LIMC*)). The Olympians reflect the binary and hierarchical gender roles seen in ancient Greece and they act as examples of expected behaviour. The Olympic Pantheon from at least the early Archaic period is very much a patriarchy that reflects the patriarchal structure of ancient Greek society. Male deities have power primarily in the public realm as creators of laws and upholders of their concomitant traditions. What are taken to be powerful, frightening and potentially destructive physical realms, namely the sky, the sea and the underworld, are ruled, not surprisingly, by the father gods Zeus, Poseidon and Hades. War is a male activity ruled by Ares. Acts of creation for the public sphere, such as literature and music, are attributed to Apollo, whereas Hephaestus oversees metalwork and ceramics, and Hermes is the primary public voice of the gods, relaying messages between gods and mortals (while the female Iris also acts as a messenger, she is far less prominent). By contrast, matters pertaining to the home and family are under the influence of female deities. These include Hestia's governance of the home, Hera's overseeing of marriage, Aphrodite's reign of love and sexuality, Artemis' dominion of rites of passage and childbirth and Demeter's of fertility. Even the earth itself from which life springs is in the female form of Gaia. The set distinction between male and female biological sex and its correlation with masculinity and femininity was further reinforced by the fourth-century BC philosophers Plato and Aristotle, arguing firmly for a biologically based norm that not only put masculine features solely in the male body and feminine features in the female, but demarcated clearly what those features were (see Ash, Kelly, Penrose and Shannon-Henderson in this volume). Masculinity included not only strength and physical domination, but rationality, creativity, technical mastery, the manipulation of forms and structures and a wilfully active existence. Features of femininity were considered to be far more corporeal, materially based and passive, the matter to be moulded and mastered by male masculinity. These hegemonic norms set out and naturalised a biological basis for gendered social identities and actions, such that even when the actions are not performed by the appropriately sexed person, the symbolic meaning of that action would remain gendered (Barnett 2012). Yet within these overarching binary structures, there are those within the divine pantheon who challenge these defined gender roles, revealing their constructed nature and the concomitant social powers that rely upon their maintenance. It is in this way that Athena and Dionysus defy gender expectations, both with respect to their physical embodiment and their actions.

Athena challenges gender expectations first of all by taking on both a masculine appearance and the purview of male influence (some notable works on Athena include Neils 1992, 1996; Clay 1997; Deacy and Villing 2001; Deacy 2008; Kennedy 2009). For while she identifies as a female goddess, she assumes the normative presentation and comportment of a man and embodies key aspects of the male gender role, such as the dynamic involvement in both the rational and the physical combat of war (Neils 2008). Athena is at first glance motherless, born from the head of Zeus fully armed. In the visual record, she is portrayed as masculine, a soldier/warrior wearing a helmet and holding a spear. Indeed, the most iconic visual attribute is her aegis emblazoned with the Gorgoneion. The aegis has a specifically militaristic meaning and is mirrored, with the Gorgoneion, in images of hoplite shields. Athena is thereby linked symbolically with a thoroughly male activity, here warfare, associated with the male Ares. Unlike Ares, however, Athena's form of warfare is not merely through physical violence. Rather, Athena is the goddess of strategic warfare. In this respect, she is more masculine than her male counterpart, for Athena is the embodiment of wisdom, and it is through this wisdom that she engages in the strategy rather than the sheer violence of war. This association of wisdom relates to her birth from the head of Zeus, directly from the mind of the king of the gods himself. Athena, a female goddess, is a masculine warrior. And the very feature that makes her so totally masculine is, ironically, that which was ultimately derived from her mother. For there is more to Athena's origin story. Her mother was Metis, the personification of wisdom, and the wisdom that is Metis was swallowed by Zeus. So 'motherless' is not entirely accurate, because given this information it becomes clear that Athena is born super-corporeally of a male god, replete with a body and the accoutrements of fighting, but given the masculine trait of wisdom by her incorporeal mother, who is now understood to be fully identified with the immateriality of wisdom. Athena takes on both a man's gender role and a masculine gender expression, despite being assigned female at her birth.

Athena presents herself in hyper-masculine terms. Not only does Athena take on the male activity of war, it is Athena among all the gods who is most closely associated with the heroes, the half-divine sons of gods who act as protectors of the mortal (public) realm. It is Athena who guides Perseus to defeat the gorgon Medusa through strategy, a deed commemorated by the Gorgoneion on her aegis. It is Athena who guides Heracles through his labours, leading the mightiest hero through deeds that require more than merely brute strength to accomplish. And it is Athena who forms a special bond with Odysseus, a hero known for his cleverness and trickery, as his guide and companion. Moreover, Athena does not simply take on the roles and activities of maleness and masculinity, but she eschews the primary expectations of women: marriage and motherhood. Athena remains a virgin goddess, without romantic attachments or interest in domestic activities (save weaving) and her virginity is connected to her interest in male pursuits. This puts her in contrast with another virgin goddess, Artemis. For while Artemis is a virgin goddess who engages in a primarily male pursuit (hunting), it is nevertheless the case that her virginity is associated with her role in childbirth and female rites of passage (as seen, for example, at the sanctuary of Artemis at Brauron). The distinction between these two virgin goddesses is also seen in their respective portrayals: Athena in her peplos, aegis and helmet, and Artemis in her short chiton. Artemis is appreciated for her beauty, while Athena alone among the Olympian goddesses is not much discussed in these terms. Unlike the other goddesses, Athena is not sexualised or objectified as such;[1] rather, she remains self-defining and self-actualising in terms of the masculine self-presentation and identity at the time, and is only known as female because of the sex she was assigned at birth.

While Athena identifies as male, Dionysus vacillates between male and female gender performances and roles (a few of the many studies on Dionysus include Carpenter and Faraone 1993; Seaford 2006; Isler-Kerenyi 2007, 2014; Bernabé et al. 2013). Dionysus' appearance is initially that of a father god, an older, bearded man similar to Zeus, Poseidon and Hades. But even in this strongly male incarnation, Dionysus is mixing things up, for he dresses in a long chiton, which has been interpreted as a female garment (Jameson 1993; see also Csapo 1997) and stands in contrast with the consistent full or partial nudity of other gods. So already the god that will become most variable in gender identities is also closest, symbolically, to the mortals reflected in them. Yet by the mid-fifth century BC there is a significant shift in the god's appearance. The older Dionysus persists in visual representations through the end of the fifth century, but a youthful, beardless, nude Dionysus co-exists with and eventually largely replaces the older representation. By the fourth century, the iconography of Dionysus is almost exclusively that of a young, beardless man, often with long curly hair. He has shifted from the *gravitas* of a father god to a beautiful young god, an appearance he is also ascribed in Euripides' *Bacchae*, a tragedy performed in Athens in 405 BC:

> Your hair is much too long to be a wrestler's
> Flowing down to your cheeks that way, and full
> Of lust. You've kept your skin quite fair, by staying
> Out of the sun, and well in the shade, to hunt
> For Aphrodite, pretty as you are.
> *Bacchae* 541–5 (trans. Gibbons and Segal)

Dionysus changes now from masculine to feminine, for not only does he appear truly feminine, with his long hair and white skin, but his appearance is a result of his own specifically feminine actions. His long hair is untamed, as a woman's would be, rather than tied back and controlled for the masculine activity of wrestling. His skin is white from remaining indoors or under the shade, as a woman's would be, and he tends to his skin carefully, as women do. And instead of hunting animals as a man, he hunts Aphrodite as a woman. Dionysus' feminine appearance is carefully crafted, the result of undertaking female activities. His gender fluidity is unique to him amongst the gods, but it is not his only fluid quality; he is very much a liminal figure with continually shifting identities across a variety of traditionally power-saturated realms. He is both male and female, young and old. He is Greek and non-Greek, a god thoroughly embedded in the Greek pantheon, but with mythologies describing him, and his cult, as being newly introduced to the Greek world. He blends the divine, mortal and bestial worlds through his human/animal hybrid followers, the male satyrs and female maenads, while Dionysus walks the line between mortal and immortal. As one of the Olympians, he is unquestionably divine, yet he alone of the Olympians had a mortal mother. And in this liminal space of divine and mortal, he crosses the boundaries between life and death as the twice-born god, having been torn from his dead mother's womb to be born again from the immortal thigh of Zeus. Further, initiates to the mystery cult of Dionysus are able to find new life through death. Thus Dionysus transforms throughout ancient Greece from old to young, Greek to non-Greek, and from masculine to feminine, all the while liminally balancing between god and mortal. Given that the gods both reflect and set an example for their mortal counterparts, Dionysus' shifting form of being suggests something more historically meaningful than a mere accident of representation: he embodies the dynamics of shifting identities and representations of social constructions of power that upset the precise institutions that demand their fixity: sex, gender, race, class, proximity to the divine, and ethnicity. For this reason, Dionysus is fully representative of the types of enquiries we put to the ancient world.

Supporting the intentional change in Dionysus is the fact that he is also the one male Olympian to be associated with fertility. Both he and Demeter are associated with agricultural fertility, he with the vine and she with crops, supplying the world with both food and drink. Fertility of crops, animals and mortals is the realm of female deities; moreover, the worship is carried out primarily by women. We can speculate that this association with fertility is foreshadowed in the story of Dionysus' (motherless) birth from Zeus' thigh. While Athena is born from his head and assumes the male attribute of wisdom (that in fact comes from her mother), Dionysus is born from his father's thigh, a birth associated with genitals, generation and fertility due to its bodily proximity. Unlike Athena, Dionysus has no maternal trace. In the birth of Athena, Zeus absorbs Metis, who then becomes a fundamental part of Athena herself. Dionysus' mortal mother, Semele, on the other hand, is removed entirely from the birth process, for when Dionysus is removed from her dead body, all of Semele is left behind, both the mortal and the maternal. Her female womb does not give birth to Dionysus, and it is only the memory of his incomplete gestation therein that connects Dionysus to her. Dionysus is his own maternal trace. In this way, Dionysus both protects his father from that symbolic gender blending (for while Zeus is mother and father, here, he is never associated with femininity), and takes on that symbolic gender blending right from the get-go.

In addition to his fluid identities, Dionysus also has a unique relationship with women. Other male deities take multiple lovers, whether the women consent or not, and in fact consent is rarely a thought, let alone a requirement. Dionysus, on the other hand, has only one consort, Ariadne, with whom he happily remains and who happily remains with him. He found her alone, sleeping on the island of Naxos, abandoned by the Athenian hero Theseus. Concomitant to the masculine Athena who protects Theseus in his quest to kill the Minotaur and return to Athens, Dionysus, in a rare turn of real pathos and loyalty towards a woman, protects the woman who helped but was abandoned by the hero.

Further, Dionysus' unique relationship with women extends to his female followers, the maenads. Maenads are regularly depicted with Dionysus in the visual record, either alone or in the company of satyrs. Outside the visual tradition, the *Bacchae* is the one literary source to provide a description of the private rites, as opposed to public state festivals, of Dionysus. In this play set in the city of Thebes, it is the women who are closest to Dionysus and perform his rites correctly. Agave (mother of the King Pentheus and sister to Dionysus' mortal mother Semele) leads the women into the mountains/woods, where they transform into maenads through rites which include wine and dancing to enter a state of *ekstasis*, another form of self-creation by 'getting outside of oneself'. In order for men to participate in these rites, they must also become or at least present as women. Cadmus (the former king, father of Agave, grandfather to both King Pentheus and Dionysus) and the seer Tiresias (himself a figure who switches gender – see Ash, Begum-Lees and Shannon-Henderson in this volume) accept the worship of Dionysus and accordingly dress as women for the rituals. But when King Pentheus rejects Dionysus and as a result incurs his wrath, the god retaliates. He convinces Pentheus to dress as a woman in order to spy on the women's secret worship. But while Pentheus appears to be a woman, his male identity is seen by the women, who, under the influence of Dionysus, subsequently tear him literally limb from limb as punishment for his attempted deception and male intrusion into female space. His transformation was not complete. Gender blending is an integral aspect of Dionysus, in a very different way than it is for Athena.

Athena and Dionysus are two primary examples of how the Olympian gods embody and enact the gender bending and gender blending addressed by the essays in this volume, and they embody this gender diversity not as outcasts incidental to their world but as fundamental figures within it. The Olympian gods, we must remember, reflect the heteronormative, patriarchal structure of society and simultaneously lead by example, much the same way twenty-first century popular culture represents not only the ways mainstream culture wants to see itself but also the dominant ways it makes available to understand itself. Those identities and expressions (no matter how numerous!) that diverge too far from the norm remain under- or unrepresented, which all too often means, as Gayatri Spivak (1999) argues, that the subaltern does not get a chance to culturally 'speak'. That is to say that, on the one hand, the Olympian gods are reflective of ideals for their world, and as such both Athena and Dionysus represent the types of gender difference that can occur, albeit marginally, within that social structure. On the other hand, and more importantly, it reveals that the hierarchical binary social structures require gender differences like the gender fluidity of Dionysus or the female masculinity of Athena in order to maintain those social structures as normative ones at all. Olympus presents the norm of a two-gendered society, where maleness and masculinity are primary to femaleness and femininity and the social structure of the gods maintains and encourages the reproduction of this social order. Yet the world of the gods also includes differences – such as the occasional outlier like female masculinity or gender fluidity – that must not be allowed into the forces of social reproduction, and are thus contained through powerful social forces, such as the law of the gods, so that the apparent outliers do not become the norm. Athena and Dionysus are not merely symbolic of how those who may not fit so well into the social structures can still be recognised, but rather they represent the fluidity that lies under the pretense of stability that is continually celebrated and must be continually reaffirmed as divine, natural, ideal and normal. Indeed, one possible conclusion is that if binary sex and gender were any of these things, they would not require such constant upkeep. Whatever else these figures may tell us, it is clear that Athena and Dionysus suggest that the ancient world was aware of gender diversity and sought ways of representing it in and as part of ancient society.

For the reasons opened to us by Athena and Dionysus, we take gender diversity to refer to a number of different ways by which individuals express their gender, how they identify with gender and gender roles, as well as what it has to do with how this relates to an individual's assigned sex at birth, their physical sex, and sometimes a person's perceived gender. Athena, for example, is assigned female at birth. Of that, there is no question. In addition, she is perceived as female by everyone, but this is the end of the alignment between the sex she was assigned at birth and her public presentation. For Athena does not express her gender as feminine; her gender presentation is masculine, from her clothing to her gender role to her comportment, and from her actions to the symbolic meaning of her actions. She is very thoroughly a masculine example of someone assigned female at birth. In fact, the most ambiguous feature of the figure of Athena is that she is recognised clearly as female while she comfortably physically presents as masculine in her body, its behaviours and its abilities, combined with her male gender role and her masculine gender expressions.

On the other hand, Dionysus represents gender fluidity: he identifies differently as male and female, and as masculine or feminine. He takes up variously male gender roles in one context, and female gender roles in another. He expresses himself as sometimes female and sometimes male; and while Dionysus is always recognised with the pronouns 'he' and 'him', he is understood through-out his narratives and visual representations to perform a gender-fluid or gen-der-creative identity that rarely aligns with traditional interpretations of male, masculine or man. Not surprisingly, Athena and Dionysus are the very models of gender diversity in the ancient world because they clearly parse the differences within gender expression, gender identity, assigned sex, physical sex, perceived sex, as well different sexualities such as Athena's asexuality and Dionysus' hetero-sexual consent-driven sexuality.

LIFTING THE CISHETERONORMATIVE METHODOLOGY FROM THE ANCIENT WORLD

Reviewing the ancient world with attention to gender expressions and gender identities leads to surprising observations that alter what we previously thought about the past and, in turn, what we thought we understood about ourselves. The feminist, queer and trans theories that these essays take up allow them to open a number of ways of looking at the world – both ancient and contempo-rary – beyond heteronormative ways of seeing and experiencing it (see especially Hughes and Sowers and Passaro in this volume). One of those ways involves distinguishing between gender identity, gender expression and the sex one is assigned at birth. In Roman iconography, as the archaeologist Ashley Barnett (2012) argues, parsing sex assignment from gender identity and gender expres-sion allows us to see, for instance, that while the phallus is a strong cultural and political symbol in ancient Rome, it is not necessarily determinate of one's gender identity. She uses the example of Priapus, god of fertility and the protection of gardens, to argue that his phallic imagery is apotropaic, cathartic and metonymic but above all synecdochal of masculine gender roles, Roman citizenry and the Roman Republic itself. Further, phallic imagery was not limited to male bodies; rather, it represented the power relations interconnecting a variety of identities and experiences. There is, in ancient Rome's phallic iconography, a differentiation between the phallus and the penis itself, showing there to be a particular set of power relations in ancient Rome that involved more than just men and women, citizens and non-citizens. In her analysis, phallic iconography was utilised to represent, encode, demarcate, protect and distinguish various types of person – child, adult, citizen, freedman, soldier and woman. It had less to do with what was between one's legs than it did with who was in a position of power in Roman society. Male sex is not identical with masculinity, for part of the purpose of the iconography is to invoke strength, protection and masculine ideals despite the gender expression (for example, smart, sacred, young, vulnerable, leader) of the individual. Nor is it identical to the gender identity of the individual, such as boy or girl or man or intersex; in fact, Barnett argues that gender roles were more attached to class in ancient Rome than to sex or sexuality.

Although the use of the Roman phallus demonstrates the distinction between power, male sex and gender identity, Mary Weismantel (2012) argues that the celebration of the divine dual-gendered Hermaphroditus suggests there was a role or respect for a diversity of gender identities. However, the space for this gender diversity was not always a positive one, for while the divine dual-sexed body was worshipped, non-conforming mortal bodies were not necessarily desirable and were at times treated with violence (Weismantel 2012: 320); there is one law for the divine gods, and quite another for mortals who see themselves ideally reflected in the gods, but who can never become god-like themselves. In this way, although nobody ever actually embodies the norms of hyperfemininity and hypermasculinity, they remain unrealisable goals that characterise masculinist and hierarchical socio-political systems such as those of much of the ancient world, and of our own (Lugones 2016; Connell and Messerschmidt 2005). According to Aileen Ajootian (1995), of the rare accounts in ancient sources that discuss non-normative bodies, some describe events such as two people identified as women but with non-conforming bodies who were reportedly burned alive in the early first century BC, and another of a series of 'androgynous' births in the mid–late Republic seen as sinister portents, drowned at sea as an act of expiation (on these passages see Penrose and Shannon-Henderson in this volume). So while the worship of divine Hermaphroditus acts as a positive, protective force, the mortal non-conforming bodies were seen as a direct threat to political and social stability that must be destroyed (Shapiro 2015 makes a similar argument with respect to the positive androgyny of the immortal Dionysus versus the negative androgyny of the mortal Athenian politician Alcibiades). This may seem to follow the theories of gender bending put forward in the late 1990s, namely that bending the rules of gender does not dismantle, and may even support hegemonic and binary gender roles (Devor 1989; Lorber 1996; Phelan 1998). Yet we stand with feminist, queer and anti-patriarchal thinkers such as Lucal (1999), Halberstam and (in some ways) Butler to argue that these figures show that gender can be (and has been!) done differently. In fact, the essays in this volume suggest that there have always been attempts to 'do gender' otherwise, challenging norms. In the case of the mortal non-conforming bodies, the disparate treatment of these bodies demonstrates both a desire and a refusal to acknowledge and accept their presence in society, and this twofold recognition underscores the ongoing need of hegemonic society to maintain the strict binary gender difference that keeps one group in power (on this point, see Deminion and McCoskey in this volume). Hermaphroditus, as a divine figure, could be accepted as belonging to another realm in which all manner of creatures existed. However, nonconforming bodies within society itself could not be so easily accepted if the symbolically phallic or masculinist order was to remain in power. One obvious outcome of this research is that if we can identify in the ancient world acts of gender violence related explicitly to queer bodies, then there existed queer bodies, whatever else we can say of them. From the point of view of trans and queer theory, denying their very being both denies the fact of queer and trans history, and also tells a very particular story of both the ancient world and of where we came from, one that conveniently leaves out the experiences of bodies we choose to invalidate. Part of the point of this volume, then, is to open a historical trajectory of trans and queer identities and representations in and through the scholarly research into ancient articulations of gender, sexuality and social bodies.

In a similar vein, Rosemary Joyce (2005) has taken up in her research the archaeological focus on the body as a site of renewed understandings of the ancient world. Joyce holds that ancient bodies can be interpreted in terms of modes of embodiment, rather than primarily in terms of symbolic features; she argues that when we consider that the 'biological person is both the medium and product of social action', then both the interiority of bodies that experienced the ancient world and the symbols that adorned and surrounded them must be understood in a new way. Her insights are important for classical scholarship because the material evidence may suggest more than the hegemonic social norms of binary genders. Rather than seeing an 'assumed stability of bodily identity', archaeological observation can attend to the objects, artworks, adornments and environments relationally: they are not static representations of an interiority, but part of the material world in which people engaged; they are not mere signals of existing identities but active agents in identity construction. These things are traces of material interaction and experience through which body practices and representation work together, either systems through which concepts and social orders became naturalised, or contested sites of agency and cultural production and reproduction. The upshot of Joyce's analysis is that when archaeologists use 'broader theories of embodiment and materiality', they can see traces of the body as a point of social action rather than an inert representation of existing social structures. Not surprisingly, Barbara Voss (2008) has championed this broader lens of viewing and interpreting material traces of the past.

Voss starts from the historically self-reflective position that any assumptions that past peoples held to the relatively modern, Western tradition of the heteronormative, cisgender, monogamous coupling of people for primarily reproductive purposes is without foundation. The proliferation of sexually explicit artefacts, jokes and stories from the ancient world denies that sex was primarily for reproduction (Voss 2008: 318). The historically and culturally shifting ideas of what counts as 'sexual' further confound our assignation of particular sexual norms onto the past. And the focus on bodies, interactions between various bodies and the celebration of bodies that used to be interpreted in terms of fertility rites has been opened by theories of embodied experience and material culture studies, such as Joyce's, to show that sometimes a naked body is just a naked body, even in ancient Greece and Rome. Given that people have been using tools, plants, acts and ideas to regulate and affect sexuality and reproduction since at least 5000 BP, all of which is material evidence that reproduction is both culturally managed and involves a fraction of 'sexual activities and relationships', it should come as no surprise that it's not only sexuality that is at issue in understandings of the ancient world, but the representation of bodies and genders as well (Voss 2008: 320). Further, just as it does more justice to the ancient world to consider the different circumstances of the past and present viewers of bodily or sexual images when we are trying to identify what and why they are, it is equally important to consider the ideological basis of who created these images, for what purpose, and in what context. For instance, when there is a thing hanging between the legs of a figure in an image of a body, it does not necessarily suggest male. Nor does it necessarily suggest masculinity. Following Barnett's analysis, sometimes the image of a phallus actually represents power, whether it is attached to a female, a woman, a non-citizen, an intersex person or a man. Sometimes it is ambiguous and the researcher has to look beyond the iconography to the audience, the maker, the materials and the provenance generally.

One of Voss's points is that when studies of prehistory find that sex and gender are varied, have varying representations and intervene continually in political power formations, and when we can recognise that this happened in the historical moments shortly after ancient Rome (as Dinshaw shows to be the case in medieval Europe in her 2012 book *How Soon is Now*), then there is little reason to assume that the ancient worlds of Greece and Rome are the lone anomaly that hold to a lack of gender and sexual diversity (Voss 2008: 322). Voss argues that recent interpretations of *kinaidoi/cinaedi* suggest that their identity was less determined by their sexual acts than by their gender liminality; looking at the iconography of penetration without ignoring the outlier images where they do the penetrating suggests a hitherto unrecognised gender diversity and shared identity (on *kinaidoi/cinaedi* see Adkins and Penrose in this volume; on the question of penetration in gender identification see Adkins, Åshede, Begum-Lees and Shannon-Henderson). And finally, Voss makes the point that those interpretations of sexuality in ancient Greece and Rome that tend to focus on the radical difference of this past from the present – effectively erasing the queerness of the past (even if the only similarity between queer past and present is queerness itself!) – are the interpretations which read contemporary heteronormative gender structures into the past. Yet those who read images of sexuality, gender and the political structures that intersect them from the standpoint of feminist, queer, trans or gender-diverse theories overwhelmingly tend to find a real continuity between past and present forms of violence, objectification, subjugation and erasure.

As mentioned, Ajootian demonstrates that the evidence which reports violence against ambiguously sexed bodies in both ancient Greece and Rome is minimal, and aside from discussions of how they were killed, they generally disappeared from history. However, she goes further to argue that although these people have been called 'hermaphrodites', after the divine Hermaphroditus, there was no connection between the divinity and the human 'monsters' (*monstra*), before Ovid's account of the joining of Hermaphroditus and Salmacis (Ajootian 1995; on Ovid's account see Kelly in this volume). Hermaphroditus is dual-sexed, and represents both a threat to dominant forms of masculinity and an apotropaic power, similar to Priapus. Yet lives which we would now call queer were still subaltern in the ancient world, and didn't always participate in the powers of their namesakes: those intersex individuals identified as 'hermaphrodite' were understood in terms of their divergence from the norm and not their similarity to the god. Queer and trans theory intersects with classics when they indicate the cultural bias by which many scholars read the ancient worlds, opening new methodologies (such as gender archaeology, embodiment theory and ethnographic studies) by which to consider and reconsider the evidence of the past, both that already well-documented and that formerly relegated to the status of anomaly.

Queer theory carries with it a strong focus on identity, for when we are considering the ways by which we behave, organise ourselves and identify ourselves, one's identity tends to determine how those behaviours will be understood, in what social groups we will be organised and what identities might be open (or not open) to us, even if we phenomenologically know we identify as a certain kind of being. This focus on identity might seem anachronistic when applying it to the ancient world, for the social categories by which we organise ourselves now may not at all have existed in the past – categories such as homosexual, transgender, femme or queer. Yet that is part of the point: categories such as nuclear family, male masculinity and essential femininity, for example, are also twentieth-century identities that may not translate so perfectly into the past. Further, queer theory integrates other social identifiers into considerations, such as class, nationality, race and citizenship, suggesting that when we look at the past we can indeed find non-heteronormative ways by which people came together. Queer theory therefore opens the analysis of the past towards (1) observing the past in surprising new ways, and thus opening abductively new ways of understanding the social structures of the past, and (2) new ways of considering what we have already observed about the embodied behaviours of the past (Dinshaw 1999; Halberstam 1998). For this reason, a reconsideration of those activities, behaviours and bodies that tend not to be universalised or brought into history – namely, gender-bending bodies, gender-blending behaviours and differently gendered identities – can unfold a new way of observing, considering and relating to the past.

NOTES ON GENDER, GRAMMAR AND TRANSLATION

Throughout this volume, we have employed a number of grammatical terms and translations that hold to the rigorous reconsideration of bodies, behaviours and histories for which the essays in this volume argue. First, we have translated *androgynos/androgynus* (in both Greek and Latin) as androgynous. We do not accept its common translation as 'hermaphrodite', a translation found in most (if not all, to our knowledge) Greek and Latin dictionaries, because the term is both derogatory and carries with it a pejorative connotation and negative value that, quite simply, the original languages do not support. The use and presence of the term in Greek and Latin dictionaries is a function of old ideas which did not recognise gender diversity; our aim is to assist in updating the canon with thoroughness and respect.

Secondly, we have taken especial care with the use of pronouns to ensure that the subjects of the following essays are not misgendered. For this reason, we use gender-neutral pronouns for Hermaphroditus (Åshede) except when discussing pre-transformation Hermaphroditus in Ovid (Kelly) because at that point, he is a boy until fused with the female nymph Salmacis. Begum-Lees also uses different pronouns for pre- and post-transformation of Iphis, as she explains in her contribution. Adkins uses feminine pronouns when she discusses the priests of Lucius' narration because they identify as 'girls', even though Lucius himself uses derogative terms and masculine pronouns to describe them. Finally, in bringing into dialogue the contemporary queer and intersectional theories with Lucian's dialogues, Ash is able to not only use but discuss in detail the shifting gender identities presented, adopted and identified in the *Dialogues*.

Finally, and in the same vein, we have found that Hermaphroditus tends to be referred to as 'he' in translations, but only because the Latin uses the masculine pronoun as default for mixed groups (as does French, for example). We hold that this use of masculine pronouns compromises the judicious presentation of Hermaphroditus and skews our understanding of hir because of the immediate default to the masculine. As Åshede indicates in her essay, the explanation for this is clearly articulated by Groves (2016: 350):

> . . . the literary text must portray him as male, in grammatical gender, if not fully in biological sex. Hermaphroditus is a *male* name after all, and the words used to describe the god and intersex people in both Greek and Latin (ἀνδρόγυνος, *androgynus*, *semimas*) are unfailingly masculine in gender . . . just as a group of mixed gender defaults to the masculine in Greek and Latin, so an individual of mixed gender does as well. There is no reason, however, for the detached reader to suspect that the masculinity of the god is anything more than a linguistic convention.

Groves (2016: 351) also notes that visual representations of Hermaphroditus are found to depict hir primarily as female (a controversial point for Åshede) and in that female presentation ze is often attacked by male satyrs or Pan. Yet in Ovid, Hermaphroditus is a boy (*puer*) and is attacked by a woman. The overarching point here is that there is no comprehensive or coherent history of Hermaphroditus' presentations that suggest one or the other gender identity or sex. For this reason, we use the pronouns 'ze' and 'hir' in reference to Hermaphroditus; while it may be more common to use the gender-neutral pronouns 'they' and 'them', this presents sometimes impassable difficulties when translating gender and tense in classical texts and for clarity and ease, we have stuck with gender-neutral 'ze' and 'hir'.

NOTES ON THE ESSAYS IN THIS VOLUME

The essays presented in this volume are grouped according to themes that abductively develop ways to observe ancient Greece and Rome anew and analyse those observations in hitherto unconsidered ways. This book is not meant to offer comprehensive coverage of all aspects of antiquity, which would be an impossible task for a single volume. Rather we seek to open up a conversation on ways to tease out gender diversity from our available sources. To this end, we have chosen to focus on a selection of literature, historical texts and material culture, each of which offers a different set of cultural representation affecting notions of gender identity and formation. We feel this represents a sufficiently broad array of sources, while still offering a variety of approaches within each grouping. One important area of study largely omitted from this volume is that of cult practice (while Adkins does address religion broadly, she does not explicitly examine cult practice). Religious rituals and practice provide particularly rich sources for the study of gender variance and would undoubtably yield valuable discussion. Interpretation of cultic practice, however, is complex and exploring the sources and interpretations of cult satisfactorily would require more space and attention than is available here. We have also included only sources which have a clear temporal/cultural context. Since the goal is to tease out gender variance within specific cultural contexts, it seems prudent to focus on sources, both textual and visual, that can be securely connected to a specific time and place for which we have a reasonably secure cultural understanding. By necessity, this means excluding prehistoric sources (such as Mycenaean and Minoan) as well as texts such as Homer, where it is unclear precisely what cultural context is being depicted.

The book begins with Walter Penrose's exploration of the virtues of courage and intelligence as locators of ancient Greek gender diversity and construction. Those with courage and intelligence – women or men – are markedly masculine, within ancient Greek heteropatriarchal notions of gender. Penrose argues for a strong distinction between gender and sexuality, holding that courageous and intelligent men are manly and masculine, and that courageous women such as Clytemnestra are not to be seen as lesbians, but as masculine women: strong, bold, dominant and ready to act with violence when needed. Men without courage, such as Aegisthus, are feminised, but are not to be seen as gay; rather, they fail to meet the requirements of male masculinity. Courage and intelligence are male qualities; thus men who bear too little are ridiculed (such as the *kinaidoi*) and women who bear too much are distanced from regular Athenian society, and both groups are considered unnatural and unAthenian. With this analysis, Penrose takes up Butler's argument that gender intersects with political and cultural formations of identity and shows how gender is produced and maintained with citizenship, status, class and nationality in a constant process of identity production that sustains the rule of particular groups. Gender identity is not born, but made in the ancient world.

Tyson Sukava reinterprets the so-called sexless body in Greek medicine and healing, by arguing for a spectrum of bodies between the two poles of maleness and femaleness through his analysis of the blending role of bodily fluids or humours. That is, ancient physicians were less interested in anatomy than physiognomy, and the way humours mixed in a body determined one's sex. In Sukava's analysis, the category of human or *anthrōpos* downplays both sex and gender to focus specifically on an ill body part, which was considered undifferentiated in human bodies that are themselves only differentiated by humoral make-up. Sukava also looks at the flip side of the unsexed body, which was the dual-sexed body, but he argues that this body appeared primarily only when reproductive organs were at issue. Sukava's analysis of a spectrum of sexed bodies – one which bears relations to current theories – suggests that notions of gender and sex were more complex in the past than they appear at first blush, and that healing practitioners actually presented new ways to consider the constructed nature, shared human nature, or at least the non-biological roots of sex and gender.

Anna Uhlig also takes up Judith Butler's performative notion of gender construction in her analysis of Pandora's 'birth by hammer', linking it with Karen Barad's post-humanist and radically materialist theory of open corporeal boundaries that are always in the process of becoming. Through a reading of two fragments of the Pandora story – Sophocles' *Pandora or Hammerers* and Pheidias' sculptural depiction of the birth of Pandora – both of which present Pandora as hammer-wrought from the earth itself, Uhlig argues against the strict and misogynistic binarism of Hesiod, who reviles her crafted body, and for a reading of her symbolism of the ambiguity of human existence. Humans are both born and made, natural and artificial; Pandora shatters the mythic binary between earth-born goddess and constructed object when she is found to construct herself out of the materials around her. Similarly, Uhlig finds the representations of Pandora surrounded by ambiguous figures such as satyrs, also wielding hammers and thereby supporting the hybrid materiality she represents in both her being and her gender. For the figure of Pandora as a woman also celebrates a body that is constructed artificially and whose artifice is her strength.

Kelly Shannon-Henderson analyses a literary device, namely the spontaneous transformation of women into men, to determine what they reveal about gender difference in the ancient world, only to find that these stories simultaneously offer alternatives to the masculinist binary norm and uphold rigorously these gender norms of the time. In the scenarios Shannon-Henderson examines, such transformation is not desired, leaving the characters the need to renegotiate family roles, legal relationships and gendered social norms. Moreover, Shannon-Henderson finds that these texts also reveal an ideological fascination with genitalia and sexual expression as determinate of both strict gender identity and male superiority. While there is no doubt, in her analysis, that the women completely transformed into men, there is also no hint that this indicates a fluidity to sex or gender, and there is no implied moral that liminal gender identities have a place in cisheteronormative patriarchal societies. The upshot of these tales is that those who transform are viewed negatively; in fact, these stories reveal the centrality of the gender binary and the social drive to destroy those who don't fit the binary gender norms because they make those who do fit the norms feel uncomfortable.

Once gender construction is situated as a fundamental theme, gender fluidity is explored in the second section of essays, beginning with two enquiries into the figure of Hermaphroditus. First, Linnea Åshede examines the visual tradition of Hermaphroditus, rejecting the conventional reading as a female figure who is surprisingly and humorously equipped with a penis. Instead, Åshede takes up the gender roles Hermaphroditus presents and argues for Hermaphroditus' gender fluidity. Åshede also takes up Karen Barad's posthumanist theory of relational construction to analyse how the anatomy, apparel, behaviour, reception and intended display contextualise the figure, showing how Hermaphroditus is best understood to be an amalgamation of conventional representations of beautiful women and boys in a gender-fluid whole.

Turning to literary sources, Peter Kelly similarly argues that the representation of Hermaphroditus in Ovid's *Metamorphoses* emerges out of the descriptions by Lucretius and Plato, but develops in a more cosmological line. Hermaphroditus is an embodiment of universal retrogression, which in this context means Hermaphroditus is a liminal figure symbolic of both universal history and of human development. The key to Kelly's argument is the gender fluidity of Hermaphroditus, for it is only as a fluid blend of sex and gender identities that the figure is representative of the discursive complexity of cosmological views in Ovid, where transformational and relational cosmic structure is played out in Hermaphroditus' transformational selfhood.

The theme of gender fluidity continues with Rebecca Begum-Lees' discussion of the character Iphis, again in Ovid's *Metamorphoses*. Iphis was assigned female at birth, but lives as a man who sexually desires women. Begum-Lees argues that Iphis' name is gender neutral, as are Iphis' actions, but rather than acting on same-sex desire, Iphis insists on acting as a man who loves Ianthe. Ovid clearly deals with the constructed nature of gender norms in this character, speaking solely about social gender and never referring to biological sex, to show ultimately the inadequacy of strict social norms when Iphis is transformed as a character into the much-longed-for male body to consummate marriage.

Jussi Rantala explores historical rhetoric around the intersection of gender ambiguity and ethnicity in the complex figure of Elagabalus. Rantala shows how this ambiguity is used as a rhetorical device by two contemporary Greek historians, Cassius Dio and Herodian. Both authors use the emperor's gender ambiguity as an entry point to explore questions of Greek ethnicity in the Roman Empire. For Herodian, Elagabalus' strange behaviour underscores the foreign, Eastern and therefore 'othered' nature of the emperor in relation to Greek culture in the eastern part of the empire. His presentation and actions were odd, but hardly dangerous. For Dio, however, Elagabalus is a much more transgressive figure. As a Roman senator who identified strongly with the Roman state, Dio views the emperor's 'womanly' presentation and behaviour as something alien to Roman identity and an insult to Roman values, values which demanded the strict binary difference of masculinity and femininity, ultimately revealing the ongoing need in Roman culture to maintain continually one's binary gender expression.

From gender fluidity, we open in section three the differences explored amongst cisgender and transgender women and men, and representations of transgender identity in general. The theme of gender ambiguity is developed in Dalida Agri's study of Flavian epic. Agri examines the allegories in the divine Virtus in Statius and Silius, linking gender liminality with forms of moral reasoning. On the one hand, Statius complicates the divine figure Virtus through a simile of Virtus as transvestite Hercules: a feminine figure with masculine meaning, dressed in female attire who seems to be reconstructing her gender deceptively. On the other hand, Silius contrasts a sternly moral and gender ambiguous Virtus with a yielding and feminine Voluptas. There is a double-coding gender analysis at work here which Agri holds points to a larger gender ambivalence that cuts through notions of a strict cultural gender binary.

Lisa Hughes revisits the characters of Omphale and Hercules in Pompeian *domus*. Normally, the representations of the domineering queen Omphale and the subordinate Hercules are figures of mockery and derision; in certain dining contexts in Pompeian *domus*, however, the figures are treated positively. Hughes argues that this is not a mistake but rather a mode of understanding difference in Neronian theatre. She argues that the blurred gender lines in these representations break down social and cultural barriers, consider the experience of those outside the binary gender norms and ultimately construct new ways to empathise and identify with the everyday domestic and public lives of those who diverge from gender norms.

Evelyn Adkins considers the transgender experience of the priests of the Syrian goddess in second century AD Roman culture, as depicted in Apuleius' *Golden Ass*. While the priests identify as female and use feminine grammatical forms, Lucius discusses them using only derogatory and male grammatical forms. In an argument that resonates strikingly with those of the contemporary world, Adkins holds that the key to their contested identity is in their speech: their words, grammatical forms, voices and intentions in speaking are derided by Lucius but are determinately feminine for the priests themselves. Lucius denies the priests' transwoman identities and instead he redefines them to conform to Roman gender expectations, where gender, class and power are all fought within the terrain of discourse and the politics of representation.

In a related argument but about a different text, Rowan Emily Ash examines Lucian's *Dialogues of the Courtesans*, and in particular the character of Megillos, who is assigned female at birth and identifies as a man. With reference to Halberstam's notion of 'female masculinities', Ash argues that the way that the audience reads emphatic particle, syntax and plot motif determines whether Megillos comes across as a lesbian or a transgender man. While at first blush the story seems to assert prevailing gender norms by showing what happens once they are defied, Ash argues that reconsidering the text with an eye to ethnicity and economic class, as well as to gender and sex, offers a stronger, intersectional reading of Megillos' gender diversity.

Female masculinity is the focus of the fourth section, beginning with Brian Sowers and Kimberly Passaro, who look at the *Acts of Paul and Thecla* to reveal a second-century AD Christian ideal of sexual asceticism that actively inhabits fluid gender identities. Thecla renounces marriage, contrary to both Greco-Roman and Jewish norms: she becomes increasingly masculine as she renounces more and more feminine duties, such as motherhood and women's clothing, to become a model Christian disciple and the ideal literary woman, who seems to identify as a man. Sowers and Passaro hold that Thecla's story reveals an unexpectedly nuanced understanding of the plurality of sexual identities promoted in the ancient Mediterranean.

Mary Deminion takes the notion of female masculinity in another direction, examining women's challenges to political gender norms in Rome. Three orators who also, and unusually, happen to be women, appear in Valerius Maximus and are presented as either gender non-conforming or even inhuman for their transgression into the masculine domain of the Roman courtroom. In arguing successfully and with courage and rhetorical skill, the three individuals are considered an *androgyne*, a monster and a mere vessel for her father's voice, respectively; that is, they are ridiculed for their defiance of heteronormative gender roles and denied propriety of their own masculinised abilities. Nevertheless, Deminion argues that the reaction to these women reveals the real anxiety about shifting gender boundaries evident in Roman public life.

Finally, Denise Eileen McCoskey examines the character of Artemisia both in Herodotus and in the 2014 film *300: Rise of an Empire*. As a Greek woman serving as advisor and commander in Xerxes' Persian fleet, Artemisia crosses boundaries of both gender and ethnicity. For Herodotus, Artemisia's role as a warrior is transgressive, crossing accepted gender roles, but he does not treat this transgression as exclusively dangerous. Rather he stresses her Greekness to set her up as a mirror of Themistocles, offering a complex calibration of gender difference and racial sameness. By contrast, the film shows Artemisia as all difference. Her gender-transgressive behaviour is now dangerous, and made even more explicit by contrast with the feminine figure of Gorgo. Her racial difference is made overt, and she herself denies her Greekness and instead identifies most closely with a black character in the film. While Herodotus' Artemisia is a remarkable and respected figure, in the film version she is only to be feared and hated. As a figure of unacceptable difference, Artemisia must be destroyed, a sentiment reflected in the brutality inflicted on her body and her eventual violent death.

NOTE

1. The one exception is Hephaestus' attempted assault on Athena, which led to the birth of the Athenian hero Erichthonios, with Athena as his nominal mother. But this is specifically an Athenian story, and even here Athena eschews the conventions of both sex and motherhood. The child is born from the ejaculate Hephaestus spills on Athena's leg, which she then flings to the earth (Gaia) from which Erichthonios will later be born. Thus Athena, the mother, remains a virgin and the child is neither conceived nor does it gestate in her womb. Nor does she take on the role of caretaker, as she hands the child immediately upon his birth over to the daughters of Kekrops to be cared for (on motherhood and Athenian autochthony see Loraux 1981; Shapiro 1995; Rauchle 2015; Surtees 2019; but see Llewellyn-Jones 2001).

PART I

Gender Construction

CHAPTER 1

Gender Diversity in Classical Greek Thought

Walter D. Penrose, Jr

In hir groundbreaking work *Transgender Warriors*, Leslie Feinberg advises that the terms 'transvestite' and 'cross-dresser' can be offensive to transgender folks because they reduce a person's entire being to clothing choice (1996: xi). In the 1990s, Feinberg's work served as activism not only by rethinking the vocabulary of gender diversity, but also by writing a history of transgender individuals. In this essay, I would like to expand upon Feinberg's analysis by underscoring that gender diversity among the ancient Greeks of the Classical Period (490–323 BC) was understood to be about more than outward appearance. While clothing choice was one factor by which the Greeks measured gender queerness, and physiognomy another, classical-era Greek authors also factored an individual's intelligence and courageousness (or lack thereof) into their gender makeup. Any one of these characteristics, or some combination thereof, may have been used to denote gender diversity. The Greeks' intentions were not always as noble or inclusive as those of Feinberg, however, as such markers were generally used to gauge transgression from perceived norms. Among the Greeks, such perceptions of gender variance were tied to misogynist, normative constructions of gender, within which men were, more often than not, expected to be courageous and intelligent, but women were often not. Within such a paradigm, women who were courageous, intelligent and also loyal could be called masculine, whereas men who lacked the characteristics of courage and strength, among other qualities, could be perceived as feminine. While Greek authors often describe the crossing of gender boundaries in a negative or pejorative fashion, occasionally we do find positive assessments, more so with respect to women who were perceived to be 'masculine' than with respect to men who were perceived to be 'feminine' (Penrose 2016: 34–61; Carlà-Uhink 2017: 9). From Greek texts we also gain insight into the attitudes of others, such as the Scythians, who, although they did not record their own histories, refreshingly seem to have revered gender-diverse individuals as shaman-type religious figures.

I will begin this essay with an analysis of prescribed gender norms in classi-cal-era Greece. Next, I will discuss how female masculinity and male femininity were constructed in relation to those norms. I will then explore variations in usage of the term *androgynos*, a term that literally translates as 'man-woman' but more often than not, meant 'feminine man'. I will also discuss how the terms *androgynos* and *kinaidos* could be used as synonymous slurs, and how both terms related to cowardice. I will then explore the very different contexts in which the term *androgynoi* was used to describe Scythian Enarees who were described as what we today would call male-to-female transgender women but were possibly also female-to-male transgender men, non-binary or intersex. Where possible, I will emphasise inconsistencies in Greek thought both with regard to the con-struction of normative gender roles and, correspondingly, gender diversity.

IDEAL WOMANHOOD AND FEMALE MASCULINITY

In Xenophon's *Oeconomicus* (7–10), a fourth-century BC Socratic dialogue on estate management, the Athenian aristocrat Ischomachus describes the ideal woman, his wife, in a discussion with Socrates. Ischomachus' wife is an aristocratic woman who capably manages the household, after having been trained by her husband to do so. Ischomachus justifies the prescription of household duties to his wife by telling her that: 'since the god [Zeus] had delegated to the woman the duty of guarding the produce that had been brought into the house, he measured out a greater portion of fear to her than to the man. And knowing that the man, work-ing outdoors, would have to defend against intruders, he gave him a greater share of courage' (7.25, ed. Pomeroy – all translations are my own). Xenophon does not see women as completely devoid of courage, however, as they must have some modicum of this trait to guard the valuables inside the house (Penrose 2016: 25). In Xenophon's understanding, prescribed gender roles are ordained by the god Zeus, and thus considered natural. In Xenophon's *Symposium* (2.12), however, Socrates asserts that courage *can* be taught 'even' to a woman (see further Pomeroy 1994: 303). Plato's Socrates goes further in asserting that men and women *can* have the same virtues, including courage (*Rep.* 5). According to Aristotle, Socrates argued that men and women *did* have the same *andreia*, although Aristotle himself disagreed, arguing in one instance that women had a lesser *andreia* than men, and, in another, that tragedians should not represent women as *andreiai* (Ar. *Pol.* 1260A 20–4; Ar. *Poet.* 1454A). Socrates was a radical; pseudo-Aristotle, in tandem with his alleged mentor Aristotle, emphasises that women are 'less cou-rageous' than men ([*Phyn.*] 809a–b) (on the Socratic idea of *andreia* as a trait shared by men and women, see Penrose 2016: 43–7).

Xenophon also asserts that women can be intelligent, even though he sees intelligence, interestingly, as a masculine trait that the ideal woman possesses:

after Xenophon's Socrates hears about what a capable household manager Ischomachus' wife has become, he exclaims 'By Hera, Ischomachus, you demonstrate what a masculine intelligence your wife has' (*Oec.* 10.1). This is a compliment, whereas when a man is called feminine, the opposite is implied (Pomeroy 1994: 303). Xenophon here shows that he is more broad-minded than other misogynist Greek authors, but nonetheless, like Semonides of Amorgos, he genders intelligence as a male trait. Semonides argues in *On Women* (1–2, ed. Lloyd-Jones) that 'In the beginning the god made the female mind separately.' (I here follow Lloyd-Jones (1975: 63–4), who persuasively argues that Semonides compares the female mind to the male mind.) Semonides goes on to classify women into different types, as though he were creating a taxonomy of animals. One of these kinds of women, he argues, 'often calls a good thing bad and a bad thing good' (10–11). Of course, Greek conceptions of gender did not necessarily match up to the reality portrayed in Greek historical accounts or even myth, where women do show intelligence. In the *Odyssey*, for example, Homer does portray Penelope as clever, and hence the gendering of intelligence as a male trait is not universal among Greek authors. In extant classical Athenian literature, however, there is a tendency to view intelligent women as masculine.

The Athenian playwright Aeschylus presents the character of Clytemnestra as a masculine woman due to both her intelligence and her boldness in his tragic trilogy the *Oresteia*, which was first performed at Athens in 458 BC. The three plays of the *Oresteia* centre around the murder of the Greek hero Agamemnon by his wife, Clytemnestra, upon his return from the Trojan War. At the beginning of the first play, *Agamemnon*, Clytemnestra is called *androboulos* 'manly-minded' because she is capably ruling Argos in her husband's stead (*Ag.* 11, ed. Page). Despite this compliment, Clytemnestra is ultimately viewed negatively for taking on other masculine prerogatives when she kills her husband in revenge for his murder of their daughter, Iphigenia. As revenge was considered to be the domain of men in ancient Greece, Clytemnestra's actions are ascribed to *tolma*, or audacity that is improper for a woman (1231–3; see further Burnett 1998: 144; McHardy 2004, 2008: esp. 37–42; Penrose 2016: 27–34).

Clytemnestra's actions disrupt the social and political order. Aeschylus' portrait of Clytemnestra negatively inscribes classical-era Athenian gender norms: Clytemnestra usurps power reserved for men, and she pays the ultimate price for doing so: death. The same may be said for Sophocles' Antigone, in the tragedy of the same name that was written in c. 441 BC (Penrose 2016: 35–7). Unlike Clytemnestra, however, Antigone is a *parthenos* (a virgin or unmarried girl). Judith Fletcher (2007: 25) argues that the 'social construct' of the *parthenos* signified 'a temporary period of wildness in a young woman's coming of age'. The ancient Greeks thought that *parthenoi* possessed 'a remarkable potency' which had to be 'incorporated within the state if the state' was to survive. The unmarried woman was considered to be *adamatos*, or 'untamed', and the only way that she could be tamed was via marriage. Fletcher (2007: 26) asserts that, in Greek thought 'when the *parthenos* becomes nubile she can turn nasty or even suicidal; the final stage of virginity, right before marriage and integration into society, is a dangerous period . . . The virgin is a powerful creature, full of a latent fecundity and incipient sexuality which cause problems unless properly channeled.' Although Fletcher focuses upon the choruses in Aeschylus in her investigation, her theoretical apparatus can be applied to Sophocles' Antigone (if not to Aeschylus' Clytemnestra, who disrupts order even after marriage). Sophocles' Antigone, betrothed but yet unwed, disrupts the social and political order by disobeying the orders of her uncle Creon, who represents patriarchal authority in the play *Antigone*. Hence she is called a man by Creon (484–5). Yet she is also called a man by her father, Oedipus, for her loyalty to him in Sophocles' *Oedipus at Colonus* (1365–9). In both plays, the reader is left to sympathise with Antigone, and thus Antigone's masculinity is held in a positive light (Penrose 2016: 35–8; see also Starkey 2012: 171). Conversely, in the *Oresteia*, the audience is led to sympathise with Clytemnestra's son, Orestes, who has killed his own mother.

While Clytemnestra and Antigone are fictional characters who transgress gender boundaries and are ultimately killed, Artemisia I of the ancient Greek city of Halicarnassus (modern Bodrum, Turkey) was a historical personage who challenged gender boundaries in real life, especially from an Athenian perspective. According to Herodotus (7.99.1), Artemisia participated in the battle of Salamis due to her *andreia* (masculinity or manly courage) and *lēmatos* (daring), fighting on the side of the Persians, even though she was the Greek tyrant of Halicarnassus in Asia Minor (see further Penrose 2016: 152–64; McCoskey in this volume). Artemisia, unlike Clytemnestra and Antigone, was not killed off and stands as a historical example of a powerful Greek woman who was perceived to be masculine, albeit one who was somewhat of an 'other' due to her role in the Persian army. Artemisia was certainly bold and outspoken in Herodotus' *Histories* (7.99, 8.69, 8.87–8), and those are the two characteristics that are used by the fourth-century BC Hippocratic author to define a masculine woman, as I will discuss below. What the Hippocratic author seems to describe, furthermore, may not be just a 'stage' that a *parthenos* traversed through, a 'tomboyism' if you will, but rather a more enduring characteristic: the bold and outspoken woman was seemingly considered to be imbued with a permanent state of masculinity.

GENDER DIVERSITY AND THE HIPPOCRATIC THEORY OF CONCEPTION

The unknown Hippocratic author of *On Regimen* viewed courage as a masculine trait, and notes that women who were bold and outspoken were called 'masculine' by his contemporaries. *On Regimen*, written in the Attic dialect in c. 400 BC (Jouanna 1999: 408–9), is a text that describes how human conception causes gender diversity (see also Sukava in this volume). Unlike Aeschylus (*Eum.* 657–66) and Aristotle (*Gen. An.* 727A–729A), who thought that only the male contributed seed to a human foetus, the Hippocratics understood that both men and women provided reproductive matter at the time of conception (Hippoc. *On Generation* 6–7; Ps.-Hippoc. *On Regimen* 1.26–9).

The author of *On Regimen* (1.28–29.1, ed. Joly) begins by explaining that men and women alike *both* produce male and female seed. Thus a man will either emit male or female semen, and a woman will similarly provide either male or female reproductive matter to mingle with the father's semen and produce a child. If both the father and mother emit female seed, the infant will be a girl, and will grow up to be 'most feminine and graceful' (*thēlukōtata/euphuestata*) (1.29.1, ed. Joly). If the mother secretes female reproductive matter but the father contributes male semen, then the two types of seed will battle in the womb. If the mother's female seed wins, the child will be a girl, but will grow up to be bolder (*thrasutera*) than in the first case but just as orderly or quiet (*kosmia*). In the case where the father emits female sperm but the mother contributes male reproductive matter and the father's female seed wins, the child will turn out to be a girl who is more audacious (*tolmērotera*) than the other two types of girls. The author notes that such women are called masculine (*andreiai*) (see further Penrose 2016: 38–43).

If the father emits male seed and the mother secretes male matter as well, the offspring will grow up to be male, and will be 'brilliant with respect to the soul and strong-bodied' (1.28.2, ed. Joly). If the father emits male semen but the mother female seed, then a battle ensues in the womb. If the father's male matter masters the female, the child will be male, but will be 'less brilliant' than the first case but still 'manly' (*andreios*) (1.28.3). Conversely, if the mother emits male seed but the father emits female seed, and the mother's male seed wins the battle, the child will be an *androgynos*. 'If male seed is emitted from the woman, and female from the man, and the male seed wins the battle, the foetus grows in the same manner as the former, while [the latter] is lessened. These become *androgynoi* and are rightly called so' (1.28.4). In other words, the child grows up to be male, because the mother's male seed has predominated in the battle of the womb but is nonetheless labelled an *androgynos*, literally a 'manwoman'. The term *androgynos* here has generally been understood to refer to a feminine man rather than an intersex individual due to the context of the entire passage, which concludes with the following sentence: 'These then . . . are the three origins of men' (Hanson 1992: 44; Gleason 1995: 62–3; Penrose 2016: 41, 41 n. 90). Greek children who were intersex were probably exposed, as the ancient Greeks perceived such infants to be ominous prodigies of ill-fate to come (Ogden 1997: 14; Brisson 2002: 2–23, 32, 37–40). In at least one case, an intersex infant was burned alive at Athens (Diod. Sic. 32.12.2). By the Roman imperial period, Brisson (2002: 38–40) argues, more tolerance towards intersex individuals developed. Garland (2010: 66, 2nd edition of Garland 1995) asserts that the burning of the intersex child at Athens in the first century BC took place under the direction of Roman authorities, and further suggests that the practice of burning intersex children was Roman, not Greek.

In any event, the Hippocratic author here understands gender diversity as related to courage/boldness, strength/weakness and possibly intelligence. While the author does not explicitly define the term *androgynos*, it is implicitly defined in contrast to both the most masculine woman and man. The masculine woman is described as bold, bolder than other women, in contrast to the feminine man, the *androgynos*, who would not have been considered bold. The most masculine male is described as both strong and *lampros tas psychas*, 'brilliant of character'. Conversely, the feminine man, the *androgynos*, would have been considered physically weak and *not* brilliant of character. The question that immediately arises is this: what did the Hippocratic author mean by the phrase *lampros tas psychas* (brilliant of soul or character)? And, perhaps more importantly for the purposes of this paper, what would the opposite be?

In Aeschylus' *Oresteia*, Clytemnestra's partner in crime, Aegisthus, is called a 'woman' (*gynē*) and accused of 'having a cowardly soul' (*psychē kakē*) by the chorus because he did not serve in the Greek army that attacked Troy, and, furthermore, because he allowed Clytemnestra to kill Agamemnon rather than do the deed himself (1625–7; 1643–5, ed. Page). Similarly, the 'female' (*thēlu*) is accused of having a soft or cowardly soul (*psychē malakē*) by Pseudo-Aristotle in the fourth century BC ([*Phgn.*] 810a). The coward at Sparta could be forced to shave half of his beard (Plut. *Ages.* 30.3), thus perhaps identifying him as an *androgynos* of sorts (see further Penrose 2016: 56–7). That term is not used in descriptions of Spartan cowards, however, who are either called *tresantes* (runaways) or *kakoi* (cowards) (e.g. Hdt. 7.231; Xen. *Lac. Pol.* 9.4). The latter correlates to the *psychē kakē*, however, the 'cowardly soul' of Aegisthus, as mentioned above.

The Athenian speech-writer Lysias (10, ed. Hude) records that one soldier by the name of Theomnestus had been prosecuted for speaking in front of the assembly after he allegedly committed the supreme act of perceived cowardice, having thrown away his weapons (*ta hopla apobeblēkota*) (10.1). Both Theomnestus and his father are described as 'strong in body but not well with respect to their souls' (*somasi dunantai tas de psychas ouk <eu> echousin*) (10.29). The 'illness' of their souls is explicitly related to cowardice, even though both men are able-bodied. Comparison of this phrase to the terminology used by the Hippocratic author of *On Regimen* (1.28.2), *lampros tas psychas* suggests that the latter could, in contrast, mean courageous.

ANDROGYNOI AND *KINAIDOI*

Hence, based upon the Hippocratic text itself as well as outside comparison, we can see that the term *androgynos*, like the slur *kinaidos*, could, at least
in some instances, be used as an epithet to denote a coward. A lost play of
Eupolis, entitled *Astreteutoi* (*Men Who Have Not Been on Military Service*) was
alternatively entitled *Androgynoi* (*Etym. Magn.* 174.50–5 (s.v. *aphados*), ed.
Gaisford=*CAF* fr. 34, ed. Koch; Dover 1989: 144, revised edition of Dover
1978), and provides an important point of comparison. The interchanging
of the titles *Astreteutoi* and *Androgynoi* further suggests that a man considered
cowardly could be called *androgynos* (Brisson 2002: 61). Cowardice in battle
was mocked in Athenian comedy, and comedy's approbation against cowardice
mirrored real life. Although Eupolis' *Androgynoi* is no longer extant, analysis of
Aristophanes' comedy *Clouds* helps to fill in the blanks. In the *Clouds* (353), one
Cleōnymus is called a 'shield-thrower' (*rhipsaspis*). Throwing away one's shield
amounted to deserting the ranks of the phalanx and retreating, and was seen
by the Greeks as a true act of cowardice (see Rademaker 2003: esp. 115–16).
Cleōnymus becomes the butt of a joke when the character Socrates instructs
his pupil Strepsiades to write Cleōnymus' name with a feminine ending, thus
changing it to Cleōnymē (*Clouds* 680). Thus the comic 'coward' is named as
an *androgynos* of sorts. In the *Timaeus* (90E–91A), Plato equates the man who
lacked courage, and thus failed to live up to the ancient Greek ideals of manhood, with a woman when he asserts that the cowardly man who lives a bad life
will be reincarnated in the second generation as a woman. An Athenian soldier
who deserted or left his post could be fined, disenfranchised and stripped of all
civic rights, including the right to address the assembly (Andocides 1.74).

The term *kinaidos* was, at least in some cases, a synonym for the term
androgynos – both could refer to men perceived to be cowardly and/or feminine
(Gleason 1990: 396). In his invective against Demosthenes, the Athenian orator
Aeschines (2.151, ed. Schultz) directly contrasts hoplites, sound of body and
mind, to *kinaidoi*: 'Which of the two would you expect they will pray for – ten
thousand hoplites like Philon, so well-conditioned with respect to his body and
so disciplined with respect to his soul, or thirty-thousand *kinaidoi* like you?' The
manly hoplite as described by Aeschines was strong and had something akin to
a 'brilliant soul', that is to say a 'disciplined soul' (*psychē sophrōn*). Like Pseudo-
Hippocrates' *androgynos*, the *kinaidos* is presented here as the antithesis of the
strong, brave, disciplined, manly male. He is thus weak and cowardly.

The author of the *Physiognomics* found in the corpus of Aristotle describes
the qualities of both the *deilos* or coward and the *kinaidos*. While the author
does not directly equate the *deilos* with the *kinaidos*, he lists weak eyes as a
characteristic that *kinaidoi* and cowards share; hence it would seem possible,
in Pseudo-Aristotle's mind, for the coward to be a *kinaidos* and vice versa. The

author asserts that the cowardly man gives himself away by his weak eyes, soft hair, a weak body, long thin hands, and a high and slack voice (806b; 807b). The author further asserts that the *semeia* or signs of the *kinaidos* include not only weak eyes, but also knocked knees, a tilted head, limp wrists, his gait (either wagging his hips or else holding them still), and finally his roaming eyes (808a). (These characteristics are almost identical to those of the *androgynos* as described by the second-century AD physiognomist Polemon. The Greek text of Polemon is only preserved in an Arabic translation and a Latin summary, making it difficult to draw definitive conclusions; the term *androgynos* may have appeared in the original Greek but we cannot be certain; see further Gleason 1990: 395; Rantala in this volume.) Pseudo-Aristotle further relates that the one characteristic shared by both the coward and the *kinaidos*, weakness of the eyes, also indicates a man who is feminine (*thēlus*) and soft (*malakos*), as well as downcast (*katēphēs*) and lacking in spirit (*athumos*) (808a). Furthermore, Pseudo-Aristotle asserts that 'the soul and the body are sympathetically affected by one another' (808b, ed. Hett), a statement that could help to explain the relationship between the 'brilliant' soul and strength of the most masculine man in Pseudo-Hippocrates (*On Regimen* 1.28.2) as well as the bad soul (*psychē kakē*) and weakness of the coward such as Aegisthus, as described above (*Oresteia* 1625–7; 1643–5).

Various etymologies of the term *kinaidos* have been handed down to us, including derivation from *kinein ta aidoia* (to move one's shameful parts) or *kenos aidous* (empty of shame) (*Etym. Magn.* 514.15–16 (s.v. *kinaidos*), ed. Gaisford; Kamen and Levin-Richardson 2015a: 453, 458 n. 22). If the former is correct, the term may have originally referred to a male dancer who shook his buttocks, perhaps to attract sexual attention (Williams 2010: 175, 335 no. 81), but if the latter is correct, the term may have had a broader meaning, one that could include cowardice. Regardless of its origin, the term was used to refer to cowardly men in the classical era. Although John J. Winkler (1990b: 171–209, esp. 177) tends to focus upon sexual passivity and sex work as defining markers of the *kinaidos*, he nevertheless notes that the *kinaidos* was perceived as a male whose behaviour deviated completely from the social norms laid down by the dominant culture. Matthew Fox (1998: 7) criticises Winkler for overemphasising the sexual passivity of the *kinaidos*, arguing that the defining sexual characteristic of an individual labelled as such was a lack of sexual restraint.

More recently, Marilyn Skinner has harkened back to Winkler's description of the *kinaidos* as an 'unreal, but dreaded, anti-type of masculinity behind every man's back' (Winker 1990b: 46; Skinner 2005: 125). Skinner further elaborates upon this, asserting that 'it is conceivable . . . that there were no actual *kinaidoî*', noting that some would argue that we can only call someone a *kinaidos* who self-identified as such. That said, Skinner (2015: 125–32) identifies the tragic playwright Agathon, a historical character, as a possible *kinaidos*. Not only was

Agathon the *erōmenos* (passive beloved) of Pausanias when already a mature man, making him, at least from an outside vantage point, the quintessential 'passive' partner, he is also presented as dressing in women's clothes in Aristophanes' *Thesmophoriazusai* (*Women at the Thesmophoria*) (111–60), first staged in 411 BC in Athens. In the play, the character Agathon claims that he dresses as a woman in order to feel the roles of the women characters for whom he writes parts (see further Medda 2017). In contrast to the character Euripides, who does drag very badly and is called a *gynnis*, a 'feminine man', Agathon is called a *gynē* or 'woman'. Demosthenes, another historical personage, is called a *kinaidos* and is accused of wearing feminine clothing, particularly undergarments, by his rival orator Aeschines (1.131, 2.151; see further Ormand 2009: 49–51).

But can we use any of this as evidence? Skinner (2005: 128) is sceptical of using comedy as historical evidence, and Amy Richlin (1993) is leery of taking invective as fact. Tom Sapsford (2015), on the other hand, has identified historical *kinaidoi* in Hellenistic Egyptian inscriptions and papyri. In two inscriptions of the first century BC, *kinaidoi* self-identify. In Egypt, it would appear that being a *kinaidos* was an occupation that involved singing, dancing or entertaining . Like the *kinaidos*, the *androgynos* appears in an historical context as well, albeit a non-Greek one. The plural of *androgynos, androgynoi*, was used by the fifth-century BC Greek historian Herodotus to describe feminine men among the Scythians, or what perhaps might be better understood from our twenty-first century vantage point as intersex persons or male-to-female transgender women.

SCYTHIAN AND PERSIAN *ANDROGYNOI*

Herodotus asserts that *androgynoi* are to be found among the Scythians, who call them Enarees (4.67.2) (on the Enarees, see Adkins in this volume). The Enarees were androgynous shaman-type priestesses who took on a role similar to that of two-spirits in North America (Feinberg 1996: 21–9; see also Williams 1986; Roscoe 1998). Herodotus does not attribute the femininity of the Enarees to conception but rather to a female disease that had been cast down upon them by the goddess Aphrodite after they pillaged her temple at Askalon (1.105.4). The Hippocratic author of *Airs, Waters, Places* (22.1, ed. Jouanna) further notes that 'Most of the Scythians become impotent [*eunouchoi*] . . . and are called Anarieis.' I translate *eunouchoi* here as 'impotent' rather than as 'eunuchs' because the preceding passage of the text (21) asserts that they become *eunouchoi* [impotent] due to several reasons, which include riding horses, the moistness of their constitution, the flabbiness of their bellies, and, after onset, the cutting of veins behind their ears to try and alleviate the condition (see further Lieber 1996: 455). The author lists neither castration nor intersexuality as reasons for their impotence.

The Anarieis 'speak like women' (22.1, ed. Jouanna), wear women's garments, act like women, and work with other women doing women's work (22.1, 7). Pseudo-Hippocrates' Anarieis are undoubtedly the same persons whom Herodotus identifies as Enarees (Littré 1840: xxxix–xlviii; Vendryes 1934: 331). The term is probably of Scythian, not Greek, origin (*LSJ* s.v. Enarees). Pseudo-Hippocrates asserts that the majority of Scythians were Anarieis, but probably overstates how many Anarieis there were. Today, intersex persons comprise up to 1.7 per cent of the population, and transgender individuals account for up to 0.6 per cent of the population (Blackness et al. 2000; Flores et al. 2016). So if the Anarieis included both intersex and transgender individuals, they could have made up to 2.3 per cent of the population (by no means a majority, but still a significant presence).

The author of *Airs* notes that these individuals are revered by others in Scythian society, who prostrate themselves before the Anarieis and attribute the cause of their femininity to divine ordinance (see further Lieber 1996). Similarly, Herodotus (4.67.2) notes that the Enarees said that Aphrodite endowed them with the gift of prophecy, further suggesting that the Anarieis and Enarees were the same group of persons. Anthropological studies of the Chukchi nomads of north-eastern Siberia conducted in the early twentieth century have been used to understand the Enarees (Halliday 1910/11: 97; cf. Vendryes 1934). Among the Chukchi, intersex, male-to-female and female-to-male transgender persons served as 'diviners' or 'shamans' in roles that seem to correspond to those of the ancient Scythian Enarees (Bogaras 1901: 98–9). It would appear that, like the Chukchi, Scythian society created a safe space for transgender and/or intersex individuals that ancient Greek society of the classical period did not. Although instances of Greek cross-dressing are recorded in both textual and iconographic evidence, they are usually linked with rituals (see further Lissarrague 2002: 11–13; Carlà-Uhink 2017; Facella 2017; La Guardia 2017). Gender-queer eunuch priestesses of the goddess Cybele do appear in a Greek context in Apuleius' second-century CE *The Golden Ass* (8.24–30; see Adkins in this volume). They wander from town to town, seemingly without a home, and Apuleius writes of them in a pejorative manner. One suspects that Scythians may have been more tolerant of gender non-conforming persons.

The question which immediately arises is this: were some or all of the Scythian Enarees intersex, and, if so, is this why they were called *androgynoi* by Greek authors? Or, since they were alleged to have been men inflicted with a 'female disease', were they the ancient Scythian equivalent of male-to-female transgender women? The answer may be both (Hart 2017). Archaeological evidence may suggest that the Scythians, unlike the Greeks, raised intersex individuals rather than exposing them. I make this hypothesis by drawing a comparison to the noted presence of grown disabled individuals among the Scythians in the archaeological record, which suggests that the Scythians did not practice infanticide as did the Greeks. Eileen Murphy has proven that Scythians did raise children with genetic abnormalities by comparing several accounts of such persons in Herodotus to burials in Amyrlag, Siberia. Herodotus (4.13) describes a race of the one-eyed Arismaspians who lived at the 'furthest edges' of the earth, but his claims were dismissed as sheer fantasy until excavations at Amyrlag unearthed individuals who were born with genetic differences from other Scythians. Specifically, they had one eye rather than two due to cebocephalus or Cyclops malformation (Murphy 2004: 179). Herodotus must have heard reports of these individuals, who lived among other peoples rather than being a race unto themselves, and exaggerated them (Murphy 2004: 177–80). Similarly, persons with clubfoot have been found at Amyrlag, and serve to explain the basis of Herodotus' description of a 'goat-footed' race in this region (4.25). Whereas the Greeks are thought to have had a tendency to commit infanticide because they saw deformities as marks of divine disfavour (Ogden 1997: 9–14; Penrose 2015: 509–11; Garland 2010: 13–16; cf. Rose 2003: 29–40), the Scythians and related peoples did not (Murphy 2004: 181). The same may have been true of intersex children – whereas the Greeks tended to expose them, perhaps the Scythians did not. (And it should be here noted that not all infants who were disabled were necessarily exposed by the Greeks, as Patterson (1985: 114), Garland (2010: 13–16), Ogden (1997: 16–17), and Rose (2003: 29–40) have discussed).

In any event, archaeological evidence suggests that disabled children were raised by the Scythians, and thus intersex individuals may have also been reared by them. A burial of what may have been an Enaree has been found at Tilya Tepe in Afghanistan, but the individual was male to female, not intersex according to Jeanine Davis-Kimball (2000: 226–7). Another burial discovered in the permafrost of Siberia is of even more interest. The deceased was buried with both weapons and fertility amulets and other objects deemed to be 'feminine' by Russian archaeologists (Moss 2015). At first, it was assumed that the burial was of an 'Amazon' warrior woman. DNA testing has revealed that the interred had XY chromosomes, however, and thus must have been intersex, a male-to-female transgender woman, or otherwise 'gender non-binary'. The grave goods suggest that the remains are of an elite warrior.

Was the deceased a male-to-female transgender 'Amazon' or an armed Enaree? As noted above, Pseudo-Hippocrates tells us that the Enarees spoke like women. Could this indicate that at least some of them were intersex? This remains a possibility. It has been suggested, however, that the Enarees may have been transgender women who drank mare's urine to help them transition from male to female. Pregnant mare's urine contains high levels of oestregen and is still used today to make a hormone replacement therapy drug called premarin. The name of this drug is a contraction of 'pre(gnant) mar(e's ur)in(e)', and it is widely used today by female-to-male transgender individuals to transition (Savage 2006: 74–5; Taylor 1996: 212–13). According to Timothy Taylor (1996: 213), it is 'not at all unusual for pastoralist people to drink the urine of their animals'. Thus the Enarees may have transitioned to womanhood by drinking an extract of pregnant mare's urine. That said, other theories have been posited. Murphy suggests that the Enarees may have had slipped femoral capital epiphysis, a condition in which sexual characteristics in males are delayed, or an 'abnormality of the sex chromosome' (Murphy 2004: 180). Additionally, queer persons today may exhibit speech patterns that differ from others (Bigham 2014), and so perhaps did the Enarees. Stephanie West (1999) asserts that Pseudo-Hippocrates' understanding of the Scythians is far from reliable, yet the 'female disease' of the Enarees may have been a Greek way of understanding intersex individuals, transgender women or otherwise gender non-binary persons who were Scythian Enarees. What is clear is that the Scythians not only tolerated, but celebrated sex/gender diversity in a way that the Greeks did not.

Not surprisingly, the Greeks tended to understand gender diversity as something foreign, whether among the Scythians or others. Ctesias (*Excerpta de Virtutibus et Vitiis* I: 330, 5, ed. Büttner-Wobst=Nicolas of Damascus *FGrHist* 90 F4), a Greek physician and historian who lived at the Persian court in ca. 400 BC, tells us that the Babylonian satrap Nanarus was called an *androgynos* by his rival Parsondes. Nanarus, Ctesias tells us, lived in luxury wearing feminine clothing, shaving himself and using cosmetics, but nonetheless took offense to being called an *androgynos* by Parsondes (see further Hart 2018: 62–6). Ctesias suggests that the term *androgynos* held bad connotations for Nanarus, but of course, if there is any truth to this story, the conversation was probably not conducted in Greek. What is important here is that Ctesias' usage of the word confirms that an *androgynos* may have been a person who engaged in cross-dressing and other gender non-conforming behaviours.

Filippo Carlà-Uhink (2017: 10) has recently asserted that among the Greeks and Romans there was a 'widespread idea that cross-dressing' was 'practiced by other barbarian cultures', which were 'victims of their *tryphe* [luxury] and unable to correctly draw the distinction between male and female'. While truly gender-queer individuals, the Enarees, are located by the Greeks among the Scythians, when we hear of 'cross-dressing' among the Greeks, it is often described or portrayed in a ritual context, or on the stage (e.g. Lissarrague 1990: 11–13; Miller 1999; Smith 2010: 191; Surtees 2014; La Guardia 2017; Facella 2017; Medda 2017; Carlà-Uhink 2017: 12–13), rather than as part of an ongoing, transgender-type identity. Nevertheless, *androgynoi* are understood in the Hippocratic text *On Regimen* as existing universally, both in Greece and beyond its shores.

CONCLUSION

The term *androgynos*, from a Greek point of view, referred to feminine men or male-to-female transgender women. In extant texts of which I am aware, the term is used in two ways: (1) to problematise 'feminine men' who were perceived as weak and lacking in courage, and (2) to describe intersex persons or male-to-female transgender persons, such as the Enarees. The Greeks understood male femininity as a defect of character or 'illness' of sorts of the soul. Similarly, they understood the Scythian Enarees as men who have a 'female disease'. While we cannot know what the Scythians themselves would have thought, the fact that they revered the Enarees suggests that they were more tolerant and understanding of intersex and transgender persons than the Greeks. According to Judith Butler (1999: 6), 'it becomes impossible to separate out "gender" from the political and cultural intersections in which it is invariably produced and maintained'. Extant literary descriptions of the Enarees or Anarieis, however, were 'produced' in the cultural and political intersections of Greece, even if the Enarees were Scythians. Whereas the Scythians created a space for intersex or transgender individuals to occupy within society, the ancient Greeks appear to have been less tolerant of sexual and gender diversity, and less understanding of it when viewed in others such as the Scythians or Persians. It would be the Greek understanding of Enarees that would be recorded for posterity, not the Scythian. In ancient Greek sources, we see early vestiges of the Western medicalisation of intersexuality and transgender identification as diseases or abnormal conditions, a phenomenon that is still, unfortunately, occurring today (on contemporary medicalisation of transgender and intersex bodies, see further Holmes 2008, 2009; Feder 2014; Johnson 2015).

In a different, more Greek context, the term *androgynos* could be used as a synonym for the epithet *kinaidos*. Both words were pejoratively hurled as slurs against men perceived to be cowards. While the terms *kinaidos* and *deilos* could also be used as synonyms, the differentiation drawn by the Aristotelian author of the *Physiognomics* between the two types of men is of interest. Both had 'weak eyes' (a condition that was associated with femininity), but otherwise could be recognised by other bodily characteristics and movements which were not the same. This suggests that the two were not necessarily the same, even if a coward might be called a *kinaidos*.

In correlation, courage was a primary factor in identifying masculinity in women. Halberstam (1998: 46) suggests that we avoid prevalent modern assumptions that historical female masculinities 'simply represent early forms of lesbianism,' and rather search for 'meanings of early female masculinity within the history of gender definition and gender relations'. Female masculinity in classical Athens was apparently measured by the presence of both courage and intelligence in women, because courage and intelligence were considered male qualities, that, when manifested in women, were often perceived as anomalies by male authors. We must also avoid positing our own associations between homosexuality and femininity on the ancients as well. The gender-deviant *kinaidos* may have been marked in part by either passive sexuality or sexual excess, but he could also, like the *androgynos,* be marked by cowardice and/or transgender behaviour.

CHAPTER 2

Blending Bodies in Classical Greek Medicine

Tyson Sukava

In his influential book *Making Sex: Body and Gender from the Greeks to Freud* (1992), Thomas Laqueur posited that the binary sexual classifications of male and female are relatively recent concepts in the Western world.[1] In antiquity, females were imagined as imperfect versions of males; female genitalia, key markers of sex, were reductively envisioned to be inverted versions of male sexual organs. The product, Laqueur argues, was a 'one-sex body' model. This claim has been successfully critiqued by Helen King (2013b), who has pointed out, among other problems, Laqueur's reliance upon the relatively late physician Galen (second century AD) when examining ancient material. King argues instead that both one-sexed and dual-sexed concepts of the body have existed concurrently since antiquity.

The purpose of this paper is to examine how classical Greek physicians, in their attempts to create workable models of both one-sexed and dual-sexed bodies, produced spaces for sexual classifications to be complicated. For them, the internal body was a complex mass of vaguely understood parts, and physicians often obscured sexual distinctions to simplify their models. As well, following versions of the humoral theory, physicians tended to emphasise physiology over anatomy to a greater extent than in modern Western medicine. They envisioned the body primarily as a receptacle for fluids. Hidden beneath its surface were parts for production and storage of fluids, and channels for fluid transportation. Much excellent scholarly attention has been paid to how male physicians developed theories and techniques to control, regulate and subordinate the female body. Physicians' principal justification for this was a perceived overabundance of fluid in the female body, a result of the womb, relative to the male body (see for example, Hanson 1992; Dean-Jones 1994; King 1998). I am especially interested here, though, in exploring how an emphasis on bodily fluids in medical theories encouraged physicians to imagine sex, and along with it gender, as a process of blending. Although the presence of male or female genitalia could be binary anatomical indicators of sex, different types and quantities of fluids determined where an individual existed between these extremes. These differences ultimately affected one's physical state and behaviour.

I turn first to blended bodies in some classical treatises within the Hippocratic Corpus that pay special attention to bodily structures, particularly *On the Nature of Man*, *On the Places in Man* and *On Regimen*. A unifying theme held in these works, and most treatises within the Hippocratic Corpus, is that the human body is primarily a physician's area of authority and control. It is important to stress, though, that they were still members of a society and tended to align their theories to agree with cultural norms (Hanson 1992: 31–3; Dean-Jones 1994; 41–55). In early Hippocratic medicine, roughly from the mid fifth to early fourth centuries BC, physicians were concerned with justifying their right to these powers (Jones 1946; Van der Eijk 2005). For example, the author of *On Ancient Medicine* is particularly committed to demonstrating that physicians are better suited than natural philosophers to determine 'what sort of thing a human is' (*ho ti estin anthrōpos*, all translations are my own) (*VM* 20). The term *anthrōpos* (human) here and elsewhere is important because it encompasses both sexes. The author adds that a physician must limit his attention to aspects of this nature (*physis*) that are relevant to medicine, namely one's regimen (see further Schiefsky 2005: 293–4). This sentiment is echoed in *On Regimen I*, a work that examines the relationship between a human's nature (*physis*) and lifestyle in health. The first part of the work is dedicated to an account of the formation and construction of the human body. Here, the author claims that one must begin to assess a patient's regimen by thoroughly understanding 'the nature of a human' (*physis anthrōpou*), which he restricts to the knowledge of the body's material composition and the parts that control it (*Vict.* 2; see also *Loc. Hom.* 2).

There was significant disagreement among Hippocratic physicians concerning what this material is and what parts of it are important in medicine; however, the impetus for most Hippocratic writers was to reduce the number of elements that they needed to consider in the clinic, which encouraged a simplified working model of the clinical body. A common byproduct was the elision of sexual differences. Yet a persistent question for physicians was where to begin a study of the human body *per se*: every part of the body could potentially be significant for the promotion of health. The author of *On the Places in Man* mentions this crux at the outset of his treatise: 'It is my opinion that there is no beginning to the body. Rather, all [parts] are equally its beginning and all [parts] are its end, just as you cannot find the beginning of an inscribed circle' (*Loc. Hom.* 1). Implied here is that any attempt to describe the medical body, by which I mean a certain lens through which a physician views a patient with an aim to diagnosis and treatment, is to a degree arbitrary. Ideally, the starting place would be those parts that are most important to restoring health. But what might these be? The author of *Epidemics* 6, a collection of physicians' notes, articulates some of the frustration practitioners felt: 'For good physicians, similarities [produce] wanderings and obstacles, but so do opposites [when investigating] what sort of actual cause there is [for a phenomenon]. But this is difficult to comprehend even for one knowing the method [of medical practice]' (*Epid.* 6.8.26; see also *Loc. Hom.* 41). He follows this comment with a list of observable features and habits – a sharp head, flat nose, difficulty with vomiting, decadent lifestyle – and questions how these could possibly be connected. A patient assails the physician with an overwhelming number of observable details: the problem is identifying those that matter.

One important way of limiting important details in the medical body was to adopt some variation of the humoral theory, the notion that health (both physical and mental) was promoted through the regulation of fluids, or occasionally other elements, within the body. Different bodies contained different proportions of fluids that allowed for multiplicity in individual natures, which we shall see has some important ramifications. The material body, on the other hand, is composed of parts that provide structure, locomotion and a means to refine, store and convey the humours within the body (Gundert 1992; Craik 2009). As Mirko Grmek (2002: 248) writes, 'For nearly all Hippocratic authors, disease was the expression of a disorder – not in the primary constituents, but in the fluid components of the human body.' In other words, most Hippocratic interest in the body emphasised physiology over anatomy.

Although traces of the humoral theory are evident throughout the Hippocratic Corpus, the fullest articulation of the humoral theory is contained in *On the Nature of Man*. The work is especially notable for its authorship. Aristotle attributes it to Polybus, the son-in-law of Hippocrates, which offers the securest connection between a Hippocratic treatise and the theories of the historical Hippocrates (Arist. *HA* 512b with Langholf 2004). At sections 4 and 5 of the treatise, the author explains that the human body (*sōma anthrōpou*) contains four types of fluid: blood, phlegm, yellow bile and black bile (on the Hippocratic humoral theory, see further Jouanna 1999: 314–17 and Schöener 1964). Importantly, the author does not say that these are only components of the body's nature; they are the essence of it (*taut' estin autōi hē physis tou sōmatos*). At the conclusion of section 5, we find that all of these fluids are contained within every body at birth. Furthermore, one is born from and nurtured by a human being (*anthrōpos*, specifically a woman) who contains all of these elements within her.

The author of *On the Nature of Man* follows through with this reductionist approach in his study. The humoral method he adheres to is an elegant one, which is a large reason for its enduring popularity: instead of being overwhelmed by the vast array of possibly extraneous details, a physician can focus on observing expelled fluids and restoring the balance of a patient's four humours. There is an important derivative from such an approach. In the attempt to simplify much of the medical art to a harmonisation of bodily fluids, the sexualised body becomes obscured and, at times, nearly erased (see also *Loc. Hom.* 42). The author of *On the Nature of Man* is obligated by his explanation for the origin of these fluids to hold that both males and females contain each of the four in varying proportions. At its base, the nature of a body is defined by the fluids it contains. Since the ratios of these fluids can differ (whether between individuals or across time in the same person), there is the potential for a spectrum of human natures. That is, the emphasis on blended bodily fluids in Hippocratic medical thought allowed for fluidity in any one person's constitution, whether male or female.

We shall see later how this becomes used in other works as a means to place individuals on sexual spectrums. In *On the Nature of Man*, though, there is virtually no trace of a sexualised body. The author created a homogenised medical body to explain why humans as a class respond to natural stimuli and treatment in similar predictable ways. To treat male and female bodies separately within the treatise would be akin to fighting a battle on two fronts: he would need to provide different accounts for the humours in each sex for each external factor explored (for example, the seasons and climate). This is messy science. The only place where the treatise explicitly contrasts men and women is in a passage that elides any differences. In section 9, the author makes a distinction between diseases caused by regimens (*diaitēmata*) – that is, diet and lifestyle – and those caused by the air. Diseases caused by regimen are idiosyncratic, but those caused by air affect everyone – younger and older, men and women – equally. Later in the same section, the author provides a similar list of factors important to a physician in the case of regimen: the kind of disease, the patient's constitution and age, the season and the patient's nature (*physis anthrōpou*). This last criterion, the patient's nature, could perhaps be interpreted as some hint of sex distinction, but this could equally apply to the spectrum of humour ratios across human bodies, regardless of sex.

Two more examples of possible yet superficial sexual distinctions in *On the Nature of Man* are worth noting for the sake of completeness. Near the end of the work in a description of bloodletting, the author traces the jugular veins (*sphagatides*) from the neck to the testes (*orchies*) and thighs (11). The use of the word *orchies* might suggest that the author is defaulting to a male body as his model; however, it is clear from the context that mention of the testes was intended as a reference point for the path of the veins and has little to do with the author's theory (see also *Oss.* 15 with Harris 1973: 67). As Vivian Nutton (2004: 100) correctly notes, the gynaecological treatises in the Hippocratic Corpus were written by and for men; we can probably extend this comment to all writings in the collection. It would therefore make sense for the author to refer to anatomical parts of the intended readership to guide their understanding. In the following section, another set of vessels are neutrally described as terminating at the private parts (*to aidoion*), a term regularly associated with both male and female genitals. The final instance of possible sexual distinction appears in section 12. Here, the author begins by remarking that after the age of thirty-five, people become softer from decreased physical activity, which contributes to disharmony within the body. He continues to remark that children are susceptible to kidney stones, but men (*andres*) are not. The reason for this is the body is its hottest at birth (heat is necessary for growth, he explains) but as the body decays, it necessarily cools. But, perhaps as a correction to his default to the male body, the author then generalises his account by including the term *anthrōpos* (human) when clarifying his statement. Here too, we see an impulse towards generalising the human body: both male and female bodies apparently undergo similar changes as they age.

Certainly, Hippocratic medicine did not always gloss over the distinctions between male and female bodies. Physicians were quite aware that there are important anatomical distinctions that affect health problems specific to the sex. Female anatomy tended to receive the greatest attention, owing mostly to the phenomenon of menstruation and women's role in childbirth. A passage from King, who has explored this topic thoroughly in several places (for example, King 1998; 2013b; 2015), is worth citing in full:

> In Hippocratic gynaecology, to be a woman is to menstruate. This poses the problem of women who do not menstruate: they may be ill, in which case drugs or mechanical procedures can be used to induce menstruation; they may be pregnant, in which case there is no danger to their health because the excess blood is contributing to the foetus; or they may be past the menopause, that natural process of 'drying out' which transforms even a wet and spongy female body into something that does not bleed. (1998: 76)

The *locus classicus* for classifying a female body in Hippocratic writings is at *On the Diseases of Women* 1.26. Here, the author uses the comparatives *araiosarkoterē* (more spongy) and *apaloterē* (more soft) to describe the female body in relation to the male body. Similar comments can be found elsewhere in the Corpus (see for example, *Gland.* 1 and 16 with King 1998: 28–9, and Hanson 1992: 36). What is notable for our purposes is that the distinction here is one of quality, not of kind.

Gynaecology for the Hippocratics is mostly limited to the study and treatment of the womb (*hysterē* or *mētrē*). Because of their limited access to the internal body, physicians were encouraged to examine bodily effluence – for example, faeces, urine and vomit – as indications of internal health (see for example, *Prog.* 11 and 12). The coincidence of the womb and process of menstruation offered reasons to inflate the effects of both upon the sex (Hanson 1992: 38–9). The author of *On the Places in Man* concisely limits this sphere of treatment: 'The so-called women's sicknesses: [their] wombs are the cause of all of these sicknesses' (46; see also Arist. *HA* 497b). Indeed, the treatments that are described in gynaecological works such as *On the Diseases of Women* and sections of *On Generation/On the Nature of the Child* leave the impression of a polarised distinction between female and male bodies. (It is notable that the author of *On the Diseases of Women I* is probably the same author of *On Generation/On the Nature of the Child* [Jouanna 1999: 385, 392].) Other anatomical differences are incidental to the presence of the womb: the author of *On Airs, Waters, and Places*, for example, notes that females are less inclined to have kidney stones because they have shorter and wider urethras (9). Such circumscribed attention to the womb in delineating anatomical differences left opportunities for significant overlap between the sexed bodies.

Indeed, the author of *On the Nature of Women* argues that there is also a spectrum of body types for women that can intersect to some degree with the qualities of male bodies. In the introduction to this work, the author is careful to use the plural 'women's natures' (*hai physies tōn gynaikōn*) to denote the object of his study, thereby suggesting diversity among them. He then continues to describe three types of women's natures based on their complexions (*chroai*): extremely white women are moister (*hygroterai*); women with dark complexions are drier (*xēroterai*); and wine-coloured women are a blend of the two previous types (*meson ti amphoterōn echousin*). As a woman ages, she becomes drier and has less blood, an explanation likely based on the process of menopause (*Nat. Mul.* 1). This fluidity of female body constitutions provides the opportunity for a spectrum of classification that, beyond the hypothetical asexed medical body, can allow for significant overlap with male bodies.

We can see this more clearly in three other Hippocratic works, *On the Places in Man*, *On Regimen 1* and *On Generation*. Just as with *On the Nature of Man* discussed above, the author of *On the Places in Man* concentrates on a homogenised model of the body. At its outset, the author states that bodies that are dry are more susceptible to sickness than wet bodies. The reason is that a moist constitution compels the sickness to flow more readily throughout the body and weaken, since it lacks an opportunity to become fixed in one place. If the author of this treatise adheres to the common Hippocratic belief that women are 'wetter' than men, this would commit him to the belief that female bodies are healthier than males. There is, however, no explicit trace of this in the work. What follows is a series of anatomical, physiological and pathological accounts that contain no mention of sexed bodies. Only at the conclusion is there specific attention to sex anatomy, the aforementioned comment that 'women's sicknesses' are a product of the womb (47). The incongruent addition of this section has been seen by some as intrusive, though, and convincing arguments have been made for it being a later addendum to a work on an otherwise exclusively asexed medical body (Craik 1998: 218–19 with bibliography).

A comparable approach is adopted by the author of *On Regimen 1*, yet here we see the spectrum between male and female bodies more carefully articulated. As with other works explored above, the author here argues that his study of bodily regimen must begin with an assessment of a human's nature (*physis anthrōpou*, section 2). Because his work concentrates on a person's daily habit, he goes on to clarify that both natural and artificial exertion can produce changes in one's fleshes (*sarkes*). In other words, every body is subject to fluidity. As an extension of this, the author states that the flesh of both male and female bodies – one of the distinguishing qualities mentioned in *On the Diseases of Women* – can become increased or reduced. In sections 1 and 4, the author diverges from the four-humour theory to claim that all living beings, including humans, are composed of two things: fire and water. Each is needed to exist within a person, and each contains specific qualities. Fire is hot and dry, whereas water is cold and wet. Both elements, however, can share in each other's qualities of moistness and dryness. This communication between binaries is what produces the various things in the universe. Hynek Bartoš (2015: 98 and n. 424) observes that the balance of these opposing elements becomes the author's core theory of dietetics. Therefore, there is no specific distinction made between male and female bodies in his account of regimen, with one exception. In section 27, he recapitulates the common Hippocratic belief: female bodies incline towards water, and are therefore best suited to cold, wet and soft food and drinks, whereas male bodies, inclining toward fire, are drawn to dry and warm ones. He then explains that both sexes contribute secretions (*apokrithes*) to the production of offspring. The sex of children can therefore be altered prior to conception by both the male's and the female's intake of food and drink with specific qualities. An increase of the 'fire' element within a parent promotes a male child; that of 'water' promotes a female.

This ability to increase female and male qualities within a body regardless of sex has interesting repercussions. In the following section (28), the author claims that both the female (*thēlu*) and the male (*arsen*) can be fused together (*synistasthai . . . pros allēla*), since defining elements of both sexes are contained within each. A further reason for this fusion is that the soul (*psychē*) is of a similar synthesis within all animate things. The specific qualities of the soul are determined by the admixture of secretions from the male and female: the strongest children are those from male secretions from both partners; blending of male secretion from male and female from female produces a male (for the stronger absorbs the weaker); female from a male and male from a female produces *androgynes* (literally 'men-women'). A similar process occurs with the production of females. Most notable are instances when a male secretes female material and a female contributes male. The products of such unions are manly (*andreiai*) women (29). This theory of blended elements, a fluidity of body/soul types, therefore is disruptive to sexual polarisation. Nevertheless, there are still strong traces of cultural gendered power dynamics here, since, everything being equal, male elements will consistently subjugate the female.

The author of *On Generation*, a shorter work concentrating on the process of procreation, posits a similar account of the contest between male and female secretions in the production of children. This is the only other work in the Hippocratic Corpus to articulate such a theory explicitly (Dean-Jones 1994: 168–9; on this passage, see also Penrose in this volume). In section 6 of the treatise, he posits that each partner possesses both male and female seeds (*spermata*), although only one type of seed is contributed by each partner during copulation. It is taken as axiomatic that the male is stronger (*ischyroteron*) than the female, and he concludes from this that it is a necessity (*anagkē*) that the male seed will overpower the female during copulation. If a male and female both contribute male seeds, then a male is produced; if only female, then a female is produced. He continues to posit, though, that if either the male or female contributes more of the female seed than male, then the weaker seed (female) will overpower the stronger (male) by its volume. The product is then a female. It is clear from the sections that follow, though, that he does not mean that a partner's victorious seed completely displaces the losing seed; rather, there is a blending of the two during which the stronger becomes more dominant in the formation of the child. The author, exhibiting his fondness for demonstrable analogies, explains that this is clear from the admixture of fat and wax. When both are combined and melted and more fat than wax is present, the ratio is unclear; however, when the mixture cools, it is apparent which substance has the greater proportion. We can extrapolate from this that bodies, outside of pure male/male and female/female seed combinations, are blends of sexual elements in different proportions.

There are several conceptual difficulties in this account, at least *prima facia* (see Lonie 1981: 125–6; Dean-Jones 1994: 168 for useful comments). The most relevant one here is the problem of what is meant by a 'stronger' (*viz.* male) seed, if the amount of the contribution seems to be the deciding factor. A probable solution for this can be found by looking outside of the work itself. As Iain Lonie has observed, the same author writes in *On the Nature of the Child* that the male seed is thicker (*pachyterē*) and the female is moister (*hygroterē*) (*Nat. Puer.* 20). If the author is being consistent across the two treatises, by 'stronger' he probably means that it would take a greater contribution of the female seed to overpower the male because it is less concentrated (Lonie 1981: 128–30). Once again, this author aligns his theory with the common Hippocratic belief that the male sex is naturally denser, thus stronger. By analogy, he transfers these attributes to the primordial elements of ancient embryology: the seeds of sexual determination.

Unlike *On Regimen 1*, *On Generation* does not elaborate upon the possible offspring that arise from various pairings of seeds; however, in section 8 the author does observe that children tend to have specific features that appear more similar to either the father or the mother. This, he argues, is proof that a child is produced from a mixture of material from both parents. When a child has a feature that appears to be more like the father's, it is because more from that part of the father's body has entered the seed than the mother's, and vice versa. Never, he asserts, does it occur that a child is entirely similar to one or the other parent. The author here thus posits a version of pangenesis: the belief that the seed produced by either a male and female is derived from every part of the body (see also *Aër.* 14). The resulting blending and struggle of male and female elements therefore lead to results similar to those in *On Regimen 1.* As Ann Hanson (1992: 43–4) remarks, following the classifications in *On Regimen 1,* 'the sexually bivalent seeds from the father and mother vied for mastery within the womb to result either in the "masculine boy" and the "feminine girl", or in the "wimpy boy" and the "manly girl"'. She further notes that this spectrum of potential outcomes allowed for medical intervention to prevent and correct aberrant outcomes of males presenting female qualities, or females presenting male ones.

So far, we have seen medical descriptions of didactic, hypothetical 'human' bodies where sex markers have been all but erased; we have also seen attempts to explain the messier business of real-world differences between people. The practising physician would have been inundated with the latter in his clinic, and navigating the spectrum of body types was often difficult. King (2015: 260) has demonstrated this in her analysis of a certain Phaëthousa of Abdera, described in *Epidemics* 6 (6.8.32) (on Phaëthousa and Nanno, see Shannon-Henderson in this volume). Phaëthousa had stopped menstruating (presumably earlier than menopause) some time after having children. Following this, her body became masculine (*to te sōma ēndrōthē*): she became hairy and grew a beard, and her voice became rough. The author notes that a similar thing happened to Nanno of Thasos, who could become re-feminised (*viz.* normalised) only if her menstruation started again. King concludes that because Phaëthousa had given birth, she still must have been considered a woman by physicians because she possessed a womb and had menstruated; no complete revolution in sexual classification had occurred. The note therefore may be a caution that a doctor can be misled by external observations.

Here was a crux for physicians: does the existence or absence of a specific body part, the genitalia in particular, or physiological process affect how a patient should be classified and treated? At least in some cases this is not so. In one example from *Aphorisms* (3.11), the author describes illnesses that follow dry winters and rainy springs. In such years, the summers produce acute fevers, eye disease and dysentery, 'especially in women and men with moist natures (*physes*)' (see also *Aër.* 19–20 and *Aph.* 3.17). In other words, men who display female qualities of moistness are inclined to suffer similar health issues and, presumably, would receive similar treatment. We see then that both in conceptions of the idealised medical body and in practice, there are opportunities for overlapping male and female qualities.

I conclude with a brief example to illustrate how these representations of bodies in classical Greek medicine might have influenced broader concepts of sex. There unfortunately is little evidence external to the Hippocratic writings; however, a possible glimpse of diffusion among at least some members of the larger community can be found in Plato's *Republic*. It is clear that Plato was interested in medicine and its relationship with his ethical philosophy (Levin 2014). There appear to be traces of this in his description of Guardian types – overseers in his ideal city – in Book 5 (5.451c ff.). Here, Plato's Socrates explores the potential contribution of both men and women in the Guardian class. The example of hunting dogs is first introduced, in which the interlocutor Glaucon is compelled to say that there is no sexual difference influencing the abilities of dogs: the distinction rests on training. Glaucon claims that they are similar in every way (*koinēi . . . panta*) except in degree: the female is weaker and the male is stronger (451e1–2), qualities that the Hippocratics have cast back to the seeds of life itself.

Socrates next offers that the same can be said for humans: there is a difference between a female's and male's nature (*physis*, 453a), but this alone does not preclude them from sharing pursuits (453e). Indeed, the traditional male/female binary possibly obscures important similarities between the natures (454b). To illustrate this, Socrates offers an analogy comparable to individual body classifications we have seen in the Hippocratic Corpus: if a man is bald and a cobbler in the city, he asks, does this exclude long-haired men from the profession? Do these sorts of extraneous differences between individual natures matter? The answer is ultimately 'no'. Likewise, that a female bears children and the male begets – or generative physiology – has no bearing on their topic. As we might expect from Plato, it is the soul (*psychē*) that matters. By way of further proof, he observes that a female can possess a physician's soul (*iatrikē psychē*) just as a male can (454c–e). Socrates concludes from the discussion that similar natures are distributed to both sexes; one (the female) is just usually weaker than the other (the male), a notion very similar to *On Regimen 1* and *On Generation* above. A person must decide whether such a male/female distinction is significant in a specific context, and in this case it is not. Thus, as in Hippocratic theories, both nature and lifestyle can influence a person's definition.

As with others that we have seen, Plato's assessment of sex and gender here clearly falls short of the equality we today would want to see. Socially derived gender distinctions attached to the sexualised body seem to have directed his theory, as they directed medical concepts. It is unfortunate that we have such limited evidence of ancient medical debate on this issue and of the public's reaction to these ideas. Nevertheless, Greek medical approaches to sex and gender do help to illustrate two strong factors in the development of a scientific idea: an impetus towards classification and generalisation, even in the face of great multiplicity; and a successful idea's alignment with broader cultural beliefs. Some Hippocratic authors appear to have explored the practicality of dogmatic binaries between male and female bodies for their medical theories and practices. From a cultural perspective and superficial observations there are differences; but exactly what are they and how do they come to be? Physicians observed that there is significant overlap between male and female anatomy that allowed them to speak of a 'human nature'. Moreover, beyond the polarisation of sex organs, differences become fluid: female bodies are generally wetter, colder and softer than males, but here too there are opportunities for specific bodies to overlap boundaries. Such phenomena created perceived problems, but also explanations, when one sex displayed qualities of another; the humoral theory also provided avenues for doctors to assess the seriousness of the problem and develop corrective treatments. Even in descriptions of a sexual spectrum, individual bodies still found placement in relation to extremes, producing such classes as 'manly women' and 'effeminate men' that satisfied cultural views.

There is always a risk of making too close an analogy between antiquity and today; however, there do seem to be points of similarity in how Western science has regularly attempted to quantify and control sexual and gender differences. Nelly Oudshoorn (1994), for example, has examined modern medical theories of dynamic sex hormones used to categorise individual bodies. Although this hormonal spectrum allows for greater diversity than a dogmatic male/female dichotomy, a disproportionate amount of this attention, she observes, has been directed towards explaining female bodies and the gender attributes assigned to them. Perceived aberrations from the norm can be identified and corrected. In terms of intervention, this is not far off from the Hippocratic humoral models: both admit spectrums of body/behaviour types and both leave space for medical manipulation to restore bodily aberrations to perceived normality. Chandler Brooks et al. (1962) have even proposed that ancient medical concepts of the balanced humours were early crude versions of modern endocrine homeostasis. Although any similarities are probably incidental, both ancient and modern Western medical models of sexual spectrums are products of individual bodies' resistance to being pigeonholed into any one group, which complicates both culturally determined categories and attempts at scientific simplicity.

NOTE

1. I would like to express my gratitude both to the editors of this volume, Jennifer Dyer and Allison Surtees, and to the anonymous reviewer for their excellent suggestions, challenging questions and keen insights. I also single out Allison Surtees specifically for her encouragement and advice from the very inception of this project. What follows hopefully does some justice to the time and effort that each has expended on bringing it to light; any errors of course remain my own.

CHAPTER 3

Birth by Hammer: Pandora and the Construction of Bodies

Anna Uhlig

If gender, as Judith Butler (1993) has persuasively argued, is a performance played out with and through the body, the study of gender in the ancient world is, in important respects, dependent upon the bodies that have left their traces in the historical record. That this record is partial, biased and prone to the erasure of non-normative forms should come as no surprise. Nevertheless, the broad diversity of ancient bodies to which we still have access is, as the contributions to this volume make clear, something to celebrate. The specific form of celebration that I pursue here does not seek to retrieve previously disregarded figures from the margins of our historical record, but rather to recover, and reflect on, the often-unacknowledged corporeal diversity of ancient representations of Pandora, the 'first woman' whose body has shaped our modern notions of ancient gender for over a century. The complicated picture of Pandora that emerges serves not only as a prompt to revisit other apparent exemplars of 'traditional' ancient gender structures, but also as a bridge between the diversity of ancient gendered bodies and those we construct in our own contemporary societies.

First, a brief explanation of my approach. Building on the insights of her earlier work (Holmes 2012) on the fertile intersection of ancient and modern in twentieth- and twenty-first-century gender studies, Brooke Holmes has recently called on classicists, particularly those interested in questions of sex and gender, to be more explicit about the contemporary concerns that motivate our engagement with ancient models of (what we call) gender and sexuality (Holmes 2019). Such a foregrounding of scholarly motivations helps to more overtly situate our engagement with the past in the concerns of the present, a gesture that has been something of a taboo amongst classicists for some time – even if the influence of contemporary society is no less powerful a force in academic endeavour now than it was a century ago, when scholars unabashedly viewed ancient texts through the filter of modern society. The interpretive spirit that I follow here is, quite emphatically and I believe productively, motivated by concerns of contemporary society, specifically by the increasing prominence of trans studies, and the transgender movement more broadly, in political and intellectual debates, particularly in the United States. I have been especially moved by the sophisticated theoretical interventions of trans scholars and activists who challenge us to revisit (once again) the apparent boundary between gender (understood as a socially constructed identity) and sex (understood as a biological, or at least corporeal fact) – a boundary already seriously destabilised by the work of Butler and Carolyn Dinshaw (especially Butler 1993 and Dinshaw 1999) – inviting us to see the intersection of sex and gender as a critical locus for reflection on what bodies are, and what it means to have one. The complex role of body modification, particularly through medical technologies, in the lives of many (though by no means all) trans individuals invites reflection on the way that categories such as 'natural' and 'artificial', 'agency' and 'subjectivity' shape, and potentially inhibit, our understanding of the way that sex and gender now function in our society, both for those who identify as trans and for those who do not.

One of the most compelling responses to this new landscape has found form in a strain of post-humanist theory that discards traditional boundaries of the (human) body in favour of definitions that better reflect the way that our somatic experiences and identities are bound up with other, often inert, material. This notion of a composite body, consisting of both human and non-human elements at once, has found expression in a variety of fields, most notably in the explicitly feminist cyborg reflections of Donna Haraway (1991) as well as in the radical sociological work of Bruno Latour (2004: 210), who rejects conventional subject–object relationships and, instead, speaks of collective bodies that are continuously (re)formed through the power of new 'artificial and material components'. In her own variation on post-humanist materiality, the feminist and queer philosopher of science Karen Barad notes the particular power of developing 'alternative ways to conceptualise matter' to create a new space for thinking about bodies that do not conform to, or are not well understood through, traditional notions of causation. 'Holding the category "human" fixed', Barad (2003: 826) argues, 'excludes an entire range of possibilities in advance, eliding important dimensions of the workings of power'.

Like Haraway and Latour, Barad is principally concerned with what is to come. Her model is one which celebrates a future that is 'radically open at every turn' (2003: 826). But these emphatically contemporary definitions of the body can also help us to imagine the past in new ways, and thereby to bring that past into productive dialogue with the world around us. I believe that there is no more fitting ancient body through which to begin such a dialogue than that of Pandora. The experiment that I would like to undertake here seeks to reframe the contested, reviled and unfailingly theorised body of Pandora through the lens of contemporary reassessments of corporeal boundaries. By so doing, I hope to suggest a way of productively untangling the twin binaries of male/female, natural/artificial that stand, at least at the moment, as the most enduring legacy of her appearance in Hesiod.

PANDORA AND HER HAMMERERS

Rather than begin from the canonical twin narratives of Hesiod, passages that now stand as talismans of sexual binary in ancient Greece (an excellent overview of scholarship is offered by Holmes 2012: 17–22), I turn instead to two fifth-century BC Pandoras preserved only in fragments. These uncertain glimpses of now-lost bodies are a useful reminder that the established narratives of contemporary scholarship are often built on the foundations of untold omissions. More than that, I believe that the destabilising presence of these shadowy figures, of Pandoras not quite seen, can also invite us to think about new models for thinking about bodies from the past in relation to the present. I begin with Sophocles' often-overlooked version of the myth in his now highly fragmentary satyr drama *Pandora or Hammerers*. Little is known about the play, which was staged in Athens at some point in the fifth century, beyond the fact that it dramatised some facet of Pandora's life through the raucous and ribald lens of satyr drama (Krumeich et al. 1999: 375–80). Satyr drama comprised a fourth and final performance following the three tragedies submitted by each of the playwrights competing at the City Dionysia, and was distinguished by the recurrent presence of its chorus of satyrs, half-human half-equine followers of the god Dionysus whom the plays inserted into familiar mythical scenarios such as Odysseus' encounter with the Cyclops or Heracles' enslavement to Omphale (on which see Hughes in this volume). Each outlandishly humorous scenario emerges from the basic and oft-quoted recipe of François Lissarrague (1990: 236): 'take one myth, add satyrs, observe the result'. The five surviving fragments of Sophocles' play provide little foundation for philologically defensible interpretation (though the ribald tone of fr. 483 suggests an embrace of erotic discourse that contrasts with Hesiod's stark avoidance of such matters). But it is precisely the elusive quality of the fragments that marks the play as particularly suitable to the kind of self-conscious scholarly reflection called for by queer unhistoricism. Indeed, the heart of my interest in the play comes not from the fragments themselves, but from its alternate titles, *Pandora or Hammerers* (Πανδώρα ἢ Σφυροκόποι), and the imaginative trajectories that they have and can inspire in modern critics.

My reflections emerge from the collateral role of Sophocles' play in the treatment of Pandora by first-wave feminist scholars, particularly in the work of Jane Harrison, a pioneering female scholar whose life and career have been deftly explored by Mary Beard (2000). In her ground-breaking *Prolegomena to the Study of Greek Religion,* Harrison (1908) sought to uncover evidence of the matriarchal, chthonic ritual figures that (she claimed) predated, and had been displaced by, the patriarchal system of Olympian gods. Harrison believed that the vicissitudes of history had wrongly privileged the rational structures of the Olympian order as the authentic expression of Greek religious practice. Fortunately, Harrison contended, this error could be corrected by a rigorous analysis of ancient evidence to reveal the true chthonic and magical nature of ancient Greek religion and thought. In the figure of Pandora, Harrison saw the superlative expression of the opposition between chthonic magic and Olympian rationality, a paradigm for the displacement of the more ancient (and genuine) matriarchal structure by a new (artificial) patriarchal order.

In heady and spellbinding prose, Harrison (1908: 284) claimed to have uncovered evidence that the Pandora story familiar from Hesiodic epic – the story in which Zeus instructed Hephaestus to mould Pandora out of earth as a punishment for mankind – was in fact a late innovation, a 'bourgeois, pessimistic' refashioning of the earlier, authentic myth (Harrison 1908: 284). Behind Hesiod's hollow and contemptible Pandora, Harrison claimed to have found a powerful chthonic goddess who was not an artificial object crafted by the Olympians but an autonomous, self-possessed goddess, born from the earth itself. In support of this view, Harrison adduced a series of vase paintings representing a female figure emerging from the earth, welcomed by a figure or figures in various configurations. Harrison dubbed this topos the '*anodos* of the goddess', claiming that the images were all variations on a basic, 'primitive' motif of a female goddess, whom she dubbed *kore*, emerging from her mother, the earth. On one of these vases, now in the Ashmolean collection (Oxford G 275, *BAPD* 275165, Bérard 1974: Pl. 19, fig. 71 (A)), the figures are labelled with the names Pandora and Epimetheus, respectively, leading Harrison to the conclusion that the image preserved traces of an 'earlier and more primitive' tradition in which Pandora was in fact 'a real goddess of the earth' rather than 'the handiwork of Olympian Zeus' (Harrison 1908: 284).

Harrison's identification of the *anodos* ('ascent') motif bears on Sophocles' play in two important respects. Firstly, many of the *anodos* vases contain satyrs (though none that explicitly identify the female figure as Pandora), and secondly, the figures attending to the emerging female figure in these images, whether they are satyrs or not, often carry hammers (Bérard 1974). The motif finds exuberant expression on the neck of a fifth-century Athenian volute crater, now in Ferrara, which depicts a band of hammer-wielding satyrs dancing around a female figure as she emerges from under the ground (Fig. 3.1). The iconographic pairing of *anodos* motif with satyrs and hammers is particularly enticing when one considers, as Harrison herself did, the play's alternative title, *Hammerers,* which suggests that the satyr chorus of this play were possessed of

Figure 3.1 Satyrs wielding hammers dance around a female figure emerging from the ground. The aulete at left suggests a dramatic performance. Neck of an Athenian volute krater, c. 450 BC, Ferrara T 579, *BAPD* 207095.

hammers, and that they employed these hammers in an extended and conspicuous enough fashion that someone, whether Sophocles or a later critic, considered the objects essential to the dramatic narrative. Although Harrison herself drew no firm connection between the hammering satyrs of the *anodos* vases and those of Sophocles' play, subsequent interpreters showed less restraint. Not long after the publication of Harrison's *Prolegomena*, it became common to strongly suggest, and even to assert outright, that the vases were evidence that Sophocles' play depicted Pandora as born from the earth, not crafted by Hephaestus, and that the hammer-wielding chorus employed their tools as 'clod busters' to facilitate her emergence (Robert 1914; Guarducci 1929; Brommer 1959: 51–2; Trendall and Webster 1971: 33–6; Simon 1982: 145–6).

There are a number of reasons to be hesitant about such claims, not least in light of fr. 482, where the instruction to begin moulding clay (πηλὸν ὀργάζειν) points strongly towards a fashioning of Pandora rather than an autonomous *anodos*. Recently, the critical pendulum seems to be swinging in this sceptical direction, with Christina Heynen and Ralf Krumeich declaring the claim that Sophocles' Pandora emerged from the earth 'extremely hypothetical' (Heynen and Krumeich 1999: 379). Although I tend to agree with the growing consensus that Sophocles' Pandora was, in the main, cast in the mould of her Hesiodic predecessor, there nevertheless remains much to be said about the largely unacknowledged legacy of Harrison's work in the way that we think about this play, and the body of Pandora more broadly. Again, it is the play's double title that motivates my thinking, since one of the most confounding features of the twofold description (*Pandora or Hammerers*) is the degree to which both of the paired terms stubbornly resist resolution. In the case of Pandora, the idea of a double figure – at once earth goddess and artisan craft, 'natural' body and 'artificial' object – is the heart of Harrison's argument. Even if one does not accept Harrison's outdated developmental model, the iconographic evidence of an earth-born Pandora cannot be gainsaid. The duality of the second title, *Hammerers* (Σφυροκόποι), is (to me at least) somewhat more surprising, and it is this discursive tool that I will use as my own 'clod buster' in aid of bringing a queer, unhistorical body to light.

References to the *sphyra*, the substantive that lends the 'hammer' element to the title of Sophocles' play, reflect a twofold usage of the instrument, as a tool of metallurgy on the one hand, and of agricultural labour on the other. Like the artisanal Pandora which it would signal, the former is far more common, and gives rise to a number of compounds relating to smithery. The familiar adjectival form *sphyrēlatos* is regularly used to describe armour and, more pertinently for the discussion at hand, metal sculpture produced by hammering sheets of metal (rather than through the lost-wax technique). Although it has been suggested that the hammering satyrs of Sophocles' play may have used their tools to fashion Pandora's clay form (Jebb 1917: 136), given Hephaestus' role in crafting Pandora's crown in Hesiod (*Theog.* 578–80), and the frequent association of satyrs with the fiery work of the god (Jebb 1917: 136; Simon 1982: 134–6; Hedreen 1992), one might plausibly conjecture that the hammers of Sophocles' play were put to such a metallurgical use, with the chorus endeavouring to fashion the elaborate adornments for the newly born first woman. However, since, as I have said, my interest here is not to reconstruct the details of Sophocles' fragmentary drama, but rather to consider the implications of its double title for our understanding of Pandora, I will resist dismissing the agricultural resonances of the tool, even if I think it unlikely that the *sphyrai* of the play were used in such a way. Whatever their specific purpose in the drama, the presence of the implements activates a range of associations that extend not only to (presumably unseen) the rural sphere, but to the *anodos* iconography in which the tools so frequently appear. Indeed, it is easy to imagine that an audience familiar with images of an earthborn Pandora surrounded by hammer-wielding figures, often satyrs, would have perceived this tradition as a subtext to the hammer-wielding chorus of Sophocles' drama. The suspicion that this duality was intentionally cultivated by the playwright gains some weight in light of Aeschylus' pointedly paradoxical description of (Pandora as) a 'mortal woman [born/created] from a seed of moulded clay' (ἐκ πηλοπλάστου σπέρματος θνητὴ γυνή fr. 369).

More importantly for my present concerns, the double function of the *sphyra* calls our attention to the fact that artisan tools – indeed, the *same* artisan tools – are central to the Pandora narrative in both of its configurations. As a crafted object, Pandora gains her additional adornments through the manipulation of the *sphyra*, but/and, in her guise as an earthborn goddess, she is brought to the light by the same. Hammers are, as Harrison herself made clear, a recurrent motif in *anodos* imagery. What Harrison does not say, although it is an inescapable implication of this fact, is that the presence of hammers – of craftsman's tools – within the *anodos* tradition falsifies the rigid binary between earthborn goddess and manufactured object, and between the oppositional spheres of nature and culture to which Pandora's two bodies are said to belong.

One need not rely on Sophocles to arrive at this observation. But Sophocles' play, with the inbuilt duality of its double title mirrored in twentieth-century critical discourse, offers a particularly productive window through which to reflect on the implications of Pandora's non-binary bodies. The value of the play stems in part from its highly fragmentary nature, which demands an unusually acute sensitivity to the motivations behind our modern speculations about the text. But the power of Sophocles' drama also lies in the figures with whom Pandora shares the theatre and the play's title: the chorus of satyrs whose hammer-wielding antics are somehow critical to, and synonymous with, the appearance of the first female body. As I have argued elsewhere, the satyrs of fifth-century Athenian drama provided the theatre-going audience with an unusually charged site for reflecting on bodies, especially the way that bodies articulate the unstable binary of 'nature' and 'artifice' (Uhlig 2018). In the theatre, the satyrs' own hybrid form – part human, part horse or donkey – finds material expression in a composite costume that highlights the combination of 'natural' and 'artificial' elements in order to transform Athenian choreuts into the mythical slaves of Dionysus. Critical to this metamorphosis are the distinctive shorts, or *perizomata*, that reveal the choreuts' own nude limbs and torsos (likely for the first time in their nearly completed performances) while providing them with fabricated genitals and equine tail. This unsettling conjunction of inborn and constructed elements is a persistent theme of somatic reflection in fifth-century Athens, both within satyr dramas themselves and in vase painters' frequent depictions of conspicuously costumed theatrical satyrs. The iconographic power of the *perizoma* is highlighted by the ease with which the distinctive contours of the satyr costume can be identified, even on highly fragmentary figures such as those found on a group of fifth-century Athenian sherds, now in Bonn (Fig. 3.2). The large circular marks (possibly horse brands) commonly adorning the side of *perizomata* in fifth-century vase illustrations call attention to the complex conjunction of human and animal, flesh and artefact. The costumed nudity joins the living flesh of the choreut with the tanned and sewn skin of a dead animal to produce a new, composite form; a naked body that is at once more 'natural' and more 'artificial' than the other bodies of the theatre, performers and audience alike.

The composite form of theatrical satyrs – part living flesh, part fabricated skin and organ – calls the nature of their bodies into question, and in doing so opens the boundary of their somatic forms to further artificial amplification. As the familiar satyrs, with their familiarly composite bodies, fill the orchestra at the close of each day of tragic competition, they invent themselves anew, taking on

Figure 3.2 Fragments show the headless, but nonetheless clearly identifiable bodies of an aulete and three choreuts wearing *perizomata* to portray satyrs in the theatre. Athenian, c. 450 BC, Akademisches Kunstmuseum Bonn 1216.354-357, 1216.183, 1216.185, *BAPD* 215629.

new roles and new identities to match the particular demands of each individual drama (Seidensticker 2003: 103; Lämmle 2013: 245–91). Material objects are often critical to this transformation. The satyrs of the chorus take up new costumes – goat skins in Euripides' *Cyclops*, or women's dress in Ion's *Omphale* – or new tools – nets in Aeschylus' *Nethaulers*, wrestling gear in his *Cercyon* or hammers in Sophocles' *Pandora* – and thus become the figures of a new drama. The physical objects grant the chorus a new identity, and with it new bodies that conform to their role in each specific play. Sometimes the transformation is marked within traditional somatic boundaries, as when the chorus of Aeschylus' *Theoroi* adopt the physique of athletes to participate in the Isthmian games (fr. 78a 29–31). But seemingly external accessories such as robes or nets also result in corporeal shifts. If we take seriously the expanded definition of the body put forth by contemporary theorists, the fabricated objects that theatrical satyrs wield and wear are no less a part of their somatic identity than the fabricated *perizomata* that produce their naked, hybrid form (Uhlig 2018).

The conjunction of Pandora and a chorus of theatrical satyrs in Sophocles' play helps to foreground certain parallels between these two types of conspicuously crafted bodies. The satyr chorus are a kind of somatic analogue to Pandora herself. The double body of her two birth narratives finds its match in the satyrs' material hybridity. Both have bodies that inhabit an uncertain territory between nature and artifice, between organic body and constructed form. At the same time, both simultaneously unsettle and epitomise what it means to have a (human) body and both are explicitly defined by sexual identity (if not function). This somatic symmetry finds its most compelling symbolism in the hammers by which both of their bodies are crafted, and which, consequently, form part of the corporeal identity of both, since the transformative effect of these tools on Pandora integrates them into her body – on which they work, or for which they help to fashion adornments – no less than for the satyrs who wield them.

OTHER HAMMERERS, AND ANOTHER PANDORA

Hammers, as we have seen, are central to Sophocles' understanding of Pandora, though their precise role in the drama remains nebulous for modern critics. The broader connection between hammers and corporeal generation is attested by the striking regularity with which the implements appear in *anodos* images, whether in depictions of Pandora or of other earth-born figures. The role of hammers in the creation of bodies is, in a somewhat different register, also underlined by the frequent description of metallic sculpture, whether of bronze or gold, as *sphyrēlatos* (wrought by hammer). The two perspectives, corresponding to the 'natural' and 'artificial' bodies of Pandora, underline the shared properties of both through their common reliance on instrumental intervention.

Two further instances of generative hammers help to round out the picture. The first emerges around the unusual birth of Helen from an egg. A well-known fourth-century BC Apulian crater depicts a comic staging of the moment of her 'delivery', in which the new-born Helen, still standing inside the egg, is attended to by a male figure (generally thought to be Tyndareus) holding a hammer above his head (Fig. 3.3). Notably, the comic costumes in the image recall the *perizomata* of the performing satyrs; their prominently displayed prosthetic phalloi and artificially nude limbs accentuate the ways by which dramatic bodies are constructed. A similar theme – without costumed figures, though with the presence of a satyr – is struck by another fourth-century Italian vase, now in Boston, on which Helen's brother carries the unhatched egg in one hand and a hammer in the other (Boston 07.862, Padgett 1993: no. 167). The suggestion in both images is that the hammer has been or will be used to break open the shell, much as the same implements serve to break open the earth to facilitate the emergence of earthborn goddesses. Helen, whose extreme bodily beauty and corresponding destructive powers align her in important ways with Pandora (Blondell 2013: 26–8), replays the double birth of her predecessor by merging 'natural' and 'artificial' elements in the unusual genesis of her body.

The hammer that frees Helen from the egg is mirrored by another hammer familiar from the iconographic tradition: that wielded by Hephaestus at

Figure 3.3 Tyndareus(?) stands wielding a hammer after helping(?) Helen to emerge from her egg. Apulian krater attributed to Dijon painter, c. 350 BC, Bari 3899; De Agostini Picture Library/G. Dagli Orti/Bridgeman Images.

the birth of Athena. The popular motif of Hephaestus' instrumental assistance in the goddess's unusual birth is nicely illustrated by a fifth-century Athenian *pelike*, now in the British Museum, which shows the craftsman god, tool in hand, standing immediately to the left of Zeus and the new-born Athena (Fig. 3.4). Scholars often refer to the implement as a double axe, perhaps under the influence of Pindar's O.7, where Hephaestus makes use of a 'bronze axe' (χαλκέλατος πέλεκυς 36) to free Athena from the head of Zeus. The iconographic tradition, however, does not distinguish between the instrument used to extract Athena and the familiar hammer, often paired with tongs, that marks Hephaestus as a worker of metal (on two-sided hammers, see Raubitscheck 1998: 120 n. 8). Like Pandora, the new-born Athena is marked as a craft product, fully clad in the metal armour – another material/corporeal product of the hammer – that signals not only the goddess's martial nature but her unsettling masculine qualities. Where Pandora's material artifice is thought to align her with the race of women, Athena's ornamentation is traditionally assimilated to her rejection of female concerns, a position that finds its clearest expression in

Figure 3.4 Hephaestus stands with his hammer after helping Athena emerge from the head of Zeus. Athenian *pelike*, c. 450 BC, British Museum E410, *BAPD* 205560.

her famous claim, in Aeschylus' *Eumenides*, to side with the masculine in all things (τὸ δ' ἄρσεν αἰνῶ πάντα 737).

The parallels between the crafted, hammer-born bodies of Athena and Pandora did not, it seems, go unnoticed in fifth-century Athens, though the conjunction of the two – like that of Pandora and the hammering satyrs of Sophocles' play – survives only in fragmentary traces of bodies that were once on full view. By contrast with Sophocles' satyr drama, the pairing of Athena and Pandora was on permanent display in the heart of the city, inscribed into the base of Pheidias' great chryselephantine statue of Athena Parthenos, the cult image located inside the Parthenon. This often-overlooked fact is recorded by Pausanias in his description of the sculptural program of the Parthenon, where he notes that the birth of Pandora (Πανδώρας γένεσις) was worked onto the support for the towering sculpture (1.24.7). Pausanias gives no details about the scene, connecting the image to the accounts of Pandora as the first woman found in 'Hesiod and others' without further elaboration. But even if we cannot speak with confidence about the form that the depiction took, we should not underestimate the significance of Pandora's inclusion, confronting viewers at eyelevel, in the preeminent representation of Athena in Athens.

As Jeffrey Hurwit, one of the few contemporary scholars to consider the role of Pandora in the complex iconography of the Parthenon, has elegantly observed, the import of such a powerful and surprising juxtaposition cannot be reduced to a single definitive interpretation (Hurwit 1995: 182). Hurwit argues that the inclusion of Pandora is primarily motivated by a desire 'to say something about her gender – "the race of female women," as Hesiod puts it' (Hurwit 1995: 178). Following the binary, misogynistic logic of Hesiod's account, the Parthenon Pandora stands as a 'visual articulation of the male-female antithesis', a reminder that the city of Athens, like Athena herself, was defined by the subjugation and exclusion of women (Hurwit 1995: 185). In the self-replicating iconographic patterns of the Parthenon, Pandora stands as a correlate to the Amazons so conspicuously subdued on the temple's west metopes. But there is, as Hurwit also acknowledges, another discourse of the Parthenon imagery into which Pandora just as readily fits, one which is emblematised by the depiction, now lost, of the birth of Athena that adorned the east pediment. 'Anyone entering the temple from the east could not have missed the parallel' between the miraculous births of these two female figures (Hurwit 1995: 182). The crafted body of Pandora thus takes on another form, as a celebration of Athena *Ergane*, an artificially crafted mortal body replicating the corporeal artifice of Athena herself. The presence of Pandora on the sculpture base points to the analogy between the technical accomplishment of Pheidias' chryselephantine Athena, with its radical proportions and complex manipulation of material, and the crafted body it represents. The temple encourages visitors to contemplate hammer-born figures brought to life in forms that are quite literally *sphyrēlatos* ('hammer-wrought').

LEARNING FROM PANDORA'S FRAGMENTED BODIES

The fragmentary Pandoras of fifth-century Athens, the theatrically constructed body of Sophocles and the sculpted form of Pheidias, suggest a further alternative narrative of Pandora. They do not present us with a prior, more 'authentic' or 'natural' body born from the earth, but rather a body whose artificiality is celebrated as a source of power, whose construction through tools is not a sign of dependence but a deliberate means of bringing a new form into the light. The hammer-wielding Hephaestus remains a shadowy figure in the Parthenon images, his presence, and that of his tool, presumed but never confirmed. But his counterparts, the dancing satyrs in the theatre of Dionysus, invite us to consider the ways in which the construction of bodies establishes a certain corporeal symmetry between craftsman and craft object, a shared somatic experience that is effected through the tools common to both. It is surely not by chance that Athena, the virgin goddess, produces her only offspring together with Hephaestus (Hurwit 1995: 183). The son of two artisan gods, the new-born Erichthonius is regularly figured in fifth-century Athenian vases emerging from the earth in a scene that mirrors the female *anodos* images linked to Pandora by Harrison. In place of hammers, the skilled hands of Athena, the mother who gave him form, aid his passage up from the ground.

These alternative narratives of female (and male) bodies blended together with tools and ornament do not erase the deep-seated misogyny that characterises Hesiod's canonical versions of the Pandora story, but they do suggest that the rigid binaries that structure his narratives can be reimagined in ways that open a productive dialogue with contemporary thinking about trans bodies, and bodies more broadly. Such a reading would allow us to view Hesiod's disdain for Pandora's crafted body, and not the body itself, as a product of his misogynistic binary. Rather than posit a purer, 'natural' Pandora whose true form is obscured in Hesiod's account, we could redeem the artificial woman of his accounts, reclaiming the beauty so demonised there as something truly and authentically valuable, not despite but because of its fabricated nature. In his seminal interpretation of Hesiod's Prometheus, Jean-Pierre Vernant (1996: 199) observed that the central role of Pandora in both accounts stems from the fact that her 'double nature is, as it were, the symbol of the ambiguity of human existence'. This symbolism is all the more pointed when one considers that Hesiod provides no account of the creation of man to contrast or complement that of woman in his poems. Pandora's birth, the artificial creation of the human form, stands for all. Indeed, as Vernant notes elsewhere (1989: 47–8), tradition often attributed to Prometheus the creation of both men and women from clay. It is this inclusive perspective that seems to inspire Ovid, in the otherwise strongly Hesiodic opening narrative of the *Metamorphoses*, when he recounts the creation of mankind, sown into earth by the craftsman of things (*ille opifex rerum*) and shaped by Prometheus as moulded clay (*Met.* 1.79–83). In his pointed revision Ovid not only negates the gender binary of Hesiod's narratives, but with it the opposition between 'natural' and 'artificial' generation.

In the final chapter of the *Generation of Animals*, Aristotle interrupts his lengthy consideration of the form and purpose of teeth to reflect on the many ways that breath works within bodies. 'It is fitting,' he observes 'that many things are worked by breath, as by a tool (*hōs organō*); just as certain tools of the crafts serve many purposes, like the hammer and anvil in metalwork, so too does breath in those things formed by nature' (789b8–12). Aristotle draws the connection between differently constructed bodies by means of the broad resonances of the term *organon*, which can connote both artisanal instruments and the mechanisms of living creatures. But in invoking the hammer, and its partner the anvil, in the elaboration of this correspondence, Aristotle inadvertently calls to mind a tool which, perhaps more than any other, served to underline the complex interdependence of animate and inanimate bodies in Classical Athens. It goes without saying that hammers no longer hold such a place in our twenty-first century somatic imaginations, but we too rely on bodily tools that are as powerful as breath itself.

CHAPTER 4

Life after Transition: Spontaneous Sex Change and Its Aftermath in Ancient Literature

K. E. Shannon-Henderson[1]

There are several well-known characters in classical mythology who experience a change of sex, such as Tiresias (see Brisson 1976; Ugolini 1995) and Hermaphroditus (Ovid, *Metamorphoses* 4.285–388, with Robinson 1999). But there are also reports of girls and women who spontaneously acquire anatomical markers of maleness, not in myth but in real life, at specific times and places (Doroszewska 2013a: 224–5). It is these accounts of 'real-life' change of sex, particularly as related by authors active between the first century BC and the second century AD, that will be my focus in this essay. Their stories differ not only from mythical accounts of sexual transformation, but also from accounts of intersex children found in Roman historians' reports of prodigies (e.g. Livy 27.11.4–5, 27.37.5–7, 31.12.6–10; Julius Obsequens 46, 81, 92, 94, 96, 107, 108, 110; see Krauss 1930: 130–3). Whereas the birth of intersex children inspired fear in a Roman population that viewed them as signs of severe divine displeasure (MacBain 1982: 127–35; Allély 2003), the reports of sexual transformation I consider are different. Intersex people – born with genitals that appear to combine masculine and feminine characteristics – display 'simultaneous dual sexuality'; people born with one set of genitalia that change to the opposite exhibit 'successive dual sexuality' (Brisson 2002: 2). Unlike the intersex infants drowned at sea during the Roman Republic, the people I will discuss were born as and assigned female at birth but transitioned across the gender boundary, lived to tell the tale, and even lived openly as men after transformation.

Reports of spontaneous sexual transformation are relatively rare in ancient literature. The most detailed narratives appear in the fragments of book 32 of Diodorus Siculus (32.10–12), written in the first century BC and preserved in the *Bibliotheca* of Photius, written in the ninth century AD (on Photius as a reader of Diodorus, see Botteri 1992: 28B9; Wirth 2008: 9B10; Rathmann 2016: 152). There are also shorter reports in Pliny the Elder's *Natural History* (7.36), a massive first-century AD work on aspects of the natural world, and the

Περὶ θαυμασίων (*On Marvels*) by Phlegon of Tralles, a freedman of Hadrian active in the mid-second century AD. Scholars have attempted to explain what the ancient texts present as spontaneous transformations in terms of modern medical diagnoses, for example as disorders of sexual differentiation misunderstood by ancient observers (e.g. Hansen 1996: 124). My goal in examining these accounts is to understand what they reveal about ancient conceptions of gender difference. I will analyse these texts from several angles: their attitude to the anatomy and the gender and sexual expressions of the transformed individuals; the interpretive frameworks through which they seek to understand them; and their descriptions of the transformed individuals' attempts to re-navigate community and family life after transformation. People who spontaneously change from female to male would seem like the perfect place to look for gender nonconformity in ancient culture. But, as we shall see, these stories broadly confirm rather than challenge three widespread ancient ideas: (1) that there are two distinct sexes, male and female; (2) that a person must belong to one sex or the other; and (3) that of those two sexes, the male is definitively superior.

PHAËTHOUSA AND NANNO: CHANGE AND DIE

I begin with an older case study: a report in the Hippocratic text *Epidemics*, composed substantially earlier than my other source texts (fourth century BC), of two women, Phaëthousa and Nanno, who suddenly develop male characteristics. The way this text discusses how Phaëthousa and Nanno's bodies change is fundamentally different from, and provides an instructive contrast with, the later stories of sexual transformation. In the later stories, the women truly and fully become men; but Phaëthousa and Nanno remain fundamentally female throughout the changes they undergo.

> In Abdera, Phaëthousa the wife of Pytheas, who kept at home, having borne children in the preceding time, when her husband was exiled stopped menstruating for a long time. Afterwards, pains and reddening in the joints. When this happened, her body became manly (ἠνδρώθη) and grew hairy all over, she grew a beard, her voice became harsh, and though we did everything we could to bring forth menses they did not come, but she later died after surviving (βιώσασα) a short time. The same thing happened to Nanno, the wife of Gorgippus, in Thasos. All the physicians I met thought that there was one hope of becoming feminine (γυναικωθῆναι): if normal menstruation occurred. But in her case (ταύτη), too, it was not possible, though we did everything, but she died quickly. (*Epidemics* 6.8.32; trans. adapted from Smith 1994: 275)

This account shows some similarities with the later sex change stories, but the *Epidemics*' discussion of Phaëthousa and Nanno's bodies suggests that their experiences are a fundamentally different type of change from the complete transformations of the later accounts. Phaëthousa loses some biological markers of femaleness (menstruation) and acquires markers of maleness (beard, body hair, deep voice). These two symptoms are connected, according to the principles of Hippocratic thought about menstruation: women's menstrual blood was thought to be a way of expelling excess moisture from the body, whereas in men, who were constitutionally hotter and physically more active than women, such moisture would be consumed by the body and manifested as hair (e.g. Aristotle *GA* 582b30–583a4; Dean-Jones 1994: 133–4; King 1998: 56–7, 154–5, 163). The claim that Phaëthousa's body 'became manly' probably indicates not that a change occurred in her genitalia (such as the growth of a penis or testicles), but that her body lost the wet, spongy nature characteristic of women and became firmer, drier, hotter – i.e. more masculine (King 2013a: 129).

Helen King has shown that two details are key to understanding Phaëthousa's ailment: her husband's absence, and her previous experience of childbearing. The text suggests that Phaëthousa's menses cease because she has no husband around to ensure she experiences frequent sexual intercourse and possibly conception (King 1998: 56–7). Nevertheless, Phaëthousa's essentially female reproductive anatomy remains unchanged: she may have a beard, but she still possesses a womb that has borne children (King 2013b: 111). So, although Phaëthousa's body changes in ways that make her appear less feminine and ultimately lead to her death, she does not actually become male (King 2015: 256). Indeed, even at the moment of death, both she and Nanno remain grammatically feminine in the text (βιώσασα, ταύτη); this indicates that the author does not consider either of them to have truly become men, but to have retained their female identity throughout (King 2013a: 128). The Hippocratics saw sex as a continuum, with male and female at opposite poles; on this rationale, it was possible to be a manly woman or a womanly man without fully transforming into the opposite sex (*Regimen* 1.28; see Gleason 1990: 390–1, 394–5; Cadden 1993: 15–21; King 1998: 9; Dreger 2000: 32). Yet ultimately both Phaëthousa and Nanno die as a result of their conditions. Losing female traits (especially menstruation) in exchange for male characteristics is not the same as becoming a man; but it is also impossible for a woman to continue living in such a state. The boundary between male and female cannot be crossed, and even attempts to approach it are deadly. The story, in other words, suggests the ultimate impossibility of exactly the types of sexual transformation that occur in the later texts.

DIODORUS, PLINY AND PHLEGON: A PENIS MAKES A MAN

The stories in Diodorus, Pliny and Phlegon are also concerned with physical changes, but of a different type. The *Epidemics* passage mainly focuses on secondary sexual characteristics (beard, body hair, timbre of voice), and the women never acquire male sex organs. This is a vast point of difference between the

Hippocratic text and our later authors, who focus on anatomical changes to the genitals of the women who transform. These anatomical details – specifically, the sudden presence of a penis and testicles where none had been visible before – are the key to assigning a new identity to the transformed person. In all cases, it is male genitalia that come first, and a new gender identity and social role that follows the physical changes. The individuals who transform are not viewed as an intermediate category in the no-man's-land between male and female, but cross the gender boundary completely thanks to their altered genitalia.

Not all of our texts provide much detail on the physical aspect of the transformation, but even the sparest accounts make clear that male genitalia do appear. Pliny, citing Licinius Mucianus (an author from the Flavian period, on whom see Ash 2007), describes a man named 'Arescon, who had been called Arescusa and had actually gotten married, but . . . eventually a beard and a penis came forth (*barbam et virilitatem provenisse*) and he took a wife' (*HN* 7.36, all translations are my own unless otherwise stated). Arescusa, like Phaëthousa and Nanno before her, grows a beard; this time the transformation does not stop there, but proceeds to the appearance of *virilitas*, indicating a penis and/or testicles as the male sexual organs *par excellence* (*OLD* s.v. *virilitas* 1b and ancient references there cited; Adams 1982: 69–70). Similarly, in Phlegon's shorter narratives of sexual transformations (*Mir.* 7–9), he specifically states that the woman acquired male anatomy. In AD 53, Philotis, a girl betrothed to be married, 'became a man when male genitals appeared on her' (*Mir.* 7, μορίων αὐτῇ προφανέντων ἀρρενικῶν ἀνὴρ ἐγένετο). Note that Philotis is described using a feminine pronoun, but immediately upon the appearance of male μόρια, a word frequently used to denote genitalia (*LSJ* s.v. μόριον A.II.2; Adams 1982: 45, 58), she transforms into a man. Similarly, in AD 116 the married woman Aitete 'changed her shape (μετέβαλε τὴν μορφὴν) . . . and upon becoming a man (ἀνὴρ γενόμενος) changed her name to Aitetos' (*Mir.* 9). In *Mir.* 6, the sudden appearance of a penis is part of a more detailed narrative. In AD 45, a girl from Antioch suffers severe abdominal pains for several days before her transformation; the symptoms perplex her physicians, until 'suddenly male parts burst forth on her and the girl became a man' (*Mir.* 6, ἄφνω αὐτῇ ἀρσενικὰ μόρια προέπεσεν καὶ ἡ κόρη ἀνὴρ ἐγένετο).

This focus on genitalia underlines the idea that, for Phlegon and Pliny, there is no physical middle ground between male and female: the sudden appearance of a penis is enough to make someone a man. Phlegon refers to the women with feminine pronouns up until the moment the male genitals appear, but from that point forward he says simply that they 'became men' using the language ἀνὴρ ἐγένετο (*Mir.* 6, 7) or ἀνὴρ γενόμενος (*Mir.* 8, 9); Pliny the Elder similarly says that they were changed into men or boys (*HN* 7.36 *puerum/virum factum* or *mutatum/mutari in marem*). For both writers, women who spontaneously become men are distinct from individuals who possess both male and female genitalia simultaneously. Pliny describes what he calls *hermaphroditi* or *androgyni*, who possess ambiguous genitals from birth, in a separate chapter (7.34) alongside other portentous births (e.g. women who give birth to snakes or elephants). Phlegon similarly distinguishes transforming women from infants born with two sets of genitalia mentioned elsewhere in his text. Compare, for example, Phlegon's description of a child, born in Boeotia in the fourth century BC (*Mir.* 2), as 'possessing two sets of genitals, male and female (αἰδοῖα ἔχον δύο, ἀνδρεῖον τε καὶ γυναικεῖον), which differed amazingly in their nature: The upper parts of the genitals were complete and masculine, but the parts around the thighs were womanly and softer' (*Mir.* 2.3). In this unusually detailed description, almost medical in character (Doroszewska 2013b: 382–3), Phlegon gives far more information about the appearance of the child's genitals than he does about the transformed women's new male genitals. This suggests that he views the women not, like the two infants (whose unusual genitals need to be carefully explained for the audience), as being of indeterminate sex, but as having thoroughly unambiguous and unremarkable, and thoroughly male, genitalia. For both Pliny and Phlegon, then, these women who spontaneously change sex are viewed as a decidedly different category of being from people born with genitals that display both male and female characteristics simultaneously: women who spontaneously grow penises are not intersex, but male.

Diodorus' narratives offer a more complex account of spontaneous transformation, in that his characters Heraïs and Kallo (whose transformations are said to have occurred in 145 BC and 115 BC respectively) require medical intervention to bring manhood to physical completion. Nevertheless, his descriptions suggest that these women truly become men. Heraïs' transformation is preceded by several days of abdominal pain and fever that stymie her physicians (32.10.3), until the problem solves itself with the appearance of new genitals: 'There burst forth from Heraïs' female parts (ἐκ τῶν τῆς Ἡραΐδος γυναικείων) a male organ with testicles attached (αἰδοῖον ἀνδρεῖον ἔχον διδύμους προσκειμένους).' Later, after Heraïs begins to live as a man, doctors again examine her new genitals and offer an interpretation, along with surgical intervention:

> They believed that the masculine organ (φύσις ἄρρενος) had lain hidden in an egg-shaped space within the feminine organ (φύσεως θηλείας), and that, since skin was surrounding the organ (τὴν φύσιν) in an unusual way, a passage had formed through which excretions could exit; for this reason, they had to make an incision and cicatrise the perforated area, and after putting the man's organ in good order (τὴν . . . ἀνδρὸς φύσιν εὔκοσμον ποιήσαντας) they received credit for giving treatment as permitted by the situation. (Diodorus 32.10.7)

Heraïs' case displays certain similarities with the Hippocratic Phaëthousa: both transformations occur during a period when a woman's husband is absent (King 2008: 162–3; King 2013b: 106–7) and are accompanied by fever (King 2008: 162). This suggests that the intellectual underpinnings of Diodorus' story lie in the Hippocratic notions of higher male body heat and the necessity of regular intercourse for women. But whereas Phaëthousa's fever was accompanied only by the growth of a beard, Heraïs is explicitly stated to transform fully into a man thanks to the presence of male genitalia: φύσις, the word Diodorus repeatedly uses, designates genitals in medical, magical and literary texts (Winkler 1990a: 217–20; *LSJ* s.v. φύσις 7.2). The adjective εὔκοσμον, 'well-ordered', used to describe Heraïs' new penis after the doctors' intervention, suggests that the surgery is merely cosmetic: the doctors did not create these new genitalia, but only helped to make them more visually perfect (Garland 1995: 131).

King argues that the doctors' interpretation of Heraïs' case – that her penis had been there all along, but had lain concealed – amounts to an assertion that Heraïs did not truly transform, but had secretly been a man all along (King 2008: 165–6). But this interpretation papers over the nuances of Diodorus' account. The doctors never explicitly say that Heraïs was always a man, and indeed acknowledge that she possessed female genitalia (φύσις θηλεία) before the incident in question. Indeed, when her illness first begins, doctors assume that the cause is an ulceration 'at the neck of the uterus' (32.10.3 περὶ τὸν τράχηλον τῆς μήτρας); whatever they saw between Heraïs' legs, it was evidently not so unusual in appearance as to lead them to believe that she possessed anything other than the typical female anatomy of vagina and womb. Furthermore, the way Diodorus tells Heraïs' story suggests he views her as female: even after the moment her penis first appears, he continues to refer to her as Heraïs, using feminine pronouns and participles (e.g. 32.10.4 ἀπολυθεῖσαν, 5 ἐκείνης, 6 δεινοπαθοῦσαν) and even calling her a woman (32.10.5 γύνη). Only in the sentence after the doctors' surgical intervention, with the change of name, does her grammatical gender change: 'Heraïs, changing her name to Diophantus (τὴν δ᾽ Ἡραΐδα μετονομασθεῖσαν Διόφαντον), enlisted in the cavalry, and after serving with the king (παραταξάμενον) retired with him to Abae' (32.10.8). In Diodorus' portrayal of her, then, Heraïs was not secretly a man, but a woman whose anatomy was for all intents and purposes female, and later suddenly replaced by male genitalia and perfected with medical help, at which point she transitioned to a fully male identity. When male genitals become apparent, she becomes male just as completely as she had once been female.

Kallo's story follows a similar pattern: she suffers from a tumor that causes abdominal pain and perplexes her doctors (32.11.1). Instead of bursting spontaneously to reveal the male genitalia inside, Kallo's tumor must be cut by an 'apothecary' (φαρμακοπώλης), who also operates on Kallo's new penis to perforate it and performs catheterisation to release trapped secretions (32.11.3). Diodorus' description does not suggest that Kallo is at an indeterminate stage between male and female before the surgery, but rather that she has a decidedly male physical appearance which has not quite attained perfection on its own. Kallo's new genitalia are explicitly described as 'man's parts' (ἀνδρὸς αἰδοῖα), enumerated as 'testicles and a penis' (δίδυμοι καὶ καυλὸς), albeit an imperforate one (32.11.2). As with Heraïs, this is a full and unambiguous physical transition from one sex to another.

Also reinforcing the idea that these transformations represent a complete shift from female to male is the texts' suggestion of a relatively smooth transition to life as a man. After the transformation of their genitalia, the women adopt various markers of male gender to accompany the 'biological' markers of male sex, apparently with relatively little difficulty. Diodorus' Heraïs is typical in that she changes her name, taking on the name of her father Diophantus. Other women adopt masculine versions of their old feminine names: Kallo becomes Kallon (Diodorus 32.11.4), Arescusa becomes Arescon (Pliny *HN* 7.36), and Sympherousa becomes Sympheron (Phlegon *Mir.* 8). The transformed women also abandon female pursuits and take on male occupations. Heraïs exchanges her female clothing for masculine dress (32.10.7) and joins the military (32.10.8), the masculine occupation *par excellence*. Kallo similarly adopts male costume, gives up wool-working, and discards her weaving equipment (32.11.4). Phlegon's bare-bones account of Sympherousa/Sympheron includes the detail that he works as a gardener after his transition (agricultural labour ideally being a male occupation, especially since women's menstrual blood was thought to harm plants; see Boatwright 1998: 72). Pliny even says that Arescusa took a wife (*HN* 7.36 *uxorem duxisse*) after becoming Arescon. These examples suggest that the sudden appearance of male genitalia pushes these individuals decidedly over the gender boundary from female into male: rather than being somewhere in the middle, they live fully as men, performing all the actions to which men are entitled.

Our texts' interest in and descriptions of the genitalia of the transformed women serve an additional purpose: underlying these physical descriptions is the notion, sometimes explicit but mostly implicit, that male genitalia are superior to female. Aristotle claims that a woman is an infertile male because her inferior anatomy prevents her from producing semen (*GA* 1.728a 17–20), and even views being a woman as the first step on the path to monstrosity (τέρας, *GA* 4.767b 8–10; Garland 1995: 153). Changing from female to male is therefore an improvement in status (Doroszewska 2013a: 236). Diodorus makes this explicit in a quip from the apothecary who treats Kallo: 'For healing her in this way, he demanded double wages: for he said that he had received a sick woman but had made her a healthy young man' (32.11.3). The same idea is inherent in the other stories of transformation: with the exception of Phlegon's discussion of Tiresias – a mythical figure and therefore a special case (Forbes Irving 1990: 150) – who changes from male to female, these texts offer *only* examples of transformations from female to male. Our authors do not include stories of men becoming effeminised, for example by castration, a situation fundamentally different from spontaneous sex change (Flemming 2000: 152 n. 54). (In fact, there is only one example in ancient literature of a man spontaneously transforming into a woman: Ausonius, *Epigr.* 76, a playful poem in which the poem's speaker recites examples of female-to-male transformations, including those recorded by Pliny, and only at the end reveals her identity as a transformed former boy.) But for Phlegon, Pliny and Diodorus, who are all seeking to report marvels, it seems that men becoming female would not be worthy of interest; it only makes a good story when the worse spontaneously becomes the better. These stories thus reveal the stamp of an ideology that believed not only in men's distinctness from, but also in their superiority to, women.

SEXUALITY AND VOYEURISM: FEAR AND SCEPTICISM

Although the women in these stories cross the gender barrier into the societally privileged and biologically superior status of manhood, this does not mean that their transformations are entirely unproblematic. At best, their transitions give rise to calamities in their personal relationships, and a voyeuristic tendency to objectify them. At worst, their transformations cause widespread panic because of the threat of divine anger they represent. The negative consequences of their transitions suggest that our authors believe it is possible, but not necessarily advisable or desirable, for a woman fully to become a man.

Some of our texts show a prurient interest in the women's sex lives in a way that reinforces the idea of male superiority. Phlegon and Pliny, whose accounts are more compressed, do not explicitly discuss how the transforming women have sex, beyond noting that before their transformations many of them were married to men; a reader would naturally assume that they consummated those marriages (Garland 1995: 130). Only Diodorus' more detailed account considers how the women's genitalia might have dictated the types of sexual intercourse they had while living as wives. Diodorus, who believes that it is impossible for someone to have both male and female genitals (32.12.1), assumes that they engaged in some type of non-vaginal sex with their husbands. Although Kallo is described as having a fistula that enabled excretion (32.11.1), Diodorus nevertheless says that she 'did not admit womanly union (τὴν . . . γυναικείαν ἐπιπλοκὴν), but was compelled to undergo unnatural intercourse (τὴν . . . παρὰ φύσιν ὁμιλίαν)'. The same is true of Heraïs: people assume she must have been incapable of 'natural intercourse' (τῆς κατὰ φύσιν ἐπιπλοκῆς) while living as a woman, and was therefore forced to have 'male intercourse' (ταῖς ἀρρενικαῖς συμπεριφοραῖς) with her husband (32.10.4). This sort of salacious gossip shows the prurient interest of the public in Heraïs' private life because of her shocking transformation. What is striking, however, is that Heraïs herself shares the gossipers' implicit assumption that it is abnormal for two men to have sex. After her transformation, Heraïs avoids her husband Samiades out of shame (32.10.5); when Samiades sues her father in an attempt to get his wife back, Diodorus describes a dramatic courtroom scene in which Heraïs removes her clothes (a motif in other ancient 'gender-reveal' scenarios; see Swancutt 2007: 22; King 2013b: 207–8) to show 'the maleness of her organ (τὸ τῆς φύσεως ἄρρεν), and spoke out in bitter complaint (δεινοπαθοῦσαν) that anyone should force a man to cohabit with another man (συνοικεῖν ἀνδρὶ τὸν ἄνδρα) (32.10.6)'. Although she has only recently become male, Heraïs has fully adopted male identity; Diodorus may still refer to her with a feminine participle, but in her own mind she is a man, made so by her male genitals. With that male identity, Heraïs has also adopted the idea, widespread in antiquity (see Williams 2010: chap. 5), that being penetrated is a feminine sexual role, demeaning for the man she has become. Immediately upon becoming male, Heraïs has internalised traditional notions of the superiority of the male anatomy, with its ability to penetrate, to the female, which must suffer being penetrated. Thus Diodorus' concern for the sex lives of Kallo and Heraïs is another way in which transformation stories actually reinforce the separation between the sexes, and the superiority of the male. When a woman married to a man suddenly becomes a man herself, to maintain sexual relations with her husband she must undergo a type of sex that undermines her new male status. If one is a man, one must become fully a man; to retain the inferior feminine sexual role is an insult to newfound masculinity.

Our texts also suggest that anyone who falls outside a strict male–female division is worthy of fear, objectification or scepticism. These transforming women are not the same as the intersex babies traditionally seen as harbingers of disaster in the Roman religious system; Diodorus, who elsewhere in his works emerges as a moralist encouraging clemency (Sacks 1990: 6), reacts against the religious interpretation in very strong terms, claiming that those who view the intersex as monsters are falling into superstition (32.12.1 δεισιδαιμονοῦσιν), and denounces as inhumane the custom of burning such people alive: 'So someone who shared a nature like ours, and was not in truth a monster (τέρας), perished undeservedly through ignorance of his illness' (32.12.2). But some trace of the religious interpretation persists in our other authors. Phlegon, in noting that the transformation of the girl from Antioch prompted the emperor Claudius to build an altar to 'Zeus the averter of evil' (*Mir.* 6), is inscribing her into that religious tradition by showing that society, even in its uppermost reaches, viewed her transformation as religiously worrisome (Garland 1995: 131). Pliny likewise notes that a maiden who became a boy in 171 BC was abandoned, presumably to his/her death, on a desert island on the advice of the *haruspices* (*HN* 7.36), but does not condemn this as Diodorus did. In his chapter on intersex births

(*HN* 7.34), Pliny does suggest a modern shift in attitudes away from the tra-ditional religious panic: 'There are born people of both sexes (*utriusque sexus*), whom we call hermaphrodites; they were once called androgynes and were considered prodigies, but now they are held as darlings (*in deliciis*).' Even this apparently more enlightened attitude is a type of objectification: the word *deliciae* is also used to describe a pet animal (Catullus 2.1), art object (Cicero *Verrines* 2.4.52) or object of sexual desire (Virgil *Eclogues* 2.2), suggesting that intersex individuals are valued only for the pleasure or excitement their exotic bodies bring to the viewer (see Adams 1982: 196–7; Pomeroy 1992: 46–9; King 2015: 255). Several ancient authors attest to this view of people with abnormal bodies as pleasantly titillating, a sensationalist attitude that some of them strongly con-demn (see Barton 1992: 85–8; Garland 1995: 52–4; Chappuis Sandoz 2008: 32; Charlier 2008: 80–8; Gevaert and Laes 2013: 221–3).

An emphasis on firsthand viewing of these individuals' bodies similarly suggests voyeurism. Pliny cites Mucianus' firsthand observation of Arescusa/Arescon (*HN* 7.36 *Licinius Mucianus prodidit visum a se . . .*), and also claims to have seen for himself one Lucius Constitius from Africa, who allegedly was a woman before transforming on her wedding day (*ipse in Africa vidi*). Similarly, Phlegon claims firsthand observation of Aitete, who became Aitetos (*Mir.* 9 τοῦτον καὶ αὐτὸς ἐθεασάμην; see further Shannon 2013: 5). Diodorus does not claim firsthand observation in the same way, but his detailed ekphrases of the genitals of Heraïs and Kallo are designed to make the story more believable by giving the reader the feeling that s/he is looking at their bodies firsthand (Langlands 2002: 94). Diodorus' doctors, who carefully inspect the women's genitals, also serve as a stand-in for the autoptic reader or author (King 2013b: 165–6). On the one hand, autopsy is simply a way authors, especially histori-ans, can verify that the information they transmit is accurate, especially when dealing with unusual phenomena (Marincola 1997: 82–3). Using this motif suggests that these people are marvels outside the realm of anything a reader might normally experience. For Phlegon, they are as wondrous as a centaur, the preserved corpse of which he also claims to have seen (*Mir.* 35; on Phlegon's use of autopsy, see Shannon-Henderson 2020). But autopsy also reinforces the notion of objectification, by implying that transformed people must be visually inspected to prove their maleness. So even where our authors reject traditional religious interpretations of individuals who transgress the anatomically defined boundary between male and female, the objectification implicitly or explicitly directed at their bodies nevertheless suggests their abnormality. Changing from female to male does not make you a sign of divine wrath, but it still makes you a curiosity worthy of attention.

Finally, our authors describe or imply negative effects on marriages, families and society produced by these transformations. All of our texts include examples of women who transform after they have already married men (Pliny *HN* 7.36;

Diodorus 32.10.3, 11.1; Phlegon *Mir.* 6–7, 9). Mostly the details of this unusual situation are not remarked upon and the reader must fill in the gaps using his/her imagination. But the fact that our authors mention the women's wifely status suggests that the relationship between gender identity and marriage is an important part of the thought-world in these transformation stories. For Diodorus' Heraïs, the transition from female to male causes conflict and tragedy (Garland 1995: 130). Her husband Samiades ultimately cannot cope with losing her and commits suicide, 'with the result that she who was born a woman (τὴν μὲν γυναῖκα γεγενημένην) took on the renown and courage of a man (ἀνδρὸς), while the man became weaker than a woman's soul (τὸν δ' ἄνδρα γυναικείας ψυχῆς ἀσθενέστερον γενέσθαι)' (32.10.9). Diodorus explicitly draws attention to the reversal of gender norms: Heraïs becomes a bold and manly soldier, while her former husband's suicide reveals his underlying effeminacy. Masculinity and femininity are a zero-sum game: in order for Heraïs to become a man, her husband has to become more feminine. Spontaneous sex change therefore has consequences for familial relationships that are destructive and tragic, reinforcing the fundamentality of the gender binary. When a married woman becomes a man, the societal fabric can be torn in ways too immense to overcome. Similarly, Diodorus notes that some of his sources claim that Kallo was put on trial for impiety because she had been a priestess of Demeter while living as a woman, and therefore saw mysteries which were forbidden to male eyes (32.11.4). This tantalising snippet of information reveals that, to some at least, after her transformation Kallo was considered to have been a man all along, further evidence that a transformed woman is viewed as fully male and not some intermediate sex. But the story also provides another example of the potentially destructive religious consequences of crossing the male–female divide. If Kallo had never transformed, the goddess would have had no cause to be upset at the profanation of her mysteries.

CONCLUSIONS: THE BINARY ALIVE AND WELL

I hope to have shown how these stories of spontaneous female-to-male transformation shed light on ancient conceptions of gender difference. These stories are extraordinary for the matter-of-factness with which the transformations are described. Even if the transformations cause social upheaval or sometimes require medical intervention, what is not in doubt is that the women concerned are truly thought to have changed completely into men. Neither medicalising nor religious discourse is able to diminish that fundamental fact. Nevertheless, the fact that women sometimes become men does not, in the authors' minds, mean that the boundary between the sexes *should* be fluid, or that women are the equals of men. Notably absent from these accounts is any consideration of how the transformed women feel about their own transformations. Our texts are not interested in their perspective; this fact on its own is suggestive, implying that these individuals are worth writing about as objects, primarily for what others think of their abnormal situations. Transition is complete (those who transform are able to fully cross the boundary), but the dehumanising, prurient gaze of the author and the negative consequences (overt or implied) of these transitions for the broader society reinforces the notion that transformations are fraught, since crossing the gender boundary can have destructive and traumatic effects. Even in these most apparently gender-b(l)ending of stories, the gender binary is alive and well.

NOTE

1. Portions of this paper were initially presented at the 2017 meeting of the Society for Classical Studies in Toronto, in a panel on the theme '[Tr]an[s]tiquity: Theorizing Gender Diversity in Ancient Contexts', sponsored by the Lambda Classical Caucus; I am grateful to the audience there for their helpful comments, to Walter Penrose and Tom Sapsford for organising the panel, and to LCC for its sponsorship. I am immensely grateful to the editors of this volume, especially Allison Surtees, and to the anonymous reviewer for their helpful critiques and feedback.

PART II

Gender Fluidity

Neutrumque et Utrumque Videntur: Reappraising the Gender Role(s) of Hermaphroditus in Ancient Art

Linnea Åshede

INTRODUCTION AND PROBLEM

As an embodied challenge to gender binarism, Hermaphroditus has fasci-nated since Hellenistic times.[1] Compared to the scarcity of literary sources, this child of Hermes and Aphrodite has primarily survived through images. With no known exceptions, these present an idealised androgynous youngster with breasts and a penis; usually long-haired, always *en déshabillé*. Although these images were being produced from the Hellenistic era into the third cen-tury AD, throughout the Mediterranean regions, Hermaphroditus' iconography remains remarkably consistent. The one notable change is the figure's inclusion into mythological group scenes set in the sphere of Aphrodite and Dionysus (Oehmke 2004: 15; Berg 2007: 68–70). This expansion of Hermaphroditus' iconographic repertoire occurs from the first century BC onwards and coincides with the start of the heyday of Hermaphroditus imagery, the period from the first century BC to the second century AD.

Ancient images of Hermaphroditus should not be understood as portrayals of atypically sexed humans, such as those listed by Livy as *prodigia* or ill omens (e.g. 27.11.4–6, 31.12.6 see Corbeill 2015: 151–68). What is portrayed is an imaginary body, akin to that of the satyrs, and set in the same uncivilised, mythi-cal landscapes. Literary sources offer few clues as to how contemporary audiences related to these images, as the texts only deal with the origin of Hermaphroditus' mixed sexual characteristics. Diodorus Siculus (4.6.5–6), the *Salmakis Inscription* (15–22, see Isager 2004), Martial (14.174) and two epigrams (*Anth. Pal.* 2.102; 9.783) describe these as the result of Hermaphroditus inheriting the traits of both hir parents. The best known literary account of Hermaphroditus – the tale of metamorphosis from *puer* or young boy to *semimas* or 'semi-man' through an unwanted merging with the nymph Salmacis (*Met.* 4.285–388; on this passage see Kelly in this volume) – is exclusive to Ovid, and not reflected in any surviving images (Berg 2007: 67; Cadario 2012: 241–4). In the most recent article to treat Hermaphroditus, Robert Groves formulates a strong case for Ovid's having taken inspiration from the artworks with which he must have been familiar, and constructing a narrative which plays with his audiences' expectations based on the same (Groves 2016: 322–6, 344–56).

Considering that the surviving testimony to Hermaphroditus' existence leaves the figure open to interpretation, it is problematic that scholarly treatments of Hermaphroditus' gender are remarkably uniform. The current consensus maintains that Hermaphroditus was portrayed as attractive but problematic – a seemingly female trap whose suddenly revealed male sex was intended to shock and surprise (Berg 2007: 71; Clarke 2011: 186; Severy-Hoven 2012: 568). Because Hermaphroditus is neither man nor woman, scholars maintain that the figure could not be considered a functional erotic partner for anyone, and that any erotic encounter thus must end in mutual frustration (Oehmke 2004: 35–7, 69–70; Cadario 2012: 237, 293). As a consequence, it is maintained that the pivotal element of Hermaphroditus imagery is the surprising discovery of the figure's true identity (examples range from Helbig 1868: 304–6 nr. 1370 to Corbeill 2015: 167; Groves 2016; see comprehensive bibliography in Åshede 2015, 24 n. 47).

These interpretations are based upon assumptions about gender and desire that are firstly tacit and unquestioned, and secondly incompatible with much of current ancient sexuality research (as noted by Oehmke 2004: 37). Scholarship has so far not seriously questioned the capacity of Hermaphroditus' unusual combination of breasts and a penis to signify gendered positions in this particular form, in its particular contexts. Instead, sexual characteristics on anthropomorphic bodies are assumed to be universal and unchanging, and as such self-explanatory, an approach to the study of sex in historical cultures which Robert Schmidt and Barbara Voss term 'sex essentialism' (Schmidt and Voss 2000: 3–5). This assumption constitutes a serious hindrance for research into the gender ideologies of any culture, particularly when based on fragmentary material objects that require extensive translation into describing, interpreting words. I suggest that the tacit assumptions about Hermaphroditus' gender circumscribe possible research on the figure, and that a different theoretical framework is required in order to question what we think we already know. In the following section, I propose the relational ontology of Karen Barad's posthumanism as a possible approach to the problem. Because it is a theoretical apparatus constructed with the unsettling of predefined categories as its primary goal, it precludes us from assuming that we already know what a penis signifies, instead spurring us to ask what specifically the penis of Hermaphroditus can signify.

WHAT POSTHUMANISM HAS TO OFFER HERMAPHRODITUS

Barad writes as a quantum physicist committed to investigating epistemo-ontological problems from a feminist-materialist point of view. Based on the particle experiments of Niels Bohr, she argues that not even atoms have distinct ontological identities, but every entity comes into being through multiple encounters that are at once material and discursive. All existence is entangled and unstable, as in undergoing continual, co-dependent transformations. This means that subjects, whether considered real or imaginary, always have multiple belongings (Barad 2007: 225; 2011: 121–5). Furthermore, relationships as such do not consist of interactions between already existing actors, but of intra-actions, encounters that simultaneously bring entities together, differentiate them, and thereby materialise them into existence (Barad 2011: 125–6, 149). Put differently, the actors do not pre-date the action. Their activity is not reducible to anything beyond themselves, but the actors are their own relational, active existence. The naming of the participants through their encounter must be understood as a local resolution: a naming-into-existence that is temporal, relative and situated in a specific encounter (Barad 2007: 80–93; 2011: 123–5).

The final point is the key to how classical studies can benefit from theoretical insights from other fields while staying sensitive to its historiocultural particularities. In regards to the Hermaphroditus artworks, Barad's ontology of entanglements cautions us against assuming either that all individual images should be understood in the same way, or that ancient Mediterranean audiences would have looked at the figure with the same preconceptions about gender as a Western viewer today. Instead of positing binary oppositions that demand a dichotomising perspective on Hermaphroditus' gender, a posthuman perspective affords us the possibility of working with continuums, a shift which promises radical new possibilities for understanding all category-challenging bodies. The following sections undertake further critical re-examinations of what we think we know about Hermaphroditus' gender, from the posthuman departure point that identity-generating and difference-making concepts such as gender should be understood as co-dependent relationships between material-discursive phenomena, rather than as inherent properties of individual bodies (Fredengren 2013: 56; Braidotti 2013: 163–5).

BELOW THE BELT: THE BE-ALL AND END-ALL OF MASCULINE EMBODIMENT?

Discussion about Hermaphroditus tends to come back to the penis, the size, visibility and significance of which have been awarded more commentary than hir other body parts taken together. This phallocentric approach is partly motivated by the images themselves – the penis has to be visible from at least one angle for Hermaphroditus to be recognisable. Among the images of hir alone, the most common type is the *anasyromenos*, where a frontally portrayed Hermaphroditus is raising a long garment to reveal hir sometimes erect penis (see Oehmke 2004: 9, 23–30, 108–26).

However, there are just as many motifs where Hermaphroditus' groin is not brought into primary focus, such as the fresco where ze is binding hir breasts before a mirror held by Eros (Fig. 5.1). Despite this, the penis emerges in scholarly discussion as the most important, or the only, identity-bearing element. This is most noticeable in the consensus that Hermaphroditus' portrayals centre on the surprising revelation of hir genitals. The narrative of surprising discovery is most often proposed for images where Hermaphroditus is either sleeping, or struggling with one or more bestial male(s). To exemplify, David Fredrick argues of Figure 5.2, where Pan is raising his hand while removing Hermaphroditus' drapery while the latter reclines on the ground, that Hermaphroditus' newly revealed, erect penis transforms Pan from sexual aggressor to a 'potential penetree' raising his hand for protection (Fredrick 1995: 281). Similarly, John R. Clarke (2007: 179–80) argues that the experience of shocking discovery offered

Figure 5.1 Hermaphroditus and Eros, fresco allegedly from Boscoreale, Stuttgart, Landesmuseum Württemberg, P. Frankenstein/H. Zwietasch, Arch 83/1c; Oehmke 2004: 135 nr. 130.

Figure 5.2 Hermaphroditus and Pan, fresco *in situ*, Pompeii, House of the Vettii, VI.15.1; su concessione del Ministero per i Beni e le Attività – Culturali; Oehmke 2004: 144 nr. 162.

by Hermaphroditus' body is the same for satyrs and human (presumed male) viewers – both are set up by the artist to be 'naturally' aroused by the sight of a seemingly female body, only to discover the penis that will 'douse his passion like a bucket of ice water'.

The insistence on Hermaphroditus' penis as something shocking to be dramatically discovered/revealed reflects, firstly, the conviction that the penis alone is perceived to misalign with the rest of hir appearance, and secondly, that the penis is awarded primary status as gender-determinant. These constant references to the surprising penis as Hermaphroditus' true sex/identity reflect a commonplace narrative trope in Western culture, described by Talia Mae Bettcher (2007: 47–8) as 'genital exposure as sex verification'. The equation of genitalia and gender-truth is further reflected in how scholars present the undressing of Hermaphroditus' penis as a sudden transformation, almost an instantaneous sex-change, which turns the presumed beautiful woman into a threatening figure – the threat being the masculine urge to sexually penetrate, which is presumed to reside in the penis and incite horror in other males (Severy-Hoven 2012: 571; Vout 2013: 77–8; Groves 2016: 328–30).

The problem with looking for Hermaphroditus' identity below the belt is that it circumscribes the range of possible conclusions. When scholars suggest that

Hermaphroditus embodies the harmonious union between man and woman, or that images of Hermaphroditus looking over hir shoulder – sometimes with a mirror aimed at hir buttocks – show the concept of hir male penis being attracted to the sight of hir 'female' backside (Stähli 1999: 272), this enforces an internal fragmentation of the hermaphroditic body. Male and female are preserved as the essential biological dichotomy, residing in individual body parts treated as independent regions. Barad (2011: 124–6, 149) specifically cautions against this type of approach, which in the present case leaves the effects of Hermaphroditus' bodily figurations unaccounted for, by beginning analysis after the gendered boundaries are already in place.

Instead of assuming that we already know what a penis signifies, we must ask what Hermaphroditus' penis can signify in relation to hir wealth of other gendered/gendering elements. To be able to consider seriously such questions, we cannot treat hir as a jigsaw puzzle pieced together from already gender-fixed building-blocks. We cannot downplay the effect of other elements in favour of a phallocentric preoccupation with genital truth, and we cannot lose sight of historiocultural specificities. The following section proposes alternative interpretations.

CHALLENGING THE 'FEMALE PLUS PENIS' VIEW OF HERMAPHRODITUS

It may seem like a biological given that certain anatomical features are pre-discursively sexed. Even on the level of DNA analysis, however, there is wider room for ambiguity than commonly recognised; an issue addressed by archaeologist Christina Fredengren:

> The find of a Y chromosome is an indication which shows a body had the possibility of being a man. However, bodies are full of potentials that may or may not be realized in various historical settings. (Fredengren 2013: 62; compare Ainsworth 2015)

Considering that this is the case with real-world human remains, we should be even warier about assuming that a penis on a body belonging to ancient myth automatically generates the gendered identity man, with associated desires. The ancient Mediterranean cultures recognised a number of penis-bearing corporealities which were nevertheless differently gendered than the normative man: certain eunuchs, not yet mature and sometimes erotically objectified boys, and the stereotype of erotically dominated or otherwise non-conforming adult males all differ from the male norm, despite having penises (see Tougher 2002; Severy-Hoven 2012: 560; Williams 2010: 193–203 with sources).

How, then, is Hermaphroditus' penis presented? Quite disparately between different images. In Figure 5.1, it is the same size as the penis of baby Eros holding hir mirror, and barely noticeable over the edge of hir low-slung drapery. In relation to this, Hermaphroditus is sporting the flat-chested appearance of most female figures in Roman frescoes. In this particular image, hir breasts are mostly noticeable because ze is in the process of binding them, and ze is further aligned with conventional representations of females through pale skin, pearl earrings and an elegant *mitra* or draped headdress (Oehmke 2007, 266–9). In contrast, two Pompeiian frescoes with the common motif of Hermaphroditus seated before Silenus – where ze is stroking his beard and seeking eye-contact while he leans over hir shoulder, grasping hir wrist and raising his free hand – shows hir unveiling a pale torso, with rosy highlights on the nipples and erection (Fig. 5.3; Oehmke 2004: 39 fig. 128). Again, the drapery, the pale skin and the long hair contrast sharply against the appearance of the dark, bearded Silenus. The former traits are more aligned with representations of female figures, but Hermaphroditus also contrasts against the maenad or feral Dionysian woman present in Figure 5.3, both through the erect penis and through hir elevated seat. This seated position is indicative of superior status to the maenad, who by standing to the side and not partaking

Figure 5.3 Hermaphroditus, Silenus and Maenad, fresco from Pompeii, House of M. Epidius Sabinus, IX.1.22, Naples, Museo Archeologico Nazionale, 27875; su concessione del Ministero dei Beni e delle Attività Culturali e del Turismo – Museo Archeologico Nazionale di Napoli; Oehmke 2004: 133 nr. 125.

in the eye contact between the pair on the platform takes on the function of what Alison Sharrock terms an 'internal viewer', a figure whose gaze directs the external audience's gazes to the central figures (Sharrock 2002: 279; also Elsner 2007: 89–90).

Visual contrast is at the forefront when Hermaphroditus appears in the company of adult males. Ze is pale where the satyric males are dark; long-haired but devoid of bodily hair where they are generally hirsute and bearded; soft and slender where they are burly. The workings of this contrasting can be observed particularly clearly in a terracotta of Hermaphroditus seated next to a standing satyr (Fig. 5.4), resembling the popular Berlin-Torlonia marble group of the same motif (Stähli 1999: 90–6; Åshede 2015: 264–86). While the large-scale, three-dimensional marbles portray Hermaphroditus wrapping hir thighs around the leg of a bearded, pine-cone-wreathed satyr, the terracotta as well as some small-scale, two-dimensional versions portray a youthfully beardless satyr (Roscher 1886–90: 2339). This younger satyr nevertheless contrasts sharply against Hermaphroditus by being short-haired and muscular – what is noteworthy is that next to his smooth face and downcast eyes, which in ancient art often communicate youthful diffidence (M. Bradley 2009: 150–9), Hermaphroditus

Figure 5.4 Hermaphroditus and Satyr, terracotta from Southern Italy, München, Staatliche Antikensammlungen und Glyptothek, NI 6781; Oehmke 2004: 132–3 nr. 123.

appears comparatively more mature. Hir hand resting on his shoulder and lifted gaze communicate confident seduction, but nothing in hir behaviour suggests that this erotic agency should be equated with phallic aggression. Rather, hir elegant coiffure with ringlets, voluptuously rounded limbs and penis peeking over the edge of low-slung drapery embody sensual invitation. The young satyr's stance – leaning away from Hermaphroditus and lowering his eyes but simultaneously reaching for hir raised hand and touching hir hip – suggests ambivalent hesitation, not horror.

The conclusion to be drawn here is that bodies in ancient art are capable of variation. If one persists in looking to penises for cues on how to understand ancient group scenes, it can be noted that just as individual replicas of the Dresden group (where Hermaphroditus is stiff-arming a satyr clinging to hir body) differ in their portrayals of Hermaphroditus' hairstyle, and Berlin-Torlonia replicas differ in the animals and objects adorning the plinth, replicas of both kind also differ in showing the satyr's penis sometimes soft, sometimes erect (see Stähli 1999, 309–40, 372–83, 431 n. 902). Likewise, individual artworks show Hermaphroditus' penis as soft or erect, hir breasts and hips more or less rounded, and hir behaviour towards others more or less assertive. It must be recognised that each recurring figure in ancient art is capable of embodying a range of possible attitudes and appearances, and that our perceptions of whether or not Hermaphroditus' breasts are bigger or smaller than those of a woman always become affected by our immediate objects of comparison. These shift constantly, and will have done so for ancient audiences as well. The fact that the exercising of individual judgement is unavoidable in connection with ambiguously gendered bodies is indeed recognised by the jurist Ulpian. He comments that *quaeritur: hermaphroditum cui comparamus? et magis puto eius sexus aestimandum, qui in praevalet*, 'on the question of which sex to assign to a hermaphrodite, I think whichever sex can be judged to prevail' (*Dig.* 1.5.10, edition Krüger: 2008; all translations are my own). This legal approach of determining the closest fit recalls second century AD physiognomic texts, that seek to determine a person's gender based not only on the genitals but on every aspect of the body, including body language, voice and overall behaviour (e.g. Polemo, edition Foerster 1893, vol. 1: 192; see Gleason 1990).

Rather than fixating on dissecting hir anatomy, a better indication of Hermaphroditus' perceived gender may be gleaned from exploring the apparent limits of hir scope for variation. By establishing that Hermaphroditus is consistently visually contrasted against humanimal male figures, that hir iconography most closely emulates those of the alluring Aphrodite and the gender-fluid, Hellenistically youthful Dionysus, and that ze is consistently portrayed with long, centrally parted hair, clinging drapery, jewellery and pale skin, we can conclude that ze adheres to pictorial conventions not associated with conventional masculinity in ancient art – if masculinity is understood as pertaining to adult, non-gender-variant men. Given this consistent non-masculine gendering, it would be incongruous to read the revelation of hir penis as overriding all other features and effecting a shocking transformation from seemingly female to threateningly masculine.

More interesting results can be reached by calling the given-ness of all aspects of Hermaphroditus into question, in the same manner as the taken-for-granted masculinity of the penis. Let us begin with that part of Hermaphroditus which is supposed by scholars to lure both satyrs and human viewers into mistaken female-oriented desire: the shapely bottom (Oehmke 2004: 55; Groves 2016: 339–40). Looking at erotically objectified females such as nymphs, Aphrodite and women in erotic scenes contemporary with Hermaphroditus, it is clear that their buttocks are frequently emphasised more than their breasts – but a nice bottom is equally strongly connected to the desirability of boys (e.g. Mart. 2.60.2, 9.67.3, 11.43; *Erotes* 27, see Williams 2010: 185, 204). In particular, Roman erotic discourse conceptualises the erotic allure of buttocks as boyish even when the buttocks in question belong to a woman. Anal penetration regardless of the recipient is referred to as *illud puerile*, 'that boyish thing'. When the confirmed boy-lover Callicratidas in the *Erotes* 14 (edition Halperin: 2002, traditionally attributed to pseudo-Lucian, though its authorship remains contested) beholds the bottom of the Knidian Aphrodite – described by the narrator as τὰ παιδικὰ μέρη τῆς θεοῦ, 'the boyish parts of the goddess' – he exclaims: τοιοῦτος ἄρα Γανυμήδης ἐν οὐρανῷ Διὶ τὸ νέκταρ ἥδιον ἐγχεῖˊ, 'so that's what Ganymede looks like as he pours the nectar for Zeus in heaven and sweetens its taste!'

This example serves as a reminder that the ancient Mediterranean cultures did not organise erotic experience solely around binary gender. Rather, the soft, youthful bodies of women/girls and boys are conceptualised as equally capable of inciting men's desires (Williams 2010: 20–9). In this culture where both women and certain categories of boys – such as slaves and foreigners – constitute erotic ideals, pictorial conventions for representing ideal beauty often overlap. Thus, not only could Hermaphroditus' buttocks equally well be read as feminine or boyish, but the same is to various degrees true about hir pale skin, flowing locks and rounded limbs (see for example Ov. *Met.* 4.354–5; Petron. *Sat.* 86.5; Stat. *Silv.* 2.1.50–1; Apul. *Met.* 5.22; Bartman 2002: 251–3). Rather than saying that these ideals are feminine or boyish in themselves, it might be more correct to understand them as a youthfully androgynous continuum of attractiveness. Hermaphroditus is capable of embodying the entire spectrum of erotic attraction, and of appearing as more or less woman, boy, both and neither to individual viewers.

The obvious interest in portraying an idealised, gender-fluid body suggests that the surprising revelation of Hermaphroditus' penis as equivalent to hir true identity has been overstated. While ze is frequently in the process of undressing or being undressed, the same pictorial convention is common in depictions of both gender-typical females and Dionysus, where it functions to voyeuristically frame a beautiful body for the viewers' delectation (Oehmke 2004: 36, 47). In the case of the *anasyromenos* or garment-lifting gesture, this is found in images of both Baubo and Priapus, suggesting that rather than revealing a hidden penis, it constitutes a ritual and/or provocative baring of genitals in general (Oehmke 2004: 9, 23–30). As Stefanie Oehmke elsewhere notes, Hermaphroditus images do not emphasise internal fragmentation but rather the seamless unity of physical traits (Oehmke 2004: 60).

If we postulate that Hermaphroditus' idealised androgyny is framed for an audience poised to understand both women and boys as erotic objects, it no longer makes sense to read the sight of hir penis as an automatic cause for male horror. Particularly not since the figures positioned as hir potential erotic partners, Pan and the satyrs, are consistently characterised in art and literature by their rampant, undiscriminating erotic appetites, literally oriented towards anything that moves (Lissarague 1990: 61–5; Marquardt 1995; Hall 1998: 15–24; Stähli 1999: 274, 389–94). As mankind's distorting mirror, these bestial creatures are at liberty to pursue even non-normative objects of desire, and can be depicted engaging in orgies with each other or fingering female genitalia (Frontisi-Ducroux 1996: 95).

As a youthfully androgynous beauty, Hermaphroditus follows ancient pictorial conventions for an erotically receptive partner. Ze is voyeuristically positioned sleeping on the ground, beautifying hirself before a mirror and struggling with bestial satyrs. The reason for the frequently raised hand of hir partners is typically interpreted as dismay at the revelation of hir penis (Groves 2016: 337). However, the same gesture occurs quite frequently in frescoes depicting related mythological scenes of Pan or satyrs undressing sleeping nymphs or Ariadne (for example Marcadé 1961: 42; Caratelli 1993: 540 fig. 120; Häuber 1999: 176 n. 38, 177 n. 65; Zanker 2004: 163 fig. 168; Lorenz 2008: 369 fig. 184). There is nothing to distinguish the expressions of the figures looking at a woman from those of a majority of the figures looking at Hermaphroditus, but the raised hand connected to a female sleeper is typically labelled in positive terms, for example as 'an eloquent gesture of wonder' (Grant 1975: 160–2). The different receptions suggest that scholars comparing the images already understand the hermaphroditic body as an impossible object of desire (for instance Oehmke 2004: 37–8; Severy-Hoven 2012: 567).

Since the raised hand is most frequently performed in connection to voyeuristic undressing, it seems plausible that it should be connected to the act of looking at nakedness in itself, perhaps functioning as the interpellation 'look at this!' – without necessarily signifying a negative or positive reaction. This reading would open the images to further ambiguity, as in the case of a now destroyed fresco from the House of the Postumii (VIII.4.4), where Hermaphroditus stands surrounded by a small *thiasos* or Dionysian party (Oehmke 2004:

97–8 nr. 41). Here, Pan moving along in the foreground has traditionally been described as fleeing the sight of Hermaphroditus, a reaction not shared by any of the surrounding figures. However, if Pan's raised hand is understood as signifying looking rather than horror, his head that is turned back to keep Hermaphroditus in his sight suggests that hir body might in fact be halting him in his tracks. Likewise, in the case of Figure 5.3, Silenus' hand grasping Hermaphroditus' wrist should probably not be understood as an act of rejection, but as a formulaic, favourable response to the chin-stroking – a set of gestures that often occur in courtship scenes between couples of varying gender constellations (Clarke 1991: 96–7; DeVries 1997: 15–20).

One exception exists, where Pan's reaction to Hermaphroditus appears to be clearly negative – not because of his raised hand, but because his entire head is averted. This fresco from the House of the Dioscuri (VI.9.6) is perhaps the most reproduced image of Hermaphroditus, but is in fact unusual in that Pan displays expressed desire to disengage from the person he has been undressing (Oehmke 2004, 50, 141 nr. 153). What sets this version apart from Hermaphroditus' other humanimal encounters, especially the similar Figure 5.2, is hir specific response. In the Dioscuri fresco, Hermaphroditus looks directly at Pan and puts a hand on his arm, thus taking erotic initiative, as opposed to demurely encouraging further contact by coyly averting hir gaze with an arm thrown over the head to signal abandon, as in Figure 5.2 (Clarke 2002: 161). The latter constitutes acceptable enactments of desirability expected of a delicate, erotically objectified body such as Hermaphroditus' – the former, however, breaks erotic protocol by interfering with the initiative of Pan, who as a hyper-masculine figure is expected to be the driving force in the encounter. He responds with unease. The problem, thus, is not Hermaphroditus' unusual body but hir unexpected behaviour.

Oehmke and Groves touch upon this alternative interpretation; however, they circumscribe its potential for communicating with the sources in a culture-sensitive manner by reducing the wrongness of Hermaphroditus' behaviour to phallic aggression (Oehmke 2004: 70–2; Groves 2016: 351). This assumption disregards the recognition primarily in literary sources of both male and female bodies 'itching' to play receptive erotic roles (for example Mart. 6.37.4) – that is, male and female bodies who actively seek their own penetration or otherwise demand erotic fulfilment. One noteworthy example is Ovid's aggressive Salmacis, who upon seizing Hermaphroditus *pugnantemque tenet, luctantiaque oscula carpit, subiectatque manus, invitaque pectora tangit*, 'holds him fast though he strives against her, steals reluctant kisses, fondles him, and touches his unwilling breast' (*Met.* 4.358–60, edition Anderson: 1996, discussed in Richlin 1992a: 165; Groves 2016: 347–52). Examples of erotically objectified, insatiable males actively seeking to be orally and/or anally penetrated abound in the *Satyrica* (for example Petron. *Sat.* 23, 87), and Deborah Kamen and

Sarah Levin-Richardson list a plethora of further examples in their critical reappraisal of the routine usage of the labels active contra passive in scholarly discussion of erotically dominated males (Kamen and Levin-Richardson 2015a: 453–6; see also their reappraisal of female sexual agency in Kamen and Levin-Richardson 2015b). Their thorough analysis of sexual Latin terminology and grammar amply demonstrates that contrary to traditional scholarly praxis, no straightforward correlation exists between active versus passive behaviour on the one hand, and the desire to penetrate versus be penetrated on the other (Kamen and Levin-Richardson 2015a: 456).

Latin literature and graffiti abound in erotically objectified bodies driven by the desire to be dominated, often specifically by being penetrated, who nevertheless take very active initiative, rather than blushingly awaiting seduction. While prolific, this behaviour is unanimously represented as transgressive, to the point of being comical or unpleasant for their would-be lovers. In relation to such a negative view on non-masculine erotic initiative, it is possible to understand Hermaphroditus' grasping hold of Pan or the Berlin-Torlonia satyr as unwelcome behaviour, without it being an expression of phallic aggression as such, which would be incongruous given Hermaphroditus' overall gender presentation. Instead, hir behaviour could be understood as consisting of overeagerness literally unbecoming of a young beauty – that is to say, behaviour seen as so transgressive in its given context that it no longer makes it possible to conceive of its enactor as desirable.

THE BEAUTY OF AMBIGUITY

Images of Hermaphroditus excel in presenting ambiguity, not just in hir youthful body but in hir encounters with others, portrayed as open-ended moments rather than linear narratives. That these artworks did elicit multiple interpretations is confirmed by two contemporary texts. Ovid, who as Groves demonstrates based his transformed Hermaphroditus on the figure familiar from art, describes the newly merged Hermaphroditus as *forma duplex, nec femina dici nec puer ut possit, neutrumque et utrumque videntur*, 'a dual form that could be said to be neither woman nor boy, but seemed to be neither and both' (*Met.* 4.378–9). This version corresponds with Hermaphroditus' existence in art, as an embodiment of the sliding scale between female and boyish beauty. In contrast, Martial (14.174, edition Heraeus and Borovskij: 1982) describes a *Hermaphroditus marmoreus* thus: *masculus intravit fontis, emersit utrumque; pars est una patris, cetera matris habet*, '[he] entered the spring male, and emerged double-sexed. One part is the father's, the rest comes from the mother'. Martial knows Ovid's story, yet describes Hermaphroditus' gendered body differently, focusing on fragmentation rather than seamlessness, and ascribing the gender ambiguity to the parentage rather than Salmacis. (As Groves 2016: 350 suggests, the masculine pronoun used about Hermaphroditus in ancient texts can likely be attributed to the masculine grammatical default used for mixed groups, even though this mixed group consists of one body; see the Introduction to this volume) The lesson from this example is that neither Ovid nor Martial has to be right. What is important is to acknowledge that all phenomena always are ontologically pluralistic – and that images of Hermaphroditus in particular hinge upon presenting viewers with multiple alternatives.

There is, however, a common limit to these alternatives, or rather a common frame: the artworks' physical contexts of display. While only a minority of the preserved images have documented find-contexts, those that have them primarily originate in connection with private gardens or public baths and theatres throughout the Roman empire. Here, they function as objects of adornment, providing audiences with both sensory and intellectual stimulation (von Stackelberg 2009: 94–6; O'Sullivan 2011: 78). Both these types of spaces and the time spent in them can be understood as firstly liminal, that is, blurring the borders between real and mythological, and secondly temporal, in that they offer a pleasant escape from the rigours of everyday life, with the expressed condition that everyone return to their duties afterwards (Hales 2003: 34–5, 156; Newby 2012: 368). As many scholars have argued, Roman gardens, baths and theatres have a further common denominator in being spaces characterised by a comparatively greater licence for gender transgressions, compared to society at large (Hales 2003: 153; Retzleff 2007: 459, 468–70; von Stackelberg 2009: 62–72; 2014: 398, 411; Platts 2011: 257–62).

Because all elements of Hermaphroditus' portrayals adhere to pictorial conventions for representing ideal, desirable bodies – including Pan's negative reaction as discussed above – hir unusual combination of sexual characteristics cannot be understood as subversive of ancient gender discourse as such. The radical potential of the figure is rather found in the many ambiguities permeating these images, allowing audiences room for speculation and fantasy, in the relatively safe space of escapist contexts, with Hermaphroditus as alluring cicerone.

NOTE

1. I offer my heartfelt gratitude to our editors and my anonymous referees, for their truly constructive and considerate assistance.

CHAPTER 6

Intersex and Intertext: Ovid's Hermaphroditus and the Early Universe

Peter Kelly

This chapter examines the story of Salmacis and Hermaphroditus from book 4 (285–388) of Ovid's *Metamorphoses*, whose two bodies are merged into one. A series of connections can be drawn between the transformation of Hermaphroditus and the representation of the primordial universe at the beginning of the *Metamorphoses*, and specifically the representation of cosmological chaos, where basic elemental oppositions such as the hot and the cold and the wet and the dry are confounded and mixed together. Likewise the Hermaphroditus narrative may be seen to undermine the ontological stability of gendered corporeal form, while the presentation of Hermaphroditus as protohuman also serves to destabilise the concept of cosmological and human evolution, or more specifically the assumption that the world moves from a state of chaos and unity to one of stability, multiplicity and division.

Ovid therefore uses the Hermaphroditus narrative not only to collapse the distinction between apparent gender categories, but also to question the notion that it is possible to hold a fixed and stable view of both the cosmos and the literary text purporting to depict it. On the one hand, Ovid's Hermaphroditus narrative stands alongside the other stories of corporeal transformation which occupy the largely 'mythological' section of the text; on the other, Ovid uses various features of this narrative to link this specific transformation with the 'scientific' opening and the description of the primordial universe. The Hermaphroditus narrative thus also highlights how the apparent boundaries and distinctions which exist in terms of textual genre are as fluid and unstable as those which are perceived to exist between genders. Ovid conveys this through the use of multiple allusions to 'scientific' discourses and specifically to accounts of 'intersex' beings in Empedocles, Plato's *Symposium* and Lucretius' *De Rerum Natura*. In this way Ovid's portrayal of Hermaphroditus performs an ontological and interacting epistemological role, as it expresses the breakdown of corporeal distinction and stability through blurring the divisions between truth and false-hood. Ovid also extends this idea to human social structures by subverting the use of opposition as a basic organising principle across the cultural spectrum.

The story of Hermaphroditus is the last of the stories recounted by the daughters of Minyas in book 4 of the *Metamorphoses* (285–388), and directly follows the stories of Pyramus and Thisbe (55–166), Mars and Venus (167–89), Leucothoe and Clytie (190–273) and Alcithoe (274–84). Here Ovid describes how the water nymph Salmacis falls in love with the teenage son of Hermes and Aphrodite, who is only at the end of the narrative referred to by the name of Hermaphroditus. When Hermaphroditus rejects the advances of Salmacis, Salmacis pretends to retreat while waiting for Hermaphroditus to enter into the pool over which she holds divine control. After Hermaphroditus unknow-ingly enters into her waters she attempts to rape him, entwining herself around his body while he strives to push her away (358–60) (Hermaphroditus will be referred to using the male pronoun prior to his transformation with Salmacis). As they struggle, Salmacis prays to the gods for him to never be taken away from her, or her from him, and their two bodies appear to be joined together (373–4). There is then a shift in the narrative, and Ovid is no longer describing the two characters but Hermaphroditus alone. The transformation, moreover, does not result in a truly double being. Instead Hermaphroditus is said to have become half a man with softened limbs, while the identity of Salmacis appears to be lost altogether, reduced to a dehumanised association with her own spring (380–2).

HERMAPHRODITUS AND THE PRIMORDIAL UNIVERSE

Ovid describes the physical merging of the bodies of Salmacis and Hermaph-roditus as they are joined together and take on a single appearance as follows:

> nam mixta duorum
> **corpora iunguntur, faciesque** inducitur illis
> **una**; velut, siquis conducat cortice, ramos
> crescendo iungi pariterque adolescere cernit,
> sic, ubi conplexu coierunt membra tenaci,
> nec duo sunt et forma duplex, **nec femina dici**
> **nec puer ut possit, nec utrumque et utrumque videntur**.

For their two bodies were mingled and joined; and they put on the appearance of one; just as, if someone puts branches through a tree's bark, he sees them joined as they grow and maturing together, so, when their bodies had come together in a clinging embrace, they were not two, but they had a dual form that could be said to be neither woman nor boy, they seemed to be neither and both (*Met.*4.377–9; edition Anderson 1996; trans. adapted from Hill 1985, used throughout).

Their two bodies fuse together (*iungere*), and they adopt a single appearance (*facies una*), yet have a dual form (*forma duplex*). They no longer appear to operate within normative conceptual distinctions: they are neither fully singular nor plural; they are neither individually male nor female; nor are they both. In being 'neither and both' the woman and the boy, the distinction of they, she, he no longer holds. Not only do we see a breakdown in perceived gender divisions, but the distinction necessary for individual identity to exist as well as our ability to describe and conceptualise it is lost. The other instance where this occurs in the *Metamorphoses* is in Ovid's description of the primordial state of the universe, where the basic elemental oppositions are confounded and physical identity can neither exist on a corporeal nor a conceptual level.

At the beginning of the *Metamorphoses*, Ovid describes *chaos*, the primordial state of the universe as follows:

Ante mare et terras et quod tegit omnia caelum
unus erat toto naturae **vultus** in orbe,
quem dixere chaos: rudis indigestaque moles
nec quidquam nisi pondus iners congestaque eodem
non bene **iunctarum** discordia semina rerum.
. . . nulli sua forma manebat,
obstabatque aliis aliud, quia **corpore** in **uno**
frigida pugnabant calidis, umentia siccis,
mollia cum duris, sine pondere, habentia pondus.

Before the sea and the lands and the sky which covers all things, there was one face of nature in her whole globe, which they called chaos: a rough unordered mass, nothing except inactive weight and joined together the discordant seeds of badly joined together things. . . . To none did its form remain, and one impeded the others, because in one body, the cold were fighting with the hot, the wet with the dry, the soft with the hard, and the weightless and the heavy. (1.5–20)

In Ovid's primordial universe the primary divisions of reality do not exist, as all of nature is said to have a single appearance (*vultus unus*). This state is directly contrasted with the formed universe based on the divisions of sea, land and sky which at this point have not yet come into existence. Primordial *chaos* operates as a singularity where the primary elements of matter (*semina*) are described as fused together (*iunctus*). The elemental opposites of the hot and the cold, the dry and the wet, the soft and the hard, and the light and the heavy are in a state of turmoil, lack stable division and occupy a single body (*unum corpus*).

There are a number of close verbal and conceptual parallels between Ovid's description of Hermaphroditus' transformed body and the depiction of the primordial universe. Both are said to be in a state of fusion (*iunctus, iungere*) where pluralities and polar opposites occupy a single body (*corpus*) and adopt a single appearance (*vultus unus, facies una*). In both cases the primary divisions or categories used to designate reality are confounded and we are faced with a state which evades precise definition. This connection is further emphasised in Ovid's description of the 'softened limbs' (**mollitaque membra**) of Hermaphroditus' body (*Met.* 4.381–2), which parallels the mixing of the elemental opposition of the soft and the hard (*mollia, duris*) in primordial *chaos*.

The connection between Hermaphroditus and primordial *chaos* becomes more apparent if we compare Hermaphroditus to another representation of the primordial universe in Ovid's *Fasti*. In book 1 of the *Fasti* the narrator is confronted with a fully fledged corporealisation of the cosmos in the guise of Janus. Janus tells the narrator that the ancients used to call him *chaos* and proceeds to describe the formation of the universe, which he identifies as his own transformation from a shapeless mass to a personified deity:

> tunc ego, qui fueram globus et sine imagine moles,
> in faciem redii dignaque membra deo.
> nunc quoque, confusae quondam nota parva figurae,
> ante quod est in me postque videtur idem.

> At that time I, who had been a sphere, a mass without form, returned into the face and limbs worthy of a god. And even now a small sign of my formerly mixed up form, what is in front and behind in me look just the same. (1.111–14; edition Alton, Wormell and Courtney: 1978; trans. adapted Wiseman 2013)

The formation of the cosmos is envisaged as the transformation of a raw spherical lump of matter (effectively another singularity) into an anthropomorphic god, as the world gains form through the development of distinct limbs. Janus reveals, however, that his double form is a sign of his previous or primordial state. Ovid uses the term *biformis* 'double-formed' to describe the body of Janus at *Fasti* 1.89. This is precisely the same term which he uses to describe Hermaphroditus at *Met.* 4.387. This strengthens the link between Hermaphroditus and the beginnings of the cosmos, with the notion of double form used specifically as a marker for this primordial state. Hermaphroditus' transformation in this context could be read as a reversal of the sequence of the development of the world. The cosmos takes shape in both the *Metamorphoses* and the *Fasti* through a process of separation, expansion and the development of distinction. In the case of Hermaphroditus, however, this essential sequence is reversed as the many become the one, through the consolidation of the separate bodies of Hermaphroditus and Salmacis and through the loss of gender opposition. At the very least, the close parallels between Hermaphroditus' metamorphosis and the primordial universe must indicate the latent chaos still present in the formed world.

PLATO'S PROTO-HUMANS AND LUCRETIUS' LOVERS

Placed next to primordial *chaos*, Hermaphroditus' transformation may be read as a retrograde shift towards an earlier stage in human or cosmological genera-tion. The transformation is the product, however, of the overwhelming desire of the lover to be completely united with the beloved. In other words, erotic desire results in a cosmic shift. On this basis and through the combination of these factors, it is likely that Ovid is referring to Aristophanes' description of the double-formed ancestors of human beings in Plato's *Symposium*. In Aristo-phanes' speech, he describes how the three different sexual orientations of his modern humans are the result of the splitting in two of the three differently gendered proto-human ancestors, namely the all male, all female and female male. This is used to explain erotic desire, where human love is understood as the need to be reunited with one's lost half. Aristophanes describes how these early human ancestors were spherical in shape: ἔπειτα ὅλον ἦν ἑκάστου τοῦ ἀνθρώπου τὸ εἶδος στρογγύλον, νῶτον καὶ πλευρὰς κύκλῳ ἔχον 'Again, the form of each human being as a whole was round, with back and sides forming a circle' (189e5). He then describes their double-formed bodies; along with hav-ing four arms and four legs, they had two faces on a single head: κεφαλὴν δ' ἐπ' ἀμφοτέροις τοῖς προσώποις ἐναντίοις κειμένοις μίαν 'there was a single head for both faces, which faced in opposite directions' (190a1). The spherical nature of Plato's proto-humans and the fact that their two faces share a single head sug-gests a close connection with Ovid's depiction of Janus in the *Fasti*, whose two faces likewise look in opposite directions. In the *Symposium*, the proto-humans are said to be the offspring of the three major cosmic bodies; the male is the child of the Sun, the female of the Earth, and the female-male the Moon, which shares the nature of both moon and earth. The cosmological correlates for the three proto-humans illustrate a further connection between gender division and the structure of the universe.

Ovid's story of Hermaphroditus and Aristophanes' account of the proto-humans also share a close connection; Salmacis attempts to fully unite her body with that of Hermaphroditus and Aristophanes' humans attempt to recombine with their lost halves after they are split. This connection is best illustrated, how-ever, by examining a potential double allusion in the *Metamorphoses* with this passage from the *Symposium* and a passage from book 4 of Lucretius' *De Rerum Natura* (*On the Nature of Things*). In the *Metamorphoses*, when Hermaphroditus enters the pool, Salmacis entwined (*implicare*) herself around him, despite his resistance: *illa premit **commissaque corpore toto*** | *sicut inhaerebat* 'she pressed on, and joined with all of her body, as she clung to him' (4.369–70). In book 4 of the *De Rerum Natura*, Lucretius describes how lovers during intercourse strive to completely join together in a single body:

> nequiquam, quoniam nil inde abradere possunt
> nec penetrare et abire in **corpus corpore toto**;
> nam facere interdum velle et certare videntur.

> It is all a waste of effort, as they cannot rub any bit of it away, nor can they get right inside that body and make their whole body disappear in it – for sometimes this is what they seem to want to do and strive for. (4.1110–2; edition Bailey: 1922; trans. adapted Godwin 1986)

The lovers attempt in vain to fully unite their bodies together, to penetrate deeper than intercourse will allow and disappear inside each other. Salmacis' desire to fuse with Hermaphroditus appears to allude to this passage from Lucretius. Salmacis does in fact lose her body in Hermaphroditus', as she appears to no longer have any form of identity following the transformation. There is a close verbal parallel between *commissaque corpore toto* (*Met.* 4.369) and *corpus corpore toto* (*DRN* 4.1111) with each phrase coming at the end of its respective line, suggesting that Ovid is specifically evoking Lucretius at this point.

This passage from the *De Rerum Natura* itself appears to be modelled on a passage from the speech of Aristophanes in Plato's *Symposium*, where humans following the split seek to do nothing else except reunite with their lost halves:

> ἐπειδὴ οὖν ἡ φύσις δίχα ἐτμήθη, ποθοῦν ἕκαστον τὸ ἥμισυ τὸ αὑτοῦ συνήει, καὶ **περιβάλλοντες τὰς χεῖρας** καὶ **συμπλεκόμενοι** ἀλλήλοις, ἐπιθυμοῦντες συμφῦναι, ἀπέθνῃσκον ὑπὸ λιμοῦ καὶ τῆς ἄλλης ἀργίας διὰ τὸ μηδὲν ἐθέλειν χωρὶς ἀλλήλων ποιεῖν.

> Now when their nature was divided in two, each half in longing rushed to the other half of itself and they threw their arms around each other and intertwined them, desiring to grow together into one, dying of hunger and inactivity too because they were unwilling to do anything apart from one another. (191a5–b1; edition Burnet: 1963 and trans. adapted Allen 1993, used throughout)

Aristophanes describes how each half so desperately longs to be physically reunited with their lost half that in their desire they can do nothing else, and they die from hunger. Philip Hardie (2002: 161) suggests Lucretius is alluding to the *Symposium* at this point, as Lucretius' lovers, like Plato's, dwindle away (*tabescere*) because they cannot do anything else (*DRN* 4.1120). Ovid's description of Salmacis' attempt to unite with the body of Hermaphroditus resembles the above passage from the *Symposium* even more closely. Ovid describes how Salmacis pours her body around (*circumfundere*) and throws her arms up under Hermaphroditus (*subiectaque manus*) (*Met.* 4.359–60), just as the lovers in the *Symposium* throw their arms around each other (περιβάλλοντες τὰς χεῖρας). Ovid also twice uses the verb *implicare* (*Met.* 4.362; 364) derived from the same verbal root as συμπλέκειν (πλέκω, *plecto*) to describe Salmacis' entwining around the body of Hermaphroditus.

Matthew Robinson (1999: 222) identifies a further allusion in the *Metamorphoses* to the *Symposium* at 192d5–e2 when Hephaestus offers to weld the lovers back together:

> Ἆρά γε τοῦδε ἐπιθυμεῖτε, ἐν τῷ αὐτῷ γενέσθαι ὅτι μάλιστα ἀλλήλοις,
> ὥστε καὶ νύκτα καὶ ἡμέραν μὴ ἀπολείπεσθαι ἀλλήλων; εἰ γὰρ τούτου
> ἐπιθυμεῖτε, θέλω ὑμᾶς συντῆξαι καὶ συμφυσῆσαι εἰς τὸ αὐτό, ὥστε δύ'
> ὄντας ἕνα γεγονέναι καὶ ἕως τ' ἂν ζῆτε, ὡς ἕνα ὄντα, κοινῇ ἀμφοτέρους
> ζῆν . . .'

> 'Is this your desire – to be in the same place with each other as much as possible, so that you're not parted from each other night and day? Because if that's what you want, I will fuse and weld you into the same thing, so that from being two you become one and, as one, share a life in common as long as you live . . .'

This desire for corporeal fusion corresponds closely with Hermaphroditus' transformation: *nam mixta duorum | corpora iunguntur, faciesque inducitur illis | una* 'For their two bodies were mingled and joined; and they put on the appearance of one' (*Met.* 4.373–5). Robinson (1999: 222) states that 'the relevance of this should be clear: the offer made by Hephaestus to the two lovers is identical to the request made by Salmacis to the gods. The idea of some divine force actually physically merging two bodies into one is far from common, and this passage of the *Met.* cannot but recall the Symposium.' Ovid's account of Salmacis and Hermaphroditus hence alludes both to Plato's *Symposium* and Lucretius' *De Rerum Natura*, and precisely to a passage in the *De Rerum Natura* which itself appears to allude to the *Symposium*. One could argue that this mixing and recombining of allusions could serve to focalise the transformation of Hermaphroditus itself. Through the mode of double allusion in particular, Ovid appears to be replicating the hybridity which we see in the body of Hermaphroditus in the composition of the text. It is also significant that in the double allusion outlined above, Ovid is mixing Greek and Latin material, while also focusing on passages in philosophical texts which centre explicitly on eroticism.

EMPEDOCLES' HYBRIDS AND LUCRETIUS' *PORTENTA*

Ovid's depiction of the transformed Hermaphroditus also shares a striking similarity with another proto-human ancestor, the *portenta*, or monstrous malformations including intersex beings which emerged from the earth in the early phase of world history in Lucretius' account of zoogony from book 5 of the *De Rerum Natura* (837–44). Lucretius describes how these *portenta* ultimately failed to reproduce due to their inability to adapt to their environment:

> Multaque tum tellus etiam portenta creare
> conatast mira facie membrisque coorta,
> androgynum, **interutrasque nec utrum, utrimque remotum** . . .

> At that time, the earth tried also to produce many monsters, and beings of amazing appearance with amazing bodies came forth: the *androgynus*, intersexual and not belonging to either sex, but separate from both. (5.837–9; edition and trans. adapted Gale: 2009)

Among the creatures to emerge from the earth in Lucretius' early stages of zoogony is the *androgynus*, which is described as distinct from both genders. These entities are grouped in the following lines with malformed creatures, some of which lack hands or feet, are dumb, blind, without faces, or are bound by limbs stuck to their whole body. They fail to reproduce since they lack the ability to join in intercourse or find nourishment. In effect they are part of an early generation whose fundamental characteristic is that they lack corporeal distinction. Gordon Campbell (2003: 111), commenting on Lucretius' depiction of the *androgynus*, describes line 5.839 (above) as 'garbled' in terms of both sense and metre in the O and Q manuscripts and prints Lachmann's correction (revised by Munro), which is also followed here. Monica Gale (2009: 171–2) has likewise characterised line 839 as highly awkward in shape and concludes that Lucretius is replicating the jarring forms of the early universe in the language of the text.

In this light, Ovid's description of Hermaphroditus at *Met.* 4.378–9 merits re-examination, for it appears to be closely modelled on the above passage from Lucretius:

> nec duo sunt et forma duplex, **nec femina dici**
> **nec puer ut possit, nec utrumque et utrumque videntur.**

> they were not two, but they had a dual form that could be said to be neither woman nor boy, they seemed to be neither and both.

Ovid's *utrumque et utrumque videntur* clearly echoes line 5.839 from the *De Rerum Natura* above: *interutrasque nec utrum, utrimque remotum,* especially given its highly awkward shape and jarring effect on the ear. This, in conjunction with the repetition of *utrum . . . utrum* introduced by a *nec* clause shows Ovid again using an allusion to Lucretius in order to link Hermaphroditus ontologically with an earlier stage in cosmic history, with the physical transformation acting as a retrograde step reversing the sequence of human evolution. Ovid also follows Lucretius in using a complex linguistic construction to replicate in his verse the transformed body of Hermaphroditus. Campbell (2003: 111–12), who likewise identifies the allusion, states that Ovid smooths out the awkward shape of the line in Lucretius 'in order to stress the unity of male and female, while still keeping the illustration of gender polarity'.

Lucretius' account of the *portenta* has been read as a response to a similar account of zoogony in Empedocles, which takes place during the phase in the cosmic cycle when Love (*Philotes*) is the dominant force in the universe. Empedocles gives an account of hybrid creatures including intersex beings that occupy an intermediary stage in the sequence of evolution:

πολλὰ μὲν ἀμφιπρόσωπα φίστερνα φύεσθαι,
βουγενῆ ἀνδρόπρωιρα, τὰ δ᾽ ἔμπαλιν ἐξανατέλλειν
ἀνδροφυῆ βούκρανα, **μεμειγμένα τῆι μὲν ἀπ᾽ ἀνδρῶν**
τῆι δὲ γυναικοφυῆ σκιεροῖς ἠσκημένα γυίοις.

Many with two faces and two chests grew, oxlike with men's faces, and again there came up androids with ox-heads, **mixed in one way from men and in another way in female form**, outfitted with shadowy limbs. (fr. Inwood 66/DK 61; trans. Inwood: 2001)

Empedocles groups the figures of mixed male and female form with monstrous hybrid creatures including the ox-faced man creatures. Campbell (2003: 111–12) notes that Lucretius' description of the *androgynus* in his account of the *portenta* alludes to this passage from Empedocles. It is likely that Ovid in his description of Hermaphroditus (*nec femina dici nec puer ut possit, nec utrumque et utrumque videntur*) is also alluding to this same passage from Empedocles and in particular the description of the figures with mixed male and female form (μεμειγμένα τῆι μὲν ἀπ᾽ ἀνδρῶν τῆι δὲ γυναικοφυῆ). This argument is strengthened if we consider that Ovid alludes at least twice to this precise passage from Empedocles elsewhere. As Hardie (1995: 214) has demonstrated, Ovid's *semibovemque virum semivirumque bovem* in the *Ars Amatoria* (2.24), a phrase which appears again in the *Tristia* (1.7.16), specifically evokes the above passage from Empedocles (see also Kelly 2018).

This evocation provides another example of Ovid imbedding a double allusion to natural philosophy, in this case to the zoogonies of Empedocles and Lucretius, in his account of Hermaphroditus' transformation. He thereby forges a further link between his depiction of Hermaphroditus and an earlier stage in the history of human and cosmic evolution. The transformation of Hermaphroditus not only distorts a series of ontological and epistemological boundaries, but it also subverts the basic temporal sequence of generation. The erotic element of the narrative again translates to the cosmic when we read Hermaphroditus in terms of Empedoclean cosmogony. In Empedocles' double cosmogony the universe cycles through two different phases: one in which Strife (*Neikos*) is the dominant force in the universe and there is a movement from unity to plurality, and one in which Love (*Philotes*) is dominant and there is a movement from plurality to unity. The reconstructions of the text by Brad Inwood (2001) and by Alain Martin and Oliver Primavesi (1999) feature a double zoogony that matches the double cosmogony. In these reconstructions, moreover, the passage from Empedocles discussed above is part of the zoogony which takes place under Love with the preceding stage involving wandering of disparate limbs. The overwhelming desire of Salmacis for Hermaphroditus can thus be read in terms of Empedoclean *Philotes* as Salmacis' love for Hermaphroditus results in the fusion of their bodies and a shift from plurality to unity.

CONCLUSION

In Ovid's depiction of Hermaphroditus the gendered human body becomes a locus for examining cosmic forces, and particularly for highlighting how binary oppositions are used in early cosmogonic texts to form an image of the universe. If we read the body of the transformed Hermaphroditus as a chaotic structure and the transformation itself as a form of devolution, what does this say about wider perspectives on intersexuality in Augustan Rome? It is difficult not to read these elements of Hermaphroditus' transformation as casting a negative light on intersexuality in antiquity. It is problematic, however, to draw further inferences about Ovid's perspective and this time period in general, and, not least of all, how or if we should disassociate the strictly negative connotations that chaos, proto-human, and devolution have in a modern context from how these would function in an ancient one. I would argue that the consolidation of gender oppositions which takes place in the Hermaphroditus narrative takes second stage in Ovid's agenda to the breakdown of the barriers between individual humans and the linking of erotic and cosmological forces. Ovid utilises the fusion of Hermaphroditus and Salmacis to raise a series of fundamental questions about how to define human identity and how the identities of separate people can combine and recombine, and form and reform each other.

He here defines the human body not only through its ability to transform, but also through the physical permeability and instability of its boundaries. Ovid's projection of Hermaphroditus' transformation onto the cosmic superstructure ultimately serves to question and undermine earlier world views based upon binary oppositions. Gender in this context is not only fluid and indefinable, but ultimately ceases to exist.

CHAPTER 7

Que(e)r(y)ing Iphis' Transformation in Ovid's *Metamorphoses*

Rebecca Begum-Lees

> But with this story, well, he [Ovid] can't help being the Roman he is, he can't help fixating on what it is that girls don't have under their togas, and it's him who can't imagine what girls would ever do without one. (Smith 2007: 97)

The story of Iphis in Book 9 of Ovid's *Metamorphoses* is unique in Latin literature.[1] Roman (male) writers make sense of female same-sex desire by casting one woman in the partnership in the active, penetrative role and characterising her as sex-mad (Hallett 1997). Ovid, by contrast, provides us with the singular tale of deep-felt desire felt by one woman or girl for another that is not reduced to this hierarchical, hyper-sexualised stereotype. That is, at least, at the story's beginning. In the end, Iphis' miraculous sex-change from female to male enables Iphis and the beloved Ianthe to marry, seemingly shutting down any possibility of a lesbian reality and reasserting the Roman heteronormative marital paradigm. This ending has therefore disappointed prominent writers such as classicist Judith Hallett and novelist Ali Smith, who gives this ancient myth an innovative take in her acclaimed *Boy Meets Girl* (2007). This chapter contends, however, that Iphis' transformation is in fact unresolved and that such disappointment is therefore misplaced. Iphis' metamorphosis can be considered in terms of biological sex (Wheeler 1997: 196, 200; Pintabone 2002: 277; Oliensis 2009: 109; Lateiner 2009: 138) but I will show that the change is strictly speaking one of social gender: regarding Iphis' biological sex the text is silent (Langlands 2002: 99–101; Ormand 2005: 99–100; Ormand 2009: 217–18; Boehringer 2007a: 254–5; Lindheim 2010: 186–8).

Moreover, the *Metamorphoses* is a poem about changing forms and Iphis' change should be considered in the context of Ovid's other transformations. Scholarship on the passage overlooks this aspect as it has focused on the rich opportunities to explore 'what the Iphis story itself can tell us about Ovidian/Roman concepts of gender and sexuality' (Kamen 2012: 22). Ovidian transformations character-istically lack resolution: as scholars repeatedly remark, no metamorphosis in the poem is fully resolved since elements of a character's final form are always-already present, such as Lycaon's lupine ferocity or Anaxarete's heart of stone. I contend that Iphis fits this pattern by resisting binary gender classification both before and after undergoing metamorphosis (*contra* Boehringer (2007a: 243–55), who insists on Iphis' femininity before and after transformation). My intervention thus restores Iphis to the poem's context of transformation and qu(e)er(ie)s Iphis' meta-morphosis by doing so.

ANDROGYNOUS YOUTH

Iphis is marked out as an androgynous youth before undergoing metamor-phosis. She is the daughter of humble parents, Ligdus and Telethusa – parents so humble that while pregnant, Telethusa is warned by her husband that they can only afford to raise a boy: regrettably, a baby girl must be exposed. When Telethusa delivers a girl, the Egyptian goddess Isis assures her that the child will be saved, and Telethusa gleefully raises Iphis as a boy, deceiving the whole community except Iphis' nurse (9.707). Before transformation, when Iphis is alone she identifies unambiguously as female, so when referring to the char-acter before transformation I use the pronouns she/her. After transformation we do not hear how Iphis identifies in private, and since my argument is that gender is unclear, I use the pronouns ze/hir.

Telethusa is delighted that Iphis receives her grandfather's name, as it can be given to both girls and boys (9.708–9). The common gender of her name is particularly noteworthy since it constitutes a significant departure from Ovid's Hellenistic model, a tale from the lost *Heteroeumena* of Nicander, known through the summary by Antoninus Liberalis (*Met.* 17) in the second or third century AD (Papathomopoulos 1968: ix). There the protagonist has an exclusively masculine name, Leucippus. Names are often determinative in the *Metamorphoses*: numerous characters are synonymous with, or etymologi-cally related to the thing into which they are transformed. A particularly apt illustration of this for our purposes, given the context of blurred gender, is the unnamed child who is said to resemble both parents equally, the gods Mercury and Venus (4.290–1). The youth's name, Hermaphroditus, is revealed only when his body is fused with that of his persistent female suitor (4.383). Although both boys and girls can be called Iphis, the name derives from Greek φι, the instrumental of ἴς, which means 'strength'. This in turn suggests the Latin linguistic cluster *vis-vir-vires* ([sexual] force-man-strength), in which masculinity and physical strength are etymologically related (Wheeler 1997: 194–5). Given the determinative importance of names in the poem, a sensi-tive reader's expectations are cued by Ovid's departure from his model, in that

Ovid allocates his hero(ine) a name that resists categorisation as either male or female but that also bears connotations of strength and virility.

Like her name, Iphis' body resists gender categorisation; here again Ovid innovates upon his Hellenistic model (as Wheeler 1997: 191 and Raval 2002: 159 have noted). In Antoninus Liberalis' version, Leucippus' feminine beauty threatens to expose the fiction of her masculinity (*Met.* 17.4). By contrast, Ovid tells us (9.712–13): 'the dress was that of a boy, but as for the face, whether you gave it to a girl or to a boy, both would be beautiful' – *cultus erat pueri; facies, quam sive puellae/ sive dares puero, fieret formosus uterque* (I use Tarrant's OCT throughout, all translations my own). An androgynous face is a common feature of a beautiful youth. We have already seen the example of Hermaphroditus (4.290–1); other gender-fluid young faces in the *Metamorphoses* belong to Hippomenes (10.631) and Atalanta of Tegea (8.322–3), and have parallels in examples such as Horace's Gyges (*ambiguoque vultu*, *Odes* 2.5.24) and Juvenal 15.137 (*ora . . . incerta*). Moreover, Ovid creates further ambiguity in the way he formulates Iphis' androgynous appearance. Very often in this poem about changing forms, the noun *facies* denotes not the face but the whole physical exterior, and the adjective *formosus* (beautiful) is found far more commonly in the feminine than the masculine (see Bömer 1976 *ad* 6.617). When *formosus* does describe males, it is the gender-fluid god Bacchus (4.18), or the object of transgressive female desires (Scylla on Nisus, 8.26, and Byblis on Caunus, 9.476). Iphis also blends genders at a grammatical level. While Richard Tarrant's Oxford Classical Text consistently describes Iphis with feminine pronouns and adjectives, the manuscript tradition is actually unresolved in three places, so that there is evidence of both grammatically masculine and feminine Iphis (*Iphide mutata/ mutato* 9.668, *ambarum/ -orum*, 9.720, and *quamque/ quemque*, 9.723 – see Lämmle 2005: 199; see Strauss Clay 1995: 146–8 for a similar treatment of Attis in Catullus 63).

IMPOSSIBLE LESBIANS

The key manner in which Iphis bends Roman gender norms is in her sexual desire for another girl. There is now scholarly consensus around a basic model of Roman sexual encounters that involves an active, penetrative partner, who is by necessity male, and a passive, penetrated partner, who could be male or female (if male, then ideally an adolescent, whom Romans characterised as gender-fluid). According to this model, there is no conceptual space for female homoerotic encounters, since 'female' is equivalent to 'passive' in Roman gender ideology. The few (of course, male-penned) instances of female same-sex erotic encounters from extant Latin literature impose this structure upon women's practice (Hallett 1997, first printed in 1989 (*Helios* 16.1: pp. 59–78), and critiqued by Brooten 1996: 42–50). Women who had sex with women were envisaged as trying to take an active – i.e. a man's – sexual role. As Kirk Ormand (2005: 84) notes, a sexually active woman (often labelled a 'tribas' in post-Ovidian literature) could be envisioned to desire a boy or a woman; what was considered deviant was not the sex of her desired object but her pretension to play the active role.

A model of Roman sexuality based solely on acts, penetration and hierarchy (although well-intentioned, as it tries to avoid ascribing identities which Romans did not use) is far from satisfactory, and scholars have added further nuance to the paradigm (e.g. Langlands 2006; Levin-Richardson 2013; Kamen and Levin-Richardson 2015a). Iphis is of course not Roman but Cretan, a place the Romans often associated with female sexual deviance and deceit (see Armstrong 2006). As her wedding with Ianthe approaches, however, it is the Roman model that provides the terms in which Iphis understands and chastises her desire, which is configured as outside the gender norms relevant to Ovid's Roman audience. For some scholars, Iphis is indifferent as to whether she plays the active or passive role (e.g. Pintabone 2002: 275), and for other scholars she is determined to play the active, masculine role (e.g. Ormand 2005: 97). The currently accepted reading is that the metamorphosis reassigns prescribed sexual roles by supplying Iphis with the necessary apparatus. I will show that the way that Iphis configures her desire blends active and passive elements, and thus masculine and feminine elements, so that hir ambiguous gender after metamorphosis is actually a continuation of her ambiguous gender before metamorphosis.

Iphis despairs of being able to 'enjoy' Ianthe (*Iphis amat, qua posse frui desperat* (9.724) or 'possess' her (*nec tamen est potienda tibi*, 9.753), using verbs that in Latin connote the male orgasm (Adams 1982: 188, 198; Wheeler 1997: 198) and thus imply that Iphis desires to play the *active* sexual role. In the same tortuous monologue, Iphis views her love as even more transgressive than that of her compatriot Pasiphae, the Cretan queen who famously copulated with a bull to produce the legendary Minotaur. With the assistance of the inventor Daedalus, Pasiphae is disguised as a cow so she could 'suffer' the bull (*imagine vaccae/passa bovem est*, 9.738–9). The verb *patior* – 'suffer' – is the standard term for sexual submission (Adams 1982: 189–90), suggesting that here Iphis envies Pasiphae's ability to play the *passive* role. Continuing with the theme of disguise, Iphis asks whether Daedalus could turn either Iphis or Ianthe into a boy (9.743–4). Her request is indifferent as to whether Daedalus transforms herself or Ianthe, and thus Iphis appears indifferent as to who plays the active and who the passive role. Ormand (2005: 93) writes that 'Iphis' bombast is meant to be taken as amusing, coming as it does from a thirteen-year-old.' But the sentiment, however comical the language, also pinpoints the fundamental difference between cross-dressing and sex-change that is critical for Iphis' situation. Disguise is a sufficient strategy for the needs of Pasiphae, whose bovine outfit Daedalus designed, as well as for

Daedalus, who successfully took to the sky on self-fashioned wings (even if his son was less successful, 8.183–235). Although Iphis' current disguise suffices for Ianthe to believe that Iphis is a man and therefore a potential husband (*quamque virum putat esse, virum fore credit Ianthe*, 9.723), it cannot allow her to fulfil the relationship with Ianthe, once married, in the way that gender transition would (*contra* Langlands 2002: 105 and Lindheim 2010: 185–6).

Another way in which Iphis' desire blends genders is the way in which her monologue positions Iphis as an elegiac *amator* (Ormand 2005: 96–7). Although a part played by men, the elegiac *amator* takes on a feminised role, portraying himself as the passive slave of his mistress, and thus also combining masculine and feminine genders. Indeed, a male elegiac lover by the name of Iphis takes to the stage in Book 14. Rejected by his 'hard' mistress (*dura*, 14.704), Iphis ultimately kills himself by hanging. This is 'the tragic way for women to kill themselves', and this *amator*'s 'gender-crossing' is a 'trace' left by the hero(ine) of our investigation, Iphis' Book 9 namesake (Hardie 2002: 250).

Since Iphis' desire does not fit a strict dichotomising framework of active versus passive, it seems that either she or Ianthe needs to grow a member for this relationship to survive. But it is possible that Ovid gestures to a place in which Iphis and Ianthe can marry as they are: Egypt (for a fuller appreciation of the roles of Isis and Egypt in this passage, see Panoussi 2019). Diane Pintabone (2002: 277) fleetingly suggests that by replacing the goddess Leto in Nicander's version with the Egyptian goddess Isis, Ovid could have led a Roman audience to expect the tale to 'end with two female spouses', since as Bernadette Brooten (1996: 332–6) shows, female same-sex marriages – however unofficial – may have been associated in Roman thought with Egypt. For Pintabone, this possibility is immediately foreclosed by the transformation, 'so that we have instead a heterosexual wedding sanctioned by the traditional Roman deities of marriage'. But by foregrounding Egypt, not just by replacing Leto with Isis but also by referring to Egyptian gods (9.690–4), the Egyptian rattle (*sistra*, 9.693, *sistrum*, 9.784) and Egyptian landmarks (9.773–4), Ovid potentially reminds the audience of a place where Iphis' desire can be realised without the radical solution of sex-change. The idea that Ovid is sensitive to such cultural relativism is evident from the words of another character in the *Metamorphoses* who feels a sexual desire that violates cultural norms: Myrrha laments that she was not born in a place that permits, or even celebrates, marriage between relatives (10.331–5). The potential allusion to female same-sex marriage is even more important given that Iphis' transformation is not fully resolved, as I will now demonstrate.

METAMORPHOSIS

Isis fulfils her promise to Telethusa that all would turn out well for her child, as Iphis follows hir mother from the temple looking and acting substantially more masculine. My translation is deliberately literal, showing how often in English we require a gendered pronoun where there is none in the Latin:

> mater abit templo. sequitur comes Iphis euntem,
> quam solita est, maiore gradu; nec candor in ore
> permanet et vires augentur et acrior ipse est
> vultus et incomptis brevior mensura capillis,
> plusque vigoris adest habuit quam femina. nam quae
> 790
> femina nuper eras, puer es. date munera templis,
> nec timida gaudete fide. dant munera templis,
> addunt et titulum; titulus breve carmen habebat:
> DONA PUER SOLVIT QUAE FEMINA VOVERAT IPHIS
> postera lux radiis latum patefecerat orbem,
> 795
> cum Venus et Iuno sociosque Hymenaeus ad ignes
> conveniunt, potiturque sua puer Iphis Ianthe.
> 9.786–97

The mother departed from the temple. Iphis accompanied and followed as she went, with a longer stride than was her habit. Facial glow does not remain, strength is increased, the very facial expression is sharper and dishevelled hair is shorter. More strength is present than was had as a female person. For you who recently were a female person, are now a boy. Donate gifts at the temple, and rejoice in confident faith. They donate gifts at the temple, and add an inscription. The inscription had a short verse:

IPHIS GIVES AS A BOY GIFTS WHICH WERE PROMISED AS A FEMALE PERSON

Later the light had lain open the broad world with its rays, when Venus and Juno and Hymenaeus congregated at their associated torches, and the boy Iphis possessed/penetrated his/her Ianthe.

On a first reading, it might seem absurd to suggest that Iphis' transformation is not fully resolved. Ze has all the markers of Roman masculinity: a long stride, dark skin, physical strength, sharp facial features and short hair. Not only that, the narrator explicitly tells us that Iphis has gone from a female person to a boy (*nam quae/femina nuper eras, puer es*, 9.790–1). One can press, as scholars have done (e.g. Wheeler 1997: 200–1), the sexual connotations of *potior* at 9.797, and assume that Iphis now physically penetrates Ianthe (*potiturque sua puer Iphis Ianthe*) – though Vassiliki Panoussi (2019) cleverly points out that *potitur* is incongruent with *puer*, a term also used to described sexually submissive slaves. In Iphis' monologue, shortly after she despairs of being able to penetrate/possess

Ianthe, she blames nature alone for obstructing her: *at non vult natura . . ./quae mihi sola nocet* (9.758–9). The noun *natura* can be a euphemism, 'generally acceptable in the educated language', for genitalia (Adams 1982: 59). In the *Fasti*, Ovid's Attis uses the same expression after he breaks his vow of chastity. 'Ah! Perish the parts that harmed me!' he cries (*a! pereant partes, quae nocuere mihi!* 4.240), before castrating himself. This vocabulary, then, can be associated both with sexual intercourse and with genital alteration. These few indications (and the *Fasti* comparison is not one I have seen other scholars make) perhaps imply that Iphis has genuinely changed sex.

One might object that Ovid is not concerned with Iphis' sexual anatomy, for the epic genre's decorum veils the question of what Iphis may or may not have acquired. This is indeed a valid explanation for Ovid's failure to mention, unlike Antoninus Liberalis (*Met.* 17.6), any private parts, especially since Ovid's metamorphoses usually pay very close attention to anatomical details (note too that Leucippus' mother explicitly prays to Leto to turn Leucippus into a boy (*Met.* 17.4), whereas Ovid's Telethusa merely prays to Isis for help just before the wedding, 9.773–81). However, 'phallic symbolism' is 'part of the surface texture' of this and of other stories despite the fact that 'the Roman sense of decency kept the literal penis under wraps' (Oliensis 2009: 108; cf. Lindheim 2010: 187). With this licence, Ellen Oliensis (2009: 109) interprets the many references to 'horns' in the passage (e.g. 9.689, 9.774, 9.784) to imply that Iphis emerges from Isis' temple, 'though Ovid decorously refrains from specifying this key feature, newly equipped with his own virile appendage'. Many other scholars interpret from these lines that a physical sex change has occurred, either through puns (Wheeler 1997: 196, 200), through recourse to ancient medical theory (Lämmle 2005: 203–6) or pure assumption (Pintabone 2002: 277; Lateiner 2009: 138). Even when scholars acknowledge that Iphis' transformation is subtler than others and/or foregrounds performative markers of gender over biological indications, they conclude that ultimately, anatomy and performance are aligned (Raval 2002: 163–4; Lämmle 2005: 196, 198, 208; Walker 2006: 217–18; Volk 2010: 93–4).

The text, in fact, resists a firm conclusion. As Ormand (2009: 217–18) writes, Iphis' transformation of '*social* gender' rather than '*biological* sex' is symptomatic of the Roman view of masculinity as 'not a biological fact, but a hard-won social position that had to be continually bolstered and reinforced' (Ormand's emphasis). Let us examine more closely the markers that confirm that only Iphis' outward gender and not hir biological sex has changed. Extensive research has demonstrated that Roman orators viewed body language such as gait and facial expression to be entirely manipulable (e.g. Gleason 1995; Corbeill 2004; Fögen 2009). This is one way in which Iphis' stride could be understood to be deliberately made longer (*maiore gradu* 9.787), and hir face sharper (*acrior ipse est/*

vultus, 9.788–9). The physical strength that Iphis has acquired (*vires augentur*, 9.788; *plusque vigoris adest*, 9.790) can certainly be built up through exercise: see e.g. Cicero, *Brutus* 313–16 and Seneca, *Controversiae* 9 pr. 4.

The *candor* that Iphis loses from hir face is the pale glow that emblematises Roman youth (such as that of Caelius in Cicero, *Pro Caelio* 36, Hylas in Propertius 1.20.45 or Alexis in Virgil, *Eclogue* 2.15–19). When Athena transforms Odysseus from an old beggar back into his adult prime, he becomes 'dark-skinned' (μελαγχροιής, *Odyssey* 16.175), which suggests that the idea that the association between a ruddy complexion and manhood has a long literary pedigree. Iphis' loss of *candor* can thus be taken in line with readings that interpret this to be a coming-of-age story. Such an interpretation reads the transformation as not only from female to male, but also as from youth to adult (Forbes Irving 1990: 154, 170). This reading certainly accords with Iphis' longer stride and increased strength, but falls down when we remember that Iphis has not become an adult man – a *vir*, as Ianthe already presumed hir to be – but only a *puer*, a boy – who, as we saw above, might in any case be presumed to have ambiguous features. Skin can be darkened by environmental factors: Seneca, for example, bemoans people spending their lives baking their bodies in the sun (*De Brevitate Vitae* 13.1), and Celsus warns how skin colour changes according to an individual's health (*De Medicina* 2.2.1). Elaborate hairstyles are an external mark of an elegiac *puella*, and Iphis does not need to change sex to sport the shorter, dishevelled hair (*incomptis brevior mensura capillis*, 9.789) that signifies male presentation. I do not suggest here that Iphis simply exercises, sunbathes, has a haircut and learns to alter hir expression and gait, but rather I am emphasising that hir transformation involves only performative signifiers (cf. Langlands 2002: 99–100; Boehringer 2007a: 254–5; Lindheim 2010: 187–8).

Something else that the narrative lacks – quite apart from a phallus – is an aetiological component. Ovid's metamorphosis narratives explain the origins (*aetia* in Greek) of things. Antoninus Liberalis' version explains the origin of the Ekdysia festival (for the debate concerning what this festival celebrates, see Leitao 1995 and Heslin 2005: 207–9, 226). Ovid's *Metamorphoses*, which tends to favour aetiologies of natural phenomena over cultural institutions (Myers 1994: 34), does not refer to this festival. A potential natural *aetion* in the Iphis story could possibly be found among Roman prodigy records. This argument is suggested by Hallett (1997: 267), who cites Roman reports of women miraculously growing penises (in some stories, on the eve of their wedding day to a man, on which see Shannon-Henderson in this volume). Modern research shows that certain hormonal conditions have precisely this effect (see e.g. Zucker 1999: 20; for speculation that this explains ancient tales of female-to-male transformation see Charlier 2008: 294). Indeed, tales similar to Iphis' circulate in other cultures: for example, a recent anthropological study entitled *Changing Sex and Bending Gender* opens with an Indian myth that reads eerily like the story of Iphis (Shaw and Ardener 2005: 1). Alison Shaw (2005: 2) states that 'the anthropological record shows that changes of sex and transformations of gender occur in a wide range of social contexts and have probably taken place in all known human societies'. While it cannot be ruled out that real, non-normative bodies would have contributed to the cultural anxiety about enforcing gender norms that produces tales such as Iphis', it is not possible to make retrospective medical diagnoses (Graumann 2013: 200). Though modern parallels are striking (in Dominican, *guevedoce* means 'testicles-at-twelve' and Iphis is about to turn thirteen, 9.714), our passage also resonates with other modern gender scenarios that do not involve penises naturally developing at puberty. Examples include Afghani *bacha posh* (girls born to families without sons and raised as boys, see Nordberg 2014), or homosexual individuals who undergo gender reassignment surgery in countries that criminalise homosexuality (see e.g. Bluck 2012).

If we compare Iphis' transformation with other characters in the poem who retain their humanity but change sex or age, we see that Ovid could have been much more conclusive about Iphis' final gender had he so wished. The poem contains two parallels that demonstrate a reverse transition from manhood to youth, firstly in Medea's rejuvenation of Aeson, and secondly Iolaus, in the very same book as the Iphis narrative. Among the many changes that Aeson undergoes, his beard loses its greyness and regains its dark colour (*barba comaeque/canitie posita nigrum rapuere colorem*, 7.288–9). The only marker of Iolaus' rejuvenation in Book 9, apart from the assignation *puer*, is facial hair ('covering his cheeks with barely there down', *dubiaque tegens lanugine malas*, 9.398). In both rejuvenation tales, then, facial hair is an important signifier of return to youthful masculinity, and Ovid could have given some to Iphis if he wanted explicitly to turn hir into a young man (cf. Boehringer (2007a: 255) notes that Ovid does not refer to 'pilosité, musculature, silhouette, changement du sexe').

Other sex-change narratives are also more conclusive about the final outcome. The first sex-change in the *Metamorphoses* is that of Tiresias, transformed into a woman when he prods a pair of copulating sacred snakes, and when she sees them again seven years later she does not hesitate to strike them again and return to his original form. Tiresias' experience makes him an ideal consultant in Jupiter and Juno's marital squabble over the question of whether men or women derive more pleasure from sexual intercourse. As Ovid tells us, 'both Venuses were known to him' (*Venus huic erat utraque nota*, 3.323), where the goddess of love's name is a double entendre for sexual desire or pleasure, as it is twice in Iphis' monologue (9.728, 9.739). We can clearly intuit the clinical details of Tiresias' double transformation, without indecorous references to certain parts of the body. Similarly, Ovid draws attention to how Hermaphroditus' body changes after it fuses with Salmacis: 'they were no longer two people but a double form that could be called neither a woman nor a boy; they seemed neither and both' (*nec duo sunt sed forma duplex, nec femina dici/nec puer ut possit, neutrumque et utrumque videntur*, 4.378–9, on which see Kelly in this volume). Caenis, after being raped by Neptune, prays no longer to be a woman (*da femina ne sim*, 12.202). She suddenly gains 'the voice of a man' (*viri vox*, 12.204): ancient rhetorical handbooks suggest that while men can alter their voices through training, women cannot completely overcome their vocal deficiency (Gleason 1995: 91; Flemming 2000: 225–6). The newly named Caeneus also acquires the masculine grammatical gender (*saucius*, 12.206, *laetus*, 12.208), which seems to confirm that full gender transition has taken place (on grammatical gender to confirm sex change see also Shannon-Henderson in this volume).

In contrast with Caeneus, Iphis receives no grammatical markers of masculinity after metamorphosis except the assignation *puer* (feminine *solita* in 9.786 refers to before the transformation). And this label, *puer*, does not reveal much. As Maud Gleason (1995: 59) famously demonstrates, Roman masculinity was 'an achieved state, radically underdetermined by anatomical sex'. Masculinity is a state earned after a *puer* has made the transition to adulthood. Roman *pueri* are characterised by their beauty and feminine softness. And Iphis was already, to all except hir mother and nurse, a *puer* before transformation. Other than some performative alterations, it is hard to see how much has changed. Ormand (2005: 99) underlines the point by noting that '*puer es* is almost an anagram of *nuper eras*'. To this we may add some wordplay analysis in the style of Frederick Ahl (1985), on the basis that *nuper* contains an anagram of the word *puer*: that a word meaning 'recently' can be reshuffled to produce the word 'boy' perhaps conveys the instability of being a boy. This continuity between what Iphis was before and after transformation is utterly in keeping with other Ovidian transformations.

CONCLUSION

Many scholars have stressed the themes of continuity of characteristics and lack of resolution in Ovid's metamorphoses. It is typical for certain traits to persist even after the form of a character has changed (see e.g. Anderson 1963; Solodow 1988: 174–86). In the programmatic example of Lycaon, it is often remarked that Ovid points to the preservation of his hallmark features: *canities eadem est, eadem violenta vultus,/ idem oculi lucent, eadem feritatis imago est* (the same white hair is there, the same violence of expression, the same eyes glint, and there is the same image of ferocity, 1.238–9). Sometimes the continued characteristic will persist despite incompatibility with the new form, such as Niobe's continued tears after she has been petrified (6.310–12). Sometimes the preserved trait will be emotional or habitual, rather than corporeal, such as Cycnus' everlasting hatred of fire after he becomes a swan (2.379–80), or Aesacus' repeated seaward plunges as a diving bird (11.795). Sometimes it is simply the character's name, and we had cause above to note Ovid's penchant for onomastic determinism, a feature that is commonly inherited from the Greek source (e.g. Cycnus 'κύκνος' swan), but also applies to Roman examples (for example, Picus is the Latin, not the Greek, for 'woodpecker'). We also noted that Ovid pointedly changes the masculine name of his source's protagonist to a name that can be allocated to males or females. That this move suggests an ongoing gender-fluid future for Iphis is supported by Philip Hardie's (2002: 250) comment on the narrative's finale: 'The interchangeability of male and female is given permanent expression in Iphis' votive inscription . . . The single name 'Iphis' is masculine in apposition to *puer*, and feminine in apposition to *femina*.'

Continuity of characteristics also leads to a sense of unresolvedness: some aspects of, for example, Lycaon, have changed, but some have not. A particularly strong proponent of the unresolved quality of metamorphosis is Marie von Glinski (2012: 13), who states: 'The transformed victim both is and is not his new form . . . The victim has ceased to be human from the perspective of his environment; nonetheless, his human identity lies dormant in the transformed body'. Von Glinski (2012: 12) is so focused on how the unresolved quality of metamorphosis is the result of 'crossing the physical and not just figurative boundary of human and animal' that her study overlooks examples where the transformed victim does not lose 'his' humanity but instead undergoes a sex change. Although Iphis does not cross the boundary of human and animal, von Glinski's thesis that both similarities and differences hold between pre- and post-transformed states equally applies. After transformation, Iphis gains the status of husband, but it is not possible to determine that a full gender transition has taken place. Scholars repeatedly point to the singularity of the Iphis narrative, both for its unique depiction of female same-sex love, and for its 'unusually happy ending' (Hallett 1997: 263). Instead, Iphis' final metamorphosis is unresolved and produces the continued characteristic of resistance towards binary gender classification. In these two defining aspects of Ovidian transformation the passage is in keeping with the remainder of the poem. Ultimately, far from being the exception to the following concession in *Girl Meets Boy*, Ovid's Iphis perfectly illustrates that 'Ovid's very fluid, as writers go, much more than most. He knows, more than most, that the imagination doesn't have a gender' (Smith 2007: 97).

NOTE

1. I would like to thank the editors and the external reviewer for their helpful comments and suggestions, as well as Emily Gowers, Caroline Vout, Kirk Ormand and Vassiliki Panoussi for their feedback on earlier drafts, and James Barker for proofreading. I am also grateful to the audience at the Classical Association of Canada's 2015 'Gender B(l)ending' panel, where this paper was originally presented, and to the Arts and Humanities Research Council, the Faculty of Classics, Cambridge and Newnham College, Cambridge for funding my attendance there. Thanks for particular references are owed to Olivia Elder, Joe Grimwade, Talitha Kearey, George Koukovasilis and Henry Tang.

CHAPTER 8

Ruling in Purple . . . and Wearing Make-up: Gendered Adventures of Emperor Elagabalus as seen by Cassius Dio and Herodian

Jussi Rantala

INTRODUCTION

The reign of Emperor Elagabalus (AD 218–22) is one of the most peculiar episodes in the history of the Roman Empire. Elagabalus, whose birth name was Varius Avitus Bassianus, was the third ruler of the Severan dynasty. Born in AD 203, he had been a priest of the sun-god El'Gabal in his native city, Emesa of Syria, before becoming emperor. As a ruler, he was officially known as Marcus Aurelius Antoninus Augustus; it appears that only after his death was he called Elagabalus. From a governmental point of view, his short reign has not been considered very significant, and it seems that he was personally not that interested in governing issues (Arrizabalaga y Prado 2010: 278–80; Halsberghe 1972: 71). Instead, he took a great interest in religion, promoting El'Gabal to become the supreme god of Roman state religion and also taking a Vestal Virgin, Julia Aquilia Severa, as his wife. For many Romans in that time, these were probably acts of sacrilege, and in AD 222 his soldiers mutinied. Elagabalus was murdered and his cousin Alexianus, now known as Severus Alexander, was declared the new emperor (Potter 2004: 148–57).

Elagabalus is particularly famous for his controversial behaviours not only in religious matters, but also with respect to gender expression, gender identity and sexuality in particular. The intention of this chapter is to approach this specific aspect of his portrayal in two accounts of the early third century AD; *Roman History* by Cassius Dio (c. 155–235 AD) and *History of the Empire from the Death of Marcus* by Herodian (died probably in the 250s AD). Thus, the purpose of this chapter is not to trace actual, 'real' actions of historical Emperor Elagabalus as such. Indeed, tracing 'real' Elagabalus would require many more sources than just historical narratives. Ancient historiography

was, by its nature, highly rhetorical and ideologically normative, often holding strong links to earlier literary traditions. Consequently it does not provide
enough 'factual' information about a figure as controversial as Elagabalus (see
Arrizabalaga y Prado 2010). Instead, I provide a literary analysis of the two historical accounts, focusing on the issues of gender identity and expression in the
acts of Elagabalus as portrayed by Dio and Herodian, and comparing these two
narratives from that point of view (see Kemezis 2016 for similar comparison in
the context of political propaganda). As a result, this study takes a closer look
at intellectual discourse on gender, masculinity and femininity in the context
of the early third century AD: how did the historians of the period present the
young emperor as a transgressor of the line between masculinity and femininity, or even the line between 'being a man' and 'being a woman'? How can we
explain the different attitudes that can be traced from these stories? What do
these attitudes tell us about the aims and audiences of the authors?

While both historians have received some criticism from modern scholars
(for Dio, see Millar 1964: 118 and Bowersock 1975: 230; for Herodian, see
Birley 1999: 204), most recent research considers them to be valuable sources
when tracing intellectual attitudes of the early third century AD. Despite their
possible factual shortcomings, it is nowadays widely accepted that Dio in particular provides us with a view of elite writers of the period on many interesting and important topics (see, for example, Lange and Madsen 2016: 1–4; for
Herodian, see Potter 2004: 232). In addition to Dio and Herodian, there exists
a third biography on Elagabalus, included in the *Augustan History*. However,
this collection of imperial biographies, probably a product of a single author
and written in the late fourth century AD, falls out of the scope of this study –
not only because it is generally considered to be highly unreliable, contradictory
and full of fiction, but also because it was written almost 200 years after Dio and
Herodian, and thus belongs to a very different cultural, intellectual and political environment (for Elagabalus in the *Augustan History*, see Bitarello 2011 and
Mader 2005; all three major traditions are dealt with in Sommer 2004).

HISTORIANS AND THEIR TASKS

Cassius Dio was the son of Cassius Apronianus, a Roman senator from Nicaea
in Bithynia. Appointed as consul in c. 205 AD, Dio left Rome for provincial
duties in Smyrna in AD 218 and returned to the capital about ten years later
(Hose 2007: 462). His massive literary work, Roman history from the traditional foundation of the city in 753 BC to his own times, was probably written
between AD 220–31 (Birley 1999: 203–4).

The traditional view of Cassius Dio has considered him a prime example of
a member of the Greco-Roman elite of the late second or early third century, a

Romanised Greek representing the Hellenistic-Roman empire (Millar 1964; for more recent study see De Blois 1998). While some scholars have challenged this view and stressed his Greek identity (Sidebottom 2007: 76–7), it is important to keep in mind that Dio was a Roman senator who identified himself very strongly with the senatorial class of the capital. All in all, in his writings Dio appears to us as a rather conservative member of the Roman senatorial class and, despite his Greek cultural roots, should therefore be considered a 'true' Roman (Rantala 2016: 174–5). Indeed, Greek-speaking senators such as Dio were not a rarity in the Roman senate during the early third century AD. It has been estimated that, by the beginning of the third century AD, about a quarter of all Roman senators came from the eastern provinces, where the Greek language dominated (Potter 2004: 68–9).

Compared to Cassius Dio, we know much less of Herodian. Generally, he seems to write from 'outside' – in contrast to Dio, who observed many imperial phenomena from the very core of the empire. It appears that he, like Dio, came from Roman Greece but was not a senator; instead, he was probably an official of a lower rank (Rantala 2017: 10–11). His history, covering the period of AD 180–238, relied heavily on Dio's work; indeed this close relationship makes the differences between the two histories even more remarkable (Osgood 2016: 177–8; for Herodian in general, see Hidber 2006 and Polley 2003).

Herodian's audience is hard to trace as well. Some suggestions have been made that he wrote for the Greek nobility residing not in the capital but in Greece, and that his work was part of the discourse among Greek elite regarding Greek identity within the Roman empire (Sidebottom 2007: 80–1). Adam Kemezis (2014: 266–70) has recently disputed this view and rightly points out that the Greek features in Herodian's work do not refer primarily to Hellenic identity as such; rather his history follows the general trends in literature in the whole of the Roman empire. Herodian holds a somewhat pessimistic view on the proceedings of his time, but he was first and foremost a storyteller who wished to entertain his readers. Herodian was not interested in the causes of the political crisis, but simply wanted to describe its symptoms in an entertaining manner (Kemezis 2014: 271–2).

PHOENICIAN IN PURPLE

As noted above, Elagabalus is probably most famous for his disregard for Roman sexual taboos and gender roles, as presented by both Cassius Dio and Herodian. From the works of the historians, we can trace three themes related to these issues: his physical appearance, some of his religious acts, and his sexual behaviour.

Of the two writers, it is Herodian who pays particular attention to Elagabalus' appearance. In his account of the emperor (5.3.6), the historian refers many times to the appearance of the young ruler, stressing that the emperor looked very strange in the eyes of Romans. Herodian begins his account by

describing the eastern appearance of the future emperor. He relates that Elagabalus, while still residing in his native Emesa, performed publicly in 'barbarian
clothing' wearing a long-sleeved, gold and purple tunic, and how his lower half –
from waist to toes – was covered by clothes with gold and purple ornaments.
Herodian continues by describing that Elagabalus wore a crown with colourful
jewels, and notes that the emperor looked very beautiful, comparing the young
ruler to the god Dionysus (cf. SHA *Heliog.* 23.3–4). Herodian further highlights the 'un-Romanness' of Elagabalus by commenting that interested Roman
soldiers watched the 'barbaric' ritual dances of the beautiful young man.

Up to this point, Herodian himself does not seem to be overly critical of
the future ruler. However, his assessment does become more critical when he
continues his account. This is possibly due to the fact that he begins to describe
events that occurred after Elagabalus had become the emperor and started his
journey to Rome; in other words, the historian now starts a new part of his narrative. Herodian states that, whenever possible, Elagabalus conducted laughable
rituals and wore only the most expensive clothing and jewellery, and that he
appeared both as a 'Phoenician priest' and a 'Persian living in luxury' (5.5.4).
Herodian's negative comments on the appearance of Elagabalus grow stronger
as his account progresses. The historian describes (5.6.10) how the emperor
painted his cheeks red and wore black make-up around his eyes which eventually destroyed his beautiful looks, and how Elagabalus, just before his ejection
from power, wore such extensive make-up that 'even a modest woman would
have been ashamed' (5.8.1). Indeed, these sentences may serve a dramatic purpose, forecasting the sad fate of Elagabalus.

Cassius Dio, on the other hand is less vocal about the appearance of the
emperor. According to Dio (80[79].14.3), Elagabalus presented more or less as
a man while leading court, but otherwise he preferred to appear as a woman by
showing 'affectation in his actions and quality of his voice'. Furthermore, Dio
remarks on the feminine appearance of Elagabalus when he describes the relationship of the emperor and a young man named Zoticus (cf. SHA *Heliog* 10.2–7).
According to Dio, Elagabalus desired this man from Smyrna because of his very
large penis. He further asserts that Zoticus, when he met the emperor for the first
time, greeted him with words 'hail my Lord', as was the custom. To this, Elagabalus replied by taking a feminine pose and saying that Zoticus should not call
him lord, as he was a lady. To this end, Dio also claims that the emperor used to
dance everywhere: while giving speeches, receiving salutations, sacrificing, even
while simply walking (80[79].16.7). The feminine nature of Elagabalus, both in
appearance and activities, is evident in other passages by Dio as well:

And finally, – to go back now to the story which I began, – he was
bestowed in marriage and was termed wife, mistress, and queen. He
worked with wool, sometimes wore a hair-net, and painted his eyes,
daubing them with white lead and alkanet. Once, indeed, he shaved his

chin and held a festival to mark the event; but after that he had the hairs plucked out, so as to look more like a woman; and he often reclined while receiving the salutations of the senators. (Cass. Dio 80[79].14.4; translated by E. Cary)

If we compare the accounts provided by Cassius Dio and Herodian, there are some differences. At first glance, Herodian does not appear as critical as Dio when describing the personal beauty of Elagabalus. However, for Herodian, the general appearance of Elagabalus seems to be connected to the idea of an 'eastern luxury', itself an old *topos* in Greco-Roman literature (see Isaac 2004 for discussion). Within this literary tradition, describing someone as 'eastern' could refer to a variety of negative qualities, and often specifically pointed to gender presentation. This is evident in Dio's account, as he often calls Elagabalus a 'Sardanapalus' with deep contempt (Dio also uses other mocking names, such as 'Pseudo-Antoninus'; cf. SHA *Heliog.* 17.4). In Greek and Roman literature, Sardanapalus was considered to be a prime example of a woman-like eastern male, as witnessed, for example, in a passage from the first-century BC historian, Diodorus Siculus:

Sardanapalus, the thirtieth in succession from Ninus, who founded the empire, and the last king of the Assyrians, outdid all his predecessors in luxury and sluggishness . . . he lived the life of a woman, and spending his days in the company of his concubines and spinning purple garments and working the softest of wool, he had assumed the feminine garb and so covered his face and indeed his entire body with whitening cosmetics and the other unguents used by courtesans, that he rendered it more delicate than that of any luxury-loving woman. He also took care to make even his voice to be like a woman's, and at his carousals not only to indulge regularly in those drinks and viands which could offer the greatest pleasure, but also to pursue the delights of love with men as well as women; for he practiced sexual indulgence of both kinds without restraint, showing not the least concern for the disgrace attending such conduct. (Diod. Sic. 2.23; translated by C. H. Oldfather)

In his description of the Assyrian king, Diodorus follows the long tradition of Greek and Roman attitudes towards eastern peoples. They were widely described as passive, soft, treacherous, feeble and feminine, whereas westerners were thought to be masculine, brave, strong and active (Isaac 2004: 308). By describing Elagabalus as 'Sardanapalus', Dio thus connects the emperor to the tradition of woman-like men, whose masculinity was very much in doubt. So while Herodian is not as direct in his critiques as Dio, connecting Elagabalus with 'eastern luxury' was probably to his readers a clear reference to the emperor's rather feminine gender expression, if not his non-conforming gender identity.

The identification of Elagabalus as an easterner is further articulated through the religious policies for which he was famous. While Dio makes few direct connections between cult practice and gender presentation, he hints obviously in this direction when he combines Elagabalus' eastern appearance with his religious activities. Dio describes in a very hostile and disgusted manner the worship of El'Gabal and some of its cultic practices: circumcision, refusal of eating pork, and Elagabalus' public appearance dressed in Syrian priestly clothes. Moreover, Dio (80[79].11) claims that young boys were sacrificed in 'barbaric rituals', and that animals were fed in the temple with cut genitals. Cutting off genitals is an interesting detail as such, because it obviously points to eunuchs – a group indeed often associated with easterners, such as the eunuch priests of eastern cults such as Cybele (cf. SHA *Heliog.* 7.1; see also Rauhala 2008). From the aspect of gender, it has sometimes been claimed that eunuchs were considered to be 'half-men' with no manly qualities (Isaac 2004: 338). While this might be an exaggeration, ancient sources do point out that the presence of eunuchs upset Roman cultural notions of masculine identity in the western part of the empire and that, because of their castration, eunuchs were perpetually considered to be 'other' in the Roman west (Kuefler 2001: 31–2). Accordingly, Dio strengthens the picture of Elagabalus as a dangerous, degenerate 'other', by his very nature as a feminine easterner.

SEX AND POLITICS

Perhaps the most famous deeds of Elagabalus are related to his sexual behaviour. Nevertheless, Herodian remains rather silent on the subject, and the only more or less direct reference to Elagabalus' femininity in Herodian's work is not even related to sex. In his history, Herodian (5.7.4–5) compares Elagabalus to his successor, Severus Alexander. According to the story, Elagabalus wanted to encourage his cousin and heir to learn the same things he practised himself, such as dancing and other activities required in the worship of the sun-god El'Gabal. However, Julia Mamaea, mother of Alexander, considered these acts disgraceful and directed her son towards more manly activities (cf. SHA *Heliog.* 8.2–4). This detail deserves some attention, as it presents Elagabalus and Julia Mamaea as antagonists who compete over which direction the future emperor should be led. In doing so, they are at least in principle breaking gender boundaries. Elagabalus, a man, encourages Alexander to pursue more feminine activities, while Julia, a woman, tries to provide her son with a more traditional and masculine education. Yet as Julia eventually wins the 'battle' between gender conforming and non-conforming behaviours, the hierarchy of a dominant man over a submissive woman is broken even more clearly. This is a noteworthy detail, as gender hierarchy is something we should not underestimate when examining Greek and Roman culture. In sexual relationships, for example, we can observe a strict hierarchy in which a 'real' man should always be active and act as a dominant partner compared to a 'non-man' (a woman, a boy, a man seeking to play a receptive role in penetrative acts or a slave; Williams 2010: 180–3). Here, gender-conforming behaviour is at once emphasised by Julia and undermined by her taking the upper hand with Elagabalus.

While Herodian is not that straightforward about the issue, sexual hierarchy and its importance seems to be clearly present in Cassius Dio's text. The historian starts mocking Elagabalus (80[79].9.1) for his lack of manhood when reporting on the emperor's marriage to his first wife, Cornelia Paula. Dio comments ironically that Elagabalus wanted a wife in order to become a father, even if he 'could not even be a man'. The historian also reports (80[79].13.1) that Elagabalus was married to and divorced from five different women and that the young emperor had sexual relationships with many others, ignoring imperial moral laws altogether. However, for Dio, this was not a sign of Elagabalus' manliness; rather the historian claims that Elagabalus had intercourse with women simply because he wanted to learn how to please his (male) lovers. In other words, he wanted to learn how to act as a woman in his relationships with other men.

Dio continues his story (80[79].13.2) by reporting that Elagabalus' 'most conspicuous act' was to perform as a female sex worker. He paints a vivid picture of an emperor who would go to taverns wearing a wig and portraying himself as a woman; an emperor who would go to notorious brothels to practice his 'profession'. Eventually, Dio continues, Elagabalus would act as a sex worker in the imperial palace, 'always standing nude at the door of the room, as the harlots do, and shaking the curtain which hung from gold rings, while in a soft and melting voice he solicited the passers-by' (80[79].13.3). It is impossible for us to know if Elagabalus indeed provided sex to male customers, although it is very likely that the story is a fabrication of Dio (or other opponents of Elagabalus). After all, in Roman thinking, sex workers were part of the lowest, most despised social group, akin to actors, players and singers. Thus, this may well be Dio's attempt to portray the emperor in as bad a light as possible, and the story is based perhaps on gossip, or simply fabricated by the historian himself, something more recent studies highlight (see, for example, Arrizabalaga y Prado 2010; Icks 2011). However, for our purposes, the veracity of the story is not important. The significant detail is Dio's overtly hostile attitude towards the emperor's feminine role. Dio makes it clear that the young emperor's behaviour differs remarkably from the ideal behaviour of a Roman man in the sexual hierarchy. Moreover, it should also be understood that gender roles normatively associated with sexual behaviour were closely connected to the socio-political hierarchy in the Greek and Roman world (Halperin 1990a: 266). With respect to Rome in particular, two concepts were particularly central in this aspect, *virtus* and *imperium*. *Virtus* pointed to proper manly moral values, such as valour, excellence, courage, character and worth, as opposed to those characteristics typically associated with women, such as excessive softness and lack of self-control. *Imperium*, on the other hand, signified the dominant role of a proper Roman male, who had to keep control in his relationships with women or 'non-men', but also, on a wider scale, with foreign peoples (Williams 2010: 145–8). Thus, for Dio, it was bad enough that Elagabalus behaved contrary to the ideal image of a proper Roman man. Even more despicable for the historian, who too was a conservative Roman senator, was that a ruler of the people, the *Pater Patriae* himself, was in fact a man who took the role of a woman in his relationships.

BECOMING A WOMAN?

So far, we have dealt primarily with issues associated with Elagabalus acting as a woman in a culturally defined field of normative binary gender, for he is portrayed performing acts traditionally reserved for 'non-men'. However, there is one more twist in the story. Dio states (80[79].11.1) that Elagabalus pondered having himself castrated, not for religious reasons (as castration was traditionally associated with some eastern cults), but because of his feminine nature. Later in his history Dio provides a similar statement, describing how Elagabalus asked the doctors to contrive a woman's vagina in his body (80[79].16.7). What we witness here is a step beyond merely challenging traditional gender roles and gender expression towards the actual changing of one's sex in order to become female, presumably to match a feminine expression and a female gender identity. While it is very probable that Dio's primary motif was simply to mock Elagabalus by hyperbolically presenting his actions to be as extreme as possible, this is perhaps not the whole story. Reading Dio's account in context of the cultural ideas of his own lifetime indicates that the question of 'being a man' or 'being a woman' was not as straightforward as one might think for the Romans of the day. Indeed, in deciding if one was a 'man' or a 'woman', the biological aspect was not the only one; there were other important considerations.

By the early third century AD, at least upper-class Romans were quite familiar with the science of physiognomics, according to which the character of a person could be decided from one's behaviour and physical appearance. This was also true in deciding one's masculinity and femininity (Montserrat 2000: 156–7). Indeed, during the times of Dio, Herodian and Elagabalus, physiognomics was already a very old idea. The subject had been addressed by Aristotle in the fourth century BC, and continued to be studied through the centuries, perhaps reaching its high point in the second century AD with Marcus

Antonius Polemon (AD 88–145), an ambassador in Rome to the Emperor Trajan. His handbook on physiognomy was influenced by earlier traditions, but he himself was an acknowledged figure in this field of study as well (Evans 1969: 6–11; for Polemon and physiognomy in general, see Gleason 1995). Indeed, in his work Polemon underlines very directly the importance of physical appearance when determining if one is a man or a woman (Pol. 2.1.192F). After Polemon, we can find direct interest in physiognomics in the fourth century AD (Evans 1969: 15–17), but despite the lack of sources there is no need to think that it was out of fashion during the reign of Elagabalus. After all, one of the most important written sources of the early third century AD, Philostratus, gave an account of Polemon's life in his works (Swain 2005: 126), but also had a close relationship to the imperial circles during the Severan period (Rantala 2017: 11–12).

Even if physiognomy is clearly relevant to the narratives of both historians, it is difficult to trace exact passages in either Dio or Herodian that refer directly to Elagabalus in physiognomic terms. The main problem is that, for Polemon at least, physiognomics is particularly related to involuntary physical characteristics of a person; that is, negative aspects of character that a person might want to conceal, but which can reveal one's 'true' character when noticed. On the other hand, while Herodian seems to consider the feminine character of Elagabalus to be more or less a voluntary one, there is at least one passage in Dio's history that is more vague. According to Dio, when Elagabalus met the aforementioned Zoticus for the first time, he 'sprang up with rhythmic movements' (80[79].3), that is, in a rather feminine manner, quite spontaneously, an act which could point to 'involuntary' action. Moreover, as Dio provides a large number of examples in which Elagabalus behaves like a woman, it is not always possible to separate 'voluntary' and 'involuntary' actions, even if Dio does mention that Elagabalus generally displayed 'affectation' in his actions and in the quality of his voice (80[79].3). All in all, physiognomy is perhaps not distinctively present in historical narratives, but it still offers a more nuanced view of Dio and Herodian, as it surely was part of the intellectual context of early third century AD. Indeed, if we widen the picture from strict physiognomy to more general cases of 'gender-blending', we should also note that even if Elagabalus is in a class of his own with respect to gender issues, Dio also applies femininity to Nero (AD 37–68), another ruler he strongly dislikes. For example, at one point Dio directly states (72[71].6) that Nero was not a man but a woman, as witnessed by his voice, lyre-playing and beautiful appearance; he returns to this theme in other parts of his history as well (70[69].9; 70[69].28). The *topos* of portraying a bad emperor such as Nero as a woman can also be found in the stories of other Roman historians (especially Suet. *Ner.* 28–9; Tac. *Ann.* 15.37), but Dio's views on the subject are by far the most extreme.

CONCLUSION

Generally, when we evaluate Elagabalus and his gender-blending activities in the account of these two third-century historians, it appears there is not much we can take at face value. Both historians have their own agenda, and eventually both portray the emperor in a way that fits their respective literary missions as much as possible. Thus, we must be extremely careful when we try to understand the 'real' Emperor Marcus Aurelius Antoninus Augustus beyond the character of Elagabalus. On the other hand, it is very likely that Elagabalus was indeed seen by many Romans of the period as a foreigner, an exotic easterner. Given the traditional stereotype of easterners as soft, feminine people in Greek and Roman literature, this would have given the historians a weapon to use against Elagabalus who was, after all, a Syrian prince and a priest of an oriental sun-cult. Of the two historians, Dio certainly used this weapon more critically.

In the bigger picture, both historians see the young emperor as an 'other', someone strange and alien, but the similarities tend to end there. For Herodian, Elagabalus' otherness is primarily connected to his appearance, to his alien looks. There are hints of femininity, especially since everything eastern had by nature some feminine connotation in the Greco-Roman literary tradition. Nevertheless, Herodian is silent on issues such as the emperor's same-sex relationships, or his hopes of changing sex. For Herodian, the acts of Elagabalus were ridiculous, but that was simply because the emperor was a young fool who did not realise the damage he did to himself through his eastern appearance and exotic behaviour. Herodian's Elagabalus was an entertaining figure, a subject of a good tale, but hardly a dangerous character.

If we compare Herodian's account to that of Cassius Dio, we can indeed notice clear differences. As we have seen, it was particularly the ambiguity around masculinity and femininity in Elagabalus' behaviour that irritated Dio. At first glance, his very strict condemnation seems somewhat odd. During the reign of Elagabalus, Dio did not reside in the capital, but worked in the provinces and returned to Rome for senatorial and consular duties only after the fall of the emperor. Thus, Dio could not have been shocked by any personal experience of an emperor behaving badly. Dio's attitude, then, can perhaps be explained by the simple fact that gender and, more specifically, the idea of 'proper' or traditional gender roles and behaviour had a tremendous significance for Roman society and social order. The most obvious aspect of this is the highly patriarchal nature of Roman society, demonstrated in part by the limited authority and participation of women in many public and private duties (see, for example, Cantarella 2003; Mustakallio 2013; Thomas 1996). However, the significance of gender was much broader than that. It was present not only as a legal, but also as an 'unofficial' entity in all spheres and strata of the Roman Empire; it can be found not only in the literature of the Roman elite, but also in sources related to everyday life, such as inscriptions or papyri. Gender deeply affected the ways Romans behaved, but also how they thought and remembered and, as a result, how they built their identities (see Rantala 2019).

Accordingly, as Dio, a conservative Roman senator, creates an image of true Romanness by portraying it against the 'other' (in this case, the Emperor Elagabalus), he does so by relying heavily on gender issues, and particularly on gender expression and gender identity. While he does criticise the feminine gender expressions, such as the clothing, appearance and religious views of the young emperor, it is Elagabalus' unmanly, unchaste sexual behaviour combined with his dismissal of clear gender identity that seems to be the defining factor in deciding who is a true Roman and who is not. Ultimately, Dio stresses that the most important thing, particularly for the emperor, is to act as a real Roman. For Dio, a central part of this self-presentation was to avoid crossing the line between the strict binary ideals of masculinity and femininity – something that Elagabalus was unable to do.

PART III

Transgender Identity

Allegorical Bodies: (Trans)gendering Virtus in Statius' *Thebaid* 10 and Silius Italicus' *Punica* 15

Dalida Agri

INTRODUCTION

In Statius' *Thebaid* and Silius' *Punica* (produced in the Flavian era of the first century AD), gender ambiguity is a striking and defining trait of divine Virtus, which bears much hidden significance. First, it flags gender as a key point of interest in both depictions of the allegory. Personified allegories are traditionally gendered as female (with the exception of *Somnus* in *Metamorphoses* 11), so the gender instability which seems to characterise Flavian depictions of Virtus would make it less controllable in terms of unity of meaning. Second, such a feature brings these two Flavian texts together in a way that compels us to read one alongside the other. In this chapter, I would like to indulge in some 'experimental' reading by looking at one passage through the other, since it is not clear which passage takes historical precedence (though Statius most probably does), and see how the notion of gender is being used, articulated and manipulated in order to reconfigure the meaning of epic *virtus* for the Flavians.

This reading practice implies, to borrow Stephen Hinds' words (1998: 10), a 'shift [in] the balance of power away from the poet and towards the reader' since 'poetic meaning is always, in practice, something (re)constructed *by the reader* at the point of reception'. If there is a period in Roman literary history where this type of reading can be exercised without risking the charge of going 'off track' or being 'far-fetched', it is the Flavian period – even more so in the context of the literary relationship between Statius and Silius. As contemporaries, it is not inconceivable that Statius may have edited a particular passage in reaction to Silius, or vice versa (on recent scholarship discussing Statius and Silius' literary relationship, see Manuwald and Voigt 2013; Ripoll 2015). And, concomitantly, as discussed in the introduction to this volume, newly posited or renewed enquiries into gender representations in classical media also contribute to the opening of (potentially) new interpretations which may have eluded our attention so far. Here, both notions of gender and poetic influence are coterminous and enhance the analysis of one through the other, as we shall see.

That both Statius and Silius chose to define personified Virtus in such concrete physical terms as to favour fluidity in gender, a relatively unobserved trait in the gendering of allegorical figures, is too conspicuous not to be seen as indicative of literary interaction. It is worth noting at this point that the development of personification allegory in Augustan poetry (27 BC to AD 19) has made it an obvious site of intertextual engagement for the Flavians, much owing to Ovid's and Virgil's innovative contributions to the field (Lowe 2008). The passages under study are Statius' *Thebaid* 10.632–49 and Silius' *Punica* 15.20–31. In the first two sections, I will explore Statius' and Silius' use of gender ambivalence in their depiction of personified Virtus and how key intertexts and allusions highlight links between gender and morality. In section two, I will also look at how Silius' passage specifically engages with that of Statius through the lens of gender and the impact on Silius' own conception of divine Virtus. A third section will focus on a cross-reading of the two texts in order to assess how one is potentially reworking the other, and how bringing these two texts together creates new and larger meanings in either direction.

CROSS-DRESSING VIRTUS IN *THEBAID* 10

In Statius' *Thebaid* 10, the fratricidal war opposing Eteocles and Polynices is raging, and Thebes is now facing a long siege by the Argive army led by Polynices. Menoeceus, Creon's youngest son, is in the midst of a successful *aristeia*, when disguised Virtus appears to the youth and persuades him to commit suicide in order to save Thebes from destruction. Menoeceus' suicide is now commonly read as an act of failed *devotio*, as it subsequently creates a whole new range of problems for Thebes (Heinrich 1999; Ganiban 2007: 148; Bernstein in Manuwald and Voigt 2013: 151). The appearance of Virtus closely tails Tiresias' prophecy, urging the death of the 'latest-born descendant of the serpent's race'. Creon understands that the life of his son, Menoeceus, is at stake and tries to silence the seer. Too late, Fama, the incarnation of rumour, is on its way spreading the dreaded oracle across Thebes. This is the moment Virtus chooses to appear to Menoeceus (*Theb.* 10.632–49):

> Diva Iovis solio iuxta comes, unde per orbem
> rara dari terrisque solet contingere, Virtus,
> seu pater omnipotens tribuit, sive ipsa capaces
> elegit penetrare viros, caelestibus ut tunc
> desiluit gavisa plagis – dant clara meanti
> astra locum quosque ipsa polis adfixerat ignes;

iamque premit terras, nec vultus ab aethere longe.
sed placuit mutare genas, fit provida Manto,
responsis ut plena fides, et fraude priores
exuitur vultus. abiit horrorque vigorque
ex oculis, paulum decoris permansit honosque
mollior, et posito vatum gestamina ferro
subdita; descendunt vestes, torvisque ligatur
vitta comis (nam laurus erat); tamen aspera produnt
ora deam nimiique gradus. sic Lydia coniunx
Amphitryoniaden exutum horrentia terga
perdere Sidonios umeris ridebat amictus
et turbare colus et tympana rumpere dextra.
(ed. D. R. Shackleton Bailey, Loeb Classical Library 2003)

Divine Valour is a close attendant to the throne of Jupiter, whence she is accustomed to approach the earth, though rarely to be lavished upon the world, whether the omnipotent father sends her down or she herself chooses to penetrate the heart of worthy men, as now when joyful she descends from the celestial regions! The bright stars give way to her travel, and those fires that she herself had affixed to the heavens. She strides the earth now, and yet her face is not far removed from the sky; but it pleased her to change her appearance, and she becomes vatic Manto, so that genuine belief would be granted to her speech, and by deceit she sheds her former demeanour. The horror-inducing look, the glow of vigour were gone from her eyes, something of charm remained, and a softer beauty; the sword cast aside, she took instead the prophet's wand. Her dress falls to her feet, and the sacred fillets are bound over her unkempt hair (where before the laurel was); yet her fierce countenance and unbridled gait betray the goddess. And so laughed the Lydian mistress at Amphitryon's son, when deprived of his bristling hide he spoiled the delicate Sidonian tunic with his vast shoulders, threw the distaff into confusion and smashed the small drums with his hand. [All translations are mine, unless stated otherwise.]

Here, the use of the simile (*sic Lydia coniunx* . . . 10.646) is rather puzzling, to say the least, because it is both unexpected and disruptive in tone. Richard D. Williams even describes it as 'wholly inappropriate in the context of the transformation of the majestic goddess Virtus' (Williams 1972: 109). However, what the simile essentially does is allow Statius to suggest that Virtus' change of appearance amounts to cross-dressing, which in itself indicates an attempt to alter her gender identity. But what does it mean? Technically, the Latin term *virtus* sits between two genders: though *virtus*, as a quality, is etymologically

defined as exclusively male (*vir*-tus), it is grammatically gendered as female
(Cic. *Tusc. Disp.* 2.18.43). There were questions already in antiquity regarding
this inconsistency between *virtus* meaning literally 'manliness', which came to
designate 'martial courage' and 'bravery' and its feminine grammatical category.
The passage above shows Virtus, shortly before her encounter with the Theban
youth. Following conventional divine behaviour, Virtus unsurprisingly takes
human appearance, and in the process she dresses like Manto, the seer's daughter, thus becoming the wearer of human female attire. But it is through the use
of the simile that she is paradoxically stamped with the charge of cross-dressing.
In fact, the simile alludes to a particular scene in Ovid's *Fasti* 2.317–26, which
describes Hercules dressed in queen Omphale's clothing and struggling to look
the part of a woman (on this passage see also Hughes in this volume):

> dumque parant epulas potandaque vina ministri,
> cultibus Alciden instruit illa suis.
> dat tenuis tunicas Gaetulo murice tinctas,
> dat teretem zonam, qua modo cincta fuit.
> ventre minor zona est; tunicarum vincla relaxat,
> ut posset magnas exeruisse manus.
> fregerat armillas non illa ad bracchia factas,
> scindebant magni vincula parva pedes.
> ipsa capit clavamque gravem spoliumque leonis
> conditaque in pharetra tela minora sua.
> (ed. J. G. Frazer, Loeb Classical Library 1976)

While the attendants were making ready the viands and the wine for the
celebration, she arrayed Alcides [Hercules] in her own garb. She gave
him delicate tunics dipped in Gaetulian purple; she gave him the dainty
girdle, which had girded her waist. For his belly, the girdle was too narrow; he broke the clasps of the tunic as he tried to thrust out his large
hands. He shattered the bracelets unfit for his arms, his big feet split the
little shoes. She herself took the heavy club, the lion's skin, and the lesser
weapons placed in their quiver.

In this passage of the *Fasti*, Hercules is not very successful in his attempt to
fit into Omphale's clothes: his large hands have made the clasps of the tunic too
loose, the queen's girdle is too small for his belly, and his arms are too bulky for the
delicate bracelets. Even though Hercules is made to dress like a woman, it only
reinforces his hyper-masculine idealised body, which clearly is not the 'correct'
body for the hyper-feminine clothing of the queen. Returning to Statius' passage, the Ovidian simile, whose focal point is cross-dressing, implies that by
tampering with her appearance, Virtus is voluntarily attempting to tweak her

gender. In fact, the simile depicts Virtus as if she were covering herself with female otherness, and not successfully either – which is rather odd, since she is textually gendered as female.

At this point, Virtus is very much like and unlike Hercules, the cross-dresser. The simile seems to suggest that, like Hercules, Virtus is attempting to appear as another gender by dressing like Manto, in a way that highlights a gap in the performance. Simultaneously, unlike Hercules, she is encoding herself in the language of gender rather deceptively. Yet deception is also another point of contact between the simile and its hosting narrative. In the *Fasti*, Hercules unwittingly deceives Faunus, the god of the Lupercalia, when the latter attempts to rape queen Omphale at night and instead finds himself in bed with the transvestite hero, having been tricked by the soft fabric of Hercules' dress. Unlike Hercules in the *Fasti*, where the hero's deception of the god is not deliberate, Statius' Virtus is purposefully seeking to deceive young Menoeceus through her borrowed looks. In the *Fasti*, the comedy of cross-dressing turns into a sexual comedy, and deception plays a crucial role in enabling it. Faunus climbs into Hercules' bed, thinking it is the queen's, but upon discovery, humiliation ensues for the god as the improbable couple burst into laughter. In *Thebaid* 10, the passage is very serious in tone, but the simile does not seem to be.

There is also a startling contrast between the bleak exterior of Virtus as she morphs into Manto and the light-hearted playfulness of the Ovidian simile, which leaves the reader rather puzzled as to how to reconcile the two. For instance, every detail of Virtus' description in Statius contributes to her creation as a conflation of multiple sinister models, which have been previously pointed out: Denis Feeney (1991: 382–5) sees Homer's towering Eris (*Il.* 4.442–5) and Virgilian Fama (*Aen.* 4.175–7), Elaine Fantham (1995) is reminded of Allecto in *Aeneid* 7, where the Fury also puts on the *vittae* to disguise her cruel features (*torva facies*), and Virtus' infernal connections with Virgil's furies, the Dirae (*Aen.* 12.845–9) have led Randall T. Ganiban (2007: 142) to coin the expression 'intertextual fury'. As one reads on, Virtus' behaviour also consolidates her chthonic associations. After she has exhorted Menoeceus to forsake combat and embrace death, she touches his hand and releases herself into his heart, like Allecto with Turnus. Even Virtus' choice of Manto as her mortal medium is an arresting thought in itself. From the outset, this is justified as the goddess' attempt to foster belief (*fides*, 640) in Tiresias' prophecy within her victim. What better substitute than the seer's daughter to act as her father's spokesperson? But such a choice is equally telling and worrying given Manto's necromantic skills in *Thebaid* 4, strongly evocative of Lucan's dreadful Erichtho.

Going back to the Ovidian simile, how does one reconcile its farcical, absurd tone with the dark, hellish background of Virtus? It is a tricky one to account for, but we could look for links. For instance, if Virtus is transvestite Hercules, then who is the fool? Who plays the part of Faunus, the god who gets tricked in the end? Is it Menoeceus who dies with the (false) belief that his death will save Thebes? And/or personified Pietas, who foolishly sweeps in at the end to retrieve Menoeceus' dead body alongside Virtus (*Theb.*10.780–2)? Indeed, Virtus' speech is rhetorically crafted to sell self-inflicted death to the youth as an act of *pietas* to his city, to the gods; Apollo demands it, she claims (*hoc urguet Apollo*, 10.667). The deception is far-reaching: one could include all of the Thebans who tragically believe the prophecy, as Fama spreads it, apart from Creon who resists the oracle.

And so what begins as an Ovidian farce turns into a *comédie noire* with the death of Menoeceus, a casualty that will call for more. The failure of Creon's kingship ultimately rests upon his inability to cope with the loss of his youngest son. His grief blinds his judgement, goading the king into revenge. The resulting effect, a fatal decree that forbids burial of the fallen enemy, leads to yet another war and Creon's death at the hands of Theseus. Even Capaneus is misled by the oracle as he provocatively uses the spot of Menoeceus' fall to test the power of the prophecy ('*hac*', *ait*, '*in Thebas, hac me iubet ardua virtus/ire, Menoeceo qua lubrica sanguine turris./experiar quid sacra iuvent, an falsus Apollo*', 845–7), a test that will prove fatal to the Argive hero.

On the metapoetic level, it can be argued that Virtus is actively seeking comparison with morally dubious models, conceivably as a way to account for her distorted use in an epic that concerns itself with civil war: her loaded touch of Menoeceus, and self-revealing mode of departure openly align Virtus with other destructive deities, such as Allecto, of course, but also Iris (*Aen.* 9.14–15). Even the Ovidian simile points in the direction of Virtus' intertextual awareness: just as Hercules is aware of what he is doing as he attempts to slip into Omphale's clothes, so is Virtus as she conscientiously rethinks her appearance to resemble her sinister 'models'.

The motif of cross-dressing as a *comparandum* to the divine practice of switching appearance before approaching mortals raises questions not just about how successful Virtus is in her attempt to disguise herself, but also about the appearance of gender. What she loses in excess of austerity (*horrorque vigorque/ex oculis*), she gains in softer beauty (*honosque/mollior*) – perhaps to appear less threatening, and therefore more feminine. She discards the sword (perhaps too phallic a symbol) and feigns virginal modesty as her robe falls to her feet (*descendunt vestes*). Her cover-up still falls short of the mark, as her hard (masculine?) features (*aspera ora*) and wide gait (*nimiique gradus*) retain something of her divine/virile personification. The difficulty to determine which traits pertain to her divinity and which to gender underscores her liminality. Fantham (1995) observes: 'with the *aspera ora* of Virtus we can compare the "asperity" of the warriors Mezentius and Thybris (*Aen.* 7.647, 729) and the three females dignified by the epithet: Juno *Aen.*1.279, Allecto, the *pestis . . . aspera* of 7. 505, and Camilla, 11.664'. Male, divine, virile woman, it is all

there. Virtus' liminality in gender and status stigmatises her attempt at morph-
ing into a definite gender as a fraud. The Latin *fraude* unequivocally describes
her enterprise in borrowing Manto's identity and covering herself with 'female
otherness' as an imposture. This particular imposture could be read as a metaphor for the incongruity of *virtus* in the context of civil war. Perhaps the idea
here is that any expression of *virtus* in the *Thebaid* is a perversion because it
operates within a war so unnatural that any kind of heroism is tainted; a view
that would deeply resonate with a Roman audience given Rome's historical
record of civil wars. That divine Virtus should encode herself so deviously in
the language of gender speaks of Statius' conception of Virtus as an avatar of
the chthonic feminine forces ruling the *Thebaid.*

ANDROGYNISING VIRTUS IN SILIUS' *PUNICA* 15

In *Punica* 15, Virtus is morally far less ambiguous and emphasis on her gender
duality tends to highlight the male component of *virtus* as a quality. Is this
Silius' attempt to replace the *vir* at the heart of *virtus*? Possibly. Statius' Virtus is
thought-provoking but gets rather bad publicity, something that Silius is moved
to rectify – assuming that he is reacting to Statius. Like Statius, Silius brings in
personified Virtus at a turning point of the narrative (or perhaps it does emerge
as a turning point in Statius, after reading Silius). At the beginning of *Punica* 15,
Scipio, a young aspiring hero, is pondering the role he should play in the war
between the Romans and the Carthaginians led by Hannibal. Rome is losing
and personal tragedy has struck: both his father and uncle were killed fighting
the Carthaginians. Scipio wants revenge but he is too young. The youth is very
much conflicted. This is the moment when Virtus and Voluptas approach the
Roman youth: both allegories represent opposites in life choices. The first advocates a life of hardship eventually crowned with deserving glory, the second, a
life filled with easy pleasures and the absence of pain. Each woman bears specific
features that portend a set of moral trappings (or lack of thereof), clearly playing
with Roman cultural expectations of what a morally acceptable or unacceptable
woman looks like (*Pun.* 15.20–31):

> cum subito assistunt, dextra laevaque per auras
> allapsae, haud paulum mortali maior imago,
> hinc Virtus, illinc virtuti inimica Voluptas.
> altera Achaemenium spirabat vertice odorem,
> ambrosias diffusa comas et veste refulgens,
> ostrum qua fulvo Tyrium suffuderat auro;
> fronte decor quaesitus acu, lascivaque crebras
> ancipiti motu iaciebant lumina flammas.
> alterius dispar habitus: frons hirta nec umquam

composita mutata coma; stans vultus, et ore
incessuque viro propior laetique pudoris,
celsa humeros niveae fulgebat stamine pallae.
(ed. by J. D. Duff, Loeb Classical Library 1968)

Suddenly, stood to his right and left two figures flown down from the
sky, and exceeding by far mortal stature: Virtue was on one side, and on
the other, the enemy of virtue, Pleasure. The latter exhaled Persian scents
from her head's crown, her ambrosial hair flowing free, and she shined in
her dress, wherein Tyrian purple was embroidered with shimmering gold;
her hair pin gave to her brow a studied beauty; and her roving wanton
eyes shot forth flame upon flame. The appearance of the other was different: her brow and hair were unkempt, not fashioned by ordered locks,
her eyes were steady, in face and gait she was more like a man, and she
revealed a cheerful modesty. Her tall stature was enhanced by the snow-
white robe she wore.

Here, Voluptas is unequivocally female, and a seductress, morally dangerous
for the ethos of the epic hero. In contrast, the blending of male and female features within Virtus raises questions in terms of gender-based moral reasoning.
The entire passage is an obvious replay of Prodicus' didactic tale 'On Heracles',
as recounted by Socrates to Aristippus in Xenophon's *Memorabilia* 2.1.34. In
the tale, Heracles, on the cusp of manhood, similarly meditates the proper path
to take in life, when he is approached by two women, Arētē (Virtue) and Kakia
(Vice), each striving to win him over (Xen. *Mem.* 2.1.21–3):

φησὶ γὰρ Ἡρακλέα, ἐπεὶ ἐκ παίδων εἰς ἥβην ὡρμᾶτο, ἐν ᾗ οἱ νέοι
ἤδη αὐτοκράτορες γιγνόμενοι δηλοῦσιν, εἴτε τὴν δι' ἀρετῆς ὁδὸν
τρέψονται ἐπὶ τὸν βίον εἴτε τὴν διὰ κακίας, ἐξελθόντα εἰς ἡσυχίαν
καθῆσθαι ἀποροῦντα, ποτέραν τῶν ὁδῶν τράπηται: [22] καὶ φανῆναι
αὐτῷ δύο γυναῖκας προσιέναι μεγάλας, τὴν μὲν ἑτέραν εὐπρεπῆ τε ἰδεῖν
καὶ ἐλευθέριον φύσει, κεκοσμημένην τὸ μὲν σῶμα καθαρότητι, τὰ δὲ
ὄμματα αἰδοῖ, τὸ δὲ σχῆμα σωφροσύνῃ, ἐσθῆτι δὲ λευκῇ, τὴν δ' ἑτέραν
τεθραμμένην μὲν εἰς πολυσαρκίαν τε καὶ ἁπαλότητα, κεκαλλωπισμένην
δὲ τὸ μὲν χρῶμα, ὥστε λευκοτέραν τε καὶ ἐρυθροτέραν τοῦ ὄντος δοκεῖν
φαίνεσθαι, τὸ δὲ σχῆμα, ὥστε δοκεῖν ὀρθοτέραν τῆς φύσεως εἶναι,
τὰ δὲ ὄμματα ἔχειν ἀναπεπταμένα, ἐσθῆτα δὲ, ἐξ ἧς ἂν μάλιστα ὥρα
διαλάμποι, κατασκοπεῖσθαι δὲ θαμὰ ἑαυτήν, ἐπισκοπεῖν δὲ καὶ εἴ τις
ἄλλος αὐτὴν θεᾶται, πολλάκις δὲ καὶ εἰς τὴν ἑαυτῆς σκιὰν ἀποβλέπειν.
[23] ὡς δ' ἐγένοντο πλησιαίτερον τοῦ Ἡρακλέους, τὴν μὲν πρόσθεν
ῥηθεῖσαν ἰέναι τὸν αὐτὸν τρόπον, τὴν δ' ἑτέραν φθάσαι βουλομένην
προσδραμεῖν τῷ Ἡρακλεῖ καὶ εἰπεῖν: ὁρῶ σε, ὦ Ἡράκλεις, ἀποροῦντα
ποίαν ὁδὸν ἐπὶ τὸν βίον τράπῃ. ἐὰν οὖν ἐμὲ φίλην ποιησάμενος, ἐπὶ

τὴν ἡδίστην τε καὶ ῥᾴστην ὁδὸν ἄξω σε, καὶ τῶν μὲν τερπνῶν οὐδενὸς ἄγευστος ἔσῃ, τῶν δὲ χαλεπῶν ἄπειρος διαβιώσῃ.

(ed. E. C. Marchant, Loeb Classical Library 1923)

When Heracles was passing from boyhood to the state of youth, wherein the young, now becoming their own masters, show whether they will approach life by the path of virtue or the path of vice, he went out into a quiet place, and sat pondering which road to take. And there appeared two women of great stature coming towards him. The one was fair to see and of high bearing; and her limbs were adorned with purity, her eyes with modesty; sober was her figure, and her robe was white. The other was plump and soft, with high feeding. Her face was made up to heighten its natural white and pink, her figure to exaggerate her height. Open-eyed she was, and dressed so as to disclose all her charms. Now she eyed herself; anon looked whether any noticed her, and often stole a glance at her own shadow.

When they drew closer to Heracles, the first kept an even pace; but the other, all eager to outdo her, ran to meet him crying:

'Heracles, I see that you are in doubt as to which path to take towards life. Make me your friend; follow me, and I will lead you along the pleasantest and easiest road. You shall taste all the sweets of life; and hardship you shall never know.'

(trans. E. C. Marchant with adaptations)

In Silius, the passage mostly reads as a duplication of the Prodicean tale, with Scipio substituted for a young Heracles. Mostly a duplication, but not entirely: the b(l)ending of Virtus' gender is nowhere to be seen in Prodicus, but it is unmissable in Silius: 'in face and gait she was more like a man' (*orel incessuque uiro propior*). Also in Silius, the motif of Virtus' hair 'seeking no borrowed charm from ordered locks' does not feature in Prodicus, but it is mentioned in Statius where the goddess binds her dishevelled hair with the priestess's customary fillets of white wool (*torvisque ligaturl vitta comis, Theb.*10.644–5). Is this Silius engaging with Statius' image of Virtus taming her hair, and implying that, unlike his own Virtus, Statius' creation is counterfeiting a more appropriate look? If so, Silius could very well have used Statius' Virtus as a model for his own Voluptas, whose hair-pin is said to convey the look of propriety (*fronte decor quaesitus acu, Pun.* 15.26).

The Prodicean traces in Silius' handling of his allegories are equally telling. In Silius' passage, Virtus is purposefully made to look like Greek Arētē, and as such, she is meant to stand as her Roman equivalent. Further similarities between the two allegories abound. The tall stature, the look of modesty and the white robe all point out their moral credentials, except for the male face and gait, which feature only in Silius. Here, Virtus' undisguised virility acts as a reminder that

Roman *virtus* is deep-down culturally constructed as a male quality, repositioned as a positive masculine ideal through *pudor* mirroring Arēte's *aidos* in Prodicus. In fact, the purpose of Prodicus in Silius is to reinstate Virtus as a moral agent, as if to redeem her Statian subversive past. Unlike in Statius, Virtus' gender duality is not framed as transgressive: there is no ambiguity regarding her moral affiliation. Her speech even repeats that of Arēte. She is clearly marked as the opposite of Voluptas.

READING SILIUS THROUGH STATIUS AND VICE VERSA

Although intertextuality is usually framed as one poet trying to outdo his competition, there is the possibility that one poet is not automatically reacting *against* but rather elaborating on/paying tribute to the work of another, as if in a dialogue. This thought is all the more inviting given that our two Flavian poets were solid contemporaries. It is not impossible that Statius may have edited a particular passage to engage specifically with Silius' poetry, and Silius may have just done the same. This could potentially explain the incongruity of the *Fasti* simile in Statius' passage as a later addition. There is, of course, no way of knowing, but this should not prevent us from trying to read one passage through another and see where it leads. For instance, when Silius writes 'in face and gait she was more like a man', is this a 'gloss' (to borrow Hinds' word) of the Ovidian simile in Statius? As mentioned above, there is no sign of gender ambivalence in Prodicus' depiction of his allegories. Therefore, Silius must be reacting to Statius, who so emphatically manipulates the gendering of Virtus. In that case, it is tempting to read this 'gloss' (if it is what it is) as Silius' attempt to undercut the memory of the Ovidian simile and to reassign to Virtus all the moral trappings of her Prodicean self. The emphasis on *ore incessuque viro propior* ('in face and gait she was more like a man', *Pun.* 12.29–30) is somewhat amending Statius' Virtus whose *honos* (beauty, 10.642) is said to be *mollior* (softer) – too elegiac in tone perhaps for Silius' conception of epic divine Virtus.

If we were to go back to Statius' passage with Silius in mind, similarities between Statius' Virtus and Silius' Voluptas quickly emerge. It is remarkable, for instance, that Virtus, in exhorting Menoeceus to reject combat (*linque humiles pugnas, Theb.* 10.664), is aligning herself with Voluptas, who equally seeks to dissuade young Scipio from martial pursuits (*quis furor hic, non digne puer, consumere bello/florem aevi, Pun.* 15.33–4; *ni fugis hos ritus, Virtus te saeva iubebit/ per medias volitare acies mediosque per ignes, 40–1*). In Statius, Virtus also promises quick immortality (*rape mente deos, rape nobile fatum,/ i, precor, accelera, Theb.* 10.670–1); in Silius, the path leading to Virtus' abode, and immortal glory, is steep, *ardua* (*celso stant colle penates,/ ardua saxoso perducit semita clivo, Pun.*15.101–2), not easily accessible, it is a strenuous (Herculean?) journey that takes time. But according to Statius' Virtus, the path to glory is immediate and not so steep, although ironically it is, quite literally even, since

Menoeceus must ascend to the walls from which he leaps to 'glory'. In that regard, Statius' Virtus is still closer to Silius' Voluptas, whose road metaphor privileges the image of an easy route (*at si me comitere, puer, non limite duro/iam tibi decurrat concessi temporis aetas, Pun.* 15.46–7). The rhetorical comparability between Statius' Virtus and Silius' Voluptas clearly reinforces the former's subversiveness. Even when Statius' Virtus is likened to her actual equivalent in Silius, it is not to her advantage. For instance, when Voluptas accuses Virtus of driving Scipio to an untimely death as she did his father and uncle (*Pun.* 15.42–5), it is also true of Statius' Virtus vis-à-vis Menoeceus:

haec patrem patruumque tuos, haec prodiga Paulum,
haec Decios Stygias Erebi detrusit ad undas,
dum cineri titulum memorandaque nomina bustis
praetendit nec sensurae, quod gesserit, umbrae.

She it was who sent your father and uncle down to the Stygian waters of Erebus, she who threw away the lives of Paulus and the Decii, while holding out a glorious epitaph on the tomb that covers his ashes to the ghost that cannot even be conscious of the great deeds he did on earth.

So much so that, in Statius, when Virtus exhorts Menoeceus to send his soul to heaven (*caeloque animam*, 10.665), she is/becomes what Voluptas makes her out to be in Silius. Is this Silius manipulating Statius, or is it Statius deriving his Virtus from Voluptas? If Statius is reacting to Silius, then the moral ambiguity of Virtus, and *virtus* as a quality overall in the *Thebaid*, is further reasserted. If Silius is reacting to Statius, then there is a clear attempt to rehabilitate *virtus* as an epic ideal that improves on all his forbears/contemporaries. These are the possible readings. Yet one question remains: is it possible that Prodicus is already there in Statius' passage and that Silius is raising it to the level of intertext by borrowing it so extensively? I am not entirely convinced by it, although the Ovidian simile in Statius shows a post-Prodicean version of Hercules who seems to have failed to live by his choice. If we were to read Statius with Silius in mind, Statius might have inserted the *Fasti* simile as a way to create ambiguity that is not directly available in the Prodicean contest. Statius, by having his Virtus (falsely) take the didactic role of Arēte, and resembling so closely Silius' Virtus and Voluptas all at once, complicates the picture and undercuts the possibility of an exclusively positive reading of *virtus* as an ideal, not just within the *Thebaid*, but anywhere else.

Silius, by contrast, is keen to salvage *virtus* once it becomes associated with Scipio. The emphasis on Virtus' virile face and gait in *Punica* 15 redefines her as a male-gendered physical ideal, mindful of the need for a Roman physical victory over the treacherous Carthaginians. But the overly determined female modesty (e.g. cheerful *pudor* and snow-white dress, which stands for moral incorruptibility), is really what lends *virtus* moral substance. So the Romans, by claiming *virtus* to their side, can also reclaim a sense of moral agency. In Silius, Virtus' blending of gender is paradoxically not so blended together in the detail as each attribute is clearly gender-specific, and made explicitly so, which speaks volumes in terms of gender-based moral reasoning. In Statius, Virtus is distinctly gender-ambivalent. As a result, it is worth observing that, unlike Karla Pollmann (2008: 365), who argues that the poet 'removes *virtus* from *viri* (or the other way round)', rather the gender confusion of personified Virtus seems to actively align the *vir* with the feminine chthonic agents of *nefas*, thus making any display of masculine *virtus* in civil war narrative deeply problematic.

CONCLUSION

In Statius, the Ovidian simile characterises Virtus' endeavour to inscribe herself in the language of 'another' gender as an imposture, but it also makes it all the more difficult to visualise what Virtus really looks like, and this is the point. Her gender instability further reflects her potential for manipulation. In Silius, Virtus' duality in gender is more clearly defined. The female gendered 'purity' of the snow-white dress and immaterial *pudor* assign to the male physicality of *virtus* a sense of moral agency that is so lacking in her Statian self.

Statius, by perhaps deliberately having Virtus speak like Silius' Voluptas (or is it the other way round?), is paradoxically turning her into a parody of herself: stripped of its moral trappings, epic *virtus* is a form of lust – lust for death. Following Virtus' departure, Menoeceus is driven to the wall by a love of death (*amor leti*, 10.677). The devaluation of epic *virtus* is semantically signalled through the transfer of elegiac terms such as *amor* and *mollior* (as in *honosque mollior*, 42–3) into epic context, subverting Virtus into a demanding but sinister mistress.

The question of gender draws attention to the fact that, in both narratives, female allegories are used as models/sources of inspiration for male heroic behaviour, however morally justifiable or successful the underlying intention or response is. Variations in gender identity flag up the issue of liminality as culturally double-edged. This has a lot to do with gender difference in moral orientation, which stems from gender-typed constructs of morality grounded in Roman social structures and expectations of gender-based behaviour. Gender liminality is either perceived as dangerous, which then leads to a demonisation of the powerful female element (Statius' Virtus), or conveys a more balanced sense of moral reasoning (e.g. Silius' Virtus). In any case, both passages distinctly argue against the notion of a culturally strict gender binary in epic.

CHAPTER 10

Performing Blurred Gender Lines: Revisiting Omphale and Hercules in Pompeian Dionysian Theatre Gardens[1]

Lisa Hughes

Select Pompeian homes displayed Dionysian-themed visual representations linked to gender reversal in or near garden settings. For the purposes of this study, I focus on two key mythological characters, the foreign Lydian Queen, Omphale, and the hero, Hercules, who offer a glimpse into how this gender reversal can potentially reinforce or break down perceived social and cultural barriers for ancient Roman diners. While ancient visual culture was not intended to be a precise reproduction of literary accounts, I suggest that an adaptation of Ovid's *Fasti* 2.313–31 is pertinent to our understanding of the visual representations of the pair in or near garden settings, which I call 'Dionysian Theatre Gardens'. When Omphale and Hercules appear with visual representations of Dionysus and his retinue, I maintain that the pair serve as props in the backdrops of small-scale Julio-Claudian performances (for example, pantomime, poetic recitations) that were part and parcel of the convivial experience. The inclusion of the cross-dressed pair in a theatrical context, I will argue, made gender reversal an intrinsic part of both domestic and public life.

CONSTRUCTING THE DIONYSIAN THEATRE GARDEN

The connections between the foreign deity Dionysus, gardens and dining spaces help to garner a better understanding of the potential for Omphale and Hercules' theatrically staged presence within Pompeian *domus*. Dionysus was an omnipresent figure in the ancient Mediterranean, worshipped as the embodiment of transformation through wine, revelry and performance (Henrichs 2013: 560). These multiple personae appear in visual representations of many Pompeian homes, primarily as wall paintings and sculpture in or near garden spaces, where dining took place. The representations include the deity himself, satyrs, maenads and theatrical masks, as well as subsidiary characters related to the Dionysian mythic cycle (Neudecker 1988: 47–51; von Stackelberg 2009: 27). In order to explain the presence of such imagery within garden settings, two explanations emerge, which, as will become more apparent below, are not mutually exclusive. The first maintains that the garden evokes or represents a bucolic setting for cultic or ritual performances that were synonymous with the god Dionysus (Dwyer 1982; Mastroroberto 1992; Seiler 1992; Zanker 1998: 171; von Stackelberg 2009; Petersen 2012). The second connects garden space to theatre space in order to convey a means of self-representation for the patron of the home (Zanker 1998: 21–3; von Stackelberg 2009: 82–3). Rather than separating these two explanations, I argue that both the cultic and theatrical aspects of the deity together make up what I call the 'Dionysian Theatre Garden', and that this will be an integral component in understanding Omphale's and Hercules' theatrically staged presence. Dionysian cultic and theatrical connections have been linked specifically to Pompeian wall fresco contexts (e.g. Dionysian faux marble masks and frescoed pinakes that make up the garden decorations of the 'Blue Cubiculum' in Pompeii's House of the Orchard, I.9.5–7, Tronchin 2012: 269). More work needs to be done, however, in terms of integrating actual garden spaces thematically with other architectural features and material remains found in select Pompeian homes.

Based on the preliminary findings of residential contexts in the Bay of Naples area, the study for the 'Dionysian Theatre Garden' is part of a larger project, 'The Art of Performance in the Theatre Gardens of Ancient Rome'. I have found four distinctive features that constitute the 'Dionysian Theatre Garden': (1) dining areas (*triclinia, oeci, cenationes, cenacula* – here I acknowledge the problematic nature of these terms with respect to function and space; see Allison 1993; Leach 2004) located in or in close proximity to garden spaces; (2) stages/ raised platforms; (3) sculpture, frescoes, mosaics and other artefacts related to Dionysian myth; and/or (4) plantings or representations of plantings related to Dionysus. Dionysian-themed decorative schemes also figure into the placement of theatrical architectural forms and gardens within select smaller scale *domus*, the focus of this discussion. It has been established that dining rooms and gardens proper were used for performance within the *domus* (Csapo 2010: 185–6), and other areas such as porticoes and stage-like structures (permanent or temporary) could have added to the performative experience (von Stackelberg 2009: 95; Csapo 2010: 186). Dionysian-themed artworks in these areas were also part and parcel of the performative experience (Dunbabin 2003: 8–9). As Katharine von Stackelberg (2009: 82–3) notes, 'The popularity of Dionysian imagery as garden ornaments may have been inspired by this connection between garden space and theatre space, both created by artifice and allusion.' If we take the multifaceted Dionysus as the god of theatre and wine, his presence in addition to that of his retinue in the visual representations in and around the dining areas of select Roman homes could also do more than act as a subtle reference to the theatre. One could argue that spaces allotted for visual representations of

Dionysus and other mythic characters associated with the deity could serve as backdrops and props for actual small-scale performances, such as pantomime.

These features provide a basis for understanding further the representations of Omphale and Hercules selected for this study. In what follows, the goal is to situate the performative roles of Omphale and Hercules within the Pompeian 'Dionysian Theatre Garden', which echo the elements of sartorial exchange, grove setting and sexual comedy found in Ovid's *Fasti* 2.313–31. This, in turn, suggests a possible rationale for performing pantomime plays or other small-scale performances of Omphale and Hercules in a domestic setting. In doing so, we are able to catch a glimpse into how these small-scale performances provide a social role for gender reversals in both domestic and public contexts.

SITUATING OMPHALE AND HERCULES WITHIN THE POMPEIAN DIONYSIAN THEATRE GARDEN

The following discussion of Omphale and Hercules focuses on a sample of Pompeian artistic representations of the pair: three fresco paintings and one full-length sculpture in the round, all dating roughly to the Julio-Claudian period (the first half of the first century AD). First, in Figure 10.1, from the House of M. Lucretius (IX. 3.5, Dyer 1891, room 14, fresco, central panel, east wall), we see the cross-dressed pair. A frontal Hercules dons select pieces of Omphale's wardrobe in the centre, and Omphale, wearing his Nemean lion headdress, stands to the right propped by his club, and looks back to him. The pair stands in the presence of Dionysian characters such as erotes, maenads and Dionysus himself. To the viewer's left of Hercules stands Priapus. Second, Figure 10.2, from the House of the Golden Cupids (VI.16.7, Seiler 1992, garden peristyle), is a marble statue depicting a standing figure of Omphale, represented in a similar fashion to the representation found on the fresco painting from the House of M. Lucretius (Fig. 10.1). Dressed in a long tunic, she appears with Hercules' Nemean lion headdress. Although the arms on this statue have been damaged, it is very likely, on the basis of Omphale's stance and the position of the left arm, that she propped herself with Hercules' club. Third, in Figure 10.3, from the House of the Prince of Montenegro (VII.16.10, Strocka 1984, fresco, '*oecus*'), Omphale and Hercules appear convivially in a grove setting. Here, Omphale, seated with female attendants at her side on the viewer's upper left, watches the activities of one group of erotes carrying off Hercules' club and another group who draw away his quiver while standing on the altar. A drunken Hercules reclines on the viewer's lower left side of the panel. Finally, Figure 10.4, from the House of Siricus (VII.1.47, Niccolini 1854, fresco, room 7), shows a variant of the representation found on Figure 10.3. Again set within a grove, female attendants accompany Omphale, seated on the viewer's upper left. She watches two groups of erotes: one carries away Hercules' club below the

Figure 10.1 Pompeii, IX.3.5, Room 14, House of M. Lucretius, Naples, Museo Archeologico, Inv. 8992, fresco, first century AD, Zanker 1999: 123.

Figure 10.2 Pompeii, VI.16.7. Statue of the Omphale, within the physical garden, House of the Golden Cupids, marble, second century BC to first century AD. H. 0.625 m. Naples, Museo Archeologico, Inv. 1483, Ridgeway 207–8; Seiler 1992, 117, 124.

Figure 10.3 Pompeii, VII.16.10, *Oecus*, House of the Prince of Montenegro, Naples, Museo Archeologico, Inv. 9000, fresco, first century AD, Lorenz 2007: 674.

Figure 10.4 Pompeii, VII.1.47, Room 7, House of Siricus, fresco, first century AD, Lorenz 2007: 674.

altar, the other, the quiver while standing atop the altar. The drunken Hercules reclines on the viewer's left. In contrast to the episode depicted in figure 10.3, we see the addition of a group of five male convivial figures reclining on the viewer's upper right side. In addition, these four examples appear in houses that feature gardens, dining areas and Dionysian-themed artefacts, which, in turn, formulate Dionysian Theatre Gardens. As will become more evident, situating the representations of Omphale and Hercules near or within these spaces is highly suggestive of the pair's performative roles as seen in the *Fasti*.

Compositional, sartorial and symbolic attributes serve to identify the pair as Omphale and Hercules. In this sample, Omphale can appear standing (Figs 10.1, 10.2) or seated (Figs 10.3, 10.4). Her sartorial features include: Hercules' Nemean lion headdress covering her head (Figs 10.1, 10.2) or lying near her side (Figs 10. 3, 10.4); Hercules' club appearing in her hand (Figs 10.1, 10.2) or near her side (Figs 10. 3, 10.4); an ankle-length tunic (Figs 10.1–10.4) and a mantle draped around her body (Figs 10.1–10.4). Hercules can appear standing (Fig. 10.1) or reclining (Figs 10.3, 10.4). Sartorial features include a mantle draping his otherwise unclothed body (Fig. 10.1), or Omphale's tunic (Figs 10.3, 10.4). Other wardrobe markers include a vine wreath (Fig. 10.1) and sandals (Fig. 10.1).

The representations in my analysis feature one of two distinctive settings that may allude to Ovid's reference to the pair dining in a garden/grove in the *Fasti* (see below), either directly (Figs 10.3, 10.4) or indirectly (Figs 10.1, 10.2). These representations, moreover, substantiate the presence of the Dionysian Theatre Garden. Figure 10.1 indirectly situates Omphale and Hercules in a grove on the basis that the dining room where the painting was found is set directly off the garden. Hercules leans against the figure of Priapus, the god of fruit plants and guardian of gardens, identified by his tunic laden with fruit. The visual reference to Priapus provides not only an allusion to physical gardens/ groves, but also conflated references to other comic rape narratives involving this deity in Ovid's *Fasti* (for example, Lotis and Vesta, Ov. *Fast.*, 1.391–440, 6.319–48; Richlin, 2014: 150–2; Fantham 1983: 198–9). Other panel frescoes found in the same room as Figure 10.1 point to the thematic treatments of dining and theatrical performance whereby erotes perform pantomime and dine in outdoor Dionysian garden scenes (see Naples Archaeological Museum Inv. 9255; Naples Archaeological Museum Inv. 9205; Schefold 1957: 249; for musicians and dancers as part of the pantomime troupe, see Hall 2008: 16).

The statue of Omphale in the House of the Golden Cupids (Fig. 10.2) takes us out of the realm of fresco painting and into the physical setting of an actual garden. The statue's original findspot was in the west end of the peristyle garden, near the raised stage structure that housed a *triclinium*, and therefore in close proximity to a dining space (Seiler 1992: 117, 124). Although statuary of Hercules is not preserved in the archaeological record from this home, Omphale's presence within the garden bedecked with Dionysian-themed imagery is befitting and offers more than a prized piece of sculpture (Vorster 1999: 16). Rather, like her visual representations in fresco, the cross-dressed Omphale offers a means to stage gender reversals, which went hand in hand with Roman dining and theatrical performance.

In contrast, Figures 10.3 and 10.4 both point directly to the garden, with the figures reclining and dining in a grove. Notably in both images Omphale and Hercules are not seated together, but recline in different areas of the composition. In addition, the presence of an altar in the centre of the composition defines the space as a sacred grove. In Figure 10.4, the outdoor convivial setting is similar to actual tripartite dining structures appearing in *triclinia*, with the notable exception that the altar replaces the conventional *mensa* (table) as the centrepiece. When entering an indoor or outdoor triclinium, viewers would face tripartite structures that could be permanent or movable couches (*lecti*) arranged around a central table (*mensa*) (Schmitt-Pantell 2006). These couches had specific names based on their position within the room. Moving from left to right we have the first position, *imus* (lowest), second, *medius* (middle) and third *summus* (highest). The Romans also carefully chose the positions where hosts and guests would sit while dining. The host and his family would be delegated to the *lectus imus*, high-status guests to the *lectus medius* and low-status guests to the *lectus summus* (Schmitt-Pantell 2006).

In Figure 10.4, there is an important difference with respect to designated gender roles and arranged seating in Roman dining practice. If we take Pedar W. Foss's reconstruction of the status designations for diners and seating arrangements, Omphale takes the primary role at the *lectus imus* and assumes the role of *domina*, blurring conventional gender lines for traditional dining practices in which the *dominus* would assume this position (Foss 1994: 52; see also Roller 2006: 155–6 for wall painting as a means to reflect on dining practices and values). Dionysus and entourage are seated at the *lectus medius*, and Hercules reclines alone and inebriated in the position of the *lectus summus*. The inclusion of not only Omphale and Hercules, but also other mythic figures within a Dionysian setting would allow diners to consider the experiences of other social classes, foreigners and women, thereby promoting a sense of identity and community (Fredrick 1995; Wilkins 2005; Roller 2006; Hales 2008; Severy-Hoven 2012; von Stackelberg 2014).

Finally, while all of these examples appear in dining areas and other rooms located in close proximity to the Dionysian Theatre Garden, there are variations of Omphale and Hercules' appropriation of each other's clothing. Clothing was a clear marker of social status in the Roman world. Kelly Olson (2014: 189) has remarked, 'Men (and women) were to be clearly distinguished by clothing; the sartorial blurring of gender boundaries was ridiculed and censured by many.' Yet sartorial blurring did indeed exist, as the examples from Pompeii show. Stefan Ritter (1996) notes a similar phenomenon when representations of Omphale and Hercules appear on Arrentine pottery and gemstones dating to the late Republic and Augustan periods. Yet, in instances where Omphale does not don Hercules' clothing and weaponry (Figs 10.3, 10.4), Katharina Lorenz (2007: 675) has concluded that 'such pictorial representations reduce the explosive potential of transvestism with regard to the subversion of social and gender roles, and instead locate it in the less controversial world of Dionysian reveling'. I do agree with Lorenz's assertion about the power 'transvestism' or cross-dressing has in its ability for subversion, but I would argue that transgender may be a more suitable term to use as it encompasses gender binaries for identity, expression and social role reasons (see, for example, the observations of Ash, p. 173, in this volume). Moreover, the roles of Dionysian allusions and contexts, as I have argued, should not be underestimated for their ability to subvert conventional social and gender roles. This is further substantiated where examples of the pair appropriating each other's clothing do appear.

SITUATING OMPHALE AND HERCULES IN OVID'S *FASTI*

And now she was reaching the grove of Bacchus and the vineyards of Tmolus, and dewy Hesperus was riding his dusky steed.

She enters a cave, its ceiling paneled with tufa and living pumice; right at the entrance there was a babbling stream. And while the attendants prepare the banquet and the wine to drink, she dresses Alcides up in her own attire.

She gives him delicate tunics dyed in Gaetulian purple; she gives him the smooth girdle which has just been round her own waist. The girdle's too small for his belly; she undoes the tunics' fastenings so he can push his great hands through; he'd broken the bracelets not made for those arms; his great feet were splitting the little sandal-straps. She herself takes the heavy club and the lion spoil, and the smaller weapons stored in their quiver. That's how they give their bodies to sleep.

They lay apart, on couches placed close to each other. Why? Because they were preparing for the rites of the god who discovered the vine, and when day dawned they would perform them in purity.

(Ov. *Fast.*, 2.313–31, trans. Wiseman and Wiseman 2011: 26–7)

Ovid's account of Omphale and Hercules sets the stage to provide a possible explanation for the scantily clad priests (*luperci*) appearing in the annual Roman purification festival known as the *Lupercalia* (Ov. *Fast.*, 2.303–58; on this passage see also Agri in this volume). In 2.310–29, we meet the pair in a vineyard dedicated to Bacchus (Dionysus). They exchange clothes, dine and take to sleep in separate beds. The *Lupercalia*'s patron deity, Faunus, enters the sleeping chamber and unsuccessfully attempts to assault the cross-dressed Hercules, mistaken for Omphale. As a result, Faunus' comical distaste for sartorial deception subsequently serves as the basis for the rites' unclothed attendees (Robinson 2011: 206–8, 224–5). Ovid's detailed comedic account of sartorial exchange not only sets the stage for both Faunus' foiled assault and the explanation for the *luperci*, but also plays into a performative reading of transvestism. The act of cross-dressing takes place when Omphale takes Hercules' club, the lion-skin headdress, and minor weaponry. Hercules, in turn, receives the foreign queen's tunic, belt, bracelets and sandals, despite the fact they are simply not quite the right fit (for the metapoetic connotations of the clothing exchange see Newlands 1995: 60; Hejduk 2011: 24–5).

My interest lies in the ways setting and sartorial exchange feature in Ovid's account of Omphale and Hercules as a way to signal the narrative cycle of the Pompeian visual representations. For example, the scene takes place in a Lydian vineyard grove dedicated to Bacchus and forms the basis for Ovid's acknowledgement of Dionysian themes (Robinson 2011: 235, 243). Moreover, in the grove there is the cave, fashioned with panelled ceilings and equipped with couches for dining and sleeping. The cave, in turn, provides the setting for Omphale and Hercules' convivial activities, their sartorial exchange, as well as for Faunus' foiled assault. Matthew Robinson (2011: 236) notes three possible allusions for the cave's presence. It could serve as a *locus amoenus* (pleasant spot), a common location for sexual assault in Latin literature; a metapoetic Virgilian allusion to the consummation between Dido and Aeneas (Fantham 1983: 184); or a Vitruvian reference (Vitr. 5.6.9) to satyr play settings (Littlewood 1975: 1064).

In the ancient world, transvestism was no stranger to ritual and theatrical performances (Robinson 2011: 237–9). For instance, the ritual associations with transvestism are linked to komastic and Dionysian revelling, as well as marriage (Fantham 1983: 195–7; Miller 1999; Robinson 2011: 237; Surtees 2014). Theatrical associations with cross-dressing appear in satyr plays, Greek comedies or mime and pantomime (Littlewood 1975; Fantham 1983: 192–201; Barchiesi 1997: 238–46; Wiseman 2002; Wiseman 2008: 217; Robinson 2011: 225). In the case of the cross-dressed pair in Ovid's *Fasti*, there is clearly a fusion between the ritual and theatrical elements (Fantham 1983: 196; Robinson 2011: 238), but most importantly, as Elaine Fantham notes: 'this passage of *Fasti* describes a sequence of events that could be only understood as pantomime by any onlookers, not because he has composed it for pantomime but most probably because he has derived it from pantomime' (Fantham 1983: 201; also see Ingleheart, 2008: 204; Zanobi 2014: 36). This fusion of ritual and theatrical elements in relation to grove setting, character wardrobe and sexual comedy may also carry over into Pompeian visual representations of Omphale and Hercules.

Existing scholarship devoted to the pair in Roman art, however, does not always align with such an interpretation. For example, Omphale and Hercules are identified symbolically as part of Octavian's anti-propagandistic campaign against Cleopatra and Antony (Varner 2008: 190; Zanker 1988: 56–8: Kampen 1996a: 235). Plutarch's *Antony and Demetrius* 3.4 serves to provide an analogy between Omphale and Hercules and Cleopatra and Antony. In his analysis of the passage, Alexander Lessie (2015: 47) states, 'Plutarch remarks that Cleopatra compelled Antony to abandon great and necessary undertakings just as we see Omphale in paintings taking away Hercules' club and stripping off his lion skin.' Lessie (2015: 46), however, questions this as an overt attack and emphasises that Plutarch likely was exploring the theatrical character of Antony. Oliver Hekster (2004) also readily and effectively dismisses the propagandistic treatment of Hercules and Omphale in art and literature, but does not provide an alternative reading for their presence.

Other scholarly references to the visual representations of Omphale and Hercules use this evidence as a means to substantiate antecedent influences of the pair in the literary or artistic traditions of the Mediterranean world. Elmer Suhr (1953: 261–2), for example, identifies briefly the comedic references and ritualistic elements of marriage in the portrayal of the cross-dressed pair, but focuses primarily on tracing the origins for the pair in the Mediterranean world. Fantham (1983: 198–200), working from Konrad Schauenberg's 1960 analysis, refers to Pompeian wall paintings thought to be derived from now-lost Hellenistic originals as possible sources for Ovid's treatment of the pair in the *Fasti*, but dismisses this interpretation on the basis that Ovid likely drew ideas from dramatic or narrative poetry. Finally, Natalie Kampen (1996a: 235–6, 244) sees Hellenistic models as possible sources for the visual representations dating to first centuries BC and AD, but emphasises that the representations adhere to the poetic traditions of this period to reinforce social disorder. Kampen (1996a: 244) does acknowledge, however, that 'the couple were associated with Bacchic cult as initiates and as figures for gender slippage and fluidity of boundaries', but this does not happen until the second century AD (for a similar treatment see also Zanker 1999). The goal of my study attempts to offer a broader cultural, historical and political understanding of the visual representations of Omphale and Hercules, particularly through the lenses of gender reversal in the private theatrical performances in the Julio-Claudian period.

It is at this point that I call for a diachronic reading of the pair that fits within the lenses of theatrical performance and Roman dining in the Julio-Claudian period. By incorporating visual representations of the pair (both fresco and sculpture) with the Dionysian Theatre Garden, I further build on Lorenz's (2007: 655) assertions that mythological wall paintings 'can lead to a better understanding of the foundations of cultural norms and ideas'. This is especially important in terms of how we may come to a better understanding of gender reversal in the Julio-Claudian period. More specifically I show how a cultural shift occurs for Omphale and Hercules' presence under the theatre-loving emperors Augustus (27 BC to AD 14) and Nero (AD 54–68) either to reinforce or break down perceived social and cultural barriers.

WEAVING OMPHALE'S AND HERCULES' THEATRICALITY IN THE JULIO-CLAUDIAN PERIOD

To garner a better understanding of the visual representations of Omphale and Hercules within the Dionysian Theatre Garden during the Julio-Claudian period, it is necessary to weave together a brief narrative that incorporates both Greek cultural tastes and Roman theatre as they pertain to the cultural milieu of the emperors Augustus and Nero. This will demonstrate the cultural relationships that exist between our cross-dressed pair, Dionysus and gardens. Furthermore it will reinforce that representations of Omphale and Hercules reinforce gender and social inclusivity not only through a ritual, but also within a theatrical setting.

Within Augustus' circle was Maecenas, a formidable patron of the Augustan poets, and a purveyor of Greek culture as well as Roman theatre. It is highly suggestive that he staged performances of Omphale and Hercules on his expansive estate, Rome's Gardens of Maecenas. Peter Wiseman (2016) has recently demonstrated, through an analysis of the *Elegia in Maecenatem,* that Maecenas performed the role of Hercules and his wife, Terentia (a known dancer), the role of Omphale. The passage refers to the classic gender reversal roles when Omphale asks Hercules to lose his power paraphernalia, the club and lion skin, in order to sport woollen flowing tunics amongst her maidens who spin wool. Although the storyline in the *Elegia* differs from the one presented in the *Fasti,* it does share similarities with Propertius, *Elegy* 4.9, where Hercules refers to himself spinning wool while wearing Omphale's Sidonian palla (Debrohun 2003: 161–2). Propertius' account of the cross-dressed pair is seen as a means to promote Julio-Claudian identity and inclusivity (Lindheim 1998; Panoussi 2016) by providing a reading of female authority to the ritual practice of spinning wool.

Maecenas was also known to play the role of Dionysus in theatrical performances. He also maintained a close relationship with his freed slave and lover, the pantomime dancer Bathyllus of Alexandria, who was known to have acted in Dionysian performances and brought pantomime to Rome (Wiseman 2016). As to where these performances would have taken place, Wiseman (2016) offers Maecenas' Hellenistic Persian-style gardens as the perfect setting, complete with auditorium, gardens and Dionysian-themed sculpture. With respect to audience, the presence of the Dionysian imagery in the Gardens of Maecenas during Augustus' reign likely appealed to a 'private sphere made up of the princeps and those closest to him, a limited number of initiates who formed an elite chosen by the god, who promised them incomparable happiness' (Wyler 2012: 8). In essence, it is suggestive, but by no means conclusive that under Augustus, Dionysus belonged to the elite sphere of Roman society. During the Augustan period, we catch glimpses of the interconnected relationships between Omphale, Hercules, Dionysus, gardens, theatrical performances and cross-dressing. They seem, however, to be contained within the circle of the emperor. Nevertheless, the seeds of inclusivity are planted with respect to breaking perceived social and gender roles.

An ideological shift, however, would occur during Nero's reign, when the emperor *qua* actor came to embody the philhellenic model, which, in turn, encompassed a much broader sphere of community and inclusivity. Dionysus became a deity open to all spheres of Roman society. Key factors in developing this shift in the Dionysian mindset would be Nero's revival of Antony's Hellenic cultural aspirations, as well as the emperor's ability to continue building associations with Dionysus. In doing so, Nero was able to reach out to and create community amongst those typically excluded from traditional elite practices, that is, the common people (Champlin 2003: 173). While evidence abounds for Nero's philhellenic predispositions (see Mratschek 2013), it is less substantive when it comes to direct associations with Dionysus. Dionysian overtones do appear in conjunction with architectural settings that relate to the historical Greek traditions of the theatre. For example, it is suggestive that Nero sought to instil the message of community and inclusivity in his refurbishment of the stage building of Athens's Theatre of Dionysus Eleuthereus in AD 60 (Sear 2006: 116). The permanent stone theatre initially constructed in the fifth century BC became the site to celebrate the *Dionysia Megala* festival (Bieber 1961: 213; Sturgeon 1977: 45). Although the nature of the festival has been the source of much attention and controversy (Goldhill 1990), it can be said that it included ritual processions involving Dionysian cross-dressing, as well as performances of tragedy and comedy to ultimately include citizens, foreigners, slaves, women and children alike (Miller 1999; Spineto 2005: 185–325; Lateiner 2009; Surtees 2014: 288–90). This coincides with Dionysus' liminal function 'as a progenitor of *communitas*' or community, whereby 'the community is stripped of all social barriers and social distinctions so that members of the community can experience one another "concretely" as equal' (Csapo 1997: 254).

Nowhere else is this notion of community better reflected than in the building of the expansive Domus Aurea, which also incorporated the Gardens of Maecenas on its eastern end (Champlin 2003: 203; Mratschek 2013: 51–2; Hauber 2014: 134–8). Built after the fire of AD 64, yet still not completed at the time of Nero's death in AD 68, the Domus Aurea provided the optimal setting to stage gender reversal roles and thereby promote community and inclusivity. As Richard Beacham (1999: 224) has noted, the 'innate theatricality' of the Domus Aurea is seen in its 'several hundred rooms, extensive colonnades, mosaic vaulting, splendidly coffered ceilings (some fashioned from ivory panels), and probably a private theatre'. Under Nero, garden and theatre space essentially became fused, as seen in his wooden amphitheatre in the Campus Martius, as well as other private stage complexes in the city of Rome (von Stackelberg 2009: 84–5; Hughes 2014: 229–31). Moreover, it was within such a setting that Dionysus came to symbolise a deity accessible to all. In reference to the Dionysian imagination in Neronian Rome, Stephanie Wyler (2012: 12) maintains that 'The fantasy of a primitive lack of differentiation between sexes and species seems to have been at the heart of the artistic experimentations of Nero himself, both in his theatrical behaviour and in the conception of his palace.' Wyler's comment does open the door to see the possibility for Nero's Dionysian theatrical proclivity as a means to promote sexual difference and social inclusion. This conclusion, however, still carries a serious negative connotation. In essence, 'the fantasy of a primitive lack of differentiation between sexes and species' is seen as going against the grain of 'traditional' Roman values and mores advocated by ancient Roman historians (for example, Tacitus and Suetonius; see Champlin 2003: 53–83; Hughes 2014: 229–32). A similar sentiment crosses over into modern scholarship when Catharine Edwards (1994: 91) states: 'acting – associated with the foreign, the female, and the fake, with licence bearable so long as lowly persons enjoyed it, but intolerable in the hands of an emperor – summed up Nero's offenses'. This negative sentiment towards Neronian performative gender blending appears to run contrary to what we see in the Pompeian archaeological record.

Performative gender blending to promote community and inclusivity goes hand in hand in Pompeii with the artistic representations of Omphale and Hercules that appeared in or near the Dionysian Theatre Gardens. The presence of the foreign queen and the feminised hero served well to reflect the performative milieu of the Neronian period. Audience and performers came from all strata of society (slave, freedman and freeborn). Performers, moreover, included pantomimes, jugglers, acrobats, *Homeristae* (performers of Homer; Starr 1987: 199–200), dancers, musicians and singers (Rosati 1999: 86). They enacted a wide array of Greek and Latin drama associated with tragedy, comedy and satyr plays, both in large-scale monumental theaters and within Roman houses (Jones 1991: 188; Beacham 1992; Jory 2002; Hunt 2008; Hughes 2014). In Neronian Rome in general and Pompeii in particular, the ability of individuals from many walks of life (including the emperor *qua* actor himself) to perform in public and private settings was acceptable practice in certain circles (Champlin 2003: 53–83; Hughes 2014: 229–32).

CONCLUSIONS

Using Omphale and Hercules as a case study only begins to scratch the surface, so to speak, to convey an understanding of the multivalent theatrical imagery and practices associated with the god Dionysus within the Roman home and garden settings. The representations of Omphale and Hercules appearing near or in the garden area are clearly connected to Ovid's *Fasti* with both metaphoric and literal allusions to the Dionysian grove. Moreover, the diverse visual representations of the pair, found in and around the garden peristyle, contributed to the diners' experiences to promote community and inclusivity beyond the dining room proper. In essence, the staged presence of Omphale and Hercules served to honour the foreign deity, Dionysus, in a setting where viniculture, dining and theatre were closely associated. It is within this convivial context that these select representations of Omphale and Hercules served to set the stage to break down perceived social and cultural barriers. Gender reversal during the Julio-Claudian period subsequently must be seen as an intrinsic part of both domestic and public life.

NOTE

1. This research was supported by the Social Sciences and Humanities Research Council of Canada. The author would also like to thank the editors of this volume, as well as the anonymous reviewers, for their generous comments and support.

CHAPTER 11

The Politics of Transgender Representation in Apuleius' *The Golden Ass* and *Loukios, or the Ass*

Evelyn Adkins

In the second-century AD novels *Loukios, or the Ass* and Apuleius' *The Golden Ass* (also known as the *Metamorphoses*), the man-turned-into-a-donkey Lucius is sold to a group of priests of the Syrian Goddess. Like the priests of Cybele with whom they are frequently linked, these figures are infamous in Greek and Latin literature for ecstatic music and dance, transvestism, self-castration, and suspect sexuality. In both the Greek and Latin novels, the first-person narrator Lucius calls them *cinaedi*, Graeco-Roman scare figures of gender and sexual deviance. The priests, however, never use this derogatory term, instead calling themselves 'girls' (*puellae*: *Met.* 8.26; *korasia*: *Onos* 36) and using feminine grammatical forms. In their own words, they construct feminine identities, adding to the evidence that some of the followers of Cybele and the Syrian Goddess – commonly referred to as *galli* – were transwomen and other assigned-male-at-birth individuals with diverse gender identities and sexual orientations (Roscoe 1996; Taylor 1997: 336, 371; Adkins 2014: 35–55; Blood 2015; Blood forthcoming; Carlà-Uhink 2017: 16–19). I argue that in the Greek and Latin novels, the primary locus of the priests' contested identities is their speech. By juxtaposing Lucius' interpretation of the priests' speech with their own words, I highlight the role of language as a mechanism of power, focusing on who has the authority to impose meaning and how this affects those whose social labels are at odds with their own identities and self-representations.

While Apuleius' Latin novel is longer and has a different ending than the Greek *Loukios, or the Ass* (hereafter referred to by its abbreviated Greek name *Onos*), both relate the story of Lucius, a Roman Greek aristocrat who is transformed into a donkey. After a year of being stolen, bought and sold, he changes back into a man. Based on the similarities between these novels and the comments of the ninth-century patriarch Photios, they are thought to derive separately from a third novel, the lost Greek *Metamorphoseis* of Lucius of Patrae (Phot. *Bibl.* 129; van Thiel 1971: 1–21; Mason 1994, 1999a, 1999b). Apuleius' narrative is frequently so similar to the *Onos* that parts of it are clearly translated from the Greek, as in this interaction between the priest Philebus and her companions:

> *Onos* 36: But when we came to where Philebus lived – for this was the name of the man who purchased me – as soon as he was before the doors he shouted loudly, 'O girls, I have purchased for you a slave, beautiful and strong and of the Cappodocian race.' (All translations my own unless otherwise noted.)

> ἐπεὶ δὲ ἥκομεν ἔνθα ᾤκει Φίληβος – τοῦτο γὰρ εἶχεν ὄνομα ὁ ὠνησάμενός με – μέγα εὐθὺς πρὸ τῆς θύρας ἀνέκραγεν, Ὦ κοράσια, δοῦλον ὑμῖν ἐώνημαι καλὸν καὶ ἁδρὸν καὶ Καππαδόκην τὸ γένος. (All Greek excerpts from the *Onos* are from MacLeod 1974.)

> *Met.* 8.26: But he led the new slave he had acquired to the house, and as soon as he was there at the threshold he shouted, 'Girls, come see the pretty little slave I've purchased for you.'

> At ille susceptum novicium famulum trahebat ad domum, statimque illinc de primo limine proclamat, 'Puellae, servum vobis pulchellum en ecce mercata perduxi'. (All Latin excerpts from the *Metamorphoses* are from Zimmerman 2012.)

The congruence here, beyond demonstrating Apuleius' translation skills, indicates that the priests' speech was expected to be recognisable to both Greek- and Latin-speaking audiences. This is supported by other literary texts that apply feminine grammatical forms to *galli* (Catull. 63; Hephaestion 12.3; Stat. *Theb.* 12.226; *Anth. Pal.* 7.223). Thus the priests' uses of feminine grammatical forms in the novels are not authorial invention, but most likely represent the real speech of some, if not all, Greek and Roman *galli*.

GALLI AND CINAEDI

Previous studies of the priests of the Syrian Goddess have focused on either the history of gender and sexuality or of religion. With respect to gender and sexuality, the priests are depicted as stereotypical *cinaedi*. Although *kinaidos/cinaedus* seems to have referred originally to a man who performed a style of dance associated with the Near East, by the Imperial period it was a derogatory term for a man who was perceived to move, speak or act in an effeminate way

(Williams 2010: 193–7). In ancient literature, *cinaedi* are portrayed as men who wear make-up and long, brightly coloured clothes, curl their hair, depilate their legs, walk with a shorter or swaying stride and speak in high-pitched voices (Edwards 1993: 68–9; Gleason 1995: 396; see also Penrose in this volume). They are often depicted as actively pursuing a penetrated/passive role in sexual intercourse, especially with men (Kamen and Levin-Richardson 2015a: 450, 453–5). For this reason, some have argued that references to *cinaedi* provide evidence for an ancient, urban subculture of homosexual men at Rome (Richlin 1993; Taylor 1997: 349–57). Others have argued that the term is better interpreted as a slur directed towards gender identity and expression rather than sexual orientation (Gleason 1995: 411–12; Williams 2010: 177–8, 230–45). The *cinaedus* serves as a scare figure, a symbol of failed masculinity (Parker 1997: 60; Williams 2010: 137–9, 196, 193–202; Holmes 2012: 94–9).

Cinaedi and *galli* are closely linked in the Greek and Roman imagination. *Galli* is the Greek and Roman term applied to some of the followers or priests of several cults of Anatolian mother goddesses, including Atargatis (the Syrian Goddess) and the more famous Phrygian goddess, called Meter in Greece, Magna Mater in Rome and Cybele in Greek and Latin literature (see especially Roscoe 1996; Roller 1999; Lightfoot 2003: 1–85). Their cults were quite different in Greece and Rome than in Anatolia, especially in the perceived nature of the *galli*. Though the origins of the term are debated, it appears first in the Hellenistic period and likely derives from the Greek name for Gauls who settled in Asia Minor in the third century BC. Their conflicts with local Greek city-states led to their depiction as 'barbarians' in Greek art and literature, a characterisation shared by the Romans in their own conflicts with western European Gauls. For Greeks and Romans, '*gallus*' thus evoked a sense of uncivilised alterity (Roller 1999: 187–234). The followers of the Anatolian goddesses also inherited long-standing Greek and Roman depictions of 'easterners' as soft, decadent, savage and effeminate, a set of stereotypes that, when combined with more recent Orientalist discourses, still lingers in modern scholarship (Roller 1999: 19–24 offers a well-articulated critique).

The Greeks and especially the Romans, who conceived of masculinity as phallocentric and physically inviolable (Walters 1997), became increasingly obsessed with the concept of the *gallus* as an effeminate easterner: in literary contexts, *galli* are frequently described as eunuchs. While the Greeks and Romans attributed voluntary castration to the eastern origins of these cults, there is limited evidence for it in the pre-Hellenistic Near East (Roller 1998, 1999: 105, 253–6). Our earliest references to eunuch followers of Cybele appear in Hellenistic Greek literature and Roman literature of the late second/early first century BC, over a hundred years after the goddess's induction into Rome (Roller 1999: 263–326; Latham 2012). Our first evidence for the worship of Cybele's consort Attis, often portrayed as the mythological model for castration, also appears in the Hellenistic period

(Roller 1999: 177–81). Thus, as Lynn Roller (1999: 318–19) has shown, the aspect of Cybele's cult that Greek and Roman authors found the most foreign and objectionable – the *galli*, who might perform femininity and/or castration – was a development of her Greek and Roman cults rather than an importation of Near Eastern practice.

Despite the ancient and modern fascination with the image of the castrated *gallus*, we do not know how widespread this practice actually was or what it meant to those who performed it. The myths related by outsiders to explain castration and the feminine dress of the *galli* depict these as a result of madness (Catull. 63), divine punishment (cf. Roller 1999: 239–41) or the avoidance of sexual wrongdoing. For the Syrian Goddess, our most extensive written source is *On the Syrian Goddess* (*De Dea Syria* = *DDS*), attributed to Lucian, the same Graeco-Syrian author to whom the *Onos* is attributed (Lightfoot 2003: 184–208). While the *DDS* provides several aetiological myths for the *galli*, the longest is the story of Combabos, a servant of the Assyrian king who accompanies his queen to Hierapolis to build a temple to Hera, who was syncretised with the Anatolian goddesses (*DDS* 19–27). Before Combabos departs, he castrates himself in case of future allegations that he has slept with the queen and leaves the evidence behind in a sealed box. When accusations are made, Combabos reveals as proofs of his innocence both the contents of the box and his own body. He returns to Hierapolis and remains as a follower of Hera.

Combabos' actions are described as the origins of the *galli*'s practices:

> Each year many castrate and unman themselves (τάμνονται καὶ θηλύνονται) in the temple, whether to console Combabos or to do favour to Hera . . . No longer do they wear male clothing, but don female robes and do women's work (εἵματά τε γυναικεῖα φορέουσιν καὶ ἔργα γυναικῶν ἐπιτελέουσιν). As I heard, the reason for this too goes back to Combabos. What happened was that a foreign woman came to a festival and, seeing him handsome and still in male clothing, was smitten with a great passion; but when she learned he was not a whole man (ἀτελέα) she did away with herself. At that, saddened because he was so unlucky in love, Combabos donned female clothing lest another woman ever suffer the same fate. And this is the reason for the female clothing of the galli (ἥδε αἰτίη Γάλλοισι στολῆς θηλείης). *DDS* 27 (Greek text and translation of the *DDS* by Lightfoot 2003: 264–7.)

This story fits within a larger body of *gallus* myths that attempt to explain why men would voluntarily become eunuchs – a state associated with slavery in Greece and Rome – and wear the clothing of women, who, even if free, had nowhere near the legal, social or economic power of men. Combabos' castration and clothing are depicted as undesirable, self-imposed punishments for excessive masculinity, in this case being too attractive to women (for the Greeks and especially the Romans, masculinity outside the norm, whether it was perceived as excessive or insufficient, was equated with effeminacy). Elsewhere in the treatise, however, Combabos has not only the clothing but also the 'shape' of a woman (*morphē: DDS* 26), and castration is depicted as a choice, not a requirement of the cult (*DDS* 42–3, 50–1). Despite the narrator's masculinist reading of Combabos and the *galli*, the *DDS* is describing gender transition, which may include changes in body, clothing and/or social role (for castration as an avenue for changing one's body to correspond with one's gender identity, see Chakrapani 2016; Blood forthcoming).

Literary depictions of the *galli* and myths like those of Combabos and Attis have led many to point out their similarities with the *hijras* of India and Pakistan (Roscoe 1996: 206–13; Taylor 1997: 332–7; Roller 1999: 320–5). *Hijras* are traditionally assigned-male-at-birth followers of a mother goddess who wear women's clothing and use feminine pronouns. Their foundational stories are so close to those of the *galli* that they likely have a historical connection (Taylor 1997: 332; Lightfoot 2003: 385–6). *Hijras* have long considered themselves a third gender; tapping into international human rights movements, some now identify as transwomen (Nanda 1990; PUCL-K 2003: 16–23, 50–5, 76–8; Narrain and Gupta 2011). Based on comparisons between *galli* and *hijras*, some have argued that the ancient Anatolian cults were likely havens for non-gender-conforming genetic males and feminine intersex individuals (Taylor 1997: 336, 371). H. Christian Blood (forthcoming) stresses that the *galli* should not be viewed as a homogeneous group, but most likely included people who would have identified, in modern terms, along a spectrum of genders and sexualities, including transwomen, cisgender transvestite men, and assigned-male-at-birth individuals who preferred a passive/penetrated role during sex; we should likely add feminine, assigned-male-at-birth, asexual individuals, who might have been marginalised if they did not marry and produce children as was expected of Greek and Roman citizen men.

The *galli*'s diversity is supported by a small body of material evidence. Roman funerary monuments for Cybelean *galli* and *archigalli* (a high priesthood added in the late first/early second century AD) depict them in a variety of gendered or gender-blended clothing (Hales 2002). *Archigalli*, whose inscriptions use masculine names and grammatical forms, are depicted wearing trousers, tunics and caps resembling those of Attis (Vermaseren 1977: nos 261, 395, 401–2, 446–8, 462). Although these would have been interpreted as masculine, their association with the Near East would have carried the baggage of barbarity and effeminacy that the Romans ascribed to this region. The best known dedication for a *gallus* is the Soterides inscription from Cyzicus, dated to 46 BC. While Soterides refers to himself in the inscription using masculine grammatical forms, he is depicted in the relief above wearing feminine clothing (Roller 1999: 332–3; see the similar

Menneas dedication in Bean 1959: 71). He makes the dedication in thanks for the safety of Marcus Stlaccius, his *symbios*, a Greek word meaning 'partner' or 'spouse' (Roscoe 1996: 203). Other images of *galli* depict them wearing the religious garb interpreted as feminine in our literary sources: robes, jewellery and curls or ribbons hanging from the head (Vermaseren 1997: nos 249–50, 466). Each of these demonstrates their subjects' status and pride in their identities as priests of Cybele, who by the second century AD had achieved a high level of visibility and a secure social position; they bear little resemblance to the frenzied, sexually depraved *galli* of Greek and Roman literature (cf. Latham 2012: 101–14).

THE POLITICS OF REPRESENTATION

The story of a man who turns into an ass is fundamentally concerned with issues of identity, language and power. Lucius' transformation into a donkey equates him with a slave in Roman law and in the Greek and Roman imagination (Bradley 2000). Deprived of human speech, he is unable to communicate his identity and social status (Adkins 2014: 111–26). Scholars of the Latin novel in particular have demonstrated that Lucius' first-person narrative, told simultaneously by an aristocrat and an enslaved ass, offers numerous hermeneutic possibilities for the reader interested in identity and authority (Winkler 1985; Selden 1994; on the *Onos*, see Hall 1995: 51–3). Some have examined how these are expressed especially through the contrast between Lucius' human mind and animal body, and Blood (forthcoming) has suggested that this sense of conflict between internal identity and external appearance makes *The Golden Ass* fruitful for understanding ancient trans* experiences. I argue that it is in the speech of the *galli* in the *Onos* and *The Golden Ass* that we see most clearly not only the existence of these ancient transgender and queer communities, but also how their lives as a visible minority were shaped by a politics of representation that often denied their self-identification. I focus on episodes where a speech event or action is understood differently by different characters. Examining how meaning is constructed and authorised in these episodes reveals cultural assumptions about gender identity and power underlying the novels.

My discussion is informed by a variety of approaches to language and power (Bourdieu 1991; Gleason 1990, 1995; Laird 1999), especially the concept of entextualisation as developed in the essays in Michael Silverstein and Greg Urban's *Natural Histories of Discourse*. Entextualisation is the process of transforming 'texts' – including speech, writing, gestures and actions – by re-presenting them within the discourse of another (Silverstein and Urban 1996a: 4, 11; 1996b). As the authors' case studies demonstrate, entextualisation is not an unchanged transfer of meaning; rather, 'a hierarchy is formed in which one mode of representing the world . . . gains primacy over others, transforming modes of representation from an array on a horizontal plane to a ranking on a vertical plane' (Mehan 1996: 253). The conflict over interpretation, especially of the identities of people and groups, is the 'politics of representation' (Holquist 1983; Wenden 2005: 90). Power is held by those who impose a definitive meaning on discourse: dominant individuals, groups or cultures authorise meaning, and marginalised individuals, groups or subcultures are defined by their distance from it (Bourdieu 1991: 53, 66–7, 167, 220–4; Foucault 1982). This is what is at stake for the priests in the *Onos* and *The Golden Ass*, and the fact that Lucius' (mis)representation of their gender and religious identities wins out has much to tell us about the power of language and labels to shape reality.

THE PRIESTS OF THE SYRIAN GODDESS

Before the priest Philebus speaks or even appears to the reader's view, Lucius describes her thus:

> *Onos* 35: For he was a *kinaidos* and an old man, one of those who carry the Syrian Goddess around into the villages and fields and force the goddess to beg.

> κίναιδος γὰρ καὶ γέρων ἦν τούτων εἷς τῶν τὴν θεὸν τὴν Συρίαν εἰς τὰς κώμας καὶ τοὺς ἀγροὺς περιφερόντων καὶ τὴν θεὸν ἐπαιτεῖν ἀναγκαζόντων.

> *Met.* 8.24: Learn what sort of man he was: he was a *cinaedus*, and an old *cinaedus*; bald, but with long, grizzled curls hanging down – one of those vulgar dregs of the common people who, making the streets and towns ring with cymbals and castanets, carry the Syrian Goddess around and force her to beg.

> Scitote qualem: cinaedum et senem cinaedum, calvum quidem, sed cincinnis semicanis et pendulis capillatum, unum de triviali popularium faece, qui per plateas et oppida cymbalis et crotalis personantes deamque Syriam circumferentes mendicare compellunt.

The priests are not only labelled but also characterised as *cinaedi* through stock literary features such as their presumed sexual preferences: in *Onos* 38 and *The Golden Ass* 8.27, they are depicted aggressively pursuing sexually passive roles with a young man, an event Lucius interprets as sexual assault, though the narrative itself leaves the man's consent ambiguous. Additionally, in *The Golden Ass*, the auctioneer at the sale of the ass mocks Philebus by suggesting she stick her face between the donkey's thighs (8.25), and the priests' male slave, described as 'their shared concubine (*partiarius . . . concubinus*)', welcomes Lucius as a source of relief for his exhausted loins (8.26).

In addition to the priests' depiction as stereotypical *cinaedi*, they are described as *galli*, though the term itself is never used. The focus throughout is on aspects of the cult of the Syrian Goddess that Greek and Roman authors found most problematic, including the ritual mendicancy described above (see also Dion. Hal. *Ant. Rom.* 2.19; Cic. *Leg.* 2.22, 2.40) and the 'Phrygian' musical instruments, rhythms and melodies played during religious rituals (*Met.* 8.30; see also Lucr. 2.618–20; Ov. *Fast.* 4.181–4, 4.189–90, 4.193–214). The priests' appearances are also remarked upon, especially in *The Golden Ass*. In addition to Lucius' comments on Philebus' hair, he describes the priests' dress at 8.27:

> On the next day, when each of them had put on multicoloured clothes and hideously beautified himself, smearing his face with caked-on foundation and outlining his eyes with paint, they set out, having put on their caps and saffron-coloured linen and silk dresses, some of them in white tunics decorated all over with flowing purple designs in the shape of lance-points, gathered up with a girdle, wearing yellow shoes on their feet.

> Die sequenti variis coloribus indusiati et deformiter quisque formati, facie caenoso pigmento delita et oculis obunctis graphice prodeunt, mitellis et crocotis et carbasinis et bombycinis iniecti, quidam tunicas albas, in modum lanciolarum quoquoversum fluente purpura depictas, cingulo subligati, pedes luteis induti calceis.

These features, commonly ascribed to *galli* and often to *cinaedi*, are depicted in Roman art and literature as characteristic of the 'effeminate easterner', particularly the distinctive caps and tunics. The image we get of the priests in *The Golden Ass* and the *Onos* – focusing on their gender expression, sexuality and the eastern origin of their goddess – depicts them as unacceptably 'other', at least in the eyes of the narrator (cf. Hijmans et al. 1985: 9; Blood forthcoming on Apuleius' possibly contrasting views).

The priests' constructions of their own identities are quite different, however, as is apparent from Philebus' first instances of direct speech in both novels. After the auctioneer's joke about Philebus' sexuality in *The Golden Ass*, she replies at 8.25:

> 'Or do you think, fool, that I can entrust my goddess to a feral beast, only for him to suddenly upset and throw off her divine image, and for me, poor girl, to be compelled to dash about with my hair loose and seek a doctor for my goddess lying on the ground?'

'An me putas, inepte, iumento fero posse deam committere, ut turbatum repente divinum deiciat simulacrum, egoque misera cogar crinibus solutis discurrere et deae meae humi iacenti aliquem medicum quaerere?'

Philebus responds to the auctioneer's sexual joke by asserting her religious devotion and gender identity. She describes herself using the feminine adjective *misera*, which I have translated as 'poor girl'. She also draws attention to her hair, marking as feminine a feature Lucius used earlier to describe her as an old *cinaedus*. Yet this first interaction demonstrates the politics of representation that affect the priests' experiences in both novels: since Philebus' speech is embedded – entextualised – within Lucius' narrative, Lucius' representation of her as a *cinaedus* predominates, especially when supported by the auctioneer.

I now return to the scene with which I begin (*Onos* 36; *Met.* 8.26). When Philebus returns with the donkey, she greets her colleagues as 'girls' in both novels; in *The Golden Ass*, she also applies to herself the feminine participle *mercata*, 'purchased'. Her friends pick up the thread of her jest:

Onos 36: Immediately they mocked Philebus with these words: 'This is not a slave, but a bridegroom for yourself! Where did you get him? May you be blessed for this fine marriage and may you soon birth for us foals just like him.'

ἤδη ταῦτα ἐς τὸν Φίληβον ἔσκωπτον, Τοῦτον οὐ δοῦλον ἀλλὰ νυμφίον σαυτῇ πόθεν ἄγεις λαβοῦσα; ὄναιο δὲ τούτων τῶν καλῶν γάμων καὶ τέκοις ταχέως ἡμῖν πώλους τοιούτους.

Met. 8.26: Turning up their noses they mocked their leader with various remarks: that in truth he had brought not a slave, but indeed a husband for himself. And they said 'Hey! Don't eat up such an obviously lovely little chick alone, but share him sometimes with us, your dovies, too.'

nare detorta magistrum suum varie cavillantur: non enim servum, sed maritum illum scilicet sibi perduxisse. Et 'Heus,' aiunt 'cave ne solus exedas tam bellum scilicet pullulum, sed nobis quoque tuis palumbulis nonnumquam inpertias.'

In Greek, the priests use feminine grammatical forms for Philebus (*sautē*, *labousa*). In both texts, they tease her about her 'husband' and add further jokes that reinforce her gender identity: in the Greek, they joke that she will give birth to foals, and in the Latin, they ask her to share her cute husband with them. With the single exception of *solus* in the Latin above (either a textual error or

Apuleius' deliberate choice to destabilise Philebus' identity), the priests in both novels employ only feminine grammatical forms and concepts, using speech to construct a shared feminine gender identity.

Other characters, however, reject this identity. When Philebus calls the priests 'girls', the narrator Lucius immediately follows:

> Onos 36: But those girls were a crowd of *kinaidoi*, the colleagues of the man Philebos . . .

> Ἦσαν δὲ τὰ κοράσια ταῦτα ὄχλος κιναίδων συνεργῶν τοῦ Φιλήβου . . .

> Met. 8.26: But those girls were a chorus of *cinaedi*, who . . .

> sed illae puellae chorus erat cinaedorum, quae . . .

Lucius reinterprets the speech of the priests not as an expression of femininity, but as proof of effeminacy (cf. Skinner 1997: 12 on 'feminine' vs. 'effeminate'). His representation is strengthened by his linguistic choices: in the *Onos*, Lucius never refers to the priests in the feminine; in *The Golden Ass*, he does so only once and only for the sake of grammatical agreement (the relative pronoun *quae* in 8.26). In all other instances, he refers to the priests using only masculine grammatical forms. Despite the priests' feminine self-representation, Lucius – and the dominant Roman culture to which he belongs – re-presents them as male, albeit unnaturally effeminate.

In *The Golden Ass*, this depiction of the priests as 'unnatural' is further conveyed through descriptions of their voices as 'broken', 'hoarse', 'effeminate', 'discordant' and 'wailing' (8.26: *fracta et rauca et effeminata voce clamores absonos intollunt*; 8.27: *absonis ululatibus constrepentes fanatice provolant*). These adjectives imply more than just an inharmonious sound: Latin authors describe the voices of women, eunuchs and *cinaedi* as 'thin' and 'broken', while the voices of men are 'sound' or 'whole' (Quint., *Inst.* 11.3.19–20, 11.3.32; Phaed. P10, 1–3; Anonymous Latin *Physiognomy* 98). Our Latin sources, coming from a tradition of rhetorical training for boys and men, assume that vocal quality reveals the truth of a speaker's gender, bodily integrity and morality (cf. Gunderson 2000; Gleason 1995). The masculine is coded as normal and admirable, while the non-masculine is abnormal. When Lucius describes the priests' voices, he is again evoking the linked ideas of the *cinaedus* and the *gallus* as physically and morally frail, and too much like women to be 'natural' (i.e., normative) men.

In both novels, Lucius' representation of the priests' alterity reaches a fever pitch in his narrative of their public rituals. In *Onos* 37, he describes how they use music to 'incite a frenzy (*ephusae . . . ntheon*)', perform an ecstatic dance, and cut their arms and tongues with swords, 'with the result that, in a moment, everything was filled with effeminate blood (*malakou haimatos*)'. Lucius depicts this religious ritual as a form of street entertainment: every time the priests cut themselves, they receive payment. Yet other than describing their blood as 'effeminate', his narrative is more observational than judgemental.

In *The Golden Ass* 8.27, the scene is much the same at first as Lucius describes the priests' ritual cutting, though here only of their arms. He then focuses on one priest:

> One of them . . . as if filled with the holy spirit of a divine power, pretended a fit of madness . . . Shouting prophetically, he begins to attack and accuse his own self with a fabricated lie, as if he had perpetrated something against the law of his holy religion, and moreover, he himself demands just punishment for his hateful crime from himself and by his own hands . . .

> unus ex illis . . . velut numinis divino spiritu repletus, simulabat sauciam vecordiam . . . Infit vaticinatione clamosa conficto mendacio semet ipsum incessere atque criminari, quasi contra fas sanctae religionis dissignasset aliquid, et insuper iustas poenas noxii facinoris ipse de se suis manibus exposcere . . .

Throughout *The Golden Ass*, Lucius depicts the priests as habitual liars: see the deceptive prophecy at 9.8 and the accusation of theft at 9.10. Here, he implies that the priest's actions are pretense rather than sincere religious expression, even using a word for 'accuse', *criminari*, that specifically indicates a false accusation (Hijmans et al. 1985: 246). To Lucius, the priests' voices not only sound wrong, they are also used in the wrong way: to lie. The priest does not defend herself through speech as an elite Roman man would and as Lucius himself has attempted to do (cf. *Met.* 3.4–7, 3.29, 7.3, 8.29). Instead, she accuses herself. Lucius' incredulousness and misgendering of the priests is marked by his language: the priest attacks *semet ipsum*, 'himself', and demands punishment *ipse de se suis manibus*, 'himself from himself by his own hands'. The priest's own words and motivations are never given, but if we strip away the layers of narratorial disgust, this is a public confession, a ritual shared by the followers of the Syrian Goddess and the cult of Isis to which the narrator himself will soon belong (Lightfoot 2003: 78–9; see Hijmans et al. 1985: 287–98 on the novel's programmatic comparison of these cults). Nor does the scene end with the priest's self-accusation: she also whips herself, subjecting her body to a physical punishment that marks her in the eyes of the Roman reader as belonging to the social classes legally subject to corporal punishment: slaves, the lower classes and *infames*, people such as sex workers, gladiators and actors who were legally disenfranchised because of the perceived immorality of using one's body for others' entertainment (Edwards 1997; Walters 1997). These figures were frequently depicted as gender-transgressive (feminised if male and masculinised if female), and in the scene above, Lucius focuses on the priest's gender, calling her whip 'the distinctive attribute of those half-men (*semiviris*)' (8.28). The final image is the same as in the *Onos*: 'You could see . . . the ground becoming wet with the filth of effeminate blood', *cerneres . . . solum spurcitia sanguinis effeminati madescere* (8.28). The verb makes us as readers complicit in Lucius' representation of the priests: '*you* could see'. Since the priests are given direct speech nowhere in this episode, our perception depends on Lucius, whose words make his reality our own: not only Lucius the ass, but you, too, could discern the truth behind the priests' false words and bodies, betrayed by their blood.

CONCLUSION

In their own words, the priests of the Syrian Goddess in the *Onos* and *The Golden Ass* identify as girls – a community of transwomen sheltered within an imported religion on the margins of Graeco-Roman society. In both novels, however, the priests' genders are redefined by Lucius, who uses their speech, voices, dress and actions to characterise them as the perverted *cinaedi* and foreign *galli* of Greek and Roman literature. Yet by putting these features in context with what we know about the followers of the Syrian Goddess and Cybele from their funerary monuments, from historical studies like those of Lynn Roller and Jane Lightfoot and from comparisons with modern communities like those of the *hijras*, we can recover the priests' representations of themselves beyond the identities ascribed to them by members of the dominant Graeco-Roman culture like the fictional Lucius. In the novels, we can see how this conflict is revealed and concealed through a process of entextualisation whereby the priests' words, actions and identities are embedded within the cultural parameters that govern Lucius' narration. The ability to impose meaning, to shape reality to one's own image, is a marker of power. The fact that our unreliable, asinine narrator Lucius can define the reality of an entire group of people through words alone reveals the role that gendered discourse played in the politics of representation in Imperial Roman literature and culture.

CHAPTER 12

Wit, Conventional Wisdom and Wilful Blindness: Intersections between Sex and Gender in Recent Receptions of the Fifth of Lucian's *Dialogues of the Courtesans*

Rowan Emily Ash

LIVING AT A CROSSROADS: INTERSECTIONAL THEORY AND LUCIAN'S *DIAL. MERET.*

The interdisciplinary field of gender studies continually challenges socially conditioned gender norms, across cultural variations and adjusting for the assumptions that any researchers will bring from their own culture. That is, it is possible to formulate a historical approach that considers how contemporary norms vary from earlier ones, but that also considers a basis for their potential similarities. Of course, the later norms that frame the discussion are themselves culturally dependent and sometimes contested. For example, J. Halberstam observes of female homosexuality that 'what we do not know for sure today about the relationship between masculinity and lesbianism, we cannot know for sure about historical relations between same-sex desire and female masculinities' (1998: 54, quoted in Rupp 2009: 5). A classical example can illustrate the temptation and difficulties of loosely applying modern terms to ancient evidence, while hopefully clarifying the significance of the latter (Halperin 2002: 14). This chapter focuses on the representation of sex and gender in Lucian's *Dialogues of the Courtesans*, a second-century AD collection of short satiric dialogues modelled on the Platonic but concentrating on the lives and relationships of courtesans and their clients instead of philosophy. I hold that a close reading of the fifth *Dialogue of the Courtesans* reveals, in the assigned-female Megillos' claim to masculinity, a greater challenge to ancient gender norms on their own rather than on modern terms. Indeed, the text's humour hinges on the disjunction between physical and putative mental markers of masculinity.

This disjunction might gradually have become more legible to ancient authors in the wake of the restructuring of Roman imperial power in the first couple of centuries of rule under emperors (the Principate), as gender positionalities were included in the negotiations of 'the imposition of authority, the shifts of status of individuals, the logic of accommodation and assimilation' (Goldhill 2001: 14–15) under the new regime. The linguistic reflex of these negotiations took the form of a pointedly, manneredly classicising Greek, modelled on usage in Athens during its heyday some six or seven centuries previously, deployed in a competitive culture of increasing(ly) rhetorical display as the range of practical political activity open to local male elites narrowed. Accordingly, it is unsurprising that in the eighty or so extant works of Lucian, display pieces ranging over fantastical ethnographies, mock legal speeches, parodic philosophical dialogues, satirical rhetorical treatises, to thematic collections of short dramatic dialogues such as the *Dialogues of the Courtesans* (*Dial. Meret.*), Lucian's stagings of the shifting contours of identity in the Roman Empire explore the intersections of sex, gender and various other axes of identity and power. However, recent scholarship on this text has often applied modern terms only loosely defined and distinguished from ancient: here, I use categories from modern gender and sexuality studies to explore the points of contact and of divergence – intersections, if one might quibble – between ancient and modern ways of thinking about sex and gender, and how such comparison highlights their specificity, without advocating for the supersession and/or assimilation of one by the other.

This challenge becomes clear if one focuses on the development of the narrative within the dialogue on its own rather than assuming its context and that its main focus is female homosexuality, in what I hope may be productively perverse literalism. I will also argue that an intersectional approach is the best by which to consider the disruption of both sex and gender norms within the dialogue, and, more briefly, the further complications introduced by, loosely speaking, class and ethnicity. I conclude by suggesting possible connections with the other *Dial. Meret.* which touch on related issues. This push at the limits of the other dialogues that can only be gestured at here is a commitment to queering the text and the theory that the *Dial. Meret.* were intended to be not only entertaining, but also, often, humorous. One might contrast, for example, simple *prosopopoeia*, or, more broadly, compare Lucian's use of 'anecdote', as defined by Graham Anderson (2009: 3), including '"literary" materials with a contemporary or realistic setting . . . with a wide range . . . either as narratives for a didactic purpose or as entertainments for their own sake'. Entertainment need not be devoid of more serious purpose, of course. Although arguably the most prominent feature of the fifteen short (averaging around three and a half pages in the OCT edition) vignettes of the *Dial. Meret.* is their low-grade titillation, interwoven through the encounters Lucian dreams up are recurrent reflections on various constraints on courtesans' lives: how to retain clients, what they want and what they offer, and several double standards, for example. These concerns intersect suggestively both within individual dialogues and through the structure of the collection as a whole, though here I focus quite narrowly on *Dial. Meret.* 5 in its own right, rather than its wider context, as most salient for Lucian's most explicit staging of the intersections between sex and gender in the *Dial. Meret.* In particular, while the question of how sex and gender might be related is not confined to the fifth dialogue, both categories at once are uniquely in question there – one might compare *Dial.* 10 and 12, which hinge largely on expected norms of masculine behaviour (gender) and female embodiment (sex) respectively – and at a further level of abstraction, as the main characters in *Dial.* 5 struggle to understand the identity of a third character outside of the frame narrative, whose lived experience as a man runs counter to his assigned sex and gender as female/woman.

I use here a minimal definition of intersectionality, a theory, building upon Kimberlé Crenshaw's foundational work (see now her retrospective in Cho et al. 2013: 787–92), by which 'one form of identity or inequality is not seen as separable or superordinate' (May 2015: ix). This means the analysis of persons' experience is complicated by overlapping and mutually constitutive identity categories. To use a canonical example, an adequate description of the experience of being (and being discriminated against as) a queer, black woman requires confronting the experiences of race in relation to gender and sexuality, and *vice versa*, relations that are often mystified or ignored: a text frequently cited in this context is 'The Combahee River Collective Statement', reprinted in Meem et al. (2010: 110–17). That is, stereotypes of race inflect those of womanhood, such that a woman's experience of sexism may also contain a racialised element (or the preponderance may be the converse), complicating the question of whether a given situation is primarily a confrontation of sexism or of racism. Similarly, one's sexuality may affect the perception of one's racial and ethnic identity. However, it has been suggested that intersections with sexuality in particular have been under-theorised (Taylor et al. 2011: 1), a matter of importance given the complications surrounding sexuality in Lucian's fifth *Dialogue of the Courtesans*. In what follows, I suggest this under-theorisation is due to a reluctance to fully confront the interrelations between sex, gender and sexuality not only within the text itself, but also in its modern reception. I invoke these categories in the most general senses, given that, for example, even within modern models of sexuality the relationships between various components (e.g. identity, desire and practice) are not determined (Fausto-Sterling 2000: 244–5, 251–2; compare Halperin 2002: 131), and that what counts as sexual is culturally contingent (Boehringer 2007b: par. 3–7, 2007a: 18–29). While intersections with sexuality in the ancient Mediterranean have recently attracted scholarly attention with regard to ethnicity, though perhaps less often race as writ large in Anglo-American late modernity (see, for example, on some varieties of putatively

'Greek' love, albeit largely implicitly, Gilhuly 2015: esp. 166ff.), with regard to sex and gender beyond the narrower limits of 'sexuality', much work remains to be done, and significantly incorporating ethnicity would call for a much larger compass than the immediate project of this chapter can span.

In keeping with the scope of this chapter, I gesture here to some specific intersections between various aspects of identity as represented and transformed by Lucian in his series of fictive dialogues, in keeping with Sumi Cho et al.'s (2013: 791) argument that 'intersectionality neither travels outside nor is unmediated by the very field of race and gender power that it interrogates'. My necessarily narrow focus here is on the possibilities that a close reading of the *Dialogues of the Courtesans*, especially the fifth, might reveal how Lucian represents various aspects of identity intersecting, and the cultural work that this representation may do. In particular, much recent work acknowledges the range of modern terminology and its utility for exploring in ancient texts what is latterly called 'sexuality', compared to antiquity's τὰ Ἀφροδίσια (*ta Aphrodisia*, perhaps 'venereal rites', tongue firmly in cheek), among others, without assuming that ancient and modern categories are coterminous. Yet, the ways by which ancient and modern categories of sex and gender intersect(ed) with those of 'sexuality' and various audiences' understanding of texts concerning the latter has attracted less attention. This is despite the long-known complications of effects such as the putative facticity of sex, even as sexuality feeds back into specific cultural understandings of the former, and *vice versa*. For instance, anxieties about queer women's womanhood, or whether homosexual practices among women are even legible as sexual (Winkler 1990a: 38–41; Rupp 2009: 4, 205–6) are notorious examples, to which one might add the implications of cultural systems in which any abstract concept of sex (as opposed to a given set of sexes) proves elusive (Winkler 1990a: 50, 224 n. 9). For a text such as Lucian's *Dial. Meret.* 5, in which sex is, at least notionally, in question, an intersectional approach sensitive to effects such as those just outlined is the most useful for a richer sense of Lucian's engagement with second-century sex and gender norms.

MEETING HALFWAY: READING CATEGORIES OF SEX, ANCIENT AND MODERN, IN *DIAL. MERET.* 5

The fifth dialogue's central event is the courtesan Leaina's account of a sexual encounter with two people, whom both she and her interlocutor Kleonarion consistently describe as women. Within the embedded narrative, however, one of Leaina's clients insists on a masculine identity, 'ἡ γνώμη δέ καὶ ἡ ἐπιθυμία καὶ τἄλλα πάντα ἀνδρός (the mind, spirit and all the other qualities of a man)' (Lucian, *Dial. Meret.* 5.4: all translations are my own, following the text in MacLeod, trans. vol. 7, 1961: 355–467, whereas ancient lexicographers are cited in the edition of the *TLG*). That character courts Leaina by asking if 'ἑώρακ[εν] ἤδη οὕτω καλόν νεανίσκον ([she has] ever seen such a beautiful young man)', and rejects the feminine/female name 'Megilla' in favour of the masculine/male 'Megillos' with the admonition, 'μή με καταθήλυνε (Don't make a woman out of me)' (5.4), when Leaina initially protests that no young man is present (5.3). However, because Megillos is introduced, with no demurral from Leaina, as τὴν Λεσβίαν Μέγιλλαν τὴν πλουσίαν '(the rich Lesbian woman Megilla)' (5.1), and does not actually participate in the conversation with Kleonarion, it seems that the text is formally structured to call attention to, and maintain, the discrepancy. Indeed, the dialogue ends with a return to the frame narrative and Kleonarion's desperate curiosity as to 'what she [*sic, sc.* Megillos] did' (5.4), as Leaina and Kleonarion still ultimately sex/gender Megillos as a female/woman.

It is thus surprising that several modern readers interpret the dialogue in terms of an unproblematic same-sex encounter, with James Davidson going so far as to call the couple Leaina entertains 'proper "modern-style" lesbians' (Davidson 2007: 407–8; cf. Dover 1978: 172; Rupp 2009: 30). If any modern notion of identity is applicable, perhaps the transgender spectrum, and transsexuality in particular, would be most useful to describe Megillos' situation, given the focus of Leaina's account of their relationship and Lucian's use of biologically marked, sexed as well as gendered, language throughout. This is in keeping with transgender as:

> an umbrella term to describe those who defy societal expectations and assumptions regarding femaleness and maleness; this includes people who are transsexual (those who live as members of the sex other than the one they were assigned at birth), intersex . . . and genderqueer . . . as well as those whose gender expression differs from their anatomical or perceived sex.
>
> (Serano 2016: 25)

This parallels clinical focus on transgender and transsexual individuals' identification with a gender other than that to which they were assigned at birth, in the latter case, often accompanied by a desire to transition to the social role of their identified sex and gender, possibly with medical assistance ([American Psychiatric Association] 2013: 451). I wish to acknowledge at the outset ongoing concerns about stigmatisation, accessibility and self-definition under this clinical model, but also that it is dominant, with all of the resulting consequences (cf. Serano 2016: 25ff, 31; Stryker 2008: 1, 18–19). In either case, gender dysphoria is a crucial diagnostic criterion, defined as 'the distress that may accompany the incongruence between one's experienced or expressed gender and one's assigned gender' ([American Psychiatric Association] 2013: 451), as such, compared to 'simple nonconformity to stereotypical gender role behavior'

([American Psychiatric Association] 2013: 458). The *DSM-5* here also specifies that a distinction should be made for 'the strong desire to be of another gender than the assigned one'. Although it is difficult to assess the significance of any distress Megillos may feel (while it is tempting to extrapolate from his difficulties with Leaina and his self-presentation as Megilla in public despite his claim to 'the mind, spirit, and all the other qualities of a man'), he certainly fits two other criteria for gender dysphoria:

> strong desire to be treated as the other gender (or some alternative gender different from one's assigned gender) [and a] strong conviction that one has the typical feelings and reactions of the other gender (or some alternative gender different from one's assigned gender).
> ([American Psychiatric Association] 2013: 452–3)

Nonetheless, many attempts to incorporate modern ideas of transgender and transsexual identities run into odd discrepancies, with one reading claiming 'Megilla is a transsexual, like Tiresias' (Gilhuly 2006: 279), eliding the fact that Tiresias' bodily transformation is a temporary situation and providing no indication that it required any emotional adjustment (for example, responding to dysphoria). Another, though cautious enough to qualify the identification as one of 'close correspondences', nonetheless concludes that Megillos' relationships represent 'transgendered lesbianism' (Haley 2002: 288, 295), denying the masculine identity that Megillos is at pains to claim, and which the dialogue itself does not strongly reject. Even the recent extended treatment most sympathetic to transgender interpretations of the dialogue, which distinguishes 'Megilla's [*sic*] own description of self as the "true" image of oneself' (Bissa 2013: 84), ultimately concludes that the 'most important issue for any study of this dialogue is what it tells us about female same-sex [*sic*] desire', and runs roughshod over Megillos' self-identification by dismissively labelling him as 'a female that identifies as male' (Bissa 2013: 97). In these readings, canonical forms of both the Tiresias myth and definitions of transsexuality, let alone identification as a 'lesbian', are treated rather heavy-handedly.

Closer examination of the fifth dialogue's development to a comic climax reveals how the previous examples of transgender interpretations may have chosen the right places to look, but stopped just short of the text's conclusion, similarly troubled by the relationships between sex, gender norms and gender identity. Fortunately, this situation does seem to be improving rapidly, though there is still a fair bit of anxiety expressed indirectly by a reluctance to commit even to consistent pronoun choices. For example, though explicitly acknowledging Megillos' male identification, Daniel Orrells (2015: 131) opts for the feminine pronoun in scare-quotes, and Walter Penrose Jr. (2014: 244) likewise hesitates between the masculine pronoun for Megillos, the contraction 's/he', and the periphrasis of 'a female-to-male transgendered person'. Kristin Mann's (2017) approach is exemplary: in adducing *Dial. Meret.* 5 as a likely parallel to a reinterpretation of Phaedrus' fable of the creation of *tribades* and *molles mares* as intentional play with ideas of sex and gender identification and assignment, Mann's discussion has opted for the singular 'they', with an explicit acknowledgement of the difficulties in deciding how to discuss Megillos.

In *Dial. Meret.* 5, then, Megillos' forthright claim to his masculinity sits uneasily with Kleonarion's dissatisfaction with Leaina's account, which may lead one to propose another explanation for Kleonarion's confusion. After all, Megillos does not leave much room for ambiguity in stating, 'τὸ πᾶν ἀνήρ εἰμι (I am all man)' (Lucian, *Dial. Meret.* 5.3). Kleonarion is experienced enough to remark that 'τοιαύτας . . . ἐν Λέσβῳ . . . γυναῖκας ἀρρενωπούς . . . γυναιξὶ δὲ αὐτὰς πλησιάζουσας ὥσπερ ἄνδρας (there are such [*or,* this sort of] masculine women in Lesbos . . . who associate themselves with women as if they were men)' (5.2) but still finds the rumours of what Leaina's been doing 'καινὰ (strange)' (5.1). One might be tempted to take Kleonarion's feeling of strangeness as due to recognising a new habitual, even identifying tendency to act in such a way, one which is comparable to modern queer identities anchored by reasonably clear-cut concepts of homosexuality, despite the scholarly commonplace of warnings against projecting categories that would not be socially salient onto other cultures (thus already Parker 1997: 47; cf. Rohy 2009: 126–30). That is, the Lesbian women Kleonarion refers to would really have become 'the sort of' women who usually love other women, rather than 'such' women who happen to do so occasionally. According to such an interpretation, Lucian's dialogue would indicate the appearance of forms of identity including a definite sexual orientation, particularly since 'λεσβιάζειν (*lesbiazein*, "to Lesbianise", act in a Lesbian way)' is attested earlier, though it is associated with general sexual impropriety rather than any particular practice (Dover 1978: 182). A further limitation is that the term is rarely contrasted with φοινικίζειν (*phoinikizein*, 'Phoenicianising'), including in Lucian (*Pseudol.* 28), in which cases the field seems more clearly to narrow to oral sex, with φοινικίζειν representing cunnilingus in particular. On its own, λεσβιάζειν remains more ambiguous (Boehringer 2007a: 61–3, citing both Lucian and Gal. 12.249).

However, the passage just cited from *Dial. Meret.* 5.2 suggests that Kleonarion's curiosity is related to the perceived masculinity of the action. In both instances in which an action is described as performed 'as' (ὡς) by a man or men (*Dial. Meret.* 5.1, 5.2), the intensifier -περ is added to the adverb, and indeed ὥσπερ is only used in such phrases throughout the dialogue. Moreover, 'ἀρρενωπούς', derived from 'ἄρρην', the biological term for 'male' (Liddell and Scott 1940: s.v.), rather than 'ἀνδρικός', is a marked choice, given Megillos' gender identity as subsequently reported by Leaina, who uses the latter form herself to express her own uncertainty, 'ἡ γυνὴ δὲ δεινῶς ἀνδρική ἐστιν (but the woman is frightfully manly)' (*Dial. Meret.* 5.1). Finally, however masculine the certain Lesbian women Kleonarion refers to may be, Leaina considers that her experience has only been similar to theirs, 'τοιοῦτόν τι (Something like that)' (5.2). As the account Leaina offers of her conversation with Megillos elaborates, Megillos occupies an ambiguous position from the other characters' perspective, even if they do have some notion of female same-sex desire.

Tellingly, Megillos' renaming of himself as a man is supported both by a literalising choice of vocabulary and a symbolically significant grammatical construction. The use of 'καταθηλύνω' (to make a woman out of, like a woman, 'to make womanish') (Liddell and Scott 1940: s.v.) in rejecting the feminine form of the name takes up the biological suggestion already seen in 'ἀρρενωπούς'; the verb is based on 'θῆλυς', the corresponding biological term for 'female' (Liddell and Scott 1940: s.v.), such that a translation bringing out the sense of the roots of the compound in Megillos' injunction 'μή με καταθήλυνε' more strongly might be, 'Don't put me down as a female'. The verb calls attention to the unequal status of male and female in the culture represented in the dialogue and consequently in Megillos' own understanding of the terms. The word may be a Lucianic coinage: in addition to here, it is only found at *De Mort. Peregr.* 19.8, *Hist. conscr.* 10.26, and four times in ecclesiastical authors from the sixth century and beyond, in the *TLG* corpus. In these other instances, the sense is not primarily biological, but rather providing variation and amplification for the idea of μαλακίζεσθαι ('going soft, weak, cowardly'), and applied in earnest to woman martyrs (John of Damascus, *Laudatio sanctae martyris Anastasiae* 21.2). θηλύνω, however, is attested some 187 times in the same corpus, with a broader range, but still less often biologically than one might expect.

Conversely, there is no 'καταρρένω', and 'κατανδρίζομαι' means to fight manfully (Liddell and Scott 1940: s.v., and see also ἀνδρίζω, which occasionally has a pejorative sense, but normally means 'to come to manhood', and cf. Cameron 1998: 141), not to be made mannish, so Lucian's word choice here indicates that the supposed masculine women in Lesbos are not necessarily attracted to other women for that reason as if they were early sexologists' 'inverts'. Inversion is perhaps most famously expressed for what would later be understood as a male homosexual context in the nineteenth-century activist Karl Heinrich Ulrichs' description of '*anima muliebris in corpore virili inclusa* (a woman's soul contained in a manly body)' (programmatic in Ulrichs 1868: v, xii, elaborated from 8ff.; quoted in Orrells 2015: 102–7). But it was not confined to that context, because such a formulation indicates how in early sexology 'the history of homosexuality and transsexuality was a shared history' (Halberstam 1998: 85, see also 76–87; Rupp 2009: 144–54). Nonetheless, Megillos' supposedly same-sex desire, based on his assigned sex and gender, cannot simply be generalised, either to women (or men!) who are only 'something like that' or to a putative general Lucianic category corresponding to homosexual people.

Moreover, Megillos goes on to claim to 'γεγάμηκ[εν] πρόπαλαι ταύτην τὴν Δημώνασσαν (have married this Demonassa very long ago)' (*Dial. Meret.* 5.3), using the active form of the verb as Greek idiom considered appropriate for men, as opposed to the middle-passive for women (Liddell and Scott 1940: s.v. γαμέω). Megillos' masculinity is thus also performative as opposed to a specifically embodied sense of sex and gender. Thus, in avoiding the temptation of retrojecting modern ideas of homosexuality onto Lucian's dialogue, one confronts another of anachronistically reading a transgender or transsexual Megillos into it instead, deploying strong social constructionist theories of gender. Nonetheless, one might bracket historical differences to assess their impact on one's interpretative possibilities, which might be considered productively ahistorical rather than anachronistic (Rohy 2009: 127ff., 139). Lucian seems to be playing with such ideas in his use of the apparently archaising word 'ἑταιρίστρια' in describing Megillos, as discussed further below.

As noted above, Leaina's attempts to come to grips with Megillos' masculine self-identification diverge in significant ways from a naive application of modern terminology. First considering whether Megillos might have been a male in disguise all along, she specifically asks about 'ὅπερ οἱ ἄνδρες (whatever men [have])' (*Dial. Meret.* 5.3), only to be told that Megillos has no need of it. Lucian's coyness suggests the importance of this claim to his joke, since the dialogue continues by clarifying that Megillos is not intersex by reference to the myth of Hermaphroditus, which offers the only definite class of sex-variant individuals mentioned in the dialogue, 'οἷοι πολλοὶ εἶναι λέγονται (of the sort which many are said to be)' (5.3). Nor is Megillos transformed from a woman to a man as Tiresias was, but has 'τι ἀντὶ τοῦ ἀνδρείου (something instead of what belongs to a man [*lit.*, the manly thing])' (5.4). In passing, one might note that the emphasis on Tiresias' *second* transformation, back to a man, further militates against Errietta Bissa's (2013: 93) otherwise interesting view of the mythological parallels cited in an attempt to understand Megillos' identity as a sequence giving decreasing importance to the phallus as a marker of physical maleness. In any case, that Megillos has something 'instead of' is a rather roundabout way of saying that Megillos does not have a penis, and, more to the immediate point, is not particularly transsexual. Megillos does not seem to wish to transition as completely as possible (in keeping with possible effects of gender dysphoria, in modern terms), compared to the broader range of identities included under the umbrella term of transgender. In addition, Megillos is able to pass as Megilla well enough that Leaina is surprised when Megillos claims the status of a 'νεανίσκον (young man)', a status that was considered to blur gendered distinctions insofar as it was not equivalent to mature adulthood (Boehringer 2010: 40).

One can recover a culturally significant point that barbs the end of the dialogue by returning to Megillos' previous statements, when he claims, 'δέομαι δὲ οὐδὲ πάνυ αὐτοῦ: . . . ἀλλὰ τὸ πᾶν ἀνήρ εἰμι (Nor do I need that [*sc.*, what other men have] at all; . . . but I am all man)' (*Dial. Meret.* 5.3). Together, these statements lead to the conclusion that a penis is a supplement to masculinity: if Megillos lacks nothing, but has 'τι ἀντὶ τοῦ ἀνδρείου (something *instead of* the manly thing)' (5.4, emphasis added), then that thing cannot have been so manly after all. Being assigned male is less important than possessing 'ἡ γνώμη δέ καὶ ἡ ἐπιθυμία καὶ τἄλλα πάντα ανδρός (the mind, spirit and all the other qualities of a man)' (5.4) – though of course one might wish to claim a male identity to top those off, if that fits one's sense of self (see Åshede's similar argument about Hermaphroditus in this volume).

The last few lines of the dialogue emphasise the point. Leaina claims to yield not only to Megillos' entreaties but because she is offered an 'ὅρμον τινά . . . τῶν πολυτελῶν καὶ ὀθόνας τῶν λεπτῶν (extravagant necklace . . . and a light linen dress)', but she says she will not go into further details because they are 'αἰσχρὰ (shameful things)' (5.4). If Leaina is not to be taken as entirely driven by greed, which would undercut the effectiveness of adding the gifts to the text, the material gifts are likewise additional, not strictly necessary, inducements to get her to cooperate, just as Megillos does not strictly need a 'manly thing'. Finally, Kleonarion's denied request for all the details ('τί ἐποίει, ὦ Λέαινα, ἢ τίνα τρόπον; (What did she do, Leaina, or in what way?)' (5.4)) forces a choice upon the audience. On the one hand, if one accepts Kleonarion's curiosity, one implicitly makes conventional, phallocentric (e.g. Halperin 1990b: 164–5 n. 67, 166 n. 83) ideas of maleness the most important marker of masculinity, losing the symbolic currency, in the classical world, of supposedly manly virtues of bravery, self-control and civic responsibility. Conversely, if one thinks that Kleonarion is missing the point, then those qualities, of 'ἡ γνώμη . . . καὶ ἡ ἐπιθυμία (the mind [and] spirit)', as Megillos puts it, are revealed as influenced by social norms, and thus less closely tied to gender and sex than the impulse to characterise them as masculine would make it.

THE MEAN STREETS OF IMAGINED ATHENS: ADDITIONAL FORMS OF CLASS IN *DIAL. MERET.* 5

Such a conclusion would be accessible to ancient readers without involving anachronistic concepts of gender identity or sexual orientation, but one may briefly draw attention to the similarly ambiguous force of the one word that places Megillos in an ancient sexual category, if not quite identity. Kleonarion says she can only understand Leaina's story if Megilla 'τις ἑταιρίστρια τυγχάνει οὖσα (happens to be some *hetaira*-lover)' (*Dial. Meret.* 5.2), a term which is only attested before Lucian in the satirical speech put in the mouth of Aristophanes in Plato's *Symposium* (191c–192b). While some late sources such as Hesychius (s.v. διεταιρίστριαι) gloss the term as 'τριβάς (tribade)', as does, possibly overlapping with Lucian's dates, the second-century Atticist Moeris (s.v. ἑταιρίστριαι), what (later) antiquity thought tribades did is rarely detailed. A gloss in the scholia on Lucian notes 'τὰς αὐτὰς καὶ τριβάδας φασίν· καὶ ἴσως ἀπὸ τοῦ αἰσχρῶς ἀλλήλαις συντρίβεσθαι (the same are also called [said (to be)] *tribades*; and justly, on account of their rubbing against each other shamefully)' (Rabe 1971: 277). However, given the rarity of attestations for 'ἑταιρίστρια', it is difficult to rule out the interdependence of glosses in lexica and scholia (Cameron 1998: 146), such that Lucian's terminology cannot be taken to have been widely interpreted as referring to tribadism in antiquity. Likewise, as Leila Rupp (2009: 38–9) notes, citing first- to second-century AD astrological texts that discuss influences on sexuality, 'τριβάς' (*tribas*) was usually reserved for the 'active' partner. Still, while there are exceptions, particularly in broadening the cultural field to the wider Roman Empire and Latinity, beyond specifically Greek contexts, the more elaborate usage in, for example, the Roman authors Seneca (*Controv.* 1.2.23) and Martial (7.67, 7.70) suggests the salience of narrower definitions (cf. Boehringer 2007a: 267–75, 286–94, and Mart. 1.90). Moreover, in Lucian, one notes that Demonassa never speaks, yet, just as Megillos does, takes an active role with Leaina, kissing and biting her (*Dial. Meret.* 5.3, cf. Boehringer 2010: 42; Bissa 2013: 89–91, 95–6). Lucian thus sets up the encounter between the three characters, all assigned female by the wider world within the text, so that the boundaries between active and passive, then masculine and feminine, and male and female, are blurred, before the dialogue playfully leaves the reader in a position opening up the gap between sex and gender.

That said, Lucian's play is not intrinsically neutral or value-free, and one should be wary of privileging a reading that elides the text's difficulties and implications in discourses that ultimately impinge on all-too-real relations of power. Although arguably *Dial. Meret.* 5 is part of a 'paradoxical discourse [that] remains coherent in its paradox because it does not produce a result' (Boehringer 2015: 280), such an aesthetic of coherent paradox has additional effects that, while perhaps not problematic for Lucian, need not foreclose other interpretative possibilities. For example, it seems to be stretching the point to suggest that in *Dial. Meret.* 5 'what is culturally and socially "masculine" (gender) circulates among three women without completely or permanently characterising any one of them' (Boehringer 2015: 273). This is particularly perverse when, once more, one recalls that Megillos himself claims that completeness, 'τὸ πᾶν ἀνήρ εἰμι (I am all man)' (*Dial. Meret.* 5.3). Lucian may have an interest in encouraging doubts in his readers, but that does not mean that one need comply, or accept his encouragement without question: one might ask what is at stake in this play of gender, and of other things, and of how and why those might intersect.

That is, one can ask why these characters should be assigned women, why Lesbian and Corinthian, and why at least one of them should be rich, which raises similar questions of the legibility of ancient categories and the relevance of the available evidence. For example, Davidson discusses the bad faith involved in classical attitudes towards ἑταῖραι, the customary fiction that their relationships with clients were ostensibly based on friendship and the voluntary exchange of gifts and favours. He leads into it with a quotation of Aristophanes' *Wealth*, according to which, compared to grasping Corinthian ἑταῖραι (*hetairai*), who only let themselves fall in love with rich clients, boys in pederastic relationships don't even love, but do it for money or gifts to avoid the stigma of mere cash (Davidson 1997: 109 (quoting Ar. *Pl.* 149–59), 111, 135). The boys end up the moral equivalents of the ἑταῖραι, but the specification of the wealthier sort of Corinthian courtesan, who has a greater degree of choice from among the men who pursue her, stresses the deception involved in her meretricious attractions. Megillos' wealth is a suggestive parallel. Passing as a financially successful woman, his private life is all the more surprising: if Megillos' appearance was always non-normative, the sloppy associativeness of stereotypical thinking would make assumptions about his identity and practices.

One may compare the role of his wealth in winning Leaina's acquiescence, as discussed above; formally, if that is not all that persuades Leaina, it is a supplement to Megillos' masculinity, just like the 'manly thing' which he does not need. However, if he is a courtesan, depending on how one is to take his description as 'ὁμότεχνος' (following the same craft) as Demonassa (*Dial. Meret.* 5.2), his wealth is not what it seems, a supplement, or, alternatively, his masculinity is also a deception. How far the connotation of 'craft' extends, and whether Megillos and Demonassa can be said to share something like the same (sexual) orientation is a crucial point (Bissa 2013: 89–90); however, the affinities here with stereotypes of transsexual people as deceptive or pathetic are suggestive, though primarily focusing on transsexual women (Serano 2016: 35–52), even though Bissa (2013: 96) is rather more sanguine about parallels with mainstream modern media images of sexual and gender minorities. If Lucian does not question the role of class and wealth in the society he depicts, this may suggest one avenue for sexual and gender norms to re-establish themselves. The dilemma of Kleonarion's question, 'What did she do, Leaina, or in what way?' (*Dial. Meret.* 5.4), which forces a choice between phallocentric ideals of maleness and symbolic values of masculinity, need not be more than rhetorical, barbing the wit of the dialogue but not intended to challenge stereotypes seriously. One can imagine that a reader might (and the recent reception suggests still often does) conclude, 'But of course Megilla *is* a woman, so it's all moot.'

Or perhaps the reader might, following Sandra Boehringer (2015: 277–9), argue for the fundamental unreliability of Leaina's account, that these are 'nothing but characters in a dialogue by Lucian', which cuts the Gordian knot. However, it is not clear what advantage Leaina might obtain by attempting to mislead her audience, nor, despite the artificiality of the likely original performance and reading contexts of the *Dial. Meret.*, that those contexts necessarily undermined the supposed naturalism of the dialogues to the extent Boehringer proposes. Taking

Lucian seriously (playing his straight man?) need not only be 'to fall into a very obvious trap' (278), but also to push him even closer to the limits of what was conceivable in his time. Alternatively, if the *True History* is programmatic for Lucian's fiction, as many have argued, including Boehringer, who makes specific reference to the *Dial. Meret.* (279), the playful exploitation of the range of fiction in *Ver. Hist.*, including lies that paradoxically tell the truth, suggests the possibility, as Karen Ní Mheallaigh argues, 'that diegetic characters are as "real" as their extra-diegetic authors' (2009: 21), and that one can extend '"the implication . . . that innovative art threatens social hierarchies"' (2014: 4, quoting Whitmarsh) beyond an author's self-imposed limits.

EXPLORING THE NEIGHBOURHOOD: POINTS OF INTERSECTION IN AND WITH THE WIDER *DIAL. MERET.*

The fifth of the *Dialogues of the Courtesans* thus opens up space to explore the intersections of sex, gender and sexuality, on which it focuses, as well as, to a degree, ethnicity and class, but that is not to say that Lucian pursues it to a liberating end. A survey of the rest of the *Dialogues* suggests that in fact he does not. Even a necessarily brief overview reveals patterns that may point towards possible extensions to the current project. The arrangement of the *Dial. Meret.* as received is particularly suggestive. The tenth is a counterpart to the fifth dialogue, if the latter was easily read in terms of stereotypical ancient conceptions of same-sex desire: in the former dialogue, a young man is ostensibly at risk of being corrupted by his tutor in philosophy (*Dial. Meret.*10.4). Compared to *Dial.* 5, the situation is familiar, but all may not be as it seems. On the one hand, this may be a joke at philosophers' expense, and especially Plato's erotics, as Kate Gilhuly discusses in relation to *Dial.* 5 (2006: 277, 286–8). On the other hand, there is a suggestion of disingenuousness as the young man distances himself from his former companion by citing his tutor's promises that 'πάνυ εὐδαίμονα ἔσεσθαί . . . καὶ ἐνάρετον καταστήσεσθαι (he will be entirely happy and established as a virtuous man)' (*Dial. Meret.* 10.3). The remark betokens either remarkable naiveté or complicity, or that he is bored with his former companion, as she surmises (10.3). One of her friends offers to help by chalking up rumours of the situation on the walls of the Kerameikos (10.4), so in this dialogue as well, things may not be what they seem, and one is reminded to ask how 'everyone knows' what the generic 'they' say. In this connection, *Dial.* 15 is also relevant, in which insane jealousy breaks down the limits of heterosexual assumption; there, his rival having escaped with his one-time companion, an angry lover attacks the flute-girl they hired, as if she was not just providing musical entertainment. The implications for Lucian's attitude to (nominally) same-sex desire (as analogously disorderly?) are not particularly flattering.

A similar outlier is *Dial.* 12; every third dialogue refers, however loosely, to the economic exigencies of a ἑταῖραι (*hetaira*)'s life. In *Dial.* 12 another scene of mistaken identity appears: a quarrelling couple are reconciled when it is revealed that it was not another man in the protagonist's bed, but one of her girl friends, because she was lonely one night without her now estranged companion (*Dial. Meret.* 12.4). This does not faze him, though the reader might think back to only a couple of dialogues previously, or back to *Dial.* 5. This, too, without additional suggestions that the protagonist may frequently share her bed with her servant, Lyde, or her perhaps ambiguous remark that she has held close to her companion as her only Phaon (*Dial. Meret.* 12.4, 12.1). As the protagonist compares her estranged companion unfavourably to other potential candidates, wealthy and/or influential, and claims her mother/madam shouts at her, presumably for imprudence (12.1), there is an economic component to the situation, but since her companion keeps away, forcing her to find comfort elsewhere, there is also a suggestion of an economy of desire unflattering to the man: not only is he not the best catch in practical terms, he's not even a reliable warm body. As with Megillos in *Dial.* 5, there appears to be a question of just what makes a man – among other things – of use.

This is not to suggest, however, that everything is in good, if rather pointed, fun, as the gestures to the often desperate lot of women who worked as ἑταῖραι reveal, and which Lucian seems to take as read. Moreover, if one folds the collection down the middle, one finds unsettling associations in the dialogues brought into juxtaposition: slander with *Dial.* 12's mistaken identity, revolting reality beneath a disguise with *Dial.* 5's highly unusual identities, and child prostitution with *Dial.* 10's anti-philosophical romp. At the very centre one finds *Dial.* 8, with its suggestion that a woman cannot be sure of her partner's love unless he is so violently jealous as to beat her: the poisoned core that perhaps most vividly reminds one of what the range of Lucian's pornography includes. This too is part of the context of Leaina's story of Megillos, and this indication of the permutations of sexuality, sex and gender, and class (wealth, status) in the arrangement of the *Dialogues of the Courtesans* must suffice for the present discussion to indicate other possible points of intersection in the collection, the connections between them and the ongoing utility of an intersectional approach to the text's study.

PART IV

Female Masculinity

CHAPTER 13

Christianity Re-sexualised: Intertextuality and the Early Christian Novel

Brian P. Sowers and Kimberly Passaro

INTRODUCTION

Early Christianity used sacred texts, including novels, to distinguish its rituals, ethics and theologies from traditional ancient Mediterranean religions, especially ancient Judaisms. One such novel, the second-century *Acts of Paul and Thecla*, hereafter *APT*, promotes its ideology – an ascetic revision of first-century Christian sexual ethics – through the adventures of its female protagonist, Thecla (Lipsius and Bonnet 1891; Barrier 2009 – all dates are AD unless otherwise specified). Scholars have approached the novel, and Thecla in particular, from various and often divergent perspectives (Hylen 2015: 1–16; Cooper 2013b: 533; Aageson 2008: 194–8). Some have seen in Thecla the daily experiences of early Christian women and female leaders residing in Asia Minor; others read the *APT* as evidence for early Christian literary history and the formation of multiple genres, including hagiography. Those interested in social and theological history have cited the apocryphal acts as supporting evidence. Others less sanguine about the reliability of these texts have read the *APT* as second-century literature (Kraemer 2011: 117–52). Regardless of approach, recent scholarly output on the *APT* has continued unabated, and the last decade has seen new editions and monographs devoted entirely or in large part to the *APT* (e.g., Davis 2001; Johnson 2006; Barrier 2009; Lipsett 2011; Hylen 2015).

Building on that essential research, we examine Thecla's sexual renunciation and repeated sexual assaults through intertexts with Hebrew bible and the first-century gospels, specifically Mary of Bethany's veneration at Jesus' feet (Luke 7:38, 10:39) and Ruth's seduction of Boaz (Ruth 3:3–6, 4:13). In our view, Mary and Ruth, who actively initiate sexualised interactions with male characters, are increasingly masculinised and hypersexualised as each episode progresses, and may be treated as Thecla's biblical predecessors. By reading Thecla's complicated gender(s) and sexual past through the (counter)feminine lenses of Mary and Ruth, Thecla becomes an allusively charged literary character, and her rejection of, for example, marriage, family and feminine attire becomes more exegetically rich. Our approach situates Thecla's sexuality within its wider literary contexts, underscores her development over the course of the novel and illuminates how the community in Asia Minor responsible for the *APT* – known now only through the *APT* itself – interpreted and updated sacred texts to advance their own ideological interests. Within the competitive register of ancient rhetoric, Thecla is intertextually transformed into the ideal literary (wo)man, the model Christian disciple. We therefore contribute to the scholarly understanding of early Christian constructions of the body, resulting in a more nuanced appreciation for the plurality of sexual identities promoted throughout the ancient Mediterranean.

SYNOPSIS OF *APT*

The *APT* opens with the apostle Paul entering Iconium and preaching an ascetic revision of Jesus' beatitudes. A young woman, Thecla, hears Paul's message from her bedroom window and, desiring conversion, breaks off her engagement, barters away her valuables and joins Paul, who had been arrested for his socially transgressive message, in jail. When the Iconian officials discover Thecla with Paul, they expel him from the city and condemn her to be burned at the stake. God saves Thecla, who cuts her hair short and leaves Iconium to join Paul as an itinerant preacher. Reluctant to accept Thecla into his entourage, Paul brings her with him to Pisidian Antioch, where a local aristocrat, Alexander, attempts to rape her. Thecla successfully fights off Alexander but is subsequently condemned to death for dishonouring him. Thecla again faces death in the arena, where she baptises herself in a pool of man-eating seals, surviving only through divine intervention and assistance from female beasts. After this second trial, Thecla dresses in masculine clothing and joins Paul before breaking away on her own to preach the gospel in her hometown. In a fourth-century expansion on the *APT*, Thecla, now an elderly anchorite in the Pisidian mountains, continues to preach the gospel and perform miracles. Her ability to heal the sick, however, threatens the livelihood of some local physicians who, presuming her celibacy to be the source of her power, hire a criminal gang to rape her. God preserves Thecla's chastity by enclosing her within the mountain, which became the centre of the late antique Thecla cult.

A NEW MARY

Early Christian authors, like most Greco-Roman literary elite, engaged in competitive rhetoric to distinguish their views, themes or characters. The author of the *APT* works within this tradition, using intertextual allusions to situate their story vis-à-vis earlier Judeo-Christian narratives (cf. *Leuc. Clit.* 2.19, 7.1; Barrier 2009: 114; Pervo 1987: 133–4). Paul in the *APT* can therefore be read as an allusively charged literary bricolage, part Paul from the *Acts of the Apostles*, part Paul from the Pauline epistles, and part Jesus from the gospel tradition. His ascetic sermon, which prompts Thecla's conversion, is an intertextual adaptation of Jesus' beatitudes that situates Paul within a prophetic tradition parallel to Jesus, and endows him with the authority to update and revise Jesus' original message. Through this allusive contrast, the Paul of the *APT* surpasses Jesus. Similarly, Thecla imitates female characters from the gospel tradition, and this complicates her gender and sexuality. This section examines Thecla's allusive and elusive gender through intertextual connections to biblical women.

The most direct of these literary intersections are the allusions in *APT* 18 to Mary of Bethany (cf. *Xanth. Polyx.* 13). After bribing her way out of her house and into Paul's jail cell, Thecla sits at Paul's feet and listens to his message (καὶ καθίσασα παρὰ τοὺς πόδας αὐτοῦ ἤκουσεν τὰ μεγαλεῖα τοῦ θεοῦ). This passage borrows heavily from Luke 10:39, where Mary of Bethany sits at Jesus' feet and listens to him (παρακαθεσθεῖσα πρὸς τοὺς πόδας τοῦ Ἰησοῦ ἤκουεν τὸν λόγον αὐτοῦ). *APT* 18 also echoes a parallel scene in which an unnamed woman anoints Jesus' feet with perfume (Luke 7:38). Here the connection is their shared act of kissing: Thecla kisses Paul's chains (καταφιλούσης τὰ δεσμὰ αὐτοῦ), while the woman kisses Jesus' feet (κατεφίλει τοὺς πόδας αὐτοῦ). Over time, the unnamed woman of Luke 7 was increasingly conflated with Mary of Bethany. In John 12:3, written a generation after Luke's gospel, this episode is recast with Mary of Bethany as the unnamed woman, a conflation fully established when the *APT* was written. By alluding to Luke 7 and 10 both lexically and syntactically, the narrator of the *APT* juxtaposes these scenes and invites a reading of Thecla through Mary of Bethany.

Within Luke's gospel, Jesus' female followers model idealised discipleship by demonstrating the social reversals of Jesus' message, providing financial support for him and his entourage, and adopting positions of humility and service (Cooper 2013a: 60–76; Cooper 1996: 63). By contrast, Jesus' male followers frequently hinder his engagement with socially marginalised groups (the poor, the disabled, women, foreigners, etc.), argue about money and compete with each other for honour and status, sometimes immediately following explicit teachings on social justice and humility. These two episodes in Luke 7 and 10 underscore the Lukan depiction of idealised (fe)male disciples, marked by their desire to listen to and venerate Jesus (contrast Malina and Rohrbaugh 2003: 271; Malone 2000: 50), and highlight Jesus' feet as the corporeal focal point for reverence and respect, a theme developed in later gospel accounts. For example, Jesus humbly washing his disciples' feet – a practice he explicitly commands them to imitate – suggests that the ideal follower was expected to pay feet more than lip service.

The image of Mary listening at Jesus' feet (Luke 10) presents the socially transgressive female disciple as the ideal, thus complicating traditional ancient Mediterranean gender roles. By prioritising Jesus' teachings over her domestic responsibilities, Mary leaves her household duties undone. Yet she is described in idealised and exemplary terms, entirely superior to Martha, who busies herself with the responsibilities of a dutiful host. Through this contrast with her sister, Mary emerges as an intimate of Jesus. As idealised disciples, Jesus' female followers were therefore not relegated to the back row or kitchen, but were front and centre, attentive pupils with the best seats in the house.

These stories about women anointing Jesus' feet prescribe normative discipleship but also contain sexually charged details that were modified in subsequent gospel accounts. The foot-anointing scene in Luke 7, for instance, focuses on the unnamed sinner's overtly erotic act of kissing Jesus' feet. Although the narrator refrains from being too explicit, possibly to avoid any implication that Jesus was sexually involved with the woman, the disapproval of Jesus' host stresses the potential inappropriateness of the woman's present behaviour in light of her sinful past (Meier 2001: 75–7). To minimise the narrative's sexual controversy, this episode undergoes several revisions in John's gospel. First, Mary of Bethany, a well-known and respectable follower of Jesus, replaces the socially liminal character of the unnamed sinner. Second, although Mary's behaviour in John 12 mirrors the Lukan account in all other respects, she never kisses Jesus' feet, strongly suggesting that early Christian readers viewed this detail with suspicion because of its sexual undertones. Finally, the ensuing disagreement between Jesus and Judas Iscariot focuses on how the proceeds from selling the perfume could have been used to feed the poor, emphasising Judas' role as chief villain rather than Mary's as idealised disciple.

Despite the elision of sexual imagery in John's version, both foot-anointing scenes share one erotic feature: spikenard/myrrh. Among its many uses, spikenard was a well-known aphrodisiac and an active ingredient in perfumes intended for apotropaic and alluring ends (Luck 2006: 514; contrast *APT* 4.10). Myrrh's erotic efficacy made it a recurring component in Greco-Roman magic spells (*PGM* XIII.1–343), with parallels in Indian traditions as early as the Atharva-Veda c. 900–700 BC (VI.102.3), in which nard attracts women and is incorporated into marriage ceremonies (Betz 1992: 172–82; Preisendanz 1931: 87–105; Schoff 1923: 218, 220). Its erotic qualities also proliferate in ancient near Eastern literature, where nard is often used to anoint lovers or in seduction or beautification scenes (Song of Songs 1:12, 4:13–14; Esther 2:12; 3 Maccabees 4:6; perhaps Ruth 3:3). Thus the centrality of myrrh in Luke 7 facilitated two interrelated conclusions: first, that the anonymous woman's behaviour was explicitly erotic, and second, that the woman was a sex worker.

Mary of Bethany's use of spikenard in John 12, an erotic vestige from the original foot-anointing scene in Luke, further reinforced the popular conflation of Mary of Bethany and Mary Magdalene into a singular, sexually ambiguous character (Schoff 1923: 222; Haskins 1993: 18). By the early third century, Origen assumed the unity of the two Marys, a position that became western dogma at the end of the sixth century under Gregory the Great (Haskins 1993: 22, 25). However, some Eastern church fathers, including John Chrysostom, continued to distinguish between the two Marys, and while the Eastern church hailed Mary Magdalene as *Myrrhophores*, it celebrated her feast on a different day from that of Mary of Bethany.

The conflation of the Marys may also be found in late antique commentaries on Song of Songs. These commentaries allegorised the poem by juxtaposing its erotic content with the Christian gospels and the *APT*. Hippolytus of Rome (*In Cant.* 24.2) compares the Shulamite woman in futile pursuit of her beloved to Mary and Martha's post-crucifixion search for Christ (Haskins 1993: 63–7), since in Hippolytus' version, Jesus appears to Mary and Martha, not Mary Magdalene (contrast the gospel accounts, e.g., John 20:1–18). While his exegetic agenda is to muffle the erotic content of Song of Songs, Hippolytus' use of 'Mary' as a desexualised lens through which to read erotic poetry underscores how sexual the poem is and how sexualised Mary had become (Haskins, 1993: 66). A century later, Gregory of Nyssa (*Hom.* 15 *in Cant.* 6.405.1–3) equates the Shulamite woman with Thecla in his allegorical exegesis on 'his lips are lilies, distilling liquid myrrh' from Song of Songs 5:13. According to Gregory, the lilies symbolise self-control and the myrrh represents Paul's words, which fall upon the welcome ears of the holy virgin, Thecla (Hylen 2015: 93). Gregory thus conflates a heavily erotic passage from Song of Songs with the account of Thecla's conversion, which itself contains a fair share of erotic imagery. These exegetical readings of the Shulamite as allegorical 'Mary' or Thecla underscore female chastity while blending erotic and continent material.

Non proto-orthodox communities, especially 'Gnostic' Christians, also conflate Mary of Bethany with Mary Magdalene and depict this singular 'Mary' as the ideal disciple. While the *Gospel of Peter* and *Pistis of Sophia* refer to Mary as Mary the Magdalene, other accounts, such as the *Gospel of Mary*, the *Dialogue of the Saviour* and the *Gospel of Thomas* simply call her Mary. That Mary is frequently paired with Martha and Salome as female equivalents to Peter, James and John suggests that this Mary is a conflation of Mary of Bethany and Mary Magdalene (Bauckham 2002: 238; Meyer 1985: 562). Gnostic circles as early as the late first century depict Mary as the disciple to whom Jesus entrusts the mysteries of the gospel, but often only after her gender is transformed; Jesus explicitly states in *Gospel of Thomas* 114 that he will 'make Mary male'. These two motifs – Mary receiving the purest form of the gospel and transcending her femininity – recur in later Gnostic texts contemporaneous with the *APT* and revolve around similar literary themes, particularly female authority to preach. In the *Gospel of Mary*, for instance, Mary and her female entourage travel abroad preaching the gospel only after Mary undergoes a gender transformation (Meyer 2007: 737–8; Anson 1974).

Thecla's conversion to sexually ascetic Christianity, marked by her broken engagement, parallels the idealised (fe)male gospel disciple in a number of ways. Like Mary in Luke 10, Thecla eschews traditional social norms for Christian(ised) ones (Aubin 1998). She alienates her immediate family through her devotion to Christianity, which she communicates by sitting at Paul's feet, a biblical echo that further underscores Thecla's role as ideal disciple. By these behaviours, Thecla and Mary explicitly obey Jesus' command that disciples reject their kinsfolk (Luke 14:26) and replace their biological family with their social/religious community (Mark 3:31–5). Over time, the incipient religious communities reflected in the gospels and the *APT* assume the role of social support system typically played by kinship groups, culminating in the religious community's adoption of kinship language. In the *APT*, Tryphaena's symbolic adoption of Thecla in Antioch, and her repeated comparisons of Thecla to her deceased daughter, return Thecla to the security of a newly converted and markedly feminine *oikos* (household).

Thecla's deviations from her literary predecessors both welcome a reading of Thecla as a competitor of her gospel models and demonstrate how her behaviour is consistent with contemporary depictions of Jesus' ideal (fe)male entourage (Hayne 1994; Hylen 2015: 100, 108). Whereas Mary of Bethany remains securely within the *oikos* despite her rejection of domestic activities, Thecla breaks out of her bedroom and travels independently in the public sphere (Bynum 1991; Sowers 2012). Her crossing the limen of the *oikos* is marked by the sale of her domestic items (mirror) and subsequent alteration of her physical appearance (cutting her hair and dressing in masculine attire, σχήματι ἀνδρικῷ). Thecla's rejection of family and abandonment of her house mirror Jesus' call to his disciples and reflect a literal application of Luke 14:26 in ways that differ from Mary's behaviour in the gospel tradition. However, as a crossdressing apostolic leader with her own missionary entourage, Thecla echoes the Mary of the gnostic tradition, particularly in regards to her gender blending and sexual ambiguity (Lipsius and Bonnet 1891: 252–3, 266; Barrier 2009; Anson 1974; Hayne 1994: 215; Fox 2006: 336). Through these intertexts, Thecla emerges as the superior exemplar, the most idealised disciple.

Collectively, these allusions complicate Thecla's chastity and sexual renunciation. As we have seen, the foot-anointing scenes are sexually charged, especially when 'Mary' kisses Jesus' feet, a feature that the *APT* directly echoes. This gives Thecla's behaviour in jail sexual connotations that are amplified by the scene's many parallels to erotic episodes typical of the Greek novel. But this presents an obvious interpretative problem within the ideological framework of the *APT*, namely that Thecla has converted to an ascetic version of Christianity which calls for lifelong vows of chastity. Said differently, as Thecla escapes from her house and joins Paul in jail, she situates herself as a devotee committed to sexual renunciation but marks herself intertextually as a sexually available disciple. Thecla's sexual agency is made more explicit through her intertextual engagement with Ruth, the topic of the next section.

Thus far we have examined intertexts between Thecla and the early Christian Mary tradition. The *APT*'s engagement with the gospel of Luke invites active readers (Pelttari 2014; Gurd 2012; Johnson 2010) to situate Thecla alongside early Christian depictions of 'Mary' as the ideal (fe)male disciple and to problematise Thecla's characterisation in light of these comparisons. As an idealised protagonist similar to Mary in Luke 10, Thecla conducts herself in idealised and therefore normative ways. By sitting at Paul's feet and heeding his every word, Thecla imitates Mary as the model female convert while adhering to Paul's updated gospel of sexual constancy, a second-century revision of Jesus' original teachings. Not rigidly bound to her literary models, Thecla transcends the precedent set by Mary in the gospels by breaking out of the confines of the *oikos*, a behaviour which distinguishes Thecla from Mary of Bethany and makes her an exceptionally ideal (fe)male disciple. It also anticipates and perhaps even foreshadows the threats Thecla will face to her newly Christianised sexual identity. Moreover, her increasingly masculine appearance – a visual parallel to her equally masculine behaviours of traversing Asia Minor, teaching and baptizing – also parallel the wider Mary tradition, especially Gnostic depictions of Mary as an exceptional apostle 'made male'.

A NEW RUTH

Since the authors of the gospels and the *APT* wrote within a wider Judeo-Christian literary tradition, the female characters in earlier texts influenced their own. Ruth, the protagonist of the eponymous account, is one such literary model. This section examines how Ruth's sexual agency and availability, particularly her seduction of Boaz, influenced the gospel tradition and, later, the *APT*. In our view, Mary's veneration of Jesus' feet in the gospels is in conversation with the Ruth narrative. Because, as we have argued above, Thecla's character explicitly builds on Mary's, it is therefore possible to read Thecla as a second-century Christianised version of Ruth, an ideal (fe)male disciple within a tradition of exemplary (and sexualised) characters from Hebrew bible.

Likely written sometime during the early Persian period (c. the late sixth to early fifth century BC), Ruth expanded on King David's ancestry and modelled a working version of the newly formed Deuteronomic legal system (Schipper 2016: 20–2; Bauckham 2002: 6–7). The story begins with the death of Elimelech and his two sons, leaving Elimelech's wife, Naomi, and his Moabite daughters-in-law, Ruth and Orpah, widows. Intending to return home, Naomi encourages the young girls to do the same, hoping they each might find new husbands. Though

Orpah obeys her suggestion, Ruth refuses to leave Naomi and travels with her to Bethlehem. Once there, in order to provide food for Naomi and herself, Ruth gleans in the fields of Naomi's relative, Boaz. Seeing that Boaz treats Ruth kindly, Naomi instructs her to seduce him. Ruth then bathes, perfumes and dresses herself before finding the drunken Boaz at the threshing floor and undressing at his feet. In so doing, Ruth successfully persuades Boaz to marry her, not only gaining security for herself and Naomi, but also perpetuating the lineage that would result in King David and, eventually, Christ.

Over the ensuing centuries, Ruth's story, especially those details which proved most influential in early Christian literature, was subject to revisionist interpretations that elide over Ruth's sexuality. For example, in his paraphrase of Ruth, the first-century Jewish historian Josephus (*Antiquities* 5.318–37) suggests that gleaning the fields alone posed no physical or sexual threat to Ruth, and that nothing sexual transpired between Ruth and Boaz at the threshing floor. By pointing out what the text does *not* contain, Josephus reveals how his contemporaries read Ruth, specifically that her travelling alone in public posed a significant risk to her safety and that her interactions with Boaz were explicitly sexual. Because Ruth's seduction of Boaz had spread widely as the background narrative to the ancestry of David, who was equally notorious for seducing Bathsheba, Ruth emerges as a central, albeit controversial, biblical character.

Roughly contemporaneous with Josephus' paraphrastic interpretation of Ruth, the gospel traditions also incorporate her character into their biographies of Jesus. In Matthew's idealised genealogy of Christ, for instance, Ruth is one of four women mentioned. That women are present in a typically patriarchal genealogy is itself significant, and has elicited some discussion by modern interpreters (Bauckham 2002: 18–24; Luz 1990: 109–10; Keener 1999: 78–80; Wainwright 1991: 64–5; Corley 1993: 149). These women – namely Tamar, Rahab, Ruth and Bathsheba – prefigure Mary, Jesus' mother, most notably as women engaged in what were, from the perspective of their ancient narrators, 'irregular' sexual relationships sometimes resulting in 'problematic' pregnancies. This is especially the case with Tamar and Bathsheba. The ethnically inclusive quality of Jesus' messianic line, evidenced by Ruth and Rahab, likely appealed to early Christianity's growing proselyte community (Smit 2010: 205–7).

In addition to being one of Jesus' ancestors, Ruth also serves as a kind of Hebrew bible template for idealised (fe)male disciples in the gospels. Specifically, the various foot-anointing scenes and the image of Mary sitting at Jesus' feet resemble the Ruth narrative in two essential ways. First, Mary positions herself at the feet of Jesus as a way to communicate humility, dependence and veneration, a gesture that parallels Ruth's posture at the feet of Boaz. Second, within the exegetical tradition surrounding Ruth, there is a line of interpretation in which Ruth anoints herself with myrrh in order to seduce Boaz

(Campbell 1975: 120; compare Song of Songs 1:3, 13, 3:6, 4:14, 5:1, 5, 13; Psalm 45:9; Esther 2:12; Proverbs 7:17). As demonstrated above, myrrh was a well-known aphrodisiac commonly used in biblical narratives, including the foot-anointing episodes from the gospels. As an intertextual imitator of Ruth, 'Mary' situates herself within a longstanding tradition, within the Davidic line, of sexually available yet markedly chaste women. This further underscores the erotic undertones of the gospel scenes and reinforces the notion that female Christian disciples may be simultaneously virtuous and sexually available. In this way, Mary both emulates and surpasses Ruth.

Since Thecla's character depends on Mary from the gospel tradition, and since Mary's veneration of Jesus' feet is also in conversation with Ruth, it is possible to read Thecla's veneration of Paul's feet alongside and perhaps even perpendicular to Ruth. Such a reading illuminates Thecla's literary ancestors and further complicates her sexual ambiguity. Moreover, the measures taken by Ruth in an effort to acquire marital security are comparable to those taken by Thecla to ensure her baptism. Each is, from the outset of her respective narrative, established as being a woman of good character. Ruth proves this by her loyalty to Naomi and by choosing not to pursue the men harvesting in the fields; Thecla, by her modest silence and initial confinement within the household (Schipper 2016: 33; Kraemer 2011: 142–3). Although it is not until the virtue of each has been established that they engage in implicitly sexual and potentially scandalous behaviour, nevertheless the first action each woman takes is essentially to reject the immediate prospect of marriage in favour of travelling to a strange land, an act which results in a crisis of identity.

Like Thecla, Ruth is a marriageable woman without a clearly defined position in society. Because Ruth is foreign and lacks a husband, when Boaz first sees her and asks whose she is, Ruth is identified by her mother-in-law, whose position is equally ambiguous, and by her ethnicity. The repeated mention of Ruth's Moabite heritage throughout the narrative perhaps foreshadows her sexualised actions at the threshing floor. Moab was the son of Lot and his eldest daughter who, not unlike Ruth, waited until her father was drunk and asleep before having sex with him. Boaz himself is the son of Rahab, the foreign sex worker, as well as a descendant of Tamar, who dresses like a sex worker in order to seduce Judah (Schipper 2016: 41).

Until Ruth's identity and sexual status are established through the solidification of her relationship with Boaz, she is explicitly vulnerable to assault: Boaz instructs his male servants not to attack or dishonour Ruth (Ruth 2:9, 16), and Naomi subsequently encourages Ruth to glean only in Boaz's fields because there she will be safe (Ruth 2:22). Paul's concerns regarding Thecla's beauty in a shameless age (APT 3.25) may suggest a similar vulnerability. Thecla's status, and the nature of her relationship to Paul, is ambiguous because the two are not explicitly sexually involved, nor can she yet be called a Christian. As a result, when Alexander attempts to bribe Paul and win Thecla who, like Ruth, is now a foreigner lacking a husband, Paul says that he does not know her, nor does he know whose she is, thereby exposing her to Alexander's advances. It is not until Thecla baptises herself and dons masculine clothing that she acquires the protection of a definite religious, gender and sexual identity. Although Paul assumes that some new misfortune has befallen Thecla when they are reunited in Myra, upon learning that she has been baptised, he expresses no lingering concerns about her vulnerability but tells her to go forth and preach. Only at this point in the narrative is Thecla's blended identity – simultaneously sexualised, as intertextual Ruth, and religious, as intertextual Mary – fully realised.

Like Ruth, Thecla attempts to acquire a new identity by arranging a private meeting with a man late at night. However, Ruth enhances her femininity through a kind of beautification ritual by bathing, perfuming and dressing herself before propositioning Boaz at the threshing floor. Although the erotic language of this scene is somewhat convoluted, and there is debate regarding whether Ruth is undressing herself or Boaz, nevertheless the act of covering/ uncovering is integral to the marriage proposal implicit in Ruth's actions (compare Ruth 3:9; Ezekiel 16:8; Deuteronomy 22:30, 27:20; Schipper 2016: 143–4, 149; Campbell 1975: 123; Carmichael 1977: 332). By contrast, Thecla divests herself of feminine possessions, selling her jewellery and mirror in order to gain entry to Paul's cell, before mimicking her predecessors by sitting at Paul's feet and kissing his chains. On the one hand, by ridding herself of material possessions, Thecla emerges as an idealised disciple (cf. Matthew 19:21). On the other, this sexualised interaction with Paul fails to win Thecla the baptism she desires, and she spends the remainder of the narrative further minimising her femininity, reasserting her chastity, and defending it against the men who pursue her. In reading Thecla through the lens of Ruth, we might view Thecla's baptism as the final beautification ritual necessary to complete her conversion, as it adheres to Ruth's tripartite practice of bathing, perfuming and dressing: Thecla bathes in the pool of man-eating seals during her self-baptism; is perfumed by the female spectators who throw scents (including nard) into the arena to protect her from the beasts; and, after the contest ends, Thecla asserts that God will clothe her before assuming the cloak of a man in the next episode. It is this ritual which ultimately wins her the right to be an itinerant Christian preacher.

Such echoes of and deviations from Ruth's standard encourage a further competitive reading of Thecla through the lens of Hebrew bible. Like Mary, Thecla's actions are comparable to Ruth's, but take them a step further and in a somewhat different direction. Both women are presented as moral, but their initial rejection of marriage and sexualised interactions with men who are not their husbands complicate this characterisation by placing them at odds with ancient Mediterranean social mores. However, because Ruth's beautification ritual increases her femininity, and because she rejects the prospect of one marriage only to accept another, she is quickly reinstated as part of the traditional feminine. By contrast, Thecla's forfeiture of jewellery and mirror, as well as her total rejection of marriage, evidences not only her first step toward increased masculinity, but also her willingness to abandon her wealth and her commitment to chastity. Whereas Ruth's combination of virtue and sexual availability makes her a more appealing future wife, the flaunting of Thecla's sexuality serves as an attempted means of preserving her chastity. Said differently, Ruth is sexual but not explicitly desirous; Thecla is desirous but explicitly chaste.

CONCLUSION

Our examination of these previously underappreciated allusions contributes to the existing scholarly understanding not only of early Christianity's conceptions of sexuality and the (fe)male body, but also its rhetoric of competition. We have seen that Thecla is a (wo)man whose gender and sexuality are not reducible to any normative ideal, but are changeable, multiple, often context-specific and ideal only insofar as they depart from the norm. From the ideological standpoint of the *APT*, this fluid identity enables her to transcend the traditional restrictions placed on her gender to become the ideal Christian. Not content with stereotypically 'feminine' silence, passivity and confinement to the home, Thecla's desire for conversion results in 'masculine' ambition. By breaking out of the female sphere, she leaves normative femininity behind and adopts 'masculine' traits as a defence against her own misogynistic society.

Though this change is met with considerable resistance from those advocating traditional gender norms, it becomes the key to entering the Christian community of the *APT*, and Thecla's baptism and preaching are dependent on a careful balance of 'masculine' and 'feminine'. Throughout the narrative, her primary allies (the newly converted Tryphaena, the women spectators and female beasts in the arena and her followers in the mountains) are explicitly feminine, and kissing Paul's chains is a sexually charged act. As intertexts between the *APT*, first-century gospels and Hebrew bible reveal, Thecla's veneration at Paul's feet imitates the posture assumed specifically by her female literary predecessors, and situates her simultaneously as a woman marked by her sensuality and sexual availability, and a disciple devoted to sexual continence. Nevertheless, Thecla cannot travel safely or preach the gospel authoritatively until she has been baptised and 'made male', with shorn hair and masculine clothing. Thecla's sexual renunciation, her rejection of domestic obligations and her commitment to hearing and preaching the gospel – ultimately enabled by her increasing masculinity and transvestism – show her commitment to the faith, and these deviations from the behavioural models of 'Mary' and Ruth demonstrate her superiority as the ideal Christian convert, surpassing all prior precedents. Thus the *APT* promotes its brand of ascetic Christianity as a chosen family in which a non-binary individual who rejects normative sexuality and behaviour is the ideal member, and by exceeding the already idealised exempla of Ruth and 'Mary', Thecla proves herself to be the disciple perfected.

CHAPTER 14

Manly and Monstrous Women: (De-)Constructing Gender in Roman Oratory

Mary Deminion

INTRODUCTION

In his anecdotal history collection *Memorable Deeds and Sayings*, Valerius Maximus records the cases of a trio of women orators who were inhibited neither by their sex nor by modesty from pleading legal cases on the public stages of the Roman forum and lawcourts. Though women were not legally barred from acting on their own behalf in trials, their foray into the male space of the Roman courtroom as orators was a gender-transgressive act met with ambivalence, even ridicule. The appearance of the three women orators in Valerius is exceptional not only for the rarity of the phenomenon at Rome but also for the paucity of accounts of women in recorded rhetorical history. Valerius reports that one of these women, Maesia of Sentinum, secured her own acquittal from unspecified criminal charges through her display of courage and rhetorical skill, but was condemned for her 'usurpation of the male role' (Marshall 1990). Maesia's performance in court represents a bending of the gender binary so alarming to her (male) audience that she is recorded for posterity as '*Androgyne*', a blending of the Greek words for 'man' and 'woman'. Harsher criticism was directed at Gaia Afrania, who thwarted the convention of relying on male kin to represent her in court and argued cases herself on multiple occasions. Afrania's repeated violation of gender norms and her assumption of the male role are so egregious that Valerius condemns her as a *monstrum*, putting her beyond not only gender categories but beyond what is regarded as human. The jurist Ulpian, writing in the third century AD, blames her example for a magistrate's edict barring all women from representing others' causes in court (*D.* 3.1.1.5). By contrast, Hortensia, daughter of the jurist Quintus Hortensius Hortalus, receives praise from Valerius and the later Appian for her speech against the war tax on Roman matrons, but only insofar as her close identification with her illustrious father allows her to transcend her gender and be seen as his living image. Whether censured or praised, the women in all three cases are presented as masculinised and gender non-conforming at best, or inhuman at worst, for breaching the gendered lines of public self-representation in political and legal matters. The ambivalence about women orators therefore reveals a deeper anxiety about gender boundaries in Roman public life and the limits of male power.

Modern feminist and queer scholarship has contributed to our understanding of gender as a set of identities and expressions that are culturally and historically situated, distinct from biological sex but related to it through social conventions. Masculinity and femininity are performed according to social codes that are fluid, mutable and historically located; gender is itself socially constructed and performative (Butler 1990; Halberstam 1998; Dinshaw 1999). Scholars have also begun to examine the field of rhetorical training as a locus of gender construction. Oratorical training in ancient Rome was concerned with the making of a man. More specifically, the goal was to make a certain kind of man – a politically engaged citizen man who would embody elite virtues and could take his place amongst the Roman ruling class. Rhetorical schools and performance halls were sites where such men are made, where 'manhood is contested, defended, defined, and indeed produced' and rhetorical handbooks, such as that of Valerius, act as 'guides to gender construction' (Richlin 2002: 74). The Latin *orator*, a third declension masculine noun, is defined by Cato the Elder as 'a good man skilled at speaking' (*vir bonus dicendi peritus*, Quintilian 12.1.1). Rhetoric and oratory in ancient Rome were practised 'in male space, by men, for men, to men, according to men's interests' (Connolly 2007: 84). By contrast, 'womanhood is constructed in Roman culture through exclusion from rhetoric' (Richlin 2002: 75). Accordingly, much classical scholarship has focused on the relationship between masculinity and rhetoric. This study aims to identify those few women in ancient Rome who proved to be the exception to the exclusionary rule. If gender is defined in ancient Rome according to a framework of inclusion/exclusion, the forced inclusion of these few women in the exclusively male domain of public oratory places tension on the construction of gender as a natural binary and poses a direct test to the limits of Roman patriarchal power.

Because of the political, cultural and social importance of public speech, the ability to speak persuasively before an audience is an exercise in power and influence largely denied women across time as well as cultures. As Cheryl Glenn (1997: 1–2) writes:

> Rhetoric always inscribes the relation of language and power at a particular moment (including who may speak, who may listen or who will agree to listen, and what can be said); therefore, canonical rhetorical history has represented the experience of males, powerful males, with no provision or

allowance for females. In short, rhetorical history has replicated the power politics of gender, with men in the highest cultural role and social rank. And our view of rhetoric has remained one of a gendered landscape, with no female rhetoricians (theoreticians) clearly in sight.

It is clear that ancient Romans were well aware of the relationship between public speech, self-representation and power. Leanne Bablitz (2007) has identified the Roman courtroom as one of a number of public 'stages' where 'Romans of elite class or those wishing to attain some measure of fame could promote and advertise themselves', activities thought immodest and inappropriate for respectable Roman women. In her chapter exploring the location of legal activities in the city of Rome, Bablitz maps the courtrooms of Rome onto the known topography of the city and finds that in both the Republican and Imperial periods court cases were most often heard in the forum, at the very heart of the city where activity would be most open and visible.

Dionysius of Halicarnassus (3.67.3) describes the Roman forum as the place where 'justice is administered, the assemblies of the people held, and other civil matters transacted' and Festus (74L) defines *forum* similarly as 'a place where lawsuits are tried, public assemblies held, and speeches delivered'. That all of these proceedings were carried out primarily by men largely to the exclusion of women is supported by Ulpian in the *Digest* (50.17.2), who observes that 'women are separated from all civic and public functions'. Indeed only Roman male citizens could vote, or serve as jurors or magistrates. Though women were not legally barred from participating in trials, convention held that men typically advocated for women who appeared as plaintiffs or defendants. Public trials were held openly in the forum, but of the cases held between 149 and 50 BC analysed by Michael Alexander (1990), fewer than 5 per cent involved women in any role. But were women excluded from the physical space of the forum itself, and to what extent can the forum be identified as a masculine sphere?

In her study 'Women and Gender in the Forum Romanum', Mary Boatwright (2011) analyses the gendered nature of public activity in the forum using literary, epigraphical and archaeological evidence. Regardless of the type of evidence used, all sources point to the problematic nature of women's involvement in civic life in the open arena of the forum. Though she assumes that spectacles such as the *ludi* and triumphal processions must have had women among their audience, Boatwright concludes that the use of the forum by women is poorly attested in the archaeological and material record. During the Republic, at least, Boatwright (2011: 108) asserts that the forum 'reinforced a masculine public civic identity by excluding women visually and ideologically'. Ancient authors overwhelmingly depict women's presence in the forum, when they were not participating in religious or funerary rituals, as 'something extraordinary, transgressive, and anomalous' (2011: 119).

Though perhaps of doubtful historicity, Plutarch's comparison between the legendary Spartan and Roman lawmakers Lycurgus and Numa reveals the strength of the taboo against Roman women speaking in the forum. Tradition, Plutarch asserts, demanded a check upon women's agency from time immemorial; the practice was upheld even during the foundation of the city and its laws. Numa, he reports, carefully preserved the standards set by Romulus towards matrons and additionally required that they 'were not to speak, even on the most necessary topics, unless their husbands were with them' (3.10f). Not only is speech constructed as a distinctly masculine purview, the absence of speech – silence – is personified as feminine in the form of the Muse Tacita, whom Numa bids the Romans to venerate (Plutarch 8.11; Brescia 2015). So unnatural was it thought to be that a woman might demand to speak on her own behalf that, according to Plutarch, 'it is said that when a woman once pleaded her own cause in the forum, the senate sent to inquire of an oracle what the event might portend for the city' (3.10f). The appearance of a woman speaking in the forum was in itself enough to trigger male anxiety, and the contravention of social and gender norms was strongly linked to fears of disaster and unrest.

VALERIUS MAXIMUS

Though little is known about Valerius' background, scholars have inferred from the preface to his work that Valerius was a professional rhetorician and teacher during the reign of Tiberius (Bloomer 1992). The work belongs to the *exempla* tradition of Roman moralising discourse and may have served as a rhetorical and ethical handbook for students and practitioners of declamation. It contains a variety of historical examples loosely organised under thematic rubrics that a Roman orator might call upon to illustrate or embellish a particular argument. As such, these examples provide a tantalising glimpse into the elite values and attitudes of their time. Though Valerius' sources are unknown, Anthony Marshall (1990) suggests that they may have included detailed collections of actual court-decisions compiled by orators to establish precedents. They therefore serve not only to reflect the values of their time, but to reinforce and replicate social and cultural mores.

In his rubric *On Steadfastness* Valerius Maximus begins by asking, 'What do women have to do with public meetings?' He answers himself, stating, 'If the customs of the forefathers are to be adhered to, nothing.' He then proceeds to establish that it is in times of sedition, violence and civil unrest that ancestral custom and proper womanly restraint are overcome. What follows is the example of Sempronia, sister of the Gracchi and wife of General Scipio Aemilianus, who was unwittingly dragged before a popular assembly in the forum in 100 BC by a tribune of the plebs who hoped she would acknowledge the pretender Equitius as the son of her late brother, Tiberius. Sempronia, daughter of the highly educated Cornelia, who, according to Quintilian in his *Institutes of Oratory* (1.1.6) was herself known for her 'extremely learned speech' and credited with influencing the eloquence of the Gracchi, is said to have resisted performing before the masses and steadfastly maintained her ancestral dignity, despite the clamour of the assembled crowd. The episode treats the appearance of a woman before the assemblies in the forum as of note precisely because of its novelty and its contravention of gendered social norms. It is a mark of political and social crisis that the customary 'domestic quiet' of women like Sempronia is upended and invaded by the violence of sedition (Milnor 2005: 276).

Little historical or social context is provided by Valerius in his discussion of the cases of Maesia, Gaia Afrania and Hortensia. We are told only that the three women are united by the fact that they were unrestrained by the condition of their nature and the modesty of the *stola*, the garb befitting a respectable Roman matron, from speaking in public (*condicio naturae et uerecundia stolae*). A breach of *verecundia* is invoked similarly by Livy (34.1.1.5) in describing the women who agitated publicly against the Oppian law in 195 BC, by thronging the streets and even blocking men's entrance into the forum. The much later *Institutes of Justinian* also reveals a concern for *verecundia* in a section identifying women's right to bring public accusations on behalf of close kin in legal proceedings (1.26.3).

MAESIA OF SENTINUM

> EXEMPLUM 1. Amesia Sentinas rea causam suam L. Titio praetore iudicium cogente maximo populi concursu egit modosque omnes ac numeros defensionis non solum diligenter, sed etiam fortiter executa, et prima actione et paene cunctis sententiis liberata est. quam, quia sub specie feminae uirilem animum gerebat, Androgynen appellabant.
> (Valerius Maximus 8.3.1, all Latin from John Briscoe 1998.)

> Maesia of Sentinum pleaded her own case in front of a large crowd at a court gathered by the praetor Lucius Titius. Having made use of all the techniques and devices of defense both diligently and boldly, she was acquitted at the first hearing nearly unanimously. Because she bore a manly spirit in the form of a woman, they called her 'Man-Woman'.
> (All translations are mine.)

The first and shortest case Valerius describes is that of Maesia of Sentinum. She is said to have been brought before the praetor, named as Lucius Titius, on an unknown criminal charge and managed to defend herself successfully. Though Valerius does not provide context, and the praetor named cannot be dated with certainty, Marshall (1990) posits that the Maesia case may have occurred in the first half of the first century BC, and her decision to represent herself may be indicative of political and social dislocation. If this is the case, it further strengthens the link between women's agency and political unrest found in many ancient accounts. She is identified as 'Sentinas', a name suggesting her origins in Sentinum, a town in Umbria, rather than following the Roman naming convention of using the genitive form of her husband or father's cognomen. A likely explanation is that Maesia had no living male kin to defend her, and she was therefore left with little recourse but to act on her own behalf. In any event, Valerius Maximus expresses grudging admiration for Maesia's masterful skill in defending herself and her knowledge of 'all the techniques and devices' (*modosque omnes ac numeros*), though these are words that also describe sexual positions, and may be insulting *double entendres*.

We are left to speculate as to how Maesia might have received her knowledge of the art of rhetoric. There is frustratingly little information about ancient women's education, but Cicero (*Brut.* 210–11) and Quintilian both praise refined women who speak eloquently. Quintilian (1.1.6) writes:

> Regarding parents, I like to see them as highly educated as possible, and I do not restrict this remark only to fathers. We are told that the eloquence of the Gracchi owed much to their mother Cornelia, whose letters testify for posterity her educated style. Laelia, the daughter of Gaius Laelius, is said to have reproduced the elegance of her father's language in her own speech, while the oration delivered before the triumvirs by Hortensia, the daughter of Quintus Hortensius, is still read and not merely as an honour to her sex.

Some elite women were perhaps therefore given private instruction in rhetoric, even if only because an eloquent mother might transmit her skill to her sons to benefit their later public careers, or an educated daughter might reflect well on the quality of her father's household. There were also slave women *lectrices* who recited Greek and Latin literary works, presumably including speeches, in affluent households such as that of the elegist Sulpicia. The literary learning they imparted may well have been employed by elite women to write funerary inscriptions for household members, as Sulpicia seems to have done for her *lectrix* Sulpicia Petale (Stevenson 2005; Hallet 2011).

Maesia, however, is remembered for having taken her technical skill beyond the appropriate feminine domestic sphere. She thereby not only breached the boundaries of feminine modesty through her self-representation in court, but also contravened the limits of nature and her sex. She dared not only to speak in her own defense before a crowd but even had the nerve to be good at it. Maesia demonstrated intelligence and courage, qualities marked as masculine, and moreover, displayed them in the form of public speech in a male sphere. The use of the epithet '*androgyne*', apparently given to her by those who acquitted her of the charges or the crowd gathered to watch (or both), points to an ambivalence and anxiety surrounding Maesia's courage in her public performance on the stage of the Roman courtroom. She is simultaneously cast as both 'same' and 'other' by the male audience, a gender-blending man–woman hybrid who has transgressed gendered boundaries both physical and ideological.

GAIA AFRANIA

EXEMPLUM 2. C. Afrania uero Licinii Bucconis senatoris uxor prompta ad lites contrahendas pro se semper apud praetorem uerba fecit, non quod aduocatis deficiebatur, sed quod inpudentia abundabat. itaque inusitatis foro latratibus adsidue tribunalia exercendo muliebris calumniae notissimum exemplum euasit, adeo ut pro crimine inprobis feminarum moribus C. Afraniae nomen obiciatur. prorogauit autem spiritum suum ad C. Caesarem iterum P. Seruilium consules: tale enim monstrum magis quo tempore extinctum quam quo sit ortum memoriae tradendum est.

Gaia Afrania, wife of senator Lucinius Bucco, being addicted to lawsuits, always argued her own causes before the praetor, not because she lacked advocates, but because she abounded in shamelessness. Because she regularly harassed the tribunals with her aberrant barking in the forum, she emerged as the most notorious example of female litigiousness, so much so that to indict the unruly habits of women one has only to throw out the name of Gaia Afrania. She lived until the year Caesar became consul for the second time with P. Servilius: indeed such a monster is better remembered by her deathdate than her birthdate.
    (Valerius Maximus 8.3.2)

Despite the more subtle unease attached to the example of Maesia, Valerius saves his true invective for one Gaia Afrania, wife of the curiously if unfortunately named senator Lucinius Bucco ('Mouth'), who served during the time of Sulla. Scholars have understandably linked this Afrania with the 'Carfania' censured by Ulpian (*Digest* III.1.1.5) for arguing cases not only on her own behalf but also for that of others, thus provoking an edictal ban on such activity for women (Marshall 1989; Benke 1996).

Valerius says nothing of Afrania acting for others, only that she elected to act 'on her own behalf always' (*pro se semper*), strongly suggesting that civil suits were her forte and that she must have pursued several of them. Of particular offense to Valerius is the fact that Afrania apparently did not lack male advocates who could have acted for her; she chose to represent herself. The language used by Valerius to describe Afrania is striking. Her public speaking in the forum is described as aberrant barking (*inusitatis foro latratibus*) and she herself is depicted as nothing short of a monster. This Scylla of the forum is further pilloried with the remark that her death date (48 BC) is more appropriately remembered than her birthdate. While Maesia is represented as defying the gender binary, Afrania has clearly broken the accepted boundaries entirely.

If we accept that the G. Afrania mentioned in Valerius and the Carfania of the *Digest* are one and the same, the example of this woman was disturbing enough to be blamed for a centuries-long ban on Roman women acting on behalf of others in the courts. Ulpian (3.1.1.5) writes that the reason women are prohibited from bringing a legal request on behalf of others is 'so that women not get themselves mixed up in other persons' legal suits contrary to the modesty befitting their gender, and so that women not perform men's duties'. The origin of this prohibition against women's legal agency is purportedly 'Carfania, a very wicked woman, who, by bringing suits without shame and disturbing the magistrate, provided the reason for the edict'.

It is worth noting that neither Valerius nor Ulpian explicitly claim that Afrania/Carfania brought suits on behalf of others, only that she brought legal requests in a manner or with a frequency that the magistrate found vexatious, and which was thought unsuitable for a woman. Jane Gardner (1986: 263) concludes that, though the memory of Afrania may have been 'burned into men's memories', she almost certainly could not have been solely responsible for the legal disability imposed on women as a class. Rather, it is the reference to prohibiting women from performing men's duties that is key to the ban; the *exemplum* of Carfania is simply a convenient scapegoat, 'an instrumental part of patriarchal strategy' (Benke 1996: 209). Under this strategy, it is necessary to view Afrania not merely as a woman who challenged gender norms, but rather as one vilified into a monster that defies and threatens the 'natural', gendered order.

HORTENSIA

> EXEMPLUM 3. Hortensia uero Q. Hortensi filia, cum ordo matronarum graui tributo a triumuiris esset oneratus nec quisquam uirorum patrocinium eis accommodare auderet, causam feminarum apud triumuiros et constanter et feliciter egit: repraesentata enim patris facundia impetrauit ut maior pars imperatae pecuniae his remitteretur. reuixit tum muliebri stirpe Q. Hortensius uerbisque filiae aspirauit, cuius si uirilis sexus posteri uim sequi uoluissent, Hortensianae eloquentiae tanta hereditas una feminae actione abscissa non esset.

> Hortensia, truly the daughter of Q. Hortensius, when the class of women was burdened with a heavy tax by the triumvirs and no man dared to lend

them his defense, pleaded the cause of the women before the triumvirs persistently and successfully: displaying her father's eloquence, she succeeded in getting the greater part of the tax remitted. Q. Hortensius lived again in the female line and inspired the words of his daughter, and if any descendants of the male sex had wished to continue this strength, such an inheritance of Hortensian eloquence would not have been cut short with the case of one woman.

(Valerius Maximus 8.3.3)

Despite the ambivalence shown Maesia and the outright contempt towards Afrania, Valerius expresses apparent praise for Hortensia. Hortensia was the daughter of the celebrated advocate and consul Quintus Hortensius Hortalus, renowned for his moving speeches on law and history. Valerius' account refers to the events of 42 BC in which Rome's wealthiest 1,400 women were subject to a tax to fund the ongoing war between the Second Triumvirate and the assassins of Julius Caesar. Outraged at being made to pay for a domestic war between political factions over which they could exert no control, the women chose Hortensia to speak on their behalf in the Roman forum. We learn from Appian's *Civil Wars* IV.32–4, though not from Valerius, that Hortensia's speech in the forum and the presumption of the women to assemble in a public meeting were regarded by the triumvirs as a socially transgressive act and subversion of gender norms. Appian (IV.34.1) writes, 'While Hortensia thus spoke the triumvirs were angry that women should dare to hold a public meeting when the men were silent.' The triumvirs ordered their lictors, or magisterial bodyguards, to drive the women away from the tribunal. However, the triumvirs were forced to relent thanks to the intercession of a large crowd who protested the treatment of the women.

The speech Hortensia delivered is recorded at length in Appian. Though she presents a 'voice of resistance' (Hopwood 2015: 305) against the male political actors of the day, Hortensia carefully begins by acknowledging that she and the other elite Roman women have tried to appeal first to their appropriate gendered networks. The women sought out the female family members of the triumvirs: they were greeted kindly by Octavia, the sister of Octavian (later the emperor Augustus), and by Julia, the mother of Mark Antony, but were rudely rebuffed by Fulvia, Antony's wife. Only after failing to find resolution through women's channels were these women driven to the male sphere of the forum as a last resort: 'As has been befitting of women of our rank when making a request of you, we had recourse to the ladies of your households; but having been treated by Fulvia in a way that was not appropriate for us, we have been driven together to the forum' (IV.32).

Hortensia is clear in stating that civil unrest has caused the women to be deprived of their rightful advocates against ill-treatment and injustice, their male kin, remarking: 'You have already deprived us of our fathers, our sons, our husbands and our brothers, indicting them for having wronged you; but if you take away our property too, you reduce us to a condition unbecoming of our birth, our behaviour, our feminine nature' (VI.32). She further asks, 'Why should we pay taxes when we do not share in the offices, the honours, the command, the state-craft, over which you contend with each other with such harmful results?' (IV.33).

With significant oratorical skill, Hortensia treads the line between acknowledging that her speech in the forum is unusual, indeed traditionally inappropriate for a respectable Roman woman, and at the same time emphasising that she is in fact making a necessary defense of the women's proper feminine status and dignity. She further appeals to the fundamental injustice of the women's having to pay taxes to fund male civil conflicts despite their formal exclusion from all other functions of state. Judging by the recorded reaction of the crowd thronging the forum, the women's cause pleaded by Hortensia was a popular one, prompting the triumvirs to change their minds.

Though her eloquence resulted in the larger portion of the tax being repealed, Hortensia's even greater success, according to Valerius, is that she allowed her father to 'breathe again in her words', speaking as she did with 'her father's revived eloquence'. Her skill thus carried on the legacy of Hortensian oratory, we are told, before it was cut short by a lack of any male descendants willing to continue the practice. Significantly, while Afrania is condemned for her usurpation of the traditional male role in court and Maesia's feminine modesty is questioned due to her masculine daring and rhetorical prowess, Hortensia suffers no such censure, perhaps because she was representing her paternal family, as 'same' rather than 'other'.

The more favourable treatment of Hortensia compared to her fellow female orators can therefore be seen as a result of Valerius' admiration for her father, Hortensius, whom she clearly evokes (Hallett 1984, 1989a). Maesia, Afrania and Hortensia all manifest traits and engage in behaviours that would be valued in Roman men, but not women, and all three do so in the male spheres of the forum or courtroom, but each woman faces a highly variable degree of praise or blame. In her analysis, Judith Hallett (1989a) finds that Hortensia, who can be seen in some significant ways as being 'the same' as her father, is accorded a legitimacy through her kinship with him and her echoing of his celebrated traits, something that is denied Maesia, and especially Afrania. Valerius is able to reconcile Hortensia's rhetorical performance with the tradition set by her father, a paragon of the genre.

CONCLUSION

Though Hortensia's feminine modesty is not impugned in the same way as Maesia's and Afrania's, acceptance of her civic activism and encroachment into the male sphere of the forum still required that she be validated through a masculine identity.

Hortensia may also be less threatening to moralistic male writers such as Valerius, because, unlike Afrania, she presented herself as assuming her role reluctantly, in the absence of available male advocates, and only after exhausting the more appropriate women's channels. She is also portrayed as having taken up a distinctly feminine cause – the tax on matrons – which she convincingly presents as a final affront to other women's dignity after the loss of their male kin. While Maesia and Afrania demonstrate their agency by actively advocating for themselves, Hortensia's actions can be viewed as being a lesser affront to the 'natural' passivity of women. She acts to restore the upended social order, not damage it further. She is also further validated by heredity: she is seen as bringing forth the legacy of her father as his living image.

Taken together, the treatment of each woman by Valerius Maximus, and other primary sources where these women appear, essentially differs only in degree, not in kind, from the others. Hortensia is depicted most positively, Afrania most negatively, Maesia most ambivalently, but all three are represented as being in violation of the traditional social norms expected of their gender. The Roman tendency to construct gender along distinct, opposing, exclusionary lines requires the swift containment of behaviour that blurs or transgresses these boundaries. In the case of our three women orators, this means that they must be recorded for posterity as cautionary *exempla* for their willingness to bend or break the gender dichotomy of public speech/silence. Hortensia and Maesia are constructed as exhibiting masculinised personae: the faithful image of an illustrious father, or a gender-blending *androgyne*, respectively; both women engage in a blending of both the masculine and feminine. Afrania, on the other hand, is rendered monstrous for wilfully and repeatedly breaking the boundary altogether. All three women orators are assumed to be anomalous, even to some degree unnatural, for their transgression onto the male stages of the Roman courts and forum.

Though Valerius presents the three women as representing a failure of feminine modesty, their success in deploying the art of oratory to their own benefit exposes the precarity of the construct of Roman masculinity. That women could display such skill in a domain formally reserved as a training ground for idealised Roman manhood demonstrates that women too could perform masculinity as the Romans conceived of it. Perhaps more threatening still is the fact that in all three cases the three women orators assumed the male role through a breakdown or failure of patriarchal political dominance. Valerius and other Roman writers explicitly link women's public speech and civic protest to periods of war and sedition when normal social restraints are dislodged. In the case of Maesia, there appears to have been no one available to assume the male role for her in court, perhaps as a result of war casualties. There is a gap in the patriarchal framework, into which Maesia has stepped competently. In Afrania's case, it is unclear whether her husband or other male relatives were unable, or simply unwilling, to rein her in. In any event, she is described as exercising her own agency to pursue her own interests. It is Hortensia, however, who makes explicit the contradictions of male political dominance. Her speech specifically problematises the notion that women should be excluded from all matters of state, yet pay the price, both in terms of financial and personal loss, for decisions made by the male ruling class. The three women orators therefore represent not merely a challenge to how oratory constructs gender, but a threat to how elite Roman men defended and reproduced their power.

CHAPTER 15

The Great Escape: Reading Artemisia in Herodotus' *Histories* and *300: Rise of an Empire*

Denise Eileen McCoskey

INTRODUCTION

In 2007, Zack Snyder's epic film *300*, recounting the ancient Spartans' heroic stand at Thermopylae in 480 BC, became a worldwide phenomenon, earning approximately 456 million dollars globally. Based on the popular graphic novel by Frank Miller, the film generated lively and often heated discussion (e.g. Cyrino 2011, Burton 2016), reportedly sparking considerable outrage in Iran (Moaveni 2007). Many critics of the film called attention, in particular, to *300*'s racially charged depictions of Persian 'difference' (Lauwers et al. 2012). As Tom Holland notes, the film version 'duly outdoes even Frank Miller in its portrayal of Persians as grotesques', with the Persian king Xerxes himself looking like 'a towering bondage queen' – '"divine" only in the John Waters sense of the word' (Holland 2007: 180; for discussion of Xerxes' varied representations over time, see Bridges 2014).

A sequel, *300: Rise of an Empire*, was subsequently released in 2014 (dir. Noam Murro), but struggled from the outset to find its voice. The film tellingly underwent a title change during production – it was originally cast and shot as *300: Battle of Artemisia* (Patten 2012) – and even beat to completion the graphic novel it was ostensibly based on (Perry 2013). Although it would eventually gross nearly 340 million dollars worldwide, *Rise of an Empire*'s more muddled ideology and convoluted narrative structure (it portrays events not only after, but also before and during the previous film) clearly dulled critical and popular reception – despite the fact that the filmmakers might be said to have started with an advantage over the original since the film's action culminates at Salamis, an actual Greek victory over the Persians, unlike Thermopylae. While *300: Rise of an Empire* shifts to the series of naval battles led by the city-state of Athens during the second Persian invasion, the Athenians' valiant undertaking – not to mention the sequel's primary themes of Greek unity and freedom – are nonetheless persistently undercut by the franchise's continuing reverence for the jingoistic and nihilistic militarism of the Spartan men in the first film.

For all its flaws, *300: Rise of an Empire* introduces a provocative vision of female subjectivity, for *Rise of an Empire* places at its dramatic core Artemisia, a Greek woman who serves as Xerxes' adviser and fleet commander. It is easy to be captivated by Artemisia in the film; indeed, Eva Green's no-holds-barred performance was one of the few elements of the film generally praised by audiences and critics alike (e.g. Gettell 2014; Labrecque 2014; LaSalle 2014). In *Rise of an Empire*, Artemisia supplants Xerxes as the main villain, and her commanding presence in the film's battle scenes explodes the limits assigned to women in the previous film (Beigel 2012; Lauwers et al. 2012). But while some critics praised Green's ability to enter the masculine arena so convincingly, others were more circumspect about the film's sexual politics, with one writer proposing that the 'macho nonsense in the first film is turned into a man's fantasised version of girl-power and feminism in the second film' (Schleicher 2014).

I do not seek here to adjudicate the thorny question of the sequel's feminism. Rather I want to use Artemisia's earlier portrayal in Herodotus' *Histories* (a work completed by 425 BC) to help shed light on some of the specific decisions made by the filmmakers. My approach focuses on the discourses of 'sameness' and 'difference' that circumscribe Artemisia's appearance in each text; that is, I want to examine how Artemisia is situated in relation to the men she fights with and against in each version, as well as vis-à-vis the audience itself. Artemisia presents an especially rich case study because her status as a Greek woman fighting on behalf of Persia raises pointed questions about race as well as gender (on my use of the terminology of race, see McCoskey 2012: 27–31, 53–6). Moreover, the stakes of Artemisia's 'difference' will ultimately prove to be much higher in the film, since *Rise of an Empire* insists that Greek unity can be achieved only, quite literally, over Artemisia's dead body.

Before turning to a closer reading of both texts, however, I want to outline what we know about Artemisia from historical sources.

ARTEMISIA IRL

During the early fifth century BC, Artemisia – not to be confused with a later queen of the same name – ruled a territory in Asia Minor that included the city of Halicarnassus (modern Bodrum). According to Herodotus, Artemisia's mother was from Crete, and her father was from Halicarnassus (7.99). She held power as a widow, and Herodotus' phrasing implies that she ascended to the throne at her husband's death (Carney 2005: 75). Halicarnassus had been founded as a Greek settlement, but the Persian empire took possession of it in the mid-sixth century BC. Artemisia thus ruled as a Persian satrap, a kind of semi-independent viceroy responsible for sending annual tribute to the Persian king. During Xerxes' invasion of Greece (480 BC) Artemisia led a cohort of five ships, and after the Persian defeat at Salamis she allegedly helped convey Xerxes' illegitimate sons to Ephesus (Herodotus 8.103, 107). She is not heard from again in contemporary sources.

Later Greek sources record mixed reactions to Artemisia's participation in the Persian wars. In Aristophanes' *Lysistrata* (411 BC), for example, the male chorus warns that the city's rebellious women might send a navy to attack 'just like Artemisia did' (674–5). More suggestive, perhaps, of Artemisia's notorious gender bending, Euripides identifies himself as 'Artemisia' when disguised as an old woman near the end of Aristophanes' *Women at the Thesmophoria* (411 BC) (line 1200; see Austin and Olson 2004: 345–6). Centuries later, Pausanias (ca. 120–180 AD) identifies Artemisia as one of the figures depicted in the Persian Stoa at Sparta, noting that she joined Xerxes' campaign 'of her own free will' (*ekousiōs*) (*Description of Greece* 3.11.3; see also Vitruvius *On Architecture* 1.1.6). Adopting a more critical tone, Plutarch (ca. 45–120 AD) mentions Artemisia only once in his narrative of Salamis (*Life of Themistocles* 14.3), having elsewhere chided Herodotus for devoting too much attention to her ('On the Malice of Herodotus' 43).

Notably, Herodotus was himself also from Halicarnassus, and his generally positive portrayal of Artemisia highlights in important ways her continuing capacity for 'escape'.

ARTEMISIA IN HERODOTUS

Artemisia makes her dramatic entrance in Herodotus' text when the historian professes that he feels the need to name none of Xerxes' fleet commanders except Artemisia, because, he contends, as 'a woman fighting against Greece' she is a 'marvel' or 'wonder' (*thoma*) (7.99.1). Herodotus notes that Artemisia took over her husband's kingship after his death and that she has a son, explicitly positioning her within the institutions of both city and family. He further underlines Artemisia's difference from Xerxes' other allies by insisting that she fights because of her spirit and 'courage' or 'manliness' (*andreia*), and not because she was compelled to do so, a direct contrast with leaders he dismissed a few chapters earlier as 'slaves' (7.96.2; on *andreia* see Penrose in this volume).

From the outset, Herodotus thus places Artemisia, the 'fighting woman', outside the roles traditionally assigned to Greek women. His very use of *andreia* – a concept derived from the Greek word 'man' (see Bassi 2003) – underlines her departure from the standard codes of Greek femininity. Even more, the rare association of *andreia* with 'wonder' in Herodotus specifically 'emerges where boundaries are blurred and categories confused' (Harrell 2003: 77). So the 'marvel' of Artemisia entails both her escape from conventional categories and her multivalent 'difference' – her sexual difference as a woman, which distinguishes her from men; her masculine *andreia* and participation in 'fighting', which distinguish her from other women (Dewald 1981; Blok 2002; Hazewindus 2004) and her autonomy, which distinguishes her from the rest of Xerxes' allies.

Once introduced, Artemisia's unique status remains a prominent part of Herodotus' narrative. During the battle of Salamis, Artemisia allegedly rams an ally when being pursued by an Athenian ship and Herodotus reports that the strategy gains her a double advantage: she fools the Athenians, and Xerxes afterwards holds her in even higher regard (8.88.1–2). Xerxes himself interprets Artemisia's bold act as the manifestation of fundamental gender inversion, proclaiming: 'My men have become women and my women, men' (8.88.3). In Xerxes' estimation, then, Artemisia's gender transgression is not so much a cause for wonder, but rather a means for overturning the entire gender system.

As the phrasing of Xerxes' outburst suggests, Herodotus employs gender as a prominent framework throughout his narrative. Herodotus openly calls into question the masculinity of the Persian forces in his earlier account of Thermopylae, proposing that Xerxes himself recognised that 'although there were many people (*anthrōpoi*), there were few men (*andres*)' in his ranks (7.210.2). Conversely, Herodotus records the Greeks' attempt to enforce strict gender boundaries when they establish a special reward of ten thousand drachmas for Artemisia's capture, purportedly resenting that 'a woman would wage war against Athens' (8.93.2). Having himself labelled Artemisia's fight against Greece a 'wonder', Herodotus immediately reassures his audience that she escaped without getting caught (8.93.2). As such approval might suggest, despite all her differences and her allegiance to Persia, Herodotus endows Artemisia with a comforting or familiar 'sameness' in relation to his Greek audience.

The Greeks of Asia Minor present a notable conundrum in ancient racial theory (Thomas 2000: 94), and any attempt to define the region of Caria (where Halicarnassus was located) 'culturally, ethnically or even geographically is itself not straightforward' (Unwin 2017: 1); for one, '(i)ts diverse population included Persians, Lydians, and especially Carians' (Munson 2014: 348). Moreover, in terms of Artemisia's own background, just as her own parents were evidently from Crete and Halicarnassus, Rosaria Vignolo Munson notes that the 'occurrence of Carian names . . . as well as Greek' in the ruling family of Halicarnassus 'suggests intermarriage' (Munson 2014: 348). Susan McWilliams posits that Herodotus' interest in 'marriage and sex across political boundaries' was part of a broader interest in representing 'hybridity' throughout his text (McWilliams 2013: 748), and this might suggest that a certain racial fluidity helps define Artemisia's 'difference' to Herodotus.

Yet despite his general interest in hybridity and his acknowledgement of the frequent porousness of borders separating groups, Herodotus treats racial groups as distinct and he defines their differences primarily through culture, that is, by 'practices, prescriptions, and prohibitions' as well as 'worldview' (Munson 2014: 350; see also Thomas 2001: 226). So Herodotus' association of Artemisia with various 'Greek' ideas and practices is critical to his construction of her Greek racial identity, even when it is at odds with other textual strategies (for the opposing argument, that she remains 'ethnically ambiguous', see Harrell 2003: 82–8). When urging Xerxes not to fight at Salamis, for example, Artemisia invokes the conventional Greek view of gender, warning the Persian king that 'their men (i.e., the Greeks') are stronger than your men at sea by as much as men are stronger than women' (8.68.1). Employing the analogy Greeks : Persians :: men : women, Artemisia is thus made to assert the Greek view of male superiority that her own actions defy, while endorsing the standard Greek association of Persians with effeminacy.

Munson identifies other features that align Artemisia closely with the Greeks: her ability to act according to her own free will (1988: 95); her stewardship of a strong navy (95, 97ff.); her prominent role as adviser, including willingness to speak what the Persian king may not want to hear (95–8); and her act of self-preservation in ramming an ally ship (98–102). Munson further argues that many of these qualities closely mirror those of the Athenian leader Themistocles himself. Themistocles, for example, frequently engages in free speech, a democratic prerogative (Munson 1988: 97), and the respective strategies Artemisia and Themistocles advocate in regard to Salamis have strong correlation (Munson 1988: 98; see also Pelling 2006: 110–12). Finally, not only does Herodotus applaud Artemisia's 'aptitude for survival through fraud' (Lateiner 1990: 232) at Salamis, but he also finds its parallel in the capacity of both Athens and Themistocles to be 'ethically and politically flexible, according to what seems most expedient' (Munson 1988: 100).

In all, Herodotus balances an abiding emphasis on Artemisia's difference – the exceptionality that sets her apart when it comes to gender – with a striking vision of her racial sameness as articulated through Greek qualities like autonomy, democratic or free speech, and skill at self-preservation. While she remains opposed to the inevitable Greek victory, Artemisia nonetheless survives, as Herodotus himself reminds us. So his ultimate take on Artemisia might by encapsulated by her propensity for escape: her escape both from the boundaries of gender as a 'woman fighting' and from the clutches of her Greek pursuers during the battle itself.

Escape will prove to be a more complicated prospect for Artemisia in *Rise of an Empire*.

ARTEMISIA IN *300: RISE OF AN EMPIRE*

Rise of an Empire opens with *300*'s iconic image of the Spartans lying dead at Thermopylae, yet the action soon moves back ten years earlier to the battle of Marathon, where combined forces from Athens and Plataea halted the first

Persian invasion in 490 BC. In an act completely invented by the filmmakers, Themistocles (Sullivan Stapleton) shoots an arrow into the Persian king Darius (Igal Naor) as his son Xerxes (Rodrigo Santoro) watches. The Spartan queen Gorgo (Lena Headey), who provides the film's narration, insinuates that the second Persian invasion will derive from Xerxes' rage, but a different source for the encounter soon emerges: female vengeance.

As the setting shifts to Persia, Artemisia, the king's 'finest naval commander', makes her dramatic entrance, striding fiercely into Darius' throne room. The camera closes in on Artemisia as Gorgo recounts her qualities of 'ferocity', 'beauty' and 'devotion' to the king. While Gorgo defines Artemisia in part by her physical appearance, Artemisia is actually far from conventionally beautiful in the terms of the franchise; unlike other female characters, she routinely wears black (she also notably wears the pants in the film, literally), heavy black eye make-up, and hair strictly parted – all in all, a 'vampiric femme fatale' (LaSalle 2014) (Fig. 15.1). Moreover, Gorgo's initial label of 'ferocity' soon trumps all other features.

Gorgo posits that Darius 'had the perfect warrior protégé' in Artemisia, but their encounter implies a more intimate bond. As Artemisia kisses the dying

Figure 15.1 Eva Green as a 'vampiric femme fatale' in *300: Rise of an Empire*, dir. Noam Murro, USA: Warner Bros. Pictures, 2014.

king's hand, Darius murmurs 'so sweet . . . my child . . . my sweet . . . child'. Artemisia becomes visibly dismayed as she hears Darius warning Xerxes that 'only the gods can defeat' the Greeks, and, with a tear running down her cheek, she leans over and pulls out the arrow still lodged in Darius' chest, hastening his death. Then, Gorgo says, Artemisia 'whisper(s) the seed of madness' to the grief-stricken Xerxes, sending him on a solitary quest that transforms him into a god as well as king, now in possession of the towering, androgynous form of the first *300*. Artemisia soon continues her verbal mastery over Xerxes. As the king addresses an enormous crowd from the palace balcony, Artemisia mouths his words along with him, then overtakes him on the final word, whispering first: 'war'. In this way, Artemisia's skill with language is radically transformed from what was advisory and democratic in Herodotus to something domineering and destabilising. Even more, Gorgo reports that Artemisia has 'cleansed' the palace of 'all Xerxes' allies', and a montage shows her brutally stabbing, strangling and drowning a series of courtiers in quick succession.

Artemisia's 'ferocity' – her lust for war and murderous rampage, not to men-tion cold dispatch of her father/king – expresses well her dangerous position with regard to gender in the world of the film. For, operating under different cultural codes, today's action film needs to account not for what Herodotus considered a 'wonder', that is, a 'woman fighting' (there are a number of female action heroes), but rather female violence itself. As Hilary Neroni (2005: 106) writes, '(f)emale violence disturbs us – and filmic narratives' because '(o)nce a woman embarks on violence, we have a sense that she may never stop'. Modern film has thus developed a specific narrative 'to provide a justification . . . for female violence' (Tasker 2002: 152), one that contains female violence, even as it allows its release: rape-revenge (Henry 2014; Heller-Nicholas 2011; Read 2000). Drawing heavily on the genre of rape-revenge, the filmmakers therefore insert a traumatic backstory of their own invention to 'explain' Artemisia's violence.

Themistocles himself recounts Artemisia's history of extreme abuse after his friend Scyllias (Callan Mulvey) reports that she 'is murderous by trade with true skill on the sea' and a 'thirst for vengeance'. When Scyllias adds, 'Rumours are her entire family was murdered by a squad of Greek hoplites', Themistocles elabo-rates, providing the voice-over for a flashback that shows first Artemisia as a young girl, crying as her city and family are destroyed and soldiers slowly advance on her; then, as a slightly older girl held captive in 'the bowels of a Greek slave ship' as a male figure glances around surreptitiously and starts to undress. Years later, Themistocles says, 'she was discarded and left for dead' and the camera lingers on the brutalised body of the young woman as she lies abandoned on a sidewalk. With heavy voice, Themistocles pronounces that 'Artemisia vowed that day to return to Greece only when she could watch it burn.'

A rape-revenge narrative was notably employed in *300* when Gorgo, having been forced into sex by a corrupt Spartan politician, takes public revenge by killing him (on Gorgo, see Tomasso 2013). Artemisia's rape-revenge plot is both more expansive and more politically radical, however. For one, rather than targeting Artemisia's dangerous aggression at an individual rapist, her vengeance is directed against all of Greece itself; it is thus, by its very nature, virtually limitless. Artemisia's quest for revenge might therefore be seen as systemic, as a response to deep-seated patriarchal structures and 'institutionalised male power' (Tasker 2002: 152). Put in that light, it is little wonder that so much of the audience found Eva Green's Artemisia so exhilarating.

The rape-revenge narrative also helps account for Artemisia's distinct look in the film. Yvonne Tasker argues that 'for the action heroine as much as the action hero, the development of muscles as a sort of body armour signifies physical vulnerability as well as strength' (2002: 152), and Artemisia's body responds to its prior exploitation not by displaying the pronounced musculature so associated with *300* (Turner 2009), but by aiming for complete impenetrability. With only one notable exception, Artemisia's body is relentlessly concealed behind heavy black clothing with metallic trim, culminating in a final costume that has actual spikes down the back. Such clothing signifies power and not merely containment, and its design is clearly meant to cast her as a kind of dominatrix as well, especially when reciting lines like, 'Today we deliver submission'. As the duality of Artemisia's clothing intimates – connoting both protection and aggression – her position in the film involves a central paradox: she is both given what should be a sympathy-producing rape-revenge plot *and* cast as the villain, a rule-breaking aberration the audience is meant to root against.

The film offsets sympathy for Artemisia, in part, by underlining her radical difference from the men in the film, a strategy that involves not just gender, but also racial frames of reference. Herodotus, as we have seen, finds no contradiction in both acknowledging Artemisia's loyalty to Persia and her 'Greekness'; nor would this combination have troubled a Greek audience who knew very well that many Greeks fought on the Persian side (Cartledge 2013: 9, 62–3). Yet *Rise of an Empire* treats the Persian wars as an encounter fought along strict racial lines, and Artemisia's status as a Greek woman fighting on behalf of Persia is raised as a problem early in the film.

The scene begins as Artemisia, sitting on the deck of her ship, brazenly carves and eats an apple (a sly echo of Leonidas in *300*). A male prisoner is dragged before her and he calls her 'a whore from the eastern seas', the film's only allusion to Halicarnassus. He then goads Artemisia's men, proclaiming, 'Your commander is a Greek. Just like me. You Persian men take your orders from a Greek woman!', intimating that gender inversion – women commanding men – is both degrading and innate to Persian order. The prisoner notably tries to highlight Artemisia's sameness to himself, labelling her 'Greek' and 'just like me', but she refuses any affinity and calmly asserts a different source for her racial identification: 'Yes, my brother. I am Greek by birth and I have Greek blood running through my veins, but my heart is Persian.' She then decapitates the prisoner, slowly kissing the unattached head on the lips before casually discarding it.

The act that concludes Artemisia's repudiation of her Greek identity is, to say the least, disconcerting; but by discounting the passive attributes of genealogy and blood, Artemisia makes the active decision to prioritise her 'heart' instead, an identification that sets 'nurture' over 'nature' and is explained by the remainder of her backstory. For, after being 'discarded', Themistocles informs us that the young Artemisia was 'found near death by a Persian emissary'. Shaking his head as he looks down on her – a subtle and moving display of disapproval within a franchise that generally glamorises violence – the emissary (Peter Mensah) tenderly lifts Artemisia up and her reconstruction begins. The flashback shifts to a stock scene of young Artemisia being trained in sword fare and concludes with the now adult Artemisia presenting decapitated heads to king Darius as the emissary proudly looks on.

The second half of Artemisia's backstory illustrates well why she would choose a Persian 'heart', but it also, I believe, raises additional questions about her racial identification in the film since the emissary who finds Artemisia is, in fact, the unnamed Black Persian messenger from *300*, the franchise's only major Black character. Thus, the film not only aligns Artemisia with the 'non-white otherness' of the Persians (Burton 2016: 14), but also gives her a Black mentor who shapes her into a powerful warrior. The inclusion of a Black character shows important recognition of the Persian empire's multiculturalism; indeed, the Greeks' first widespread encounter with Black Africans may well have been through Xerxes' army (Snowden 1997: 107). Yet black skin colour would not have had the same racial connotations in antiquity (McCoskey 2012: 8–9), and the film's decision to make the Black emissary Artemisia's saviour reinforces the outsider status of both characters for today's (White) audiences.

It is crucial not to overstate the meaning the film derives from Artemisia's connection to the emissary. For one, the film frustratingly refuses to let the adult Artemisia express any devotion to him. In fact, when she enquires of Xerxes, 'Still no word from the messenger you spent to Sparta?', she shows (like the film itself) no knowledge that he even has a name. Moreover, we should not overlook the persistence of the 'magical negro' stock character when assessing the emissary's restorative care of Artemisia (Hughey 2009: 568; see also Glenn and Cunningham 2009; on Black characters in earlier epic films, Bâ 2011; Blanshard and Shahabudin 2011: 226). Yet I believe we can witness the parallel consequences of the 'otherness' binding Artemisia and the Black emissary nonetheless, for the franchise places the death of each at the core of Greek identity formation. In *300*, after all, the cry 'This is Sparta!' comes not during the Spartan battle against Persian forces, but as Leonidas kicks the Black emissary down a well. Meaning for all *300*'s emphasis on east versus west, Spartan identity is actually articulated most concisely over the demise of the Black male body, just as Greek unity will be consolidated over the White (non-Greek) female one in *Rise of an Empire*.

In a franchise replete with bloodshed, Artemisia is also distinguished by the extreme nature of her violence. When she kisses the decapitated head, she distorts the boundaries between sexuality and violence in shocking ways. And – to ensure the audience feels authorised to judge it that way – both Artemisia's own officer and the Greek Scyllias look away in disgust. Such representations of Artemisia are troubling when placed against the backdrop of her rape-revenge narrative: to what extent might trauma inform what the film takes as her 'perversity'? On the other hand, it is noteworthy that, the captive's comment aside, male characters generally avoid objectifying her, and she is the one who initiates sexual contact with Themistocles, suggesting she views sex as a mode of power and control.

Although the film makes a failed seduction the ultimate source of conflict between Artemisia and Themistocles (rather improbably and also uncomfortably given Artemisia's backstory), it earlier hints at some of the profound similarities they share, drawing an intriguing parallel to Herodotus' text. Such a mirroring is especially meaningful because Artemisia's isolation remains one of her defining features in *Rise of an Empire*. For, contrary to Herodotus' text, the film relentlessly deprives Artemisia of both city and family. In striking contrast to Gorgo, the franchise's other major female character, for example, the adult Artemisia remains emphatically unencumbered by the private sphere. Such detachment surely allows her a radical form of autonomy, the quality she is so praised for in antiquity. Yet rather than allowing Artemisia to take any pleasure in her unique and transgressive subject position, the film insists that she experience it solely as a detriment. After being told of losses her fleet has sustained, for example, Artemisia laments that 'my disappointment is in these men of whom I stand among. 10,000. I am alone.'

Themistocles openly acknowledges his resemblance to Artemisia when, after hearing Scyllias remark that 'she (Artemisia) has sold her soul to death himself', he responds, 'some could say I've sold mine to Greece'. Moreover, like Artemisia (and unlike Leonidas in *300*) Themistocles is not bound by any obligations to family *per se*. In fact, when Artemisia probes to see why the Athenian fights, Themistocles professes, 'I've had no time for family. I have spent my entire life with my one true love, the Greek fleet, and my one passion, readying it for you.' His suggestive use of 'love' and 'passion' conveys well the erotic dimensions of Athenian political discourse (Wohl 2002), yet it also foregrounds the increasingly sexualised nature of his connection to Artemisia; indeed, he makes the confession as Artemisia is seducing him.

Wearing a revealing dress for the only time, Artemisia summons Themistocles to her ship to try to recruit him to her side. But after they engage in rough sex, each aggressively trying to dominate the other, Themistocles bluntly refuses her offer. Afterwards, he notes wryly to his men that, 'The next time we meet her, she's going to bring all of hell with her.' And with that snide comment, Artemisia's status dramatically shifts from that of Themistocles' equal and counterpart to that of woman scorned, from a larger vendetta against Greece to a more personal revenge against one man.

This redirection and narrowing of Artemisia's rage notably allows their final encounter at Salamis to serve as the film's climax. In preparing for that battle, Themistocles now defies sexist tropes and asserts that he wants to defeat Artemisia not because of some misogynist financial reward, but because of his deep respect for her skill, claiming that 'without Artemisia's command, the Persian navy is nothing'. But when he says to Artemisia, 'Who would you fight if not for me?' during their sword fight, there is a wilful erasure of the broader desires for revenge that once animated her, and I felt myself wanting to scream out on her behalf: 'All of Greece!'

As the film shrinks Artemisia's vengeance, her power diminishes and her body is once again targeted for abuse, now by both the Greek and Persian sides. During an argument, Xerxes, who was once dominated by her, now strikes Artemisia brutally across the face, knocking her to the ground. As blood trails from her mouth, Artemisia responds defiantly (Fig. 15.2), but the scene underlines her increasing loss of control by inverting their advisory relationship: it is Xerxes who now also

Figure 15.2 Artemisia (Eva Green) responds to Xerxes' blow; *300: Rise of an Empire*, dir. Noam Murro, USA: Warner Bros. Pictures, 2014.

(wisely) warns Artemisia not to engage the Greeks in battle. Themistocles soon after strikes a similarly intimate blow, punching Artemisia across the face during their final sword fight. The film underscores the significance of this moment by having Artemisia's blood splatter hit the camera lens and linger there as she herself slowly rises. But while Themistocles himself seems momentarily stunned by this sudden capitulation to the pleasure the film takes in punishing Artemisia's body, any opportunity for reflecting critically on the act of interpersonal violence evaporates when Artemisia is made simply to ridicule Themistocles' earlier sexual performance, taunting him, 'You fight much harder than you fuck.'

It is the elimination of Artemisia's cunning escape, however, that most reveals the fatal consequences of her difference in the world of today's film. For as Artemisia and Themistocles continue their fight, a fleet of Spartan ships approaches in the distance and Themistocles informs Artemisia that 'all of Greece has united against you'. To which she replies only, 'If death comes for me today, I'm ready.' It is then Themistocles who urges, 'there is still time for you to ready a launch and escape', making escape in the film a function not of Artemisia's craft and self-preservation, but a male prerogative to distribute. Artemisia adamantly refuses his offer, and her final word in the film is a disbelieving 'surrender'. After Themistocles finally pierces her stomach with his sword, she grabs his shoulder and pushes herself further onto it. When Artemisia pulls back from the sword, she falls onto her knees, and the film freezes her momentarily in a posture disconcertingly reminiscent of surrender – has Artemisia, in fact, escaped surrender with her bold act, or merely confirmed it by her death?

CONCLUSION

I can locate the origin of this article in a comment made by my friend, a TV studies scholar, as we exited the theatre: 'I don't get it,' he said. 'Why exactly are we supposed to be rooting against Artemisia?' One answer is, of course, that the franchise establishes the defeat of the Persians, and so Artemisia herself, as a precondition for the emergence of 'western values' like freedom, a theme promoted as well in ancient Greek representations of the Persian wars. Yet the film's portrayal of Artemisia's early sexual abuse at the hands of Greek soldiers and Greek slave-dealers offers a powerful opening for reconsidering both the costs and victims of such values, that is, the types of subjects who are exploited and then 'discarded' by the western 'democratic' project. Even more, the film ultimately insists on her death. So we are invited to sympathise with Artemisia, but only to an extent. What extent?

My reaction to the film became even more confused as I discovered that some of my students found it easier than I to dismiss Artemisia's violent backstory, relying mainly on the 'perversity' and power she wields as an adult combatant to cheer her defeat. Such views admittedly left me unsettled (did they really have so little compassion?), but their comments also helped me articulate more clearly the interpretive dilemma I was experiencing: how can/should the film's audience calibrate Artemisia's extreme victimisation in the past with her forceful and subversive agency in the present? Does the end of the film merely reinforce a disturbing pattern of abuse against her, or does it furnish her with a final act of resistance?

In trying to bring together a reading of Artemisia, I was fortunate that a number of friends encouraged me to grapple with the film in ways that I initially resisted. My TV scholar friend, for one, forced me to work through my initial distaste for Themistocles and admit the ways his character embodied a more complicated vision of masculinity than that of the Spartans in *300*. It is Themistocles, after all, who utters on behalf of many of us an exasperated 'Spartans' when watching the Spartans' violent training regime. And, at closer look, Themistocles' character operates in surprisingly complicated ways with and against Artemisia (bar the requisite – and quite depressing – sex scene and its locker-room denouement: you're better than that, Themistocles!).

In short, I realised I needed to account for both what I perceived as the film's deep-seated misogyny and the fact that Artemisia's presence, her unremitting defiance of the film's dominant narrative, was so electrifying. If the film asks its audience to root against Artemisia (and it does), many people I know who saw the film, myself included, did not – and surely that must also be considered a product of the film.

Finally, however, I wanted to give greater context to *300: Rise of an Empire's* confounding portrayal of Artemisia by juxtaposing it with Herodotus' account, in turn putting our own modern narrative conventions and perhaps even our own misguided sense of 'progress' in greater relief. For despite what we might think about the ancient world's strict notions of gender, Herodotus' account, unlike that of today's blockbuster film, did not imagine Artemisia's body abused in its youth nor pierced at its death. Indeed, far from seeking any form of punishment for her 'wondrous' subjectivity, Herodotus simply cheered her thrilling escape.

Selected Bibliography

Aageson, J. W. (2008), *Paul, the Pastoral Epistles, and the Early Church*, Peabody, MA: Hendrickson.

Adams, J. N. (1982), *The Latin Sexual Vocabulary*, Baltimore: Johns Hopkins University Press, London: Duckworth.

Adkins, E. (2014), *Rudis Locutor: Speech and Self-Fashioning in Apuleius' Metamorphoses*, PhD dissertation, University of Michigan, Ann Arbor.

Ahl, F. (1985), *Metaformations: Soundplay and Wordplay in Ovid and Other Classical Poets*, Ithaca: Cornell University Press.

Ainsworth, C. (2015), 'Sex redefined', *Nature*, 518.7539: pp. 288–91.

Ajootian, A. (1995), 'Monstrum or Daimon: Hermaphrodites in Ancient Art and Culture', in B. Berggreen and N. Marinatos (eds), *Greece and Gender*, Athens: Norwegian Institute in Athens, pp. 93–108.

Alexander, M. C. (1990), *Trials in the Late Roman Republic, 149 BC to 50 BC*, Toronto: University of Toronto Press.

Allély, A. (2003), 'Les enfants malformés et considérés comme *prodigia* à Rome et en Italie sous la République', *Revue des Études Anciennes*, 105: pp. 127–56.

Allen, R. E. (1993), *The Symposium*, New Haven: Yale University Press.

Allison, P. M. (1993), 'How do we identify the use of space in Roman housing?', in E. M. Moormann (ed.), *Functional and Spatial Analysis of Wall Painting: Proceedings of the 5th International Congress of Ancient Wall Painting. Amsterdam, September 1992*, Amsterdam: Peeters-Leuven, pp. 4–11.

Allison, P. M. (2015), 'Characterizing Roman Artifacts to Investigate Gendered Practices in Context Without Sexed Bodies', *American Journal of Archaeology*, 119.1: pp. 103–23.

Alton, E. H., D. E. Wormell and E. Courtney (1978), *Ovidius, Fasti*, Leipzig: Teubner.

[American Psychiatric Association, DSM-5 Task Force] (2013), 'Gender Dysphoria', in *Diagnostic and Statistical Manual of Mental Disorders: DSM-5*, Arlington: American Psychiatric Association, pp. 451–9.

Anderson, G. (2009), '"It's how you tell them": Some Aspects of Lucian's Anecdotes', in A. Bartley (ed.), *A Lucian For Our Times*, Newcastle-upon-Tyne: Cambridge Scholars, pp. 3–10.

Anderson, W. S. (1963), 'Multiple Change in the *Metamorphoses*', *Transactions and Proceedings of the American Philological Association*, 94: pp. 1–27.

Anderson, W. S. (1996), *P. Ovidius Naso, Metamorphoses*, Leipzig: Teubner.

Anson, J. (1974), 'The Female Transvestite in Early Monasticism: The Origin and Development of a Motif', *Viator*, 5: pp. 1–32.

Armstrong, R. (2006), *Cretan Women: Pasiphae, Ariadne, and Phaedra in Latin Poetry*, Oxford: Oxford University Press.

Arrizabalaga y Prado, L. de (2010), *The Emperor Elagabalus: Fact or Fiction?*, Cambridge: Cambridge University Press.

Ash, R. (2007), 'The Wonderful World of Mucianus', in E. Bispham (ed.), *Vita Vigilia Est: Essays in Honour of Barbara Levick*, London: Institute of Classical Studies, pp. 1–18.

Åshede, L. (2015), *Desiring Hermaphrodites: The Relationships of Hermaphroditus in Roman Art*, PhD dissertation, University of Gothenburg, Göteborg.

Aubin, M. (1998), 'Reversing Romance? The Acts of Thecla and the Ancient Novel', in R. F. Hock, J. B. Chance and J. Perkins (eds), *Ancient Fiction and Early Christian Narrative*, Atlanta: Scholars Press, pp. 257–72.

Austin, C., and S. D. Olson (eds) (2004), *Aristophanes, Thesmophoriazusae, with introduction and commentary*, New York; Oxford: Oxford University Press.

Avery, D. (2015), 'Siberian Princess Buried 2,500 Years Ago May Have Been Intersex or Trans', *Logo. NewNowNext* <http://www.newnownext.com/siberian-princess-buried-2500-years-ago-may-have-been-intersex-or-trans/12/2015/> (last accessed 18 July 2018).

Bâ, S. M. (2011), 'Diegetic Masculinities: Reading the Black Body in Epic Cinema', in R. Burgoyne (ed.), *The Epic Film in World Culture*, London; New York: Routledge, pp. 346–74.

Bablitz, L. (2007), *Actors and Audience in the Roman Courtroom*, Monographs in Classical Studies, London: Routledge.

Bailey, C. (1922), *Lucretius Carus, De Rerum Natura*, Oxford: Oxford University Press.

Barad, K. (2003), 'Posthumanist Performativity: toward an understanding of how matter comes to matter', *Signs*, 28.3: pp. 801–31.

Barad, K. (2007), *Meeting the Universe Halfway: Quantum Physics and the Entanglement of Matter and Meaning*, Durham, NC: Duke University Press.

Barad, K. (2011), 'Nature's Queer Performativity', *Qui Parle*, 19.2: pp. 121–58.

Barchiesi, A. (1997), *The Poet and the Prince: Ovid and Augustan Discourse*, Berkeley: University of California Press.

Barnett, A. J. (2012), 'Beyond Priapus: A Call for a Feminist and/or Queer Theory Archaeology of Roman Masculinity and Phallic Iconography', *Nebraska Anthropologist*, 27: pp. 15–23.

Barrier, J. W. (2009), *The Acts of Paul and Thecla: A Critical Introduction and Commentary*, Tübingen: Mohr Siebeck.

Bartman, E. (2002), 'Eros's Flame: Images of Sexy Boys in Roman Ideal Sculpture', in E. K. Gazda (ed.), *The Ancient Art of Emulation: Studies in Artistic Originality and Tradition from the Present to Classical Antiquity*, Ann Arbor: University of Michigan Press, pp. 249–71.

Barton, C. A. (1992), *The Sorrows of the Ancient Romans: The Gladiator and the Monster*, Princeton: Princeton University Press.

Bartoš, H. (2015), *Philosophy and Dietetics in the Hippocratic* On Regimen, Boston; Leiden: Brill.

Bassi, K. (2003), 'The Semantics of Manliness in Ancient Greece', in R. M. Rosen and I. Sluiter (eds), *Andreia: Studies in Manliness and Courage in Classical Antiquity*, Boston; Leiden: Brill, pp. 25–58.

Bauckham, R. (2002), *Gospel Women: Studies of the Named Women in the Gospels*, Grand Rapids: Eerdmans.

Bauman, R. (1992), *Women and Politics in Ancient Rome*, London: Routledge.

Beacham, R. (1999), *Spectacle Entertainments of Early Imperial Rome*, New Haven: Yale University Press.

Bean, G. E. (1959), 'Notes and Inscriptions from Pisidia I', *Anatolian Studies*, 9: pp. 67–117.

Beard, M. (2000), *The Invention of Jane Harrison*, Cambridge, MA: Harvard University Press.

Beigel, T. (2012), 'With Your Shield or On It: The Gender of Heroism in Zack Snyder's *300* and Rudolph Maté's *The 300 Spartans*', in A-B Renger and J. Solomon (eds), *Ancient Worlds in Film and Television: Gender and Politics*, Boston; Leiden: Brill, pp. 65–78.

Benke, N. (1996), 'Women in the Courts: An Old Thorn in Men's Sides', *Michigan Journal of Gender and Law*, 3.1: pp. 196–256.

Bérard, C. (1974), *Anodoi; essai sur l'imagerie des passages chthoniens*, Rome: Institut suisse de Rome.

Berg, R. (2007), 'Ermafrodito e il Gioco delle Varienti Iconografiche nella Pittura Pompeiana', in C. G. Pelegrín (ed.), *Circulación de Temas y Sistemas Decorativos en la Pintura Mural Antiqua: Actas del IX Congreso Internacional de la Association Internationale pour la Peinture Murale Antique (AIRMA), Zaragoza, Calatayud, 21–25 Septiembre 2004*, Calatayud: Gobierno de Aragón, pp. 67–75.

Bernabé, A., M. Herrero de Jáuregui, J. San Cristóbal, A. Isabel and M. Hernández (eds) (2013), *Redefining Dionysos*, Berlin; Boston; New York: De Gruyter.

Bernstein, N. (2013), '*Distat opus nostrum sed fontibus exit ab isdem*: Declamation and Flavian Epic', in G. Manuwald and A. Voigt (eds), *Flavian Epic Interactions*, Berlin: De Gruyter, pp. 139–56.

Bettcher, T. M. (2007), 'Evil Deceivers and Make-believers: On Transphobic Violence and the Politics of Illusion', *Hypatia*, 22.3: pp. 43–65.

Betz, H. D. (1992), *The Greek Magical Papyri in Translation*, Chicago: University of Chicago Press.

Bieber, M. (1961), *The History of the Greek and Roman Theater*, Princeton: Princeton University Press.

Bigham, D. (2014), 'Queer Linguistics' (5:22) <https://www.youtube.com/watch?v'OOy8A1Q8B7M> (last accessed 26 October 2017).

Birley, A. (1999), *Septimius Severus: The African Emperor*, London: Routledge.

Bissa, E. M. A. (2013), 'Man, Woman or Myth? Gender-bending in Lucian's *Dialogues of the Courtesans*,' *Materiali e discussioni per l'analisi dei testi classici*, 70: pp. 79–100.

Bitarello, M. (2011), 'Otho, Elagabalus and the Judgement of Paris: The Literary Construction of the Unmanly Emperor', *Dioalogues d'histoire ancienne*, 37.1: pp. 93–113.

Blackness, M., A. Charuvastra, A. Derryck, A. Fausto-Sterling, K. Lauzanne and E. Lee (2000), 'How Sexually Dimorphic Are We? Review and Sythesis', *American Journal of Human Biology*, 12.2: pp. 151–66.

Blanshard, A. J. L., and K. Shahabudin (2011), *Classics on Screen: Ancient Greece and Rome on Film*, London: Bristol Classical Press.

Blok, J. (2002), 'Women in Herodotus' *Histories*', in E. J. Bakker, I. J. F. de Jong and H. van Wees (eds), *Brill's Companion to Herodotus*, Boston; Leiden: Brill, pp. 225–42.

Blondell, R. (2013), *Helen of Troy: Beauty, Myth, Devastation*, Oxford: Oxford University Press.

Blondell, R., and K. Ormand (2015), *Ancient Sex: New Essays*, Columbus: Ohio State University Press.

Blood, H. C. (2015), 'Apuleius' Book of Trans Formations', *Eidolon*, 15 June <https://eidolon.pub/apuleius-s-book-of-trans-formations-b98140d11482> (last accessed 4 June 2017).

Blood, H. C. (forthcoming), '*Sed illae puellae*: Transgender Studies and *Asinus aureus* 8.24–30', *Helios*.

Bloomer, W. M. (1992), *Valerius Maximus and the Rhetoric of the New Nobility*, Chapel Hill: University of North Carolina Press.

Bluck, S. (2012), 'Transsexual in Iran: A Fatwa for Freedom?', in C. Pullen (ed.), *LGBT Transnational Rights and the Media*, Basingstoke: Palgrave Macmillan, pp. 59–66.

Blundell, S. (1995), *Women in Ancient Greece*, Cambridge, MA: Harvard University Press.

Boatwright, M. T. (1998), 'Luxuriant Gardens and Extravagant Women: The *Horti* of Rome between Republic and Empire', in M. Cima and E. La Rocca (eds), *Horti Romani: Atti del convegno internazionale*, Rome: L'Erma di Bretschneider, pp. 71–82.

Boatwright, M. T. (2011), 'Women and Gender in the Forum Romanum', *Transactions of the American Philological Association*, 141.1: pp. 105–41.

Boehringer, S. (2007a), *L'homosexualité féminine dans l'Antiquité grecque et romaine*, Paris: Les Belles Lettres.

Boehringer, S. (2007b), 'Comment classer les comportements érotiques? Platon, le sexe, et érôs dans le *Banquet* et les *Lois*,' *Études Platoniciennes*, 4: pp. 45–67 <http://journals.openedition.org/etudesplatoniciennes/902> (last accessed 16 October 2018).

Boehringer, S. (2010), 'Pratiques érotiques antiques et questions identitaires: ne pas prendre Lucien au mot (Dialogues des Courtisanes, V),' *CLIO. Histoire, femmes et sociétés*, 3.1: pp. 19–52.

Boehringer, S. (2015), 'The Illusion of Sexual Identity in Lucian's *Dialogues of the Courtesans*', *Materiali e discussioni per l'analisi dei testi classici*, 70: pp. 79–100.

Bogaras, W. (1901), 'The Chukchi of North-eastern Asia', *American Anthropologist*, 3.1: pp. 80–108.

Bömer, F. (1976), *P. Ovidius Naso: Metamorphosen Buch VI–VII*, Heidelberg: Carl Winter.

Boschung, D., H. A. Shapiro and F. Waschek (eds) (2015), *Bodies in Transition: Dissolving the Boundaries of Embodied Knowledge*, Paderborn: Wilhelm Fink.

Botteri, P. (1992), *Les fragments de l'histoire des Gracques dans la* Bibliothèque *de Diodore de Sicile* (Hautes Études du Monde Gréco-Romain 18), Geneva: Librairie Droz.

Bourdieu, P. (1991), *Language and Symbolic Power*, Cambridge, MA: Harvard University Press.

Bowersock, G. (1975), 'Herodian and Elagabalus', *Yale Classical Studies*, 24: pp. 229–36.

Bradley, J. (2009), 'Beyond Hermeneutics: Peirce's Semiology as a Trinitarian Metaphysics of Communication', *Analecta Hermeneutica*, 1: pp. 56–72.

Bradley, K. (2000), 'Animalizing the Slave: The Truth of Fiction', *The Journal of Roman Studies*, 90: pp. 110–25.

Bradley, M. (2009), *Colour and Meaning in Ancient Rome*, Cambridge: Cambridge University Press.

Braidotti, R. (2013), *The Posthuman*, Cambridge: Polity.

Bremmer, J. (2015), 'A Transsexual in Ancient Greece: the Case of Kaineus', in D. Boschung, H. A. Shapiro and F. Waschek (eds), *Bodies in Transition: Dissolving the Boundaries of Embodied Knowledge*, Paderborn: Wilhelm Fink.

Brescia, G. (2015), 'Ambiguous Silence: Stuprum and Pudicitia in Latin Declamation', in E. Amato, F. Citti and B. Huelsenbeck (eds), *Law and Ethics in Greek and Roman Declamation*, Berlin: De Gruyter, pp. 75–93.

Bridges, E. (2014), *Imagining Xerxes: Ancient Perspectives on a Persian King*, London; New York: Bloomsbury.

Briscoe, John (ed.) (1998), *Valeri Maximi Facta et Dicta Memorabilia*, Stuttgart: Teubner.

Brisson, L. (1976), *Le Mythe de Tirésias. Essai d'analyse structural*, Leiden: Brill.

Brisson, L. (2002), *Sexual Ambivalence: Androgyny and Hermaphroditism in Graeco-Roman Antiquity*, trans. J. Lloyd, Berkeley: University of California Press.

Brommer, F. (1959), *Satyrspiele*, Berlin: De Gruyter.

Brooks, C. McC., J. L. Gilbert, H. A. Levey and D. R. Curtis (1962), *Humors, Hormones, and Neurosecretions: The Origins and Development of Man's Present Knowledge of the Humoral Control of Body Function*, New York: SUNY Press.

Brooten, B. J. (1996), *Love between Women: Early Christian Responses to Female Homoeroticism*, Chicago: University of Chicago Press.

Budin, S. L., and J. M. Turfa (eds) (2016), *Women in Antiquity: Real Women across the Ancient World*, New York: Routledge/Taylor & Francis.

Burnet, J. (1963), *Plato: Opera, vol. 2*, Oxford: Oxford University Press.

Burnett, A. P. (1998), *Revenge in Attic and Later Tragedy*, Berkeley: University of California Press.

Burton, P. (2016), 'Eugenics, Infant Exposure, and the Enemy Within: A Pessimistic Reading of Zack Snyder's *300*', *International Journal of the Classical Tradition*, vol. online, 8 February, pp. 1–23 <https://doi.org/10.1007/s12138-016-0391-9> (last accessed 18 June 2017).

Butler, J. (1990), *Gender Trouble: Feminism and the Subversion of Identity*, New York: Routledge.

Butler, J. (1993), *Bodies That Matter: On the Discursive Limits of 'Sex'*, New York: Routledge.

Buxton, R. (2004), *The Complete World of Greek Mythology*, London: Thames and Hudson.

Bynum, C. W. (1991), 'Women's Stories, Women's Symbols: A Critique of Victor Turner's Theory of Liminality', in *Fragmentation and Redemption: Essays on Gender and the Human Body in Medieval Religion*, New York: Zone Books, pp. 27–51.

Cadario, M. (2012), 'L'Immagine di Ermafrodito tra Letteratura e Iconografia', in I. Colpo and F. Ghedini (eds), *Il Gran Poema delle Passioni e delle Meraviglie: Ovidio e il Repertorio Letterario e Figurativo fra Antico e Riscoperta dell'Antico. Atti del Covegno (Padova, 15–17 Settembre 2011)*, Padova: Padova University Press, pp. 235–46.

Cadden, J. (1993), *Meanings of Sex Difference in the Middle Ages: Medicine, Science, and Culture*, Cambridge: Cambridge University Press.

Cameron, A. (1998), 'Love (and Marriage) between Women', *Greek, Roman and Byzantine Studies*, 39.2: pp. 137–56.

Campanile, D., F. Carlà-Uhink and M. Facella (eds) (2017), *Transantiquity: Cross-Dressing and Transgender Dynamics in the Ancient World*, London; New York: Routledge/Taylor & Francis.

Campbell, E. F. (1975), *Ruth: A New Translation with Introduction, Notes, and Commentary*, Garden City: Doubleday.

Campbell, G. (2003), *Lucretius on Creation and Evolution: a commentary on De rerum natura: book five, lines 772–1104*, Oxford: Oxford University Press.

Cantarella, E. (1987), *Pandora's Daughters: The Role and Status of Women in Greek Antiquity*, Baltimore: Johns Hopkins University Press.

Cantarella, E. (1992), *Bisexuality in the Ancient World*, New Haven: Yale University Press.

Cantarella, E. (2003), 'Fathers and Sons in Rome,' *Classical World*, 96.3: pp. 281–98.

Caratelli, G. P. (ed.) (1993), *Pompei: Pitture e Mosaici, Vol. 5*, Rome: Instituto della Enciclopedia Italiana.

Carlà-Uhink, F. (2017), 'Between the Human and the Divine: Cross-Dressing and Transgender Dynamics in the Graeco-Roman World', in D. Campanile, F. Carlà-Uhink and M. Facella (eds), *TransAntiquity: Cross-dressing and Transgender Dynamics in the Ancient World*, London; New York: Routledge/Taylor & Francis, pp. 3–37.

Carmichael, C. M. (1977), 'A Ceremonial Crux: Removing a Man's Sandal as a Female Gesture of Contempt', *Journal of Biblical Literature*, 96.3: pp. 321–36.

Carney, E. D. (2005), 'Women and *Dunasteia* in Caria', *The American Journal of Philology*, 126.1: pp. 65–91.

Carpenter, T. H. (1991), *Art and Myth in Ancient Greece*, London: Thames and Hudson.

Carpenter, T. H., and C. A. Faraone (eds) (1993), *Masks of Dionysos*, Ithaca: Cornell University Press.

Cartledge, P. (2013), *After Thermopylae: The Oath of Plataea and the End of the Graeco-Persian Wars*, New York; Oxford: Oxford University Press.

Chakrapani, V. (2016), 'Sex Change Operation and Feminising Procedures for Transgender Women in India: Current Scenario and Way Forward', in A. Narrain and V. Chadran (eds), *Nothing to Fix: Medicalisation of Sexual Orientation and Gender Identity*, New Delhi: Sage, pp. 139–59.

Champlin. E. (2003), *Nero*, Cambridge, MA: Harvard University Press.

Chappuis Sandoz, L. C. (2008), 'La survie des monstres: Ethnographie fantastique et handicap à Rome', *Latomus*, 67: pp. 21–36.

Charlier, P. (2008), *Les monstres humains dans l'Antiquité: analyse paléopathologique*, Paris: Fayard.

Cho, S., K. W. Crenshaw and L. McCall (2013), 'Toward a Field of Intersectionality Studies: Theory, Applications, and Praxis', *Signs*, 38.4: pp. 785–810.

Clarke, J. R. (1991), 'The Decor of the House of Jupiter and Ganymede at Ostia Antica: Private Residence Turned Gay Hotel?' in E. K. Gazda and A. E. Haeckl (eds), *Roman Art in the Private Sphere: New Perspectives on the Architecture and Décor of the Domus, Villa, and Insula*, Ann Arbor: University of Michigan Press, pp. 89–104.

Clarke, J. R. (1998), *Looking at Lovemaking: Constructions of Sexuality in Roman Art, 100 BC – AD 250*, Berkeley: University of California Press.

Clarke, J. R. (2002), 'Look Who's Laughing at Sex: Men and Women Viewers in the *Apodyterium* of the Suburban Baths at Pompeii', in D. Fredrick (ed.), *The Roman Gaze: Vision, Power, and the Body*, Baltimore: Johns Hopkins University Press, pp. 149–81.

Clarke, J. R. (2003), *Roman Sex: 100 BC to 250 AD*, New York: Harry N. Abrams.

Clarke, J. R. (2007), *Looking at Laughter: Humor, Power, and Transgression in Roman Visual Culture, 100 BC – AD 250*, Berkeley: University of California Press.

Clarke, J. R. (2011), 'Erotica: Visual Representations of Greek and Roman Sexual Culture', in M. Golden and P. Toohey (eds), *A Cultural History of Sexuality in the Classical World*, Oxford: Berg, pp. 169–190.

Clay, J. S. (1997), *The Wrath of Athena: Gods and Men in the Odyssey*, Lanham: Rowman & Littlefield.

Connell, R. W., and J. W. Messerschmidt (2005), 'Hegemonic Masculinity: Rethinking the Concept', *Gender & Society*, 19.6, pp. 829–59.

Connelly, J. B. (2007), *Portrait of a Priestess: Women and Ritual in Ancient Greece*, Princeton: Princeton University Press.

Connolly, J. (2007), 'Virile Tongues: Rhetoric and Masculinity', in W. Dominik and J. Hall (eds), *A Companion to Roman Rhetoric*, Malden, MA: Wiley Blackwell, pp. 83–97.

Cooper, K. (1996), *The Virgin and the Bride: Idealized Womanhood in Late Antiquity*, Cambridge, MA: Harvard University Press.

Cooper, K. (2013a), *Band of Angels: The Forgotten World of Early Christian Women*, New York: Overlook.

Cooper, K. (2013b), 'The Bride of Christ, the "Male Woman," and the Female Reader in Late Antiquity', in J. M. Bennett and R. M. Karras (eds), *The Oxford Handbook of Women and Gender in Medieval Europe*, Oxford: Oxford University Press, pp. 529–44.

Corbeill, A. (2004), *Nature Embodied: Gesture in Ancient Rome*, Princeton: Princeton University Press.

Corbeill, A. (2015), *Sexing the World: Grammatical Gender and Biological Sex in Ancient Rome*, Princeton: Princeton University Press.

Corley, K. E. (1993), *Private Women, Public Meals*, Peabody, MA: Hendrickson.

Craik, E. (1998), *Hippocrates: Places in Man*, Oxford: Clarendon.

Craik, E. (2009), 'Hippocratic Bodily "Channels" and Oriental Parallels', *Medical History*, 53.1: pp. 105–16.

Csapo, E. (1997), 'Riding the Phallus for Dionysus: Iconology, Ritual, and Gender-Role De/Construction', *Phoenix*, 51.3/4: pp. 253–95.

Csapo, E. (2010), *Actors and Icons of the Ancient Theater*, Chichester: Wiley Blackwell.

Cyrino, M. S. (2011), '"This is Sparta!" The Reinvention of the Epic in Zack Snyder's *300*', in R. Burgoyne (ed.), *The Epic Film in World Culture*, London; New York: Routledge, pp. 19–38.

Davidson, J. (1997), *Courtesans and Fishcakes: The Consuming Passions of Classical Athens*, London: Harper Collins.

Davidson, J. (2007), *The Greeks and Greek Love: A Radical Reappraisal of Homosexuality in Ancient Greece*, London: Weidenfeld & Nicolson.

Davis, S. J. (2001), *The Cult of Saint Thecla: A Tradition of Women's Piety in Late Antiquity*, Oxford: Oxford University Press.

Davis-Kimball, J. (2000), 'Enarees and Women of High Status: Evidence of Ritual at Tillya Tepe (Northern Afghanistan)', in J. Davis-Kimball, E. M. Murphy, L. Koryakova and L. T. Yablonsky (eds), *Kurgans, Ritual Sites, and Settlements: Eurasian Bronze and Iron Age*, Oxford: BAR International Series 890, pp. 223–39.

De Blois, L. (1998), 'Emperor and Empire in the Works of Greek Speaking Authors of the Third Century AD', *Aufstieg und Niedergang der Römischen Welt*, 2.34.4: pp. 3391–443.

Deacy, S. (2008), *Athena*, London; New York: Routledge.

Deacy, S., and A. Villing (2001), *Athena in the Classical World*, Leiden: Brill.

Dean-Jones, L. A. (1994), *Women's Bodies in Classical Greek Science*, Oxford: Oxford University Press.

Debrohun, J. B. (2003), *Roman Propertius and the Reinvention of Elegy*, Ann Arbor: University of Michigan Press.

Devor, H. (1989), *Gender Blending: Confronting the Limits of Duality*, Bloomington: Indiana University Press.

DeVries, K. (1997), 'The "Frigid *Eromenoi*" and their Wooers Revisited: A Closer Look at Greek Homosexuality in Vase Paintings', in M. Duberman (ed.), *Queer Representations: Reading Lives, Reading Cultures*, New York: New York University Press, pp. 12–24.

Dewald, C. (1981), 'Women and Culture in Herodotus' *Histories*', in H. P. Foley (ed.), *Reflections of Women in Antiquity*, New York: Routledge, pp. 91–125.

Dinshaw, C. (1999), *Getting Medieval: Sexualities and Communities, Pre- and Postmodern*, Durham, NC: Duke University Press.

Dinshaw, C. (2012), *How Soon Is Now?: Medieval Texts, Amateur Readers, and the Queerness of Time*, Durham, NC: Duke University Press.

Dixon, S. (1992), *The Roman Family*, Baltimore: Johns Hopkins University Press.

Doroszewska, J. (2013a), '". . . And She Became a Man": Sexual Metamorphosis in Phlegon of Tralles' "Mirabilia"', *Prace Filologiczne – Literaturoznawstwo*, 3: pp. 223–41.

Doroszewska, J. (2013b), 'Between the Monstrous and the Divine: Hermaphrodites in Phlegon of Tralles' *Mirabilia*', *Acta Antiqua Academiae Scientiarum Hungaricae*, 53: pp. 379–92.

Dover, K. (1978), *Greek Homosexuality*, Cambridge, MA: Harvard University Press.

Dreger, A. D. (2000), *Hermaphrodites and the Medical Invention of Sex*, Cambridge, MA: Harvard University Press.

DuBois, P. (1995), *Sappho is Burning*, Chicago: University of Chicago Press.

Dunbabin, K. M. D. (2003), *The Roman Banquet: Images of Conviviality*, Cambridge: Cambridge University Press.

Dutsch, D., and A. Suter (eds) (2015), *Ancient Obscenities: Their Nature and Use in the Ancient Greek and Roman Worlds*, Ann Arbor: University of Michigan Press.

Dwyer, E. (1982), *Pompeian Domestic Sculpture: A Study of Five Pompeian Houses and their Contents*, Rome: Giorgio Bretschneider.

Dyer, H. D. (1891), *Pompeii: Its History, Buildings, and Antiquities. An Account of the Destruction of the City, with a Full Description of the Remains, and of the Recent Excavations, and Also an Itinerary for Visitors*, London: George Bell and Sons.

Edwards, C. (1993), *The Politics of Immorality in Ancient Rome*, Cambridge; New York: Cambridge University Press.

Edwards, C. (1994), 'Beware of Imitations: Theatre and the Subversion of Imperial Identity', in J. Elsner and J. Masters (eds), *Reflections of Nero: Culture, History and Representation*, Chapel Hill: University of North Carolina Press, pp. 83–97.

Edwards, C. (1997), 'Unspeakable Professions: Public Performance and Prostitution in Ancient Rome', in J. P. Hallett and M. B. Skinner (eds), *Roman Sexualities*, Princeton: Princeton University Press, pp. 66–95.

Elsner, J. (2007), *Roman Eyes: Visuality and Subjectivity in Art and Text*, Princeton: Princeton University Press.

Evans, E. C. (1969), 'Physiognomics in the Ancient World', *Transactions and Proceedings of the American Philological Association*, 59.5: pp. 1–101.

Facella, M. (2017), 'Beyond Ritual: Cross-Dressing Between Greece and the Orient', in D. Campanile, F. Carlà-Uhink and M. Facella (eds), *TransAntiquity: Cross-dressing and Transgender Dynamics in the Ancient World*, London; New York: Routledge/Taylor & Francis, pp. 108–20.

Fantham, E. (1983), 'Sexual Comedy in Ovid's *Fasti*: Sources and Motivation', *Harvard Studies in Classical Philology*, 87: pp. 185–216.

Fantham, E. (1995), 'The Ambiguity of *Virtus* in Lucan's *Civil War* and Statius' *Thebaid*', *Arachnion* 3 <http://www.cisi.unito.it/arachne/num3/fantham.html> (last accessed 9 August 2018).

Fantham, E., H. P. Foley, N. B. Kampen, S. Pomeroy and H. A. Shapiro (eds) (1995), *Women in the Classical World: Image and Text*, Oxford: Oxford University Press.

Faraone, C., and L. K. McLure (eds) (2006), *Prostitutes and Courtesans in the Ancient World*, Madison: University of Wisconsin Press.

Fausto-Sterling, A. (2000), *Sexing the Body: Gender Politics and the Construction of Sexuality*, New York: Basic Books.

Feder, E. (2014), *Making Sense of Intersex: Changing Ethical Perspectives in Biomedicine*, Bloomington: Indiana University Press.

Feeney, D. (1993), *The Gods in Epic: Poets and Critics of the Classical Tradition*, new edn, Oxford: Oxford University Press.

Feinberg, L. (1996), *Transgender Warriors: Making History from Joan of Arc to Dennis Rodman*, Boston: Beacon.

Flemming, R. (2000), *Medicine and the Making of Roman Women: Gender, Nature, and Authority from Celsus to Galen*, Oxford: Oxford University Press.

Fletcher, J. (2007), 'The Virgin Choruses of Aeschylus Revisited', in B. MacLachlan and J. Fletcher (eds), *Virginity Revisited: Configurations of the Unpossessed Body*, Toronto: University of Toronto Press, pp. 24–39.

Flores, A. R., J. L. Herman, G. J. Gates and T. N. T. Brown (2016), 'How Many Adults Identify as Transgender in the United States', Report of the Williams Institute, UCLA <https://williamsinstitute.law.ucla.edu/research/how-many-adults-identify-as-transgender-in-the-united-states/> (last accessed 9 June 2018).

Foerster, R. (ed.) (1893), *Scriptores Physiognomonici Graeci et Latini*, 1st edn, Leipzig: Teubner.

Fögen, T. (2009), '*Sermo Corporis*: Ancient Reflections on Gestus, Vultus and Vox', in T. Fögen and M. M. Lee (eds), *Bodies and Boundaries in Graeco-Roman Antiquity*, Berlin; New York: De Gruyter, pp. 15–44.

Fögen, T., and M. M. Lee (eds) (2009), *Bodies and Boundaries in Graeco-Roman Antiquity*, Berlin; New York: De Gruyter.

Foley, H. P. (ed.) (1981), *Reflections of Women in Antiquity*, New York: Gordon and Breach.

Foley, H. P. (2001), *Female Acts in Greek Tragedy*, Princeton: Princeton University Press.

Forbes Irving, P. M. C. (1990), *Metamorphosis in Greek Myths*, Oxford: Oxford University Press.

Foss, P. W. (1994), *Kitchens and Dining Rooms at Pompeii: The Spatial and Social Relationship of Cooking to Eating in the Roman Household*, PhD dissertation, University of Michigan, Ann Arbor.

Foucault, M. (1982), 'The Subject and Power', in J. D. Faubion (ed.), *Power: The Essential Works of Foucault 1954–1984*, New York: New Press, pp. 326–48.

Fox, M. (1998), 'The Constrained Man', in L. Foxhall and J. Salmon (eds), *Thinking Men: Masculinity and Its Self-Representation in the Classical Tradition*, London: Routledge.

Fox, R. L. (2006), *Pagans and Christians: in the Mediterranean World from the Second Century AD to the Conversion of Constantine*, London: Penguin.

Foxhall, L. (2013), *Studying Gender in Classical Antiquity*, Cambridge: Cambridge University Press.

Foxhall, L., and J. Salmon (eds) (1998a), *When Men Were Men: Masculinity, Power, and Identity in Classical Antiquity*, London; New York: Routledge.

Foxhall, L., and J. Salmon (eds) (1998b), *Thinking Men: Masculinity and Its Self-Representation in the Classical Tradition*, London: Routledge.

Fredengren, C. (2013), 'Posthumanism, the Transcorporeal, and Biomolecular Archaeology', *Current Swedish Archaeology*, 21: pp. 53–71.

Fredrick, D. (1995), 'Beyond the Atrium to Ariadne: Erotic Painting and Visual Pleasure in the Roman House', *Classical Antiquity*, 14.2: pp. 266–88.

Frontisi-Ducroux, F. (1996), 'Eros, Desire and the Gaze', in N. B. Kampen (ed.), *Sexuality in Ancient Art: Near East, Egypt, Greece, and Italy*, Cambridge; New York: Cambridge University Press, pp. 81–100.

Gale, M. (2009), *Lucretius: De Rerum Natura 5*, Oxford: Aris and Philips.

Ganiban, R. T. (2007), *Statius and Virgil: the Thebaid and the Reinterpretation of the Aeneid*, Cambridge: Cambridge University Press.

Gantz, T. (1993), *Early Greek Myth: A Guide to Literary and Artistic Sources*, Baltimore: Johns Hopkins University Press.

Gardner, J. F. (1986), *Women in Roman Law and Society*, Bloomington: Indiana University Press.

Garland, R. (1995), *The Eye of the Beholder: Deformity and Disability in the Graeco-Roman World*, London: Duckworth.

Garland, R. (2010), *The Eye of the Beholder: Disability and Deformity in the Graeco-Roman World*, 2nd edn, London: Bristol Classical Press.

Gettell, O. (2014), '"300: Rise of an Empire" reviews: Eva Green triumphs; film doesn't', *Los Angeles Times*, March 7 <http://articles.latimes.com/2014/mar/07/entertainment/la-et-mn-300-rise-of-an-empire-movie-reviews-20140305> (last accessed 18 June 2017).

Gevaert, B., and C. Laes (2013), 'What's in a Monster? Pliny the Elder, Teratology and Bodily Disability', in C. Laes, C. F. Goodey and M. L. Rose (eds), *Disabilities in Roman Antiquity: Disparate Bodies a Capite Ad Calcem*, Leiden: Brill, pp. 211–30.

Gibbons, R., and C. Segal (2001), *Euripides, Bakkhai*, New York; Oxford: Oxford University Press.

Gilchrist, R. (1999), *Gender and Archaeology: Contesting the Past*, London; New York: Routledge.

Gilhuly, K. (2006), 'The Phallic Lesbian: Philosophy, Comedy, and Social Inversion in Lucian's *Dialogues of the Courtesans*', in C. A. Faraone and L. K. McClure (eds), *Prostitutes and Courtesans*, Madison: University of Wisconsin Press, pp. 274–91.

Gilhuly, K. (2008), *The Feminine Matrix of Sex and Gender in Classical Athens*, Cambridge: Cambridge University Press.

Gilhuly, K. (2015), 'Lesbians Are Not from Lesbos,' in R. Blondell and K. Ormand (eds), *Ancient Sex: New Essays*, Columbus: Ohio State University Press, pp. 143–76.

Glazebrook, A. (2015), *Beyond Courtesans and Whores: Sex and Labor in the Graeco-Roman World, Helios*, special issue, 42.1.

Glazebrook, A., and M. M. Henry (eds) (2011), *Greek Prostitutes in the Ancient World: 800 BCE to 200 CE*, Madison: University of Wisconsin Press.

Gleason, M. (1990), 'The Semiotics of Gender: Physiognomy and Self-Fashioning in the Second Century CE', in D. M. Halperin, J. J. Winkler and F. I. Zeitlin (eds), *Before Sexuality: The Construction of Erotic Experience in the Ancient Greek World*, Princeton: Princeton University Press, pp. 389–415.

Gleason, M. (1995), *Making Men: Sophists and Self-Presentation in Ancient Rome*, Princeton: Princeton University Press.

Glenn, C. (1997), *Rhetoric Retold: Regendering the Tradition from Antiquity through the Renaissance*, Carbondale: Southern Illinois University Press.

Glenn, C. L., and L. J. Cunningham (2009), 'The Power of Black Magic: The Magical Negro and White Salvation in Film', *Journal of Black Studies*, 40.2: pp. 135–52.

Godwin, J. (1986), *Lucretius: De Rerum Natura 4*, Oxford: Aris and Philps.

Goldhill, S. (1990), 'The Great Dionysia and Civic Ideology', in J. J. Winkler and F. I. Zeitlin (eds), *Nothing to Do with Dionysos? Athenian Drama in its Social Context*, Princeton: Princeton University Press, pp. 97–129.

Goldhill, S. (ed.) (2001), *Being Greek under Rome: Cultural Identity, the Second Sophistic, and the Development of Empire*, Cambridge: Cambridge University Press.

Grant, M. (1975), *Erotic Art in Pompeii: The Secret Collection of the National Museum of Naples*, London: Octopus Books.

Graumann, L. A. (2013), 'Monstrous Births and Retrospective Diagnosis: the Case of Hermaphrodites in Antiquity', in C. Laes, C. F. Goodey and M. L. Rose (eds), *Disabilities in Roman Antiquity: Disparate Bodies, a Capite Ad Calcem*, Boston; Leiden: Brill, pp. 181–209.

Greene, E. (2005), *Women Poets in Ancient Greece and Rome*, Norman: University of Oklahoma Press.

Grmek, M. D. (2002), 'The Concept of Disease', in M. D. Grmek and B. Fantini (eds), *Western Medical Thought from Antiquity to the Middle Ages*, Cambridge, MA: Harvard University Press, pp. 241–58.

Groves, R. (2016), 'From Statue to Story: Ovid's "Metamorphosis of Hermaphroditus"', *Classical World*, 109.3: pp. 321–56.

Guarducci, M. (1929), 'Pandora o i Martellatori: un dramma satirico di Sofocle e un nuovo monumento vascolare', *Monumenti Antichi pubblicati per cura della Reale Accademia dei Lincei*, 33: pp. 5–38.

Gunderson, E. (2000), *Staging Masculinity: The Rhetoric of Performance in the Roman World*, Ann Arbor: University of Michigan Press.

Gundert, B. (1992), 'Parts and Their Roles in Hippocratic Medicine', *Isis*, 83.3: pp. 453–65.

Gurd, S. A. (2012), *Work in Progress: Literary Revision as Social Performance in Ancient Rome*, New York: Oxford University Press.

Halberstam, J. (1998), *Female Masculinity*, Durham, NC: Duke University Press.

Hales, S. (2002), 'Looking for Eunuchs: The Galli and Attis in Roman Art', in S. Tougher (ed.), *Eunuchs in Antiquity and Beyond*, London: Duckworth, pp. 87–102.

Hales, S. (2003), *The Roman House and Social Identity*, Cambridge: Cambridge University Press.

Hales, S. (2008), 'Aphrodite and Dionysus: Greek Role Models for Roman Homes?' *Memoirs of the American Academy in Rome. Supplementary Volumes*, 7: pp. 235–55.

Haley, S. P. (2002), 'Lucian's "Leaena and Clonarium": Voyeurism or a Challenge to Assumptions?', in N. S. Rabinowitz and L. Auanger (eds), *Among Women: From the Homosocial to the Homoerotic in the Ancient World*, Austin: University of Texas Press, pp. 286–303.

Hall, E. (1995), 'The Ass with Double Vision: Politicising an Ancient Greek Novel', in D. Margolies and M. Joannou (eds), *Heart of the Heartless World: Essays in Cultural Resistance in Memory of Margaret Heinemann*, London: Pluto Press, pp. 47–59.

Hall, E. (1998), 'Ithyphallic Males Behaving Badly, or, Satyr Drama as Gendered Tragic Ending', in M. Wyke (ed.), *Parchments of Gender: Deciphering the Bodies of Antiquity*, Oxford: Clarendon, pp. 13–37.

Hall, E. (2008), 'Introduction: Pantomime from the Performers' Perspective, A Lost Chord in Ancient Culture', in E. Hall and R. Wyles (eds), *New Directions in Ancient Pantomime*, Oxford: Oxford University Press, pp. 1–42.

Hallett, J. P. (1984), *Fathers and Daughters in Roman Society: Women and the Elite Family*, Princeton: Princeton University Press.

Hallett, J. P. (1989), 'Women as "Same" and "Other" in the Classical Roman Elite', *Helios*, 16.1: pp. 59–78.

Hallett, J. P. (1997), 'Female Homoeroticism and the Denial of Roman Reality in Latin Literature', in J. P. Hallett and M. B. Skinner (eds), *Roman Sexualities*, Princeton: Princeton University Press, pp. 255–73.

Hallett, J. P. (2011), 'Scenarios of Sulpiciae: moral discourses and immoral verses', *EuGeStA*, 1: pp. 79–97.

Hallett, J. P., and M. B. Skinner (eds) (1997), *Roman Sexualities*, Princeton: Princeton University Press.

Halliday, W. R. (1910–11), 'A Note on the ΘΗΛΕΑ ΝΟΥΣΟΣ of the Scythians', *Annual of the British School at Athens*, 17: pp. 95–102.

Halperin, D. (1990a), 'Why Is Diotima a Woman? Platonic *Erōs* and the Figuration of Gender', in D. Halperin, J. J. Winkler and F. I. Zeitlin (eds), *Before*

Sexuality: The Construction of Erotic Experience in the Ancient Greek World, Princeton: Princeton University Press, pp. 257–308.

Halperin, D. M. (1990b), *One Hundred Years of Homosexuality and Other Essays on Greek Love*, New York: Routledge.

Halperin, D. M. (2002), *How to Do the History of Homosexuality*, Chicago: Chicago University Press.

Halperin, D. M., J. J. Winkler and F. I. Zeitlin (eds) (1990), *Before Sexuality: The Construction of Erotic Experience in the Ancient Greek World*, Princeton: Princeton University Press.

Halsberghe, G. (1972), *The Cult of Sol Invictus*, Leiden: Brill.

Hansen, W. F. (1996), *Phlegon of Tralles' Book of Marvels*, Exeter: University of Exeter Press.

Hanson, A. E. (1992), 'Conception, Gestation, and the Origin of the Female Nature in the Hippocratic Corpus', *Helios*, 19.1: pp. 31–71.

Haraway, D. (1991), *Simians, Cyborgs and Women*, New York: Routledge.

Hardie, P. (1995), 'The Speech of Pythagoras in Ovid *Metamorphoses* 15: Empedoclean Epos', *Classical Quarterly*, 45.1: pp. 204–14.

Hardie, P. (2002), *Ovid's Poetics of Illusion*, Cambridge: Cambridge University Press.

Harrell, S. H. (2003), 'Marvelous Andreia: Politics, Geography, and Ethnicity in Herodotus' *Histories*', in R. M. Rosen and I. Sluiter (eds), *Andreia: Studies in Manliness and Courage in Classical Antiquity*, Boston; Leiden: Brill, pp. 77–94.

Harris, C. R. S. (1973), *The Heart and Vascular System in Ancient Greek Medicine from Alcmaeon to Galen*, Oxford: Clarendon.

Harris, S., and G. Platzner (2016), *Classical Mythology: Images and Insights*, 7th edn, New York: McGraw-Hill.

Harrison, J. E. (1908), *Prolegomena to the Study of Greek Religion*, Cambridge: Cambridge University Press.

Hart, R. (2017), Abstract of '(N)either Men (n)or Women? The Failure of Western Binary Systems', Abstracts of the 148th Society for Classical Studies Annual Meeting <https://classicalstudies.org/annual-meeting/148/abstract/neither-men-nor-women-failure-western-binary-systems> (last accessed 21 October 2017).

Hart, R. (2018), 'More than Meets the Eye: Autopsy and Physicality in Herodotus and Ctesias', PhD dissertation, University of Wisconsin, Madison.

Haskins, S. (1993), *Mary Magdalen: Myth and Metaphor*, New York: Harcourt Brace.

Häuber, C. (1999), 'Vier Fragmente der Gruppe Satyr und Hermaphrodit vom Typus "Dresdner Symplegmata" des Museo Nuovo Capitolino in Rom', in *Hellenistische Gruppen: Gedenkschrift für Andreas Linfert*, Mainz am Rhein: Philip von Zabern, pp. 157–80.

Häuber, C. (2014), *The Eastern Part of the Mons Oppius in Rome. The Sanctuary of Isis et Serapis In Regio III, the Temples of Minerva Medica, Fortuna Virgo and Dea Syria, and the Horti of Maecenas*, Rome: L'Erma di Bretschneider.

Hayne, L. (1994), 'Thecla and the Church Fathers', *Vigiliae Christianae*, 48.3: pp. 209–18.

Hazewindus, M. W. (2004), *When Women Interfere: Studies in the Role of Women in Herodotus'* Histories, *Amsterdam Studies in Classical Philology*, vol. 12, Amsterdam: J. C. Gieben.

Hedreen, G. (1992), *Silens in Attic Black-Figure Vase-Painting: Myth and Performance*, Ann Arbor: University of Michigan Press.

Heinrich, A. J. (1999), 'Longa Retro Series: Sacrifice and Repetition in Statius' Menoeceus episode', *Arethusa*, 32.2: pp. 165–95.

Hejduk, J. D. (2011), 'Epic Rapes in the *Fasti*', *Classical Philology*, 106.1: pp. 20–31.

Hekster, O. (2004), 'Hercules, Omphale, and Octavian's "Counter-Propaganda"', *Bulletin Antike Beschaving*, 79: pp. 159–66.

Helbig, W. (1868), *Wandgemälde der vom Vesuv Verschütteten Städte Campaniens*, Leipzig: Breitkopf und Härtel.

Heller-Nicholas, A. (2011), *Rape-revenge Films: a Critical Study*, Jefferson, NC: McFarland.

Henrichs, A. (2013), 'Dionysos: One or Many?' in A. Bernabé, M. H. de Jáuregui, A. I. Jiménez San Cristóbal and R. M. Hernández (eds), *Redefining Dionysos*, Berlin; Boston; New York: De Gruyter, pp. 554–82.

Henry, C. (2014), *Revisionist Rape-Revenge*, New York: Palgrave Macmillan.

Heraeus, W., and I. Borovskij (1982), *M. Valerii Martialis. Epigrammaton Libri*, Leipzig: Teubner.

Heslin, P. (2005), *The Transvestite Achilles*, Cambridge: Cambridge University Press.

Heynen, C., and R. Krumeich (1999), 'Pandora oder Sphyrokopoi', in R. Krumeich, N. Pechstein and B. Seidensticker (eds), *Das griechesche Satyrspiel*, Darmstadt: Wissenschaftliche Buchgesellschaft, pp. 375–80.

Hidber, T. (2006), *Herodians Darstellung der Kaisergeschichte nach Marc Aurel*, Basel: Schwabe.

Hijmans, B. L., Jr., R. Th. van der Paardt, V. Schmidt, C. B. J. Settels, B. Wesseling and R. E. H. Westendorp Boerma (eds) (1985), *Apuleius Madaurensis Metamorphoses Book VIII*, Groningen Commentaries on Apuleius, Groningen: Egbert Forsten.

Hill, D. E. (1985–2000), *Ovid's Metamorphoses*, Oxford: Aris and Philps.

Hinds, S. (1998), *Allusion and Intertext: Dynamics of Appropriation in Roman Poetry*, Cambridge: Cambridge University Press.

Holland, T. (2007), 'Mirage in the Movie House', *Arion*, 15.1: pp. 173–82.

Holmes, B. (2012), *Gender: Antiquity and Its Legacy*, Oxford: Oxford University Press.

Holmes, B. (2019), 'Letting Go of Laqueur: Towards New Histories of the Sexed Body', in *EuGeStA*, 9.

Holmes, M. (2008), *Intersex: A Perilous Difference*, Selinsgrove, PA: Susquehanna University Press.

Holmes, M. (ed.) (2009), *Critical Intersex*, Burlington: Ashgate.

Holquist, M. (1983), 'The Politics of Representation', *The Quarterly Newsletter of the Laboratory of Comparative Human Cognition*, 5: pp. 2–9.

Hopwood, B. (2015), 'Hortensia Speaks: An Authentic Voice of Resistance?', in K. Welch (ed.), *Appian's Roman History: Empire and Civil War*, Swansea: Classical Press of Wales, pp. 305–22.

Hose, M. (2007), 'Cassius Dio: A Senator and Historian in the Age of Anxiety', in J. Marincola (ed.), *A Companion to Greek & Roman Historiography*, Malden, MA; Oxford: Wiley Blackwell, pp. 461–7.

Hubbard, T. K. (2003), *Homosexuality in Greece and Rome: A Sourcebook of Basic Documents*, Berkeley: University of California Press.

Hubbard, T. K. (ed.) (2014), *A Companion to Greek and Roman Sexualities*, Chichester: Wiley Blackwell.

Huffman, T. (2013), 'Pragmatic Fieldwork: Qualitative Research for Creative Democracy and Social Action', *Journal of Social Justice*, 3: pp. 1–24.

Hughes, L. A. (2014), 'Sculpting Theatrical Performance at Pompeii's *Casa Degli Amorini Dorati*', *LOGEION: A Journal of Ancient Theatre*, 4: pp. 227–47.

Hughey, M. W. (2009), 'Cinethetic Racism: White Redemption and Black Stereotypes in "Magical Negro" Films', *Social Problems*, 56.3: pp. 543–77.

Hunt, Y. (2008), 'Roman Pantomime Libretti and their Greek Themes: The Role of Augustus in the Romanization of Greek Classics', in E. Hall and R. Wyles (eds), *New Directions in Ancient Pantomime*, Oxford: Oxford University Press, pp. 169–84.

Hurwit, J. (1995), 'Beautiful Evil: Pandora and the Athena Parthenos', *American Journal of Archaeology*, 99.2: pp. 171–86.

Hylen, S. E. (2015), *A Modest Apostle: Thecla and the History of Women in the Early Church*, Oxford: Oxford University Press.

Icks, M. (2011), *The Crimes of Elagabalus: The Life and Legacy of Rome's Decadent Boy Emperor*, London: I. B. Tauris.

Ingleheart, J. (2008), '*Et mea sunt populo saltata poemata saepe* (*Tristia* 2.519). Ovid and the Pantomime', in E. Hall and R. Wyles (eds), *New Directions in Ancient Pantomime*, Oxford: Oxford University Press, pp. 198–217.

Ingleheart, J. (ed.) (2015), *Ancient Rome and the Construction of Modern Homosexual Identities*, Oxford: Oxford University Press.

Inwood, B. (2001), *The Poem of Empedocles: A Text and Translation with an Introduction*, Toronto: University of Toronto Press.

Isaac, B. (2004), *The Invention of Racism in Classical Antiquity*, Princeton: Princeton University Press.

Isager, S. (2004), 'The Pride of Halikarnassos: Editio Princeps of an Inscription from Salmakis', in S. Isager and P. Pedersen (eds), *The Salmakis Inscription and Hellenistic Halikarnassos*, Odense: University Press of Southern Denmark, pp. 217–37.

Isler- Kerényi, C. (2007), *Dionysos in Archaic Greece: An Understanding through Images*, Leiden: Brill.

Isler- Kerényi, C. (2014), *Dionysos in Classical Athens: An Understanding through Images*, Leiden: Brill.

James, S. L. (2003), *Learned Girls and Male Persuasion: Gender and Reading in Roman Love Elegy*, Berkeley: University of California Press.

Jameson, M. (1993), 'The Asexuality of Dionysos', in T. H. Carpenter and C. A. Faraone (eds), *Masks of Dionysos*, Ithaca: Cornell University Press, pp. 44–64.

Jebb, R. C. (1917), *The Fragments of Sophocles*, Cambridge: Cambridge University Press.

Johnson, A. H. (2015), 'Normative Accountability: How the Medical Profession Influences Transgender Identity and Experiences', *Sociology Compass*, 9.9: pp. 803–13 <https://onlinelibrary.wiley.com/doi/pdf/10.1111/soc4.12297> (last accessed 13 June 2018).

Johnson, S. F. (2006), *The Life and Miracles of Thekla: A Literary Study*, Washington, DC: Center for Hellenic Studies.

Johnson, W. (2010), *Readers and Reading Culture in the High Roman Empire: A Study of Elite Communities*, Oxford: Oxford University Press.

Jones, C. (1982), *Sex or Symbol? Erotic Images of Greece and Rome*, Austin: University of Texas Press.

Jones, C. P. (1991), 'Dinner Theatre', in W. J. Slater (ed.), *Dining in a Classical Context*, Ann Arbor: University of Michigan Press, pp. 185–98.

Jones, W. H. S. (1946), *Philosophy and Medicine in Ancient Greece*, Baltimore: Johns Hopkins University Press.

Jory, E. J. (2002), 'The Masks on the Propylon of the Sebasteion at Aphrodisias', in P. Easterling and E. Hall (eds), *Greek and Roman Actors: Aspects of an Ancient Profession*, Cambridge: Cambridge University Press, pp. 238–53.

Jouanna, J. (1999), *Hippocrates*, Baltimore: Johns Hopkins University Press.

Joyce, R. A. (2005), 'Archaeology of the Body', *Annual Review of Anthropology*, 34: 139–58.

Just, R. (1989), *Women in Athenian Law and Life*, London: Routledge.

Kamen, D. (2012), 'Naturalized Desires and the Metamorphosis of Iphis', *Helios*, 39.1: pp. 21–36.

Kamen, D., and S. Levin-Richardson (2015a), 'Revisiting Roman Sexuality: Agency and the Conceptualization of Penetrated Males', in M. Masterson, N. S. Rabinowitz and J. Robson (eds), *Sex in Antiquity: Exploring Gender and Sexuality in the Ancient World*, London; New York: Routledge/Taylor & Francis, pp. 449–60.

Kamen, D., and S. Levin-Richardson (2015b), 'Lusty Ladies in the Roman Imaginary', in R. Blondell and K. Ormand (eds), *Ancient Sex: New Essays*, Columbus: Ohio State University Press, pp. 231–52.

Kampen, N. B. (1996a), 'Omphale and the Instability of Gender', in N. B. Kampen (ed.), *Sexuality in Ancient Art: Near East, Egypt, Greece, and Italy*, Cambridge: Cambridge University Press, pp. 233–46.

Kampen, N. B. (ed.) (1996b), *Sexuality in Ancient Art: Near East, Egypt, Greece, and Italy*, Cambridge; New York: Cambridge University Press.

Keener, C. S. (1999), *A Commentary on the Gospel of Matthew*, Grand Rapids: Eermans.

Keith, A. M. (2000), *Engendering Rome: Women in Latin Epic*, Cambridge: Cambridge University Press.

Kelly, P. (2018), 'Compounding Compound Creatures: The Catalogue of Hybrids in Tristia 4.7 and Empedocles', *Mnemosyne*, 71: pp. 667–87.

Kemezis, A. M. (2014), *Greek Narratives of the Roman Empire under the Severans. Cassius Dio, Philostratus and Herodian*, Cambridge: Cambridge University Press.

Kemezis, A. (2016), 'The Fall of Elagabalus as Literary Narrative and Political Reality: A Reconsideration', *Historia*, 65: pp. 348–90.

Kennedy, R. F. (2009), *Athena's Justice: Athena, Athens and the Concept of Justice in Greek Tragedy*, New York: Peter Lang.

Keuls, E. (1985), *The Reign of the Phallus: Sexual Politics in Ancient Athens*, New York: Harper & Row.

King, H. (1998), *Hippocrates' Woman: Reading the Female Body in Ancient Greece*, London; New York: Routledge.

King, H. (2008), 'Barbes, sang et genre: afficher la différence dans le monde antique', in V. Dasen and J. Wilgaux (eds), *Langages et métaphores du corps dans la monde antique*, Rennes: Presses universitaires de Rennes, pp. 153–68.

King, H. (2013a), 'Sex and Gender: The Hippocratic Case of Phaethousa and Her Beard', *EuGeStA*, 3: pp. 124–42.

King, H. (2013b), *The One-Sex Body on Trial: The Classical and Early Modern Evidence*, Farnham: Ashgate.

King, H. (2015), 'Between Male and Female in Ancient Medicine', in D. Boschung, H. A. Shapiro and F. Waschek (eds), *Bodies in Transition: Dissolving the Boundaries of Embodied Knowledge*, Paderborn: Wilhelm Fink, pp. 249–64.

Kleiner, D. E. E., and S. B. Matheson (eds) (1996), *I, Claudia: Women in Ancient Rome: Catalogue of the Exhibition Organized by the Yale University Art Gallery 1996*, New Haven: Yale University Art Gallery.

Kraemer, R. S. (2004), *Women's Religions in the Greco-Roman World: A Sourcebook*, New York; Oxford: Oxford University Press.

Kraemer, R. S. (2011), *Unreliable Witnesses: Religion, Gender, and History in the Greco-Roman Mediterranean*, New York: Oxford University Press.

Krauss, F. B. (1930), *An Interpretation of the Omens, Portents, and Prodigies Recorded by Livy, Tacitus and Suetonius*, PhD dissertation, University of Pennsylvania, Philadelphia.

Krüger, P. (2008), *Codex Justinianus (Corpus Iuris Civilis 2)*, Hildesheim: Weidmann.

Krumeich, Ralf, N. Pechstein and B. Seidensticker (eds) (1999), *Das griechische Satyrspiel*, Darmstadt: Wissenschaftliche Buchgesellschaft.

Kuefler, M. (2001), *The Manly Eunuch: Masculinity, Gender Ambiguity, and Christian Ideology in Late Antiquity*, Chicago: University of Chicago Press.

La Guardia, F. (2017), 'Aspects of Transvestism in Greek Myth and Rituals', in D. Campanile, F. Carlà-Uhink and M. Facella (eds), *TransAntiquity: Cross-dressing and Transgender Dynamics in the Ancient World*, London; New York: Routledge/Taylor & Francis, pp. 99–107.

Labrecque, J. (2014), '"300: Rise of an Empire": The reviews are in . . .', *Entertainment Weekly*, March 7 <http://ew.com/article/2014/03/07/300-rise-of-an-empire-critical-mass/> (last accessed 18 June 2017).

Laird, A. (1999), *Powers of Expression, Expressions of Power: Speech Presentation and Latin Literature*, Oxford: Oxford University Press.

Lämmle, R. (2005), 'Die Natur Optimieren: Der Geschlechtswandel Der Iphis in Ovids *Metamorphosen*', in H. Harich-Schwarzbauer and T. Späth (eds), *Gender Studies in Den Altertumswissenschaften: Raüme Und Geschlechter in Der Antike*, Trier: Wissenschaftlicher Verlag Trier, pp. 193–210.

Lämmle, R. (2013), *Poetik des Satyrspiels*, Heidelberg: Carl Winter.

Lange, C., and J. Madsen (2016), 'Between History and Politics', in C. Lange and J. Madsen (eds), *Cassius Dio: Greek Intellectual and Roman Politician*, Leiden: Brill, pp. 1–10.

Langholf, V. (2004), 'Structure and Genesis of Some Hippocratic Treatises', in H. F. J. Horstmanshoff and M. Stoll (eds), *Magic and Rationality in Ancient Near Eastern and Graeco-Roman Medicine*, Boston; Leiden: Brill, pp. 219–75.

Langlands, R. (2002), '"Can you tell what it is yet?": Descriptions of Sex Change in Ancient Literature', *Ramus*, 31: pp. 91–110.

Langlands, R. (2006), *Sexual Morality in Ancient Rome*, Cambridge: Cambridge University Press.

Laqueur, T. (1992), *Making Sex: Body and Gender from the Greeks to Freud*, Cambridge, MA: Harvard University Press.

LaSalle, M. (2014), '"300: Rise of an Empire" review: Not a sequel, not so good', *SFGate*, March 7 <http://www.sfgate.com/movies/article/300-Rise-of-an-Empire-review-Not-a-sequel-5293895.php> (last accessed 18 June 2017).

Lateiner, D. (1990), 'Deceptions and Delusions in Herodotus', *Classical Antiquity*, 9.2: pp. 230–46.

Lateiner, D. (2009), 'Transsexuals and Transvestites in Ovid's *Metamorphoses*', in T. Fögen and M. M. Lee (eds), *Bodies and Boundaries in Graeco-Roman Antiquity*, Berlin; New York: De Gruyter, pp. 125–54.

Latham, J. (2012), 'Fabulous Clap-Trap: Roman Masculinity, the Cult of the Magna Mater, and Literary Constructions of the *Galli* at Rome from the Late Republic to Late Antiquity', *The Journal of Religion*, 92.1: pp. 84–122.

Latour, B. (2004), 'How to Talk About the Body? The Normative Dimension of Science Studies', *Body & Society*, 10.2–3: pp. 205–29.

Lauwers, J., M. Dhont and X. Huybrecht (2012), '"This is Sparta!": Discourse, Gender, and the Orient in Zack Snyder's *300*', in A-B Renger and J. Solomon (eds), *Ancient Worlds in Film and Television: Gender and Politics*, Boston; Leiden: Brill, pp. 79–94.

Leach, E. W. (2004), *The Social Life of Painting in Ancient Rome and on the Bay of Naples*, Cambridge: Cambridge University Press.

Lee, M. M. (2009), 'Body-Modification in Classical Greece', in T. Fögen and M. M. Lee (eds), *Bodies and Boundaries in Graeco-Roman Antiquity*, Berlin; New York: De Gruyter, pp. 155–80.

Lefkowitz, M. R., and M. E. Fant (1982), *Women's Life in Greece and Rome: A Source Book in Translation*, Baltimore: Johns Hopkins University Press.

Leitao, D. D. (1995), 'The Perils of Leukippos: Initiatory Transvestism and Male Gender Ideology in the Ekdusia at Phaistos', *Classical Antiquity*, 14 (1): pp. 130–63.

Lessie, A. J. (2015), *Becoming Mark Antony: A Metabiographical Study of Characterization and Reception*, PhD dissertation, University of California, Los Angeles <http://escholarship.org/uc/item/7pq898zf> (last accessed 3 March 2017).

Levin, S. (2014), *Plato's Rivalry with Medicine: A Struggle and its Dissolution*, New York; Oxford: Oxford University Press.

Levin-Richardson, S. (2013), '"*Fututa Sum Hic*": Female Subjectivity and Agency in Pompeian Sexual Graffiti', *The Classical Journal*, 108.3: pp. 319–45.

Lewellyn-Jones, L. (2001), 'Sexy Athena: The Dress and Erotic Representation of a Virgin War Goddess', in S. Deacy and A. Villing (eds), *Athena in the Classical World*, Leiden: Brill, pp. 233–57.

Lexicon Iconographicum Mythologiae Classicae (LIMC) (1981–2009), Zurich; Munich; Düsseldorf: Artemis & Winkler <https://www.iconiclimc.ch/> (last accessed 8 September 2018).

Liddell, H. G., and R. Scott (eds) (1940), *A Greek-English Lexicon*, Oxford: Clarendon <http://www.perseus.tufts.edu/hopper/text;jsessionid'A680855B E6F6CEBC35641448F6A1CED3?doc'Perseus%3atext%3a1999.04.0057> (last accessed 14 October 2015).

Lieber, E. (1996), 'The Hippocratic "Airs, Waters, Places" on Cross-Dressing Eunuchs: "Natural" yet also "Divine"', in R. Wittern and P. Pellegrin (eds), *Hippokratische Medizin und antike Philosophie: Verhandlungen des VIII. Internationalen Hippokrates-Kolloquiums in Kloster Banz/Staffelstein vom 23. Bis 28. September 1993*, Hildesheim; Zurich: Olms-Weidmann, pp. 451–65.

Lightfoot, J. L. (2003), *Lucian, On the Syrian Goddess*, New York: Oxford University Press.

Lindheim, S. H. (1998), 'Hercules Cross-Dressed, Hercules Undressed: Unmasking the Construction of the Propertian *Amator* in *Elegy* 4.9', *American Journal of Philology*, 119.1: pp. 43–66.

Lindheim, S. H. (2010), 'Pomona's Pomarium: The "Mapping Impulse" in *Metamorphoses* 14 (and 9)', *Transactions and Proceedings of the American Philological Association*, 140.1: pp. 163–94.

Lipsett, B. D. (2011), *Desiring Conversion: Hermas, Thecla, Aseneth*, New York: Oxford University Press.

Lipsius, R. A., and M. Bonnet (1891), *Acta Apostolorum Apocrypha*, Leipzig: Hermannum Mendelssohn.

Lissarrague, F. (1990), 'The Sexual Life of Satyrs', in D. M. Halperin, J. J. Winkler and F. I. Zeitlin (eds), *Before Sexuality: The Construction of Erotic Experience in the Ancient Greek World*, Princeton: Princeton University Press, pp. 53–81.

Lissarrague, F. (2002), *The Aesthetics of the Greek Banquet: Images of Wine and Ritual (Un Flot d'Images)*, Princeton: Princeton University Press.

Littlewood, R. J. (1975), 'Lupercalia (*Fasti* 2.267–452): A Study in the Artistry of the Fasti', *Latomus*, 34.4: pp. 1060–74.

Littré, É. (1840), *Introduction to Les Oeuvres complète d'Hippocrate*, Paris: J. B. Baillière.

Lloyd-Jones, H. (1975), *Females of the Species: Semonides on Women*, London: Duckworth.

Lonie, I. (1981), *The Hippocratic Treatises 'On Generation', 'On the Nature of the Child', 'Diseases IV'*, Berlin; New York: De Gruyter.

Loraux, N. (1981), *Les enfants d'Athéna: idées athéniennes sur la citoyenneté et la division des sexes*, Paris: François Maspero.

Lorber, J. (1996), 'Beyond the Binaries: Depolarizing the Categories of Sex, Sexuality, and Gender', *Sociological Inquiry*, 66: pp. 143–59.

Lorenz, K. (2007), 'The Ear of the Beholder: Spectator Figure and Narrative Structure in Pompeian Painting', *Art History*, 30.5: pp. 665–82.

Lorenz, K. (2008), *Bilder Machen Räume: Mythenbilder in Pompeianishen Häusern*, Berlin: De Gruyter.

Lowe, D. M. (2008), 'Personification Allegory in the *Aeneid* and Ovid's *Metamorphoses*', *Mnemosyne*, 61.3: pp. 414–35.

Lucal, B. (1999), 'What it Means to Be Gendered Me: Life on the Boundaries of a Dichotomous Gender System', *Gender and Society*, 13.6: pp. 781–97.

Luck, G. (2006), *Arcana Mundi: Magic and the Occult in the Greek and Roman Worlds: a Collection of Ancient Texts*, 2nd edn, Baltimore: Johns Hopkins University Press.

Lugones M. (2016), 'The Coloniality of Gender', in W. Harcourt (ed.), *The Palgrave Handbook of Gender and Development*, London: Palgrave Macmillan.

Luz, U. (1990), *Matthew 1–7: A Commentary*, Edinburgh: T&T Clark.

Lyons, D. J. (1997), *Gender and Immortality: Heroines in Ancient Greek Myth and Cult*, Princeton: Princeton University Press.

MacBain, B. (1982), *Prodigy and Expiation: A Study in Religion and Politics in Republican Rome*, Brussels: Latomus.

McClure, L. K. (2002), *Sexuality and Gender in the Classical World*, Malden, MA; Oxford: Wiley Blackwell.

McClure, L. K. (2003), *Courtesans at Table: Gender and Greek Literary Culture in Athenaeus*, London; New York: Routledge.

McClure, L. K. (2009), *Spoken Like a Woman: Speech and Gender in Athenian Drama*, Princeton University Press.

McCoskey, D. E. (2012), *Race: Antiquity and Its Legacy*, New York; Oxford: Oxford University Press.

McHardy, F. (2004), 'Women's Influence on Revenge in Classical Greece', in F. McHardy and E. Marshall (eds), *Women's Influence on Classical Civilization*, London; New York: Routledge, pp. 92–114.

McHardy, F. (2008), *Revenge in Athenian Culture*, London: Duckworth.

McHardy, F., and E. Marshall (2004), *Women's Influence on Classical Civilizations*, London; New York: Routledge.

MacLachlan, B. (2012), *Women in Ancient Greece: A Sourcebook*, London: Continuum International.

MacLachlan, B. (2013), *Women in Ancient Rome: A Sourcebook*, London: Bloomsbury.

MacLeod, M. D. (1961), *Lucian [Works]*, vols 7–8, London: Heinemann.

MacLeod, M. D. (ed.) (1974), *Luciani Opera*, vol. 2, Oxford Classical Texts, Oxford: Clarendon Press.

MacLeod, M. D. (ed.) (1987), *Luciani Opera*, 4 vols, Oxford: Oxford University Press.

McWilliams, S. (2013), 'Hybridity in Herodotus', *Political Research Quarterly*, 66.4: pp. 745–55.

Mader, G. (2005), 'History as Carnival, or Method and Madness in the *Vita Heliogabali*', *Classical Antiquity*, 24.1: pp. 131–72.

Malina, B. J., and R. L. Rohrbaugh (2003), *Social-Science Commentary on the Synoptic Gospels*, 2nd edn, Minneapolis: Fortress.

Malone, M. T. (2000), *Women and Christianity, Volume I: The First Thousand Years*, New York: Orbis.

Mann, K. (2017), 'Gender Nonconformance in Phaedrus's *Fabulae*', Abstracts of the 148th Society for Classical Studies Annual Meeting <https://classicalstudies.org/annual-meeting/148/abstract/gender-nonconformance-phaedrus%E2%80%99s-fabulae> (last accessed 16 October 2018).

Manuwald, G., and A. Voigt (eds) (2013), *Flavian Epic Interactions*, Berlin: De Gruyter.

Marcadé, J. (1961), *Roma Amor: Studie über die Erotischen Darstellungen in der Etruskisch-Römischen Kunst*, Geneva: Nagel.

Marincola, J. (1997), *Authority and Tradition in Ancient Historiography*, Cambridge: Cambridge University Press.

Marquardt, N. (1995), *Pan in der Hellenistischen und Kaiserzeitlichen Plastik*, Bonn: Habelt.

Marshall, A. J. (1989), 'Ladies at Law: The Role of Women in the Roman Civil Courts', in C. Deroux (ed.), *Studies in Latin Literature and Roman History V*, Brussels: Latomus, pp. 35–54.

Marshall, A. J. (1990), 'Roman Ladies on Trial: The Case of Maesia of Sentinum', *Phoenix*, 44.1: pp. 46–59.

Martin, A., and O. Primavesi (1999), *L'Empedocle de Strasbourg*, Berlin: De Gruyter.

Mason, H. J. (1994), 'Greek and Latin Versions of the Ass Story', *Aufstieg und Niedergang der Römischen Welt*, 2.34.2: pp. 1665–707.

Mason, H. J. (1999a), 'The *Metamorphoses* of Apuleius and its Greek Sources', in H. Hofmann (ed.), *Latin Fiction: The Latin Novel in Context*, New York: Routledge, pp. 103–12.

Mason, H. J. (1999b), '*Fabula Graecanica*: Apuleius and His Greek Sources', in S. J. Harrison (ed.), *Oxford Readings in the Roman Novel*, Oxford: Oxford University Press, pp. 217–36.

Masterson, M., N. S. Rabinowitz and J. Robson (2015), *Sex in Antiquity: Exploring Gender and Sexuality in the Ancient World*, London; New York: Routledge/Taylor & Francis.

Mastroroberto, M. (1992), 'La Scultura dei Giardini', in B. Conticello and F. Romano (eds), *Domus-Viridaria Horti Picti*, Napoli: Bibliopolis, pp. 39–42.

May, V. M. (2015), *Pursuing Intersectionality, Unsettling Dominant Imaginaries*, New York: Routledge.

Medda, E. (2017), '"O saffron robe, to what pass have you brought me!" Cross-dressing and Theatrical Illusion in Aristophanes' *Thesmophoriazusae*', in D. Campanile, F. Carlà-Uhink and M. Facella (eds), *TransAntiquity: Cross-dressing and Transgender Dynamics in the Ancient World*, London; New York: Routledge/Taylor & Francis, pp. 137–51.

Meem, D. T., M. A. Gibson and J. F. Alexander (2010), *Finding Out: An Introduction to LGBT Studies*, Los Angeles: Sage.

Mehan, H. (1996), 'The Construction of an LD Student: A Case Study in the Politics of Representation', in M. Silverstein and G. Urban (eds), *Natural Histories of Discourse*, Chicago: University of Chicago Press, pp. 253–76.

Meier, J. P. (2001), *A Marginal Jew: Rethinking the Historical Jesus, Volume Three Companions and Competitors*, New York: Doubleday.

Meyer, M. W. (1985), 'Making Mary Male: The Categories "Male" and "Female" in the Gospel of Thomas', *New Testament Studies*, 31.4: pp. 554–70.

Meyer, M. W. (ed.) (2007), *The Nag Hammadi Scriptures*, New York: Harper-One.

Millar, F. (1964), *A Study of Cassius Dio*, Oxford: Oxford University Press.

Miller, M. C. (1999), 'Reexamining Transvestism in Archaic and Classical Athens: The Zedowski Stamnos', *American Journal of Archaeology*, 103.2: pp. 223–53.

Milnor, K. (2005), *Gender, Domesticity, and the Age of Augustus: Inventing Private Life*, New York: Oxford University Press.

Moaveni, A. (2007), '*300* Sparks an Outcry in Iran', *Time* online, March 13 <http://content.time.com/time/world/article/0,8599,1598886,00.html> (last accessed 4 August 2018).

Montserrat, D. (2000), 'Reading Gender in the Roman World', in J. Huskinson (ed.), *Experiencing Rome: Culture, Identity and Power in the Roman Empire*, London: Routledge, pp. 153–82.

Morford, M. P. O., R. J. Lenardon and M. Sham (2018), *Classical Mythology*, 11th edn, New York: Oxford University Press.

Moss, Candida (2015), 'Siberian Gender-Bending Warrior Princess', *Daily Beast* <https://www.thedailybeast.com/siberian-gender-bending-warrior-princess?ref'scroll> (last accessed 30 July 2018).

Mratschek, S. (2013), 'Nero the Imperial Misfit: Philhellenism in a Rich Man's World', in E. Buckley and M. Dinter (eds), *Companion to the Neronian Age*, Hoboken: Wiley Blackwell, pp. 45–62.

Munson, R. V. (1988), 'Artemisia in Herodotus', *Classical Antiquity*, 7.1: pp. 91–106.

Munson, R. V. (2014), 'Herodotus and Ethnicity', in J. McInerney (ed.), *A Companion to Ethnicity in the Ancient Mediterranean*, Chichester: Wiley Blackwell, pp. 341–55.

Murphy, E. (2004), 'Herodotus and the Amazons Meet the Cyclops: Philology, Osteoarchaeology, and the Eurasian Iron Age', in E. W. Sauer (ed.), *Archaeology and Ancient History: Breaking Down the Boundaries*, London: Routledge/Taylor & Francis, pp. 169–84.

Mustakallio, K. (2013), 'The Life Cycle: from Birth to Old Age', in J. H. Tullock (ed.), *A Cultural History of Women in Antiquity, Vol. 1*, London: Bloomsbury, pp. 15–32.

Myers, K. S. (1994), *Ovid's Causes: Cosmogony and Aetiology in the Metamorphoses*, Ann Arbor: University of Michigan Press.

Nanda, S. (1990), *Neither Man nor Woman: The Hijras of India*, Belmont, CA: Wadsworth.

Narrain, A., and A. Gupta (2011), 'Introduction', in A. Narrain and A. Gupta (eds), *Law Like Love: Queer Perspectives on Law*, New Delhi: Yoda Press, pp. xi–lvi.

Neils, J. (ed.) (1992), *Goddess and Polis: The Panathenaic Festival in Ancient Athens*, Princeton: Princeton University Press.

Neils, J. (ed.) (1996), *Worshipping Athena: Panathenaia and Parthenon*, Madison: University of Wisconsin Press.

Neils, J. (2008), 'Athena', in F. Malti-Douglas (ed.), *Encyclopedia of Sex and Gender, Vol. 1 A-C*, Malti-Douglas, Detroit: Macmillan Reference, pp. 104–5.

Nelson, S. M. (2007), *Women in Antiquity: Theoretical Approaches to Gender and Archaeology*, Lanham: AltaMira.

Neroni, H. (2005), *The Violent Woman: Femininity, Narrative, and Violence in Contemporary American Cinema*, Albany: SUNY Press.

Neudecker, R. (1988), *Die Skulpturen-Ausstattung römischer Villen in Italien*, Mainz am Rhein: Philipp von Zabern.

Newby, Z. (2012), 'The Aesthetics of Violence: Myth and Danger in Roman Domestic Landscapes', *Classical Antiquity*, 31.2: pp. 349–89.

Newlands, C. (1995), *Playing with Time: Ovid and the 'Fasti'*, Ithaca: Cornell University Press.

Ní Mheallaigh, K. (2009), 'Monumental Fallacy: The Teleology of Origins in Lucian's *Verae Historiae*', in A. Bartley (ed.), *A Lucian for our Times*, Newcastle-upon-Tyne: Cambridge Scholars, pp. 11–28.

Ní Mheallaigh, K. (2014), *Reading Fiction with Lucian: Freaks, Fakes, and Hyperreality*, Cambridge: Cambridge University Press.

Niccolini, F. (1854), *Le case ed i monumenti di Pompei: Volume Primo*, Napoli: Casa di Sirico.

Nordberg, J. (2014), *The Underground Girls of Kabul: The Hidden Lives of Afghan Girls Disguised as Boys*, London: Virago.

Nutton, V. (2004), *Ancient Medicine*, London; New York: Routledge.

O'Sullivan, T. (2011), *Walking in Roman Culture*, Cambridge: Cambridge University Press.

Oehmke, S. (2004), *Das Weib im Manne: Hermaphroditos in der Griechisch-Römischen Antike*, Berlin: Willmuth Arenhövel.

Oehmke, S. (2007), 'Halbmann oder Supermann? Bemerkungen zum effeminierten Priapos', in E. Hartmann, U. Hartmann and K. Pietzner (eds), *Geschlechterdefinitionen und Geschlechtergrenzen in der Antike*, Stuttgart: Steiner, pp. 263–76.

Ogden, D. (1997), *The Crooked Kings of Ancient Greece*, London: Duckworth.

Oliensis, E. (2009), *Freud's Rome: Pyschoanalysis and Latin Poetry*, Cambridge: Cambridge University Press.

Olson, K. (2014), 'Masculinity, Appearance, and Sexuality: Dandies in Roman Antiquity', *The Journal of the History of Sexuality*, 23.2: pp. 182–205.

Olson, K. (2017), *Masculinity and Dress in Roman Antiquity*, London; New York: Routledge/Taylor & Francis.

Ormand, K. (2005), 'Impossible Lesbians in Ovid's *Metamorphoses*', in R. Ancona and E. Greene (eds), *Gendered Dynamics in Latin Love Poetry*, Baltimore: Johns Hopkins University Press, pp. 79–110.

Ormand, K. (2009), *Controlling Desires: Sexuality in Ancient Greece and Rome*, Westport: Praeger.

Orrells, D. (2015), *Sex: Antiquity and its Legacy*, New York; Oxford: Oxford University Press.

Osgood, J. (2016), 'Cassius Dio's Secret History of Elagabalus', in C. Lange and J. Madsen (eds), *Cassius Dio: Greek Intellectual and Roman Politician*, Leiden: Brill, pp. 177–90.

Oudshoorn, N. (1994), *Beyond the Natural Body: An Archaeology of Sex Hormones*, London; New York: Routledge.

Padgett, M. (1993), *Vase Painting in Italy: Red-Figure and Related Works in the Museum of Arts, Boston*, Boston: Museum of Fine Arts Boston.

Panoussi, V. (2016), 'Spinning Hercules: Gender, Religion, and Geography in Propertius 4.9', *Classical World*, 109.2: pp. 179–94.

Panoussi, V. (2019), *Brides, Mourners, Bacchae: Women's Rituals in Roman Literature*, Baltimore: Johns Hopkins University Press.

Papathomopoulos, M. (1968), *Antoninus Liberalis*, Les Métamorphoses, Paris: Les Belles Lettres.

Parker, H. N. (1997), 'The Teratogenic Grid', in J. P. Hallett and M. B. Skinner (eds), *Roman Sexualities*, Princeton: Princeton University Press, pp. 47–65.

Patten, D. (2012), '"300" Prequel Given Official Title by WB', *Deadline*, September 12 <http://deadline.com/2012/09/warner-bros-gives-300-prequel-an-official-title-334848/> (last accessed 18 June 2017).

Patterson, C. (1985), 'Not Worth the Rearing: The Causes of Infant Exposure in Ancient Greece', *Transactions and Proceedings of the American Philological Association*, 115: pp. 103–23.

Patterson, C. (1986), 'Hai Attikai: The Other Athenians', *Helios*, 13: pp. 49–67.

Patterson, C. (1998), *The Family in Greek History*, Cambridge, MA; Harvard University Press.

Peirce, C. S. (1992), *Reasoning and the Logic of Things*, K. L. Ketner (ed.), Cambridge, MA: Harvard University Press.

Pelling, C. (2006), 'Speech and Narrative in the Histories', in C. Dewald and J. Marincola (eds), *The Cambridge Companion to Herodotus*, Cambridge; New York: Cambridge University Press, pp. 103–21.

Pelttari, A. (2014), *The Space that Remains: Reading Latin Poetry in Late Antiquity*, Ithaca: Cornell University Press.

Penrose, W. D., Jr (2014), 'A World Away from Ours: Homoeroticism in the Classics Classroom', in *From Abortion to Pederasty: Addressing Difficult Topics in the Classics Classroom*, N. S. Rabinowitz and F. McHardy (eds), Columbus: Ohio State University Press, pp. 227–47.

Penrose, W. D., Jr (2015), 'The Discourse of Disability in Ancient Greece', *Classical World*, 108.4: pp. 499–523.

Penrose, W. D., Jr (2016), *Postcolonial Amazons: Female Masculinity and Courage in Ancient Greek and Sanskrit Literature*, Oxford: Oxford University Press.

People's Union for Civil Liberties, Karnataka (PUCL-K) (2003), *Human Rights Violations against the Transgender Community: A Study of Kothi and Hijra Sex Workers in Bangalore, India*, Karnataka: People's Union for Civil Liberties.

Perry, S. (2013), 'Comic Book Basis for *300: Rise of an Empire* Won't Release Alongside Film', *SuperHeroHype*, December 10 <http://www.superherohype.com/news/180715-comic-book-basis-for-300-rise-of-an-empire-wont-release-alongside-film> (last accessed 18 June 2017).

Pervo, R. (1987), *Profit with Delight: The Literary Genre of the Acts of the Apostles*, Philadelphia: Fortress.

Petersen, L. H. (2009), '"Clothes Make the Man": Dressing the Roman Freedman Body', in T. Fögen and M. M. Lee (eds), *Bodies and Boundaries in Graeco-Roman Antiquity*, Berlin; New York: De Gruyter, pp. 181–214.

Petersen, L. H. (2012), 'Collecting Gods in Roman Houses: The House of the Gilded Cupids (VI.16.7, 38) at Pompeii', *Arethusa*, 45.3: pp. 319–32.

Phelan, P. (1988), 'Feminist Theory, Poststructuralism, and Performance', *TDR* 32, no. 1: 107–27.

Pierce, K. F., and S. Deacy (eds) (1997), *Rape in Antiquity: Sexual Violence in the Greek and Roman Worlds*, London: Duckworth.

Pintabone, D. T. (2002), 'Ovid's Iphis and Ianthe: When Girls Won't Be Girls', in N. S. Rabinowitz and L. Auanger (eds), *Among Women: From the Homosocial to the Homoerotic in the Ancient World*, Austin: University of Texas Press, pp. 256–85.

Plant, I. M. (2004), *Women Writers of Ancient Greece and Rome: An Anthology*, Norman: University of Oklahoma Press.

Platts, H. (2011), 'Keeping Up with the Joneses: Competitive Display within the Roman Villa Landscape, 100 BC – AD 200', in N. Fisher and H. van Wees (eds), *Competition in the Ancient World*, Swansea: Classical Press of Wales, pp. 239–77.

Polley, A. (2003), 'The Date of Herodian's History', *L'Antiquité Classique*, 72: pp. 203–8.

Pollmann, K. (2008), 'Ambivalence and Moral Virtus in Roman Epic', in S. Freund and M. Vielberg (eds), *Vergil und das antike Epos: Festschrift Hans Jürgen Tschiedel, Altertumswissenschaftliches Kolloquium 20*, Stuttgart: Steiner, pp. 355–66.

Pomeroy, A. J. (1992), 'Trimalchio as deliciae', *Phoenix*, 46: pp. 45–53.

Pomeroy, S. B. (1975), *Goddesses, Whores, Wives, and Slaves*, New York: Schocken Books.

Pomeroy, S. B. (1994), *Xenophon Oeconomicus: A Social and Historical Commentary*, Oxford: Clarendon.

Potter, D. (2004), *The Roman Empire at Bay 180–395 AD*, London: Routledge.

Preisendanz, K. (1928–31), *Papyri Graecae Magicae: Die Griechischen Zauberpapyri*, Berlin; Leipzig: Teubner.

Rabe, H. (ed.) (1971), *Scholia in Lucianum*, Stuttgart: Teubner.

Rabinowitz, N. S. (1993), *Anxiety Veiled: Euripides and the Traffic in Women*, Ithaca: Cornell University Press.

Rabinowitz, N. S., and L. Auanger (eds) (2002), *Among Women: From the Homosocial to the Homoerotic in the Ancient World*, Austin: University of Texas Press.

Rabinowitz, N. S., and A. Richlin (eds) (1993), *Feminist Theory and the Classics*, New York: Routledge.

Rademaker, A. (2003), '"Most Citizens are Euryprôktoi Now": (Un)manliness in Aristophanes', in R. M. Rosen and I. Sluiter (eds), *Andreia: Studies in Manliness and Courage in Classical Antiquity*, Boston; Leiden: Brill, pp. 115–25.

Rantala, J. (2016), 'Dio the Dissident: The Portrait of Severus in Roman History', in C. Lange and J. Madsen (eds), *Cassius Dio: Greek Intellectual and Roman Politician*, Leiden: Brill, pp. 159–76.

Rantala, J. (2017), *The Ludi Saeculares of Septimius Severus. The Ideologies of a New Roman Empire*, London: Routledge.

Rantala, J. (ed.) (2019), *Gender, Memory, and Identity in the Roman World*, Amsterdam: Amsterdam University Press.

Rathmann, M. (2016), *Diodor und seine 'Bibliotheke': Weltgeschichte aus der Provinz* (Klio Beihefte (Neue Folge) 27), Berlin: De Gruyter.

Raubitscheck, I. K. (1998), *Isthmia 7: The Metal Objects (1952–1989)*, Princeton: American School of Classical Studies at Athens.

Rauchle, V. J. (2015), 'The Myth of Mothers as Others: Motherhood and Autochthony on the Athenian Akropolis', *Cahiers Monde Anciens*, vol. 6, pp. 2–23.

Rauhala, M. (2008), 'The Greek Mother of Gods – No Model for Mortals?', in K. Alenius, O. Fält and M. Mertaniemi (eds), *Imagology and Cross-cultural Encounters in History*, Rovaniemi: Pohjois-Suomen Historiallinen Yhdistys, pp. 47–55.

Raval, S. (2002), 'Cross-Dressing and "Gender Trouble" in the Ovidian Corpus', *Helios*, 29.2: pp. 149–72.

Read, J. (2000), *The New Avengers: Feminism, Femininity and the Rape-Revenge Cycle*, Manchester; New York: Manchester University Press.

Reeder, E. (1995), *Pandora: Women in Classical Greece*, Baltimore: Trustees of the Walters Art Gallery.

Retzleff, A. (2007), 'The Dresden Type Satyr-Hermaphrodite Group in Roman Theatres', *American Journal of Archaeology*, 111.3: pp. 459–71.

Richlin, A. (1983), *The Garden of Priapus: Sexuality and Aggression in Roman Humor*, New York: Oxford University Press.

Richlin, A. (1992a), 'Reading Ovid's Rapes', in A. Richlin (ed.), *Pornography and Representation in Greece and Rome*, New York: Oxford University Press, pp. 158–79.

Richlin, A. (1992b), *Pornography and Representation in Greece and Rome*, New York: Oxford University Press.

Richlin, A. (1993), 'Not before Homosexuality: The Materiality of the Cinaedus and the Roman Law against Love between Men', *Journal of the History of Sexuality*, 3.4: pp. 523–73.

Richlin, A. (2002), 'Gender and Rhetoric: Producing Manhood in the Schools', in W. J. Dominik (ed.), *Roman Eloquence: Rhetoric in Society and Literature*, London: Routledge, pp. 74–90.

Richlin, A. (2014), *Arguments with Silence: Writing the History of Roman Women*, Ann Arbor: University of Michigan Press.

Ripoll, F. (2015), 'Statius and Silius Italicus', in W. J. Dominik, C. E. Newlands and K. Gervais (eds), *Brill's Companion to Statius*, Boston; Leiden: Brill, pp. 425–43.

Ritter, S. (1996), 'Ercole e Onfale nell'rte Romana dell'Éta Tardo-Repubblicana e Augustea', in C. Jordain-Annequin (ed.), *Heracles, Les Femmes et le Feminin. IIe Rencontre Héracléenne: Actes du Colloque de Grenoble, Université des Sciences Sociales (Grenoble II), 22-Octobre 1992. Etudes de Philologie, d'Archéologie et d'Histoire Anciennes*, 31: pp. 89–102.

Robert, Carl (1914), 'Pandora', *Hermes*, 49: pp. 17–38.

Robinson, M. (1999), 'Salmacis and Hermaphroditus: When Two Become One (Ovid, *Met.* 4.285–388)', *Classical Quarterly*, 49.1: pp. 212–23.

Robinson, M. (2011), *A Commentary on Ovid's Fasti, Book 2*, Oxford: Oxford University Press.

Rohy, V. (2009), *Anachronism and Its Others: Sexuality, Race, Temporality*, Albany: SUNY Press.

Roller, L. (1998), 'The Ideology of the Eunuch Priest', in M. Wyke (ed.), *Gender and the Body in the Ancient Mediterranean*, Oxford: Wiley Blackwell, pp. 118–35.

Roller, L. (1999), *In Search of God the Mother: The Cult of Anatolian Cybele*, Berkeley: University of California Press.

Roller, M. B. (2006), *Dining Posture in Ancient Rome: Bodies, Values, and Status*, Princeton: Princeton University Press.

Rosati, G. (1999), 'Trimalchio on Stage', in S. J. Harrison (ed.), *Oxford Readings in the Roman Novel*, Oxford: Oxford University Press, pp. 85–104.

Roscher, W. H. (ed.) (1886–90), *Ausfürliches Lexikon der Griechischen und Römischen Mythologie*, Leipzig: Teubner.

Roscoe, W. (1996), 'Priests of the Goddess: Gender Transgression in Ancient Religion', *History of Religions*, 35.3: pp. 195–230.

Roscoe, W. (1998), *The Changing Ones: Third and Fourth Genders in Native North America*, New York: St. Martin's.

Rose, M. L. (2003), *The Staff of Oedipus: Transforming Disability in Ancient Greece*, Ann Arbor: University of Michigan Press.

Rupp, L. J. (2009), *Sapphistries: A Global History of Love between Women*, Vancouver: University of British Columbia Press.

Sacks, K. (1990), *Diodorus Siculus and the First Century*, Princeton: Princeton University Press.

Sapsford, T. (2015), 'The Wages of Effeminacy?: Kinaidoi in Greek Documents from Egypt', *EuGeStA*, 5: pp. 103–23.

Savage, H. (2006), 'Changing Sex: Transsexuality and Christian Theology', PhD dissertation, University of Durham, Durham.

Schauenberg, K. (1960), 'Hercules and Omphale', *Rheinisches Museum für Philologie*, 103.1: pp. 57–76.

Schefold, K. (1957), *Die Wände Pompejis. Topographisches Verzeichnis der Bildmotive*, Berlin; Boston; New York: De Gruyter.

Schiefsky, M. (2005), *Hippocrates: On Ancient Medicine*, Boston; Leiden: Brill.

Schipper, J. (2016), *Ruth: A New Translation with Introduction and Commentary*, New Haven: Yale University Press.

Schleicher, D. H. (2014), 'The Art of Style as Substance in *Enemy*, *The Grand Budapest Hotel*, and *300: Rise of an Empire*', The *Schleicher Spin*, March 29 <https://theschleicherspin.com/2014/03/29/the-art-of-style-as-substance-in-enemy-the-grand-budapest-hotel-and-300-rise-of-an-empire/> (last accessed 18 June 2017).

Schmidt, R., and B. Voss (eds) (2000), 'Archaeologies of Sexuality: An Introduction', in *Archaeologies of Sexuality*, London; New York: Routledge, pp. 1–32.

Schmitt-Pantel, P. (2006), 'Triclinium', in H. Cancik and H. Schneider (eds), *Brill's New Pauly*, *Antiquity* <http://dx.doi.org/10.1163/1574-9347_bnp_e1220340> (last accessed 13 March 2017).

Schoff, W. H. (1923), 'Nard', *Journal of the American Oriental Society*, 43: pp. 216–28.

Schöner, E. (1964), *Das Viererschema in der antiken Humoralpathologie*, Wiesbaden: Steiner.

Seaford, R. (2006), *Dionysos*, New York: Routledge.

Sealy, R. (1990), *Women and Law in Classical Greece*, Chapel Hill: University of North Carolina Press.

Sear, F. (2006), *Roman Theatres: An Architectural Study*, Oxford: Oxford University Press.

Seidensticker, B. (2003), 'The Chorus in Greek Satyrplay', in E. Csapo and M. C. Miller (eds), *Poetry, Theory, Praxis: The Social Life of Myth, Word and Image in Ancient Greece : Essays in Honour of William J. Slater*, Oxford: Oxbow, pp. 100–21.

Seiler, F. (1992), *Casa degli Amorini Dorati*, Munich: Hirmer.

Selden, D. L. (1994), 'Genre of Genre', in J. Tatum (ed.), *The Search for the Ancient Novel*, Baltimore: Johns Hopkins University Press, pp. 39–64.

Serano, J. (2016), *Whipping Girl: A Transsexual Woman on Sexism and the Scapegoating of Femininity*, 2nd edn, Berkeley: Seal.

Severy-Hoven, B. (2012), 'Master Narratives and the Wall Painting of the House of the Vettii, Pompeii', *Gender & History*, 24.3: pp. 540–80.

Shannon, K. E. (2013), 'Authenticating the Marvellous: *Mirabilia* in Pliny, Tacitus, and Suetonius', *Working Papers on Nervan, Trajanic and Hadrianic Literature* 1.9 <http://arts.st-andrews.ac.uk/literaryinteractions/?p'573> (last accessed 17 November 2017).

Shannon-Henderson, K. E. (2020), 'Constructing a New Imperial Paradox-ography: Phlegon of Tralles and His Sources', in A. König, R. Langlands and J. Uden (eds), *Literature and Culture in the Roman Empire, 96–235: Cross-Cultural Interactions*, Cambridge: Cambridge University Press.

Shapiro, H. A. (1994), *Myth into Art: Poet and Painter in Classical Greece*, London; New York: Routledge.

Shapiro, H. A. (1995), 'The Cult of Heroines: Kekrops' Daughters', in E. Reeder (ed.), *Pandora: Women in Classical Greece*, Baltimore Trustees of the Walters Art Gallery, pp. 39–48.

Shapiro, H. A. (2015), 'Alkibiades' Effeminacy and the Androgyny of Dionysos', in D. Boschung, H. A. Shapiro and F. Waschek (eds), *Bodies in Transition: Dissolving the Boundaries of Embodied Knowledge*, Paderborn: Wilhelm Fink, 287–312.

Sharrock, A. R. (2002), 'Looking at Looking: Can You Resist a Reading?', in D. Fredrick (ed.), *The Roman Gaze: Vision, Power, and the Body*, Baltimore: Johns Hopkins University Press, pp. 256–95.

Shaw, A. (2005), 'Changing Sex and Bending Gender: An Introduction', in A. Shaw and S. Ardener (eds), *Changing Sex and Bending Gender*, New York; Oxford: Berghahn Books, pp. 1–19.

Shaw, A., and S. Ardener (eds) (2005), *Changing Sex and Bending Gender*, New York; Oxford: Berghahn Books.

Sidebottom, H. (2007), 'Severan Historiography', in S. Swain, S. Harrison and J. Elsner (eds), *Severan Culture*, Cambridge: Cambridge University Press, pp. 52–82.

Silverstein, M., and G. Urban (1996a), 'The Natural History of Discourse', in M. Silverstein and G. Urban (eds), *Natural Histories of Discourse*, Chicago: University of Chicago Press, pp. 1–17.

Silverstein, M., and G. Urban (eds) (1996b), *Natural Histories of Discourse*, Chicago: University of Chicago Press.

Simon, E. (1982), 'Satyr Plays on Vases in the Time of Aeschylus', in D. Kurtz and B. A. Sparkes (eds), *The Eye of Greece*, Cambridge: Cambridge University Press, pp. 123–48.

Skinner, M. B. (1997), 'Introduction', in J. P. Hallett and M. B. Skinner (eds), *Roman Sexualities*, Princeton: Princeton University Press, pp. 3–25.

Skinner, M. B. (2005), *Sexuality in Greek and Roman Culture*, Malden, MA: Wiley Blackwell.

Smit, P-B. (2010), 'Something about Mary? Remarks about the Five Women in the Matthean Genealogy', *New Testament Studies*, 56.02: pp. 191–207.

Smith, A. (2007), *Girl Meets Boy*, Edinburgh: Canongate.

Smith, T. J. (2010), *Komast Dancers in Archaic Greek Art*, Oxford: Oxford University Press.

Smith, W. D. (1994), *Hippocrates, Epidemics 2, 4–7*, Loeb Classical Library 477, Cambridge, MA: Harvard University Press.

Snowden, F. M., Jr (1997), 'Greeks and Ethiopians', in J. E. Coleman and C. A. Walz (eds), *Greeks and Barbarians: Essays on the Interactions between Greeks and Non-Greeks in Antiquity and the Consequences of Eurocentrism*, Bethesda: CDL Press, pp. 103–26.

Snyder, J. M. (1989), *The Woman and the Lyre: Women Writers in Classical Greece and Rome*, Carbondale: Southern Illinois University Press.

Solodow, J. B. (1988), *The World of Ovid's* Metamorphoses, Chapel Hill: University of North Carolina Press.

Sommer, M. (2004), 'Elagabal: Wege zur Konstruktion eines 'schlechten' Kaisers', *Scripta classica Israelica: Yearbook of the Israel Society for the Promotion of Classical Studies*, 23: pp. 95–110.

Sørensen, M. L. S. (2000), *Gender Archaeology*, Cambridge: Polity.

Sowers, B. (2012), 'Thecla Desexualized: The Saint Justina Legend and the Reception of the Christian Apocrypha in Late Antiquity', in J. H. Charlesworth and L. M. McDonald (eds), *'Non-canonical' Religious Texts in Early Judaism and Early Christianity*, New York: T&T Clark, pp. 222–34.

Spineto, N. (2005), *Dionysos a Teatro*, Rome: Georgio Bretschneider.

Spivak, G. C. (1999), *A Critique of Postcolonial Reason: Toward a History of the Vanishing Present*, Cambridge, MA: Harvard University Press.

Stähli, A. (1999), *Die Verweigerung der Lüste: Erotische Gruppen in der Antiken Plastik*, Berlin: Reimer.

Starkey, J. (2012), *Sophocles the Honeybee: Dramatic Context and Interaction*, PhD dissertation, University of Colorado, Boulder.

Starr, R. (1987), 'Trimalchio's *Homerist*', *Latomus*, 46: pp. 199–200.

Stehle, E. (1997), *Performance and Gender in Ancient Greece*, Princeton: Princeton University Press.

Stevenson, J. (2005), *Women Latin Poets: Language, Gender and Authority from Antiquity to the Eighteenth Century*, Oxford: Oxford University Press.

Strauss Clay, J. (1995), 'Catullus' "Attis" and the Black Hunter', *Quaderni Urbinati Di Cultura Classica*, 50.2: pp. 143–55.

Strocka, V. M. (1984), *Casa del Principe di Napoli, Häuser in Pompeji 1*, Tübingen: Wasmuth.

Stryker, S. (2008), *Transgender History*, Berkeley: Seal.

Sturgeon, M. (1977), 'The Reliefs on the Theater of Dionysos in Athens', *American Journal of Archaeology*, 81.1: pp. 31–53.

Suhr, E. G. (1953), 'Herakles and Omphale', *American Journal of Archaeology*, 57.4: pp. 251–63.

Surtees, A. (2014), 'Satyrs as Women and Maenads as Men: Transvestism and Transgression in Dionysian Worship', in A. Avramidou and D. Demetriou (eds), *Approaching the Ancient Artefact: Function, Decoration, and Meaning*, Berlin: De Gruyter, pp. 281–93.

Surtees, A. (2019), 'Autochthonous Landscape and Female Exclusion in the Athenian Democracy', in T. Tsakiropoulou-Summers and K. Kitsi-Mitakou (eds), *Women and the Ideology of Political Exclusion From Classical Antiquity to the Modern Era*, New York: Routledge/Taylor & Francis, pp. 104–19.

Swain, S. (2005), 'Polemon's *Physiognomy*', in S. Swain (ed.), *Seeing the Face, Seeing the Soul: Polemon's Physiognomy from Classical Antiquity to Medieval Islam*, Oxford: Oxford University Press, pp. 125–202.

Swancutt, D. M. (2007), 'Still Before Sexuality: "Greek" Androgyny, the Roman Imperial Politics of Masculinity and the Roman Invention of the "Tribas"', in T. C. Penner and C. Vander Stichele (eds), *Mapping Gender in Ancient Religious Discourses*, Leiden: Brill, pp. 11–61.

Tasker, Y. (2002), *Spectacular Bodies: Gender, Genre, and the Action Cinema*, London; New York: Routledge.

Taylor, R. (1997), 'Two Pathic Subcultures in Ancient Rome', *Journal of the History of Sexuality*, 7.3: pp. 319–71.

Taylor, T. (1996), *The Prehistory of Sex: Four Million Years of Human Sexual Culture*, London: Bantam Books.

Taylor, Y., S. Hines and M. E. Casey (eds) (2011), *Theorizing Intersectionality and Sexuality, Genders and Sexualities in the Social Sciences*, Basingstoke: Palgrave Macmillan.

Thesaurus Linguae Graecae Digital Library, M. C. Pantelia (ed.), University of California, Irvine <http://www.tlg.uci.edu> (last accessed 16 October 2018).

Thomas, R. (2000), *Herodotus in Context: Ethnography, Science and the Art of Persuasion*, Cambridge: Cambridge University Press.

Thomas, R. (2001), 'Ethnicity, Genealogy, and Hellenism in Herodotus', in I. Malkin (ed.), *Ancient Perceptions of Greek Ethnicity*, Cambridge, MA; London: Harvard University Press, pp. 213–33.

Thomas, Y. (1996), 'Fathers as Citizens of Rome, Rome as a City of Fathers (Second Century BC – Second Century AD)', in A. Burguière (ed.), *A History of the Family, Volume I: Distant Worlds, Ancient Worlds*, Cambridge: Belknap Press, pp. 228–69.

Tomasso, V. (2013), 'Gorgo at the Limits of Liberation in Zack Snyder's *300* (2007)', in M. Cyrino (ed.), *Screening Love and Sex in the Ancient World*, New York: Palgrave Macmillan, pp. 113–26.

Tougher, S. (ed.) (2002), *Eunuchs in Antiquity and Beyond*, London: Duckworth.

Treggiari, S. (1991), *Roman Marriage: Iusti Coniuges from the time of Ulpian*, Oxford: Clarendon.

Trendall, A. D., and T. B. L. Webster (1971), *Illustrations of Greek Drama*, London: Phaidon.

Tronchin, F. (2012), 'Introduction: Collecting the Eclectic' in F. Tronchin (ed.), *Collectors and the Eclectic: New Approaches to Roman Domestic Decoration, Arethusa, Special volume*, 45.3, pp. 261–82.

Tulloch, J. H. (ed.) (2016), *A Cultural History of Women in Antiquity, Vol. 1*, New York: Bloomsbury.

Turner, S. (2009), '"Only Spartan Women Give Birth to Real Men": Zack Snyder's *300* and the Male Nude', in D. Lowe and K. Shahabudin (eds), *Classics for All: Reworking Antiquity in Mass Culture*, Newcastle-upon-Tyne: Cambridge Scholars, pp. 128–49.

Ugolini, G. (1995), *Untersuchungen zur Figur des Sehers Teiresias*, Classica Monacensia 12, Tübingen: Gunther Narr.

Uhlig, A. (2018), 'Noses in the Orchestra' in M. Mueller and M. Telò (eds), *The Materialities of Greek Tragedy: Object and Affect in Aeschylus, Sophocles and Euripides*, London: Bloomsbury, pp. 153–67.

Ulrichs, K. H. (1868), Memnon: Die Geschlechtsnatur desmannlieben-den Urnings, Schleiz: Hugo Heyn <https://archive.org/details/bub_gb_bAkQAAAAYAAJ> (last accessed 26 Oct 2018).

Unwin, N. C. (2017), *Caria and Crete in Antiquity: Cultural Interaction between Anatolia and the Aegean*, Cambridge: Cambridge University Press.

Valentine, D. (2007), *Imagining Transgender: An Ethnology of a Category*, Durham, NC: Duke University Press.

van der Eijk, P. J. (2005), *Medicine and Philosophy in Classical Antiquity: Doctors and Philosophers on Nature, Soul, Health and Disease*, Cambridge: Cambridge University Press.

van Thiel, H. (1971), *Der Eselroman, Vol. 1: Untersuchungen*, Zetemata, 54.1, Munich: C. Beck.

Varner, E. R. (2008), 'Transcending Gender: Assimilation, Identity, and Roman Imperial Portraits', *Memoirs of the American Academy in Rome, Supplementary Volumes*, 7: pp. 185–205.

Vendryes, J. (1934), 'La couvade chez les Scythes', *Comptes rendus des séances de l'Académie des Inscriptions et Belles-Lettres*, 78.4: pp. 329–39.

Vermaseren, M. J. (1977), *Corpus Cultus Cybelae Attidisque (CCCA) III. Italia – Latium*, Leiden: Brill.

Vernant, J.-P. (1989), 'At Man's Table: Hesiod's Foundation Myth of Sacrifice', in M. Detienne and J.-P. Vernant (eds), *The Cuisine of Sacrifice among the Greeks*, Chicago: University of Chicago Press, pp. 21–86.

Vernant, J.-P. (1996), 'The Myth of Prometheus in Hesiod', in *Myth and Society in Ancient Greece*, New York: Zone Books, pp. 183–202.

Volk, K. (2010), *Ovid*, Malden, MA; Oxford: Wiley Blackwell.

von Glinski, M. L. (2012), *Simile and Identity in Ovid's* Metamorphoses, Cambridge: Cambridge University Press.

von Stackelberg, K. T. (2009), *The Roman Garden: Space, Sense, and Society*, London: Routledge.

von Stackelberg, K. T. (2014), 'Garden Hybrids: Hermaphrodite Images in the Roman House', *Classical Antiquity*, 33.2: pp. 395–426.

Vorster, C. (1999), 'La villa come museo: Sul valore delle "sculture antiche" nell'età imperial', in M. Aoyagi and S. Steingräber (eds), *Le ville romane dell'Italia e del Mediterraneo antico: Academic Meeting and the University of Tokyo*, Tokyo: Institute for the Study of Cultural Exchange Faculty of Letters the University of Tokyo, pp. 166–76.

Voss, B. L. (2008), 'Sexuality Studies in Archaeology', *Annual Review of Anthropology*, 37: pp. 317–36.

Vout, C. (2013), *Sex on Show: Seeing the Erotic in Greece and Rome*, London: The British Museum.

Wainwright, E. M. (1991), *Towards a Feminist Critical Reading of the Gospel According to Matthew*, Berlin, New York: De Gruyter.

Walker, J. (2006), 'Before the Name: Ovid's Deformulated Lesbianism', *Comparative Literature*, 58.3: pp. 205–22.

Walters, J. (1997), 'Invading the Roman Body: Manliness and Impenetrability in Roman Thought', in J. P. Hallett and M. B. Skinner (eds), *Roman Sexualities*, Princeton: Princeton University Press, pp. 29–43.

Weismantel, M. (2012), 'Towards a Transgender Archaeology: A Queer Rampage Through Prehistory', in S. Stryker and A. Aizura (eds), *The Transgender Studies Reader, Vol. 2*, New York: Routledge.

Wenden, A. L. (2005), 'The Politics of Representation: A Critical Discourse Analysis of an Aljazeera Special Report', *International Journal of Peace Studies*, 10.2: pp. 89–112.

West, S. (1999), 'Hippocrates' Scythian Sketches', *Eirene*, 35: pp. 14–32.

Wheeler, S. M. (1997), 'Changing Names: The Miracle of Iphis in Ovid *Metamorphoses* 9', *Phoenix*, 51.2: pp. 190–202.

Wilkins, J. (2005), 'Land and Sea: Italy and the Mediterranean in the Roman Discourse of Dining', in B. K. Gold and J. F. Donahue (eds), *Roman Dining, American Journal of Philology, Special Issue*, Baltimore: Johns Hopkins University Press, pp. 31–48.

Williams, C. (2010), *Roman Homosexuality: Ideologies of Masculinity in Classical Antiquity*, 2nd edn, New York, Oxford: Oxford University Press.

Williams, R. D. (1972), *P. Papini Stati Thebaidos Liber Decimus* (edited with a commentary), Leiden: Brill.

Williams, W. L. (1986), *The Spirit and the Flesh: Sexual Diversity in American Indian Culture*, Boston: Beacon.

Winkler, J. J. (1985), *Auctor & Actor: A Narratological Reading of Apuleius' The Golden Ass*, Berkeley: University of California Press.

Winkler, J. J. (1990a), *The Constraints of Desire: The Anthropology of Sex and Gender in Ancient Greece*, New York: Routledge.

Winkler, J. J. (1990b), 'Laying Down the Law: The Oversight of Men's Sexual Behavior in Classical Athens', in D. Halperin, J. J. Winkler and F. I. Zeitlin (eds), *Before Sexuality: The Construction of Erotic Experience in the Ancient Greek World*, Princeton: Princeton University Press, pp. 171–210.

Wirth, G. (2008), *Diodorus, Griechische Weltgeschichte, Fragmente (Buch XXI–XL)* (Bibliothek der griechischen Literatur 68), Stuttgart: Anton Hiersemann.

Wiseman, A. (2013), *Ovid: Fasti*, Oxford: Oxford University Press.

Wiseman, A., and T. P. Wiseman (2011), *Ovid, Times and Reasons. A New Translation of Fasti*, New York; Oxford: Oxford University Press.

Wiseman, T. P. (2002), 'Ovid and the Stage' in G. Herbert-Brown (ed.), *Ovid's Fasti. Historical Readings at its Bimillennium*, Oxford: Oxford University Press, pp. 275–99.

Wiseman, T. P. (2008), *Unwritten Rome*, Exeter: University of Exeter Press.

Wiseman, T. P. (2016), 'Maecenas and the Stage', *Papers of the British School at Rome*, 84: pp. 131–55 < https://doi:10.1017/S0068246216000040> (last accessed 3 June 2017).

Wohl, V. (2002), *Love among the Ruins: The Erotics of Democracy in Classical Athens*, Princeton: Princeton University Press.

Wyke, M. (ed.) (1998a), *Parchments of Gender: Deciphering the Bodies of Antiquity*, Oxford: Clarendon.

Wyke, M. (ed.) (1998b), *Gender and the Body in the Ancient Mediterranean*, Malden, MA: Wiley Blackwell.

Wyler, S. (2012), 'Dionysiaca aurea. The Development of Dionysiac Images from Augustus to Nero', *Neronia Electronica*, 2: pp. 3–19.

Zanker, P. (1988), *The Power of Images in the Age of Augustus*, Ann Arbor: University of Michigan Press.

Zanker, P. (1999), 'Eine römischen Matrone als Omphale', *Mitteilungen des Deutschen Archäologischen Instituts, Römische Abteilung*, 106: pp. 119–31.

Zanker, P. (2004), *Mit Mythen Leben: Die Bilderwelt der Römischen Sarkophage*, Munich: Hirmer.

Zanobi, A. (2014), *Seneca's Tragedies and the Aesthetics of Pantomime*, London; New Delhi; New York; Sydney: Bloomsbury.

Zeitlin, F. I. (1996), *Playing the Other: Gender and Society in Classical Greek Literature*, Chicago: University of Chicago Press.

Zimmerman, M. (2012), *Apulei Metamorphoseon Libri XI*, Oxford Classical Texts, Oxford: Clarendon Press.

Index

EU representative:
Easy Access System Europe
Mustamäe tee 50, 10621 Tallinn, Estonia
Gpsr.requests@easproject.com

www.ingramcontent.com/pod-product-compliance
Lightning Source LLC
Chambersburg PA
CBHW051956270326
41929CB00015B/2679